Dutchy's Diaries

Dutchy's Diaries

LIFE AS A CANADIAN NAVAL OFFICER,
IN HIS OWN WORDS :: 1916–1929

HELEN EDWARDS

Edwards Heritage Consulting
VICTORIA, BRITISH COLUMBIA, CANADA
2020

ISBN 978-0-9697282-5-2

Copyright © 2020 Edwards Heritage Consulting

All rights reserved. No part of this publication may be reproduced in any form, or by any means, electronic or mechanical including photocopying, recording, or any information browsing, storage, or retrieval system, without permission in writing from Helen Edwards.

FIRST PUBLISHED IN 2020 BY
Edwards Heritage Consulting
Victoria, British Columbia, Canada

For further information or more copies of *Dutchy's Diaries*, please write to heritagelady@gmail.com

Book design by Arifin Graham, Alaris Design
Copy editing by David Greer
Base maps by FreeVectorMaps.com

PRINTED AND BOUND IN CANADA BY VICTORIA BINDERY

This book is dedicated to the memory of John Crispo Inglis "Dutchy" Edwards, who served his country for 39 years in a distinguished naval career. May his stories live forever.

—H.E.

Contents

Preface | viii

About the Author | viii

Introduction | ix

Acknowledgements | x

Biography of John Crispo Inglis Edwards | xi

John Crispo Inglis Edwards Family Tree | xiv

The Roaring Twenties | xv

List of Images in the Journals | xvii

Glossary | xix

JOURNAL ONE :: 1916–1918 :: 1

JOURNAL TWO :: 1918–1920 :: 185

JOURNAL THREE :: 1920–1925 :: 139

JOURNAL FOUR :: 1925–1929 :: 203

Appendix A | 261

Appendix B | 282

Maps | 299

Appendix C | 302

Sources | 304

Index to the Journals | 305

Preface

THE SOURCE MATERIALS for these transcriptions are original historical documents that have not been censored, reviewed, or otherwise altered by the owner. Please be aware that some materials may contain content that is racist, sexist, or otherwise offensive. The owner is merely the custodian of archival materials; the content does not necessarily reflect the views or policies of the owner.

I understand from observation that the writer made several spelling mistakes, and for the purposes of this transcription, I have corrected a number of these errors to aid the flow of the text. In doing so, I have adhered to a policy of minimal intervention and have left variances in formatting as they were written, illustrating the different circumstances under which journal entries were recorded during and after wartime.

In some cases, I have been unable to find the modern equivalents for locations and ships mentioned in the journals but have endeavoured to ensure the appendices are as complete as possible. Any errors in transcription and research are mine alone.

About the Author

HELEN EDWARDS is the daughter-in-law of Commodore Edwards. She is a life-long historian and has written on a variety of subjects, but family history is one of her passions. She has been researching her personal family tree for over 40 years and is now working on the Edwards side of the family as well. Each new day brings discoveries, but none can top the day that she discovered these journals.

The process of transcribing and researching these journals has been thought-provoking—possibly the most thought-provoking work of her life. After reading these many pages, she now knows much more about her father-in-law. She did not meet him until 1969 when he was retired, so knew little about his personal life when he was young. Helen is pleased to share the journals with the world.

DUTCHY'S DIARIES ONLINE

To see the original scans of the pages of Dutchy's Diaries, visit our companion web site at: **https://dutchysdiaries.ca/**

Introduction

I don't remember exactly when we found my father-in-law's naval journals, but it was about six years ago. Imagine my utter delight at finding journals written during World War I and beyond—up to 1929—in a box that we had not looked at before. In digging further into the treasures, I found photographs that even pre-dated the journals and continued to the post–World War II period.

I put together a slide presentation on the World War I–era journals and presented it to the Victoria branch of the Western Front Association in the spring of 2015. I then put the material away, as I was writing a book on the history of professional hockey in Victoria. I finished that book and sent it off to be edited and designed and found myself with time to work on these journals. I have scanned all the pages of the four books and spent hours transcribing the words so that they would be easier to read.

Commodore John Crispo Inglis Edwards may have had only a Grade 8 education, but he was well schooled in handwriting, which in his case was precise, elegant and legible, and a pleasure to read. Interestingly, in the early part of his diaries, coinciding with his earliest years in the navy, his handwriting sloped to the right, the way he was undoubtedly taught at school. (In the days before computers and, indeed, common use of typewriters, instruction in handwriting was an essential part of the "three Rs"—Reading, Writing and Arithmetic. It has since fallen into disuse, all the more reason why Dutchy's handwriting was such a pleasure to read during my research.) As the years progressed, Dutchy's cursive handwriting, though still perfectly legible, became noticeably more upright—a reflection, perhaps, not only of his growing older but also of the increasing stress he was under as routine naval training gave way to increasing risk of enemy engagement and, consequently, to the necessity of hurried tasks.

I also put together a spreadsheet of all the places named in the text as well as all the ships mentioned. I then moved on to this book, which will contain only the transcripts—the scans will be on a complementary website—and some of the photographs. Apart from this short introduction, a biography of Commodore John Crispo Inglis ("Dutchy") Edwards, and the listings of ships and locations mentioned in the diaries, his words will speak for themselves. I am thrilled to be able to bring this material to a broader audience.

Helen Edwards, December 2019
VICTORIA, B.C., CANADA

Acknowledgements

I COULD NOT HAVE WRITTEN this book without the support of many people. From the attendees at a Western Front Association Seminar, where I made a brief presentation on the journals and their value, to Garry Weir, who maintains a website on naval history at http://www.forposterityssake.ca/, all have added to my depth of knowledge. Thanks to Barry Gough who gave me information on transcribing journals, precisely when I needed it and special thanks to Sherri Robinson who provided valuable information on properties owned by Esquimalt residents. My thanks also go to book designer Arifin Graham of Alaris Design, and copy editor David Greer for their contributions to the publication of this book.

Logically, I could not have written this book if my in-laws, Dot and Dutchy Edwards, had not preserved the journals intact through the myriad of moves they made during his career. They have my eternal thanks. Now Dutchy's story can be shared with the world.

Finally, thanks to my extended family, who have been with me through the research and writing process and have provided much-needed feedback. John, Susie, Edie, and Diana and their partners been great, and my wonderful husband John shared the stories he knew about his father. To you all, I appreciate your love and support.

From Dutchy's collection: Naval personnel were given British ration books to use while on leave

John Crispo Inglis Edwards

JOHN CRISPO INGLIS EDWARDS was born in Londonderry, Nova Scotia, on July 5, 1896. He was the sixth child—and fourth son—born to Major Joseph Plimsoll Edwards, a noted Canadian historian, and Emily Susan Crispo. The other children were Arthur Wellesley (1885–1971, Emily Frances (1887–1985), Grace Gwendolyn (1889–1985), Joseph Plimsoll (1891–1917), Cecil Wolfe (1894–1905), Harold Leckie (1899–1974), and Muriel Katherine Annesley (1904–1973). In his journals, Dutchy mentions his visit to his brother Joe's gravesite.

Joseph had been born in Clarence, Ontario, to a pioneer family and educated in Montreal. After his family moved there, he went into business. In 1893, he moved to Londonderry, Nova Scotia, where he managed an iron foundry. He was appointed the first income tax inspector for Nova Scotia in 1916 and moved to Halifax. He was an authority on military history and was the author of a number of historical papers and pamphlets, notably "Louisbourg: An Historical Sketch" (1895) and "The Public Records of Nova Scotia" (1920). The sale of his extensive library of Canadiana to Acadia University formed the basis of their Eric R. Dennis Special Collection.

John attended St. Alban's School in Brockville, Ontario, where his cousin's husband was the headmaster. He left there at the end of 1911—at the top of his class—to become a cadet in the second class of the Royal Naval College of Canada. On completion of his training, he was appointed Midshipman.

He went on to have a distinguished naval career, serving his country for 39 years and retiring with the rank of Commodore. His excellent work while in command of HMCS Cornwallis, the largest training base in the British Empire, was recognized when he was made Commander of the British Empire (CBE).

John Crispo Inglis Edwards was a talented athlete, excelling at many sports, and was particularly noted as a rugby and tennis player. He trained as a Physical and Recreational Training Officer in England and used this training throughout his long career.

He met Dorothy Elizabeth Symons ("D" or "Dot" in the journals) on a tennis court in Sydney, Nova Scotia, and they were married on April 26, 1926 at St. Paul's Church, Halifax. The couple's first child, Susan Elizabeth, was stillborn on February 7, 1929 and the journals contain a letter sent from Dot's sister, Marjorie ("M" or "Marge" in the journals) to Dutchy with news of the loss of the baby. They had a son born in 1932 who is still alive.

Dot died at Sidney, B.C., on February 19, 1973 and Dutchy followed her on December 31, 1978. He is buried in the churchyard at Holy Trinity Church, North Saanich, B.C.

"Hillcrest", the Edwards family home in Londonderry, NS (exterior and interior)

Dutchy with his parents, Joseph Plimsoll and Emily Susan Edwards, and his sister Muriel

Joseph Plimsoll Edwards, brother of Dutchy, who was killed in action in France on April 28, 1917

Dutchy married Dorothy Elizabeth Symons at St. Paul's Church, Halifax on April 26, 1926

DUTCHY'S DIARIES | XIII

Formal portrait of JCI Edwards

Gravestone at Holy Trinity Church, North Saanich, BC

EDWARDS — Suddenly at Saanich Peninsula Hospital, December 31, 1978, Commodore John Crispo Inglis Edwards, Royal Canadian Navy (retired), Commander of British Empire, Canadian Decoration. One of eight children born to Major and Mrs. Joseph Edwards, Londonderry, Nova Scotia. Graduated St. Alban's School, Brockville, Ontario, and Royal Naval College of Canada, Halifax. Served in World War I on numerous Royal Navy ships, also served on HMS Valiant at Malta. In World War II Commanding Officer, HMCS Stadacona, Halifax, HMCS Prince Henry, (Armed Merchant Cruiser), and HMCS Cornwallis, (Naval Training Base). Commanding Officer HMCS Naden, an outstanding tennis player, Province of Ontario and Nova Scotia Singles Title holder. Predeceased by his wife, Dorothy Elizabeth, in 1973; survived by sisters, Mrs. F. Smallwood, Montreal, Mrs. G. Stewart, Victoria, B.C., son, John and daughter-in-law, Helen, two grandchildren, John and Susanne; nieces and nephews, Commander and Mrs. Lewis, Halifax, Nova Scotia, Mr. and Mrs. Peter Evans, Halifax, Nova Scotia and Mr. and Mrs. Peter Gordon, Vancouver, B.C. Service in Holy Trinity Anglican Church, Patricia Bay, B.C. on Friday, January 5, 1979, at 1:00 p.m. Rev. Robert Sansom officiating. Interment in the Holy Trinity Cemetery. Flowers gratefully declined. Arrangements by the Sands Funeral Chapel of Roses, Sidney, B.C.
SANDS — SIDNEY

Dutchy's obituary, The Daily Colonist, *January 3, 1979, page 38*

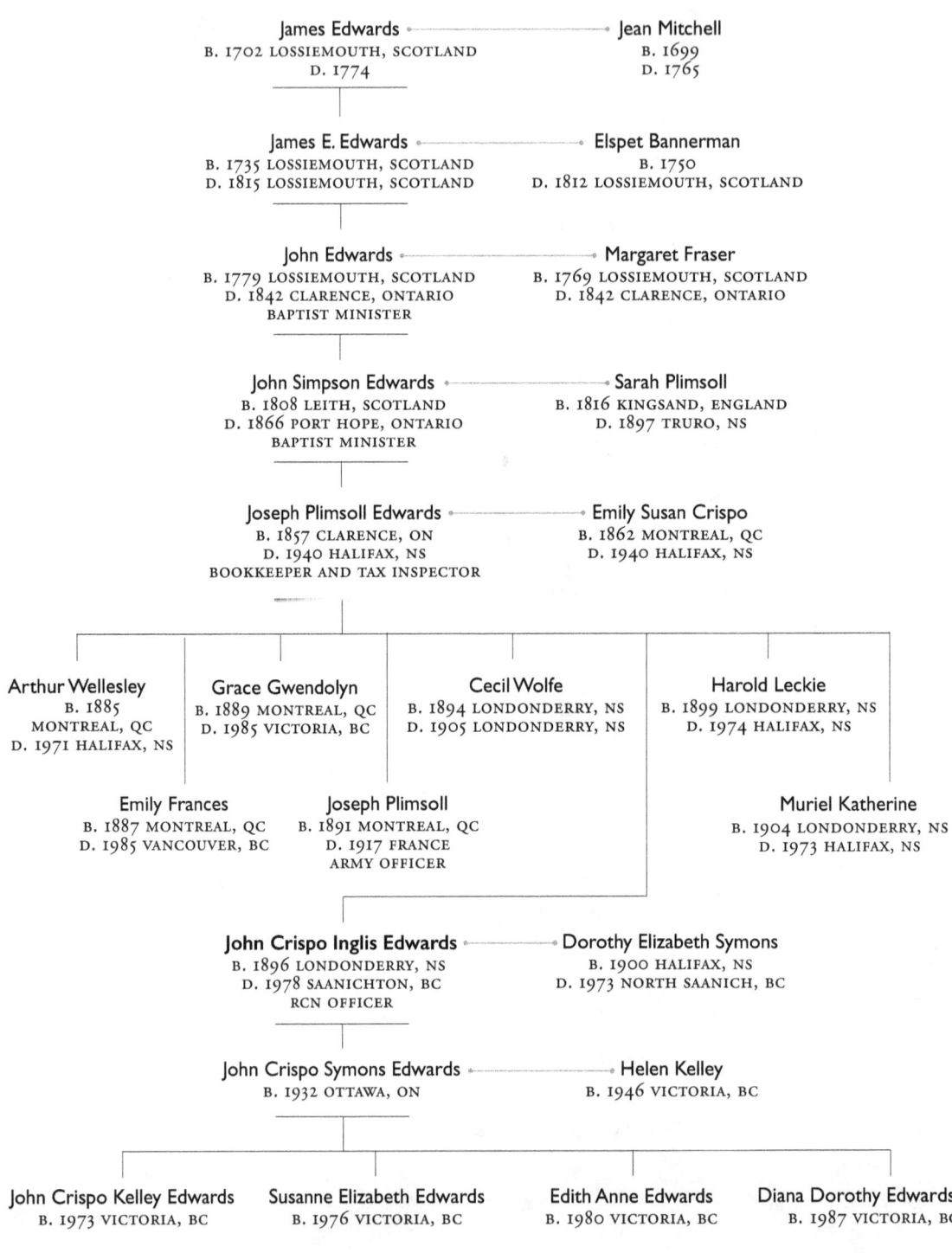

The Roaring Twenties

DUTCHY'S THIRD AND FOURTH JOURNALS give us an insight into one of the most exciting decades in Canadian—and world—history.

By 1919, World War I had finally come to an end, leaving most of the world in a post-war depression. However, in Canada, the decade would be filled with growth and change as the nation began to create a new national identity, independent of Britain. After some initial growing pains, including economic volatility and labour unrest, Canada transitioned from war to peace and prosperity. Canada granted women suffrage, launched its first radio broadcast (in 1922) and revelled in the high life of the Jazz Age. The decade was a roller coaster ride of political, cultural, and social change.

In 1928, the Canadian ship *St. Roch* became the first vessel to circumnavigate North America. Meanwhile, Canada's demand for cars steadily increased as mass production made technology affordable to the middle class. In 1918, Canada had about 300,000 vehicles, but by 1929, there were 1.9 million, and automobile parts were being manufactured in Ontario, near Detroit, Michigan. Dutchy writes in detail about his different cars and the issues he faced with them. Apparently, breakdowns were common.

Dance clubs and dancing became enormously popular in the 1920s. Their popularity peaked in the late 1920s and reached into the early 1930s. Classical pieces, operettas, folk music, etc., were all transformed into popular dancing melodies to satiate the public craze for dancing. The January 1, 1926 edition of the *Daily Colonist* noted that "at least one-third of Victoria City's fifty thousand–odd population were in attendance at the many and varied attractions held last night to bid in a New Year's manner. Perhaps the largest throng in any one place was found at the Empress Hotel where fine music, a fine supper, and the Empress management's traditional hospitality drew a crowd of merry dancers number over a thousand."

Young naval officers were in high demand at dances hosted by socially prominent Victoria citizens. The journals contain a who's who of Victoria's high society who entertained Dutchy and his fellow officers.

The Roaring Twenties was the breakout decade for sports across the modern world. Citizens flocked to see the top athletes of the day compete in new sports venues. Dutchy writes about attending the hockey games of the Victoria Cougars, who would win the Stanley Cup in 1925, long after he had returned to the east coast.

Throughout North America, the 1920s became synonymous with Prohibition, a time when the United States banned alcohol, and its illicit consumption flourished. Unlike in the United States, banning alcohol in Canada was complicated by the shared jurisdiction over alcohol-related laws between Ottawa and the provinces. The provinces controlled sales and consumption while the Canadian government was responsible for the making and trading of alcohol. In March 1918, Ottawa stopped, for the duration of the First World War, the manufacture and importation of liquor into provinces where its purchase was already illegal.

Prohibition was first enacted on a provincial basis in Prince Edward Island in 1901 and the remaining provinces, as well as in Yukon and Newfoundland, during the First World War. Prohibition was widely seen at this time as a patriotic duty and a social sacrifice, to help win the war. Québec rejected prohibition as early as 1919 and their provincial government reaped huge profits from the sale of alcohol.

In 1920, British Columbia voted "wet," and by the following year, some alcoholic beverages were legally sold there and in the Yukon through government stores. Many local entrepreneurs made fortunes as bootleggers transporting alcohol to American ports. Trade was particularly brisk along British Columbia's coastal waterways. Manitoba inaugurated a system of government sale and control of alcohol in 1923, followed by Alberta and Saskatchewan in 1924, Newfoundland in 1925, Ontario and New Brunswick in 1927, and Nova Scotia in 1930. The last bastion, Prince Edward Island, finally gave up "the noble experiment" in 1948. When Dutchy married Dot in Halifax, NS in 1926, guests consumed alcohol served in teacups.

Victoria newspapers reported with optimism on the post-war period. The *Daily Colonist* reported in its January 1, 1924 issue about the upcoming year saying, "Business and Industrial Projects Scheduled for Victoria during Next twelve Months Offer Greater Prosperity Here Than at Any Time Since Great War Disturbed World."

The Wall Street Crash of 1929 ended the era, as the Great Depression brought years of hardship worldwide.

List of Images in the Journals

Dutchy and his brother Joe in their uniforms, date unknown xxii
Journal One cover 1
Foreign stamps in Dutchy's journal, 1916–17 2
Foreign stamps in journal with Dutchy's signature, 1916–17 3
John Crispo Inglis Edwards as a sub-lieutenant, c. 1916 4
Hand-drawn illustration of HMCS *Canada* 6
HMS *Berwick* 22
Hand-drawn map of the island of Bermuda 24
Newspaper clippings about the activities of HMS *Berwick* 28/29
The *Spreewald*; German officers landing as prisoners at St. Lucia 31
Newspaper clippings about the activities of HMS *Berwick*, from 1914 32
Dutchy as a midshipman at Kingston 33
Sketch of how ship was moored at No. 3 berth 33
St. Lucia, part of the Caribbean patrol 39
HMCS *Niobe* at Clark's Harbour 49
HMS *Archer* 53
W/T transmission regarding location of possible torpedo, June 6, 1917 60
Menu from special meal on July 15, 1918 84
Journal Two cover 85
The port of Livorno, Italy 86
Memorandum from Vice-Admiral A. Calthorpe, October 9, 1918 93
HMS *Cameleon* 94
Admiralty Weekly Orders, November 13, 1918 98
The King's Message to the Fleet, November 13, 1918 99
Post-war election procedures with regard to Royal Navy personnel being
    candidates for political office, November 13, 1918 100
Congratulations to Captain Commanding, Malta Base from Admiralty 101
Message from Rear Admiral Michael Culme-Seymour 103
Orders for HMS *Cameleon* to sail to Mudros, February 3, 1919 107
Orders for HMS *Cameleon* to sail to Plymouth, England, March 14, 1919 110
Dutchy's orders to join HMS *Galatea* as Lieutenant, September 3, 1919 115
Sketch of German sailing vessel *Neptune* 118
Dutchy's written testimony before the Hebburn Salvage Arbitration, page 1 124
Dutchy's written testimony before the Hebburn Salvage Arbitration, page 2 125
Dutchy's written testimony before the Hebburn Salvage Arbitration, page 3 126
Newspaper clipping regarding Demobilization Order, March 22, 1919 127
Postcard from the Constant Spring Hotel, Kingston, Jamaica 138
Journal Three cover 139
Journal Three title page 140

Receipt for purchase of Gordon Setter puppy, September 16, 1921 ... 154
Application for Master's Certificate, 1922 ... 167
HMC Dockyard, Halifax, NS ... 171
Dutchy's dog, Peter Bangs ... 173
Coverage of Halifax Wanderers rugby team, October 24, 1922 ... 174
Halifax Wanderers rugby team, 1922 ... 175
December 26, 1922 clipping from a Halifax newspaper ... 177
Certificate presented to Dutchy, March 9, 1923 ... 181
Dutchy was a world-ranked tennis player ... 184
Officers' long course August–December 1923 ... 191
Hockey team ... 194
Rugby team ... 196
Dutchy playing hockey ... 197
Dutchy playing hockey ... 197
Journal Four cover ... 203
Series of Italian stamps that commemorate the Franciscan order ... 204
HMS *Valiant* ... 208
Journal page December 26, 1926 to January 5, 1927 ... 218
"The Battles of Coronel and Falkland Islands" video ... 225
Naval officers on camels by the Sphinx and the Pyramids ... 228
Business card from Cairo ... 229
Italian five lire note ... 229
Sketch of docking arrangement ... 253
Journal page, July 3, 1929 to July 14, 1929 ... 256
HMCS *Niobe* (detail) ... 260

Maps

East Coast of North America ... 299
West Coast of Canada ... 299
The Mediterranean Sea ... 300
The British Isles ... 300
The Caribbean Sea and Bermuda ... 301

Glossary

Abandon ship stations: Ships' companies practiced correct procedures to be used in case of emergency so that they would react correctly under pressure.

Ballast: Ballast is material that is used to provide stability to a vehicle or structure.

Cable: A cable length is the length of a ship's cable, about 600 feet.

Chronometer: A chronometer is an instrument for measuring time, especially one designed to keep accurate time in spite of motion or variations in temperature, humidity, and air pressure. Chronometers were first developed for marine navigation, being used in conjunction with astronomical observation to determine longitude.

Coaling ship: Refueling, known as coaling a ship, was one of the most grueling tasks for men of the Navy. It was a back-breaking job, accomplished by hand. Enormous piles of coal had to be moved from a dock or a collier (a ship carrying coal) into coal bunkers below the deck of the receiving ship. It took many hours to coal a ship due to the sheer volume of coal to be moved.

Collier: A collier is a bulk cargo ship designed to carry coal, especially for naval use by coal-fired warships. Coaling at sea was critical to navies and speed of coal transfer was an important factor in naval efficiency.

Court of Inquiry: A Court of Inquiry is a group of people, often with special knowledge or skill, who have been brought together in order to examine the causes of an incident. It was used in the Royal Navy to determine punishment for offences, ownership of salvage materials, and any matter of concern to the integrity of the Navy.

Cutter: A cutter is generally a small to medium-sized vessel, depending on its role and definition.

Field gun drill: Sailors were trained to disassemble and reassemble a field gun. Competitions were held between personnel of different ships.

Fire stations: Ships' companies practiced correct procedures to be used in case of emergency so that they would react correctly under pressure.

Foc'sle: The forecastle, abbreviated as foc'sle, is the upper deck of a sailing ship forward of the foremast, or the forward part of a ship with the sailors' living quarters. Related to the latter meaning is the phrase "before the mast" which denotes anything related to ordinary sailors, as opposed to a ship's officers.

Galley: A galley is a type of ship that is propelled mainly by rowing.

General quarters: General quarters, battle stations, or action stations is an announcement made aboard a naval warship to signal that all hands (everyone available) aboard a ship must go to battle stations as quickly as possible.

Jolly boat: Jolly boats were usually the smallest type of boat carried on ships and were generally between 16 feet and 18 feet long. They were clinker-built and propelled by four or six oars.

Knot: A knot measures speed. A knot is one nautical mile per hour (1 knot = 1.15 miles per hour).

Mouldy: Mouldy is a slang term for a torpedo.

Nautical mile: A nautical mile is slightly more than a statute or land-measured mile. 1 nautical mile=1.508 statute miles. Nautical miles are used for charting and navigating.

Oiling jetty: When ships changed from coal burning to oil-burning, they were fuelled at shore-based oiling jetties. It was much cleaner and quicker than coal had been.

Q ship: Q-ships, also known as Q-boats, decoy vessels, special service ships, or mystery ships, were heavily armed merchant ships with concealed weaponry, designed to lure submarines into making surface attacks. This gave Q-ships the chance to open fire and sink them. Dutchy told a tale of wearing women's clothing as part of the decoy.

Quarterdeck: The quarterdeck is a raised deck behind the main mast of a sailing ship. Traditionally it was where the captain commanded his vessel and where the ship's colours were kept. This led to its use as the main ceremonial and reception area on board, and the word is still used to refer to such an area on a ship or even in naval establishments on land.

Rigging loft: A rigging loft is a location in which rigging is prepared for use on ships.

Sea chest: A sea chest was a box or suitcase used by a sailor for storing personal property.

Splicing ropes: Rope splicing is the forming of a semi-permanent joint between two ropes or two parts of the same rope by partly untwisting and then interweaving their strands. Splices can be used to form a stopper at the end of a line, to form a loop or an eye in a rope, or for joining two ropes together.

Stern gland: Apart from stern bearings, the stern tube also houses water and oil sealing glands known as the stern glands. The stern tube is a sensitive part of the ship where the sea water can easily seep inside. The stern glands thus seal the area between the stern tube and the propeller shaft. The glands are attached at the forward end of the stern tube and prevent the passing of sea water into the ship. The glands also prevent the leaking of oil from the stern bearings into the sea.

Stern tube: The stern tube, as the name suggests, is a hollow tube-like structure at the stern or rear part of the ship. A ship needs a propeller to drive it forward against the waves. The propeller, located outside the ship, needs to be connected to the engine inside the ship's engine room. A long shaft known as the propeller shaft is used for connecting the ship's engine and the propeller. The stern tube is a narrow hole in the hull structure at the rear end (aft peak) of the ship, through which the propeller shaft passes and connects the engine and propeller.

Theodolites: A theodolite is a precision instrument used for measuring angles both horizontally and vertically. Theodolites can rotate along their horizontal axis as well as their vertical axis. They were used for mapping in World War I.

Tramp: A tramp steamer, in contrast to the liner, operates without a schedule, going wherever required to pick up and deliver its cargoes.

Trot: The Trot was a type of mooring that was quite popular in the early twentieth century. Essentially the ship was secured to a mooring buoy fore and aft so that it wouldn't move around. When ships are at anchor there is just one point holding them to the seabed and they will swing around their anchor cable based on wind and current. That fine if you have a lot of rooms to give each ship a big circle and room to swing on their anchor, but in tight harbours or anchorages, they would install mooring buoys so that they could fit more ships in a tight space without the risk of them hitting each other. It's how they use to setup/organize the convoys in Halifax Harbour (which is narrower) before they departed.

Watch: Watchkeeping or watchstanding is the assignment of sailors to specific roles on a ship to operate it continuously. These assignments, also known as watches are constantly active as they are considered essential to the safe operation of the vessel, and also allow the ship to respond to emergencies and other situations quickly. These watches are divided into work periods to ensure that the roles are always occupied at all times, while those members of the crew who are assigned to a work during a watch are known as watch keepers.

Weighed anchor: Weigh anchor is a nautical term indicating the final preparation of a sea vessel for getting underway. Weighing anchor literally means raising the anchor of the vessel from the sea floor and hoisting it up to be stowed on board the vessel. At the moment when the anchor is no longer touching the sea floor, it is aweigh.

Whaler: A whaler is a type of open boat that is relatively narrow and pointed at both ends. It was originally developed for whaling, and later became popular for work along beaches, since it does not need to be turned around for beaching or refloating.

Zig-zagging: Zig-zagging is the practice of frequently altering direction to port or starboard. The manoeuvre was designed to disguise a convoy's true course and confuse the enemy.

Dutchy, right, and his brother Joe in their uniforms, date unknown

JOURNAL ONE
February 21, 1916 – July 18, 1918

Foreign stamps in Dutchy's journal, 1916–17

Foreign stamps in journal with Dutchy's signature, 1916–17

John Crispo Inglis Edwards as a sub-lieutenant, c. 1916

JOURNAL ONE
February 21, 1916 – July 18, 1918

In which Dutchy Edwards serves in HMCS Canada *on patrol in eastern Canada, patrols the Caribbean in HMS* Berwick, *takes a torpedo course at HMS* Vernon *in England, and patrols around the English coast and then the Dardanelles in HMS* Archer.

H.M.C.S. CANADA AT YARMOUTH
FEBRUARY 1916

21st MONDAY Critchley[1] and I left Halifax by the D.A.R.[2] train at 7:15 A.M. and arrived at Yarmouth 4:45 P.M. I had been in the Niobe[3] for the last few days having joined her on the Saturday before I joined H.M.C.S. Canada who was frozen in. H.M.C.S. Starling also alongside.

22nd TUESDAY Stowing our gear and getting cabin into shape. Ship's company at rifle drill. Went ashore in the afternoon to tea at Dr. Janish's. Sent my sea chest back to Halifax by H.M.C.S. Starling.

23rd WEDNESDAY Arrived H.M.C.S. Margaret. Route march in forenoon.

24th THURSDAY Cast off from jetty & proceeded at 9 A.M. cruising Northwards through Grand Passage. Communicated with "Curlew". Anchored in Lear Bay, N.B. in 17 fathoms, quite close to American boundary. Eastport Maine and Lubeck[Lubec] are quite close and St. Andrews is further up the bay.

25th FRIDAY Exercised Fire & abandon ship stations. Arrived "Petrel". Raining all day with S.E. wind. H.W.F.&C 11h 12m. Spring rise 23½ feet Neaps 17 feet.

H.M.C.S CANADA AT WELCHPOOL
FEBRUARY 1916

26th SAT. Raining all day. Hands cleaning ship. Sent mail.

---

1 Sankey Critchley was a classmate at the Royal Naval College of Canada and a lifelong friend of Commodore Edwards.
2 The Dominion Atlantic Railway was a historic railway which operated in the western part of Nova Scotia, primarily through the Annapolis Valley.
3 To form the nucleus of its new navy, Canada acquired two ships from Great Britain. On August 4, 1910, at Portsmouth, England, the cruiser HMCS *Rainbow* was the first ship commissioned into Canada's navy. She arrived at Esquimalt, British Columbia, on November 7, 1910, and carried out fishery patrols and training duties on Canada's west coast. Another Royal Navy cruiser, HMS *Niobe*, became the second ship commissioned into the Canadian navy on September 6, 1910, at Devonport in England and arrived at Halifax, Nova Scotia, on 21 October 1910.

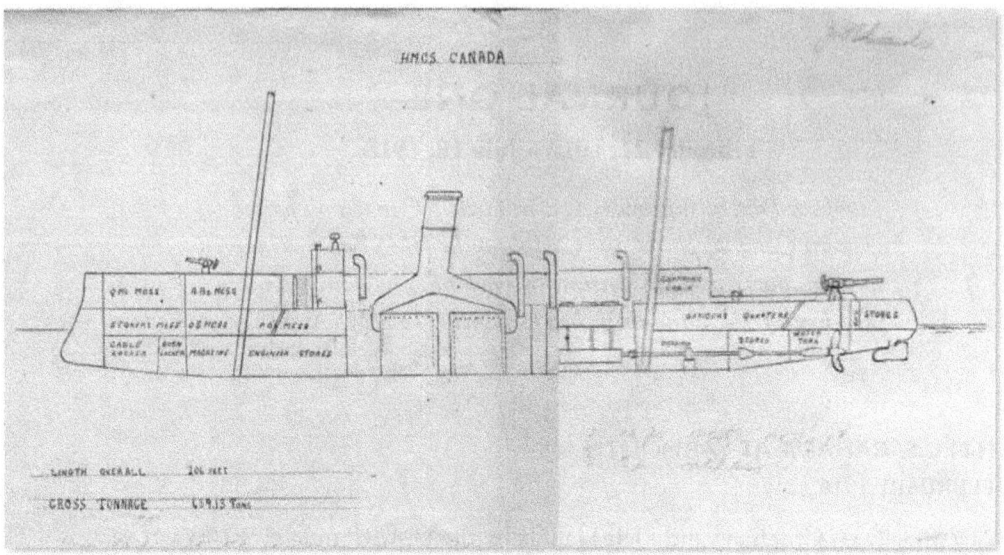

Hand-drawn illustration of HMCS Canada

27th SUNDAY DIVISIONS, went ashore in forenoon with Critchley, 1st Lieut. & Betts for a walk. Some fine summer cottages here. 1:15 Weighed and proceeded 3.05. Anchored in 11 fathoms at Letang, N.B.

28th MON. 9:20 A.M. Weighed and proceeded. Passed schooner "Clifford and White" of Jonesport. Cruising between Grand Manan Island & the Maine coast. 3:40 P.M. Anchored in 12 fathoms at Flag Cove, Grand Manan Island. Went ashore and it was very cold. Froze my ears and got pretty wet.

29th TUES. Weighed and proceed[ed] at 1:15 P.M. and at 5:30 P.M. Anchored in 10½ fathoms at Letang, N.B.

H.M.C.S. CANADA AT LETANG N.B.
MARCH 1916

1st WED. 9:00 A.M. Weighed and proceeded along the New Brunswick coast to St. John [Saint John][4]. S.S. Missanabie anchored off the entrance of harbour with troops aboard. Two other transports in the stream. Made fast alongside astern of H.M.C.S. Florence.

Sent Mr. Betts and a boarding party to the American schooner "Jessie" which sailed from New York in the early part of January & was a suspect. The Florence towed the Jessie inside the harbour at 11:00 P.M. S. S. Missanabie sailed.

2nd THURS. Sailed from St. John at 1:30 P.M. & arrived Digby at 5 P.M. Very calm sea. Went ashore.

---

4 The correct spelling of the location is Saint John.

4th SAT. Very strong wind from the North East & with high sea. Let go second anchor & kept anchor watches. Very thick all day.

5th SUNDAY Weighed & proceeded at 9 A.M., having steam in both boilers we did about 16 knots. Shaped course for Yarmouth keeping about a mile off shore & passing through Petit Passage. Arrived at Yarmouth about 2 P.M. H.M.C.S. Stadacona was here and we alongside her, saw Soulsby[5] & Lindsay. Tea party in "Stadacona".

H.M.C.S. CANADA AT YARMOUTH
MARCH 1916

6th MONDAY Shifted berth to allow the Stadacona to proceed. She had two attempts as the ice was rather heavy. Went to a recruiting meeting in the evening with Miss Janish.

7th TUES. Coaled ship. Started at 8 A.M. and finished 2:15 P.M. Took on 40 tons. We only had one brought out & it was rather slow work. Snowing quite heavily.

8th WED. At 9:00 A.M. weighed and proceeded shaped course for Digby through Petit Passage. with Capt. Pasco SNO. Patrols aboard, carried out with a few manoeuvres using the Auxiliary Patrol vessel signal book. Anchored off Digby, the wind increased during the night & we kept anchor watches.

H.M.C.S. CANADA AT DIGBY
MARCH 1916

9th THURS. I went away in the galley to bring Capt. Pasco off to the ship. He inspected the ship & seemed quite pleased with her condition. Carried out signal exercises with the Margaret.

10th FRIDAY Captain Pasco came aboard at 9:20 A.M. Exercised "fire" and "abandon ship" stations also squad drill. Boat sailing in the afternoon.

11th SAT. Weighed & proceeded at 10 A.M. with S.N.O. Patrols aboard. Exercised "man overboard" and carried out 12 and 3 pounder firing. The two 8 pounders on the foc'sle did very good shooting but we had two misfires in the afterguns & we left them for 30 minutes before extracting the cartridges. The misfires were caused by defective tubes. The twelve pounders are rather low down to do effective shooting & they are of very old mark & need re-calibrating. Arrived at St. John 2:30 P.M. & anchored in the stream. H.M.C.S. Florence here. The S.S. Matatua caught fire about midnight she is loaded with automobiles, carbides, etc.

---

5 Henry Wilkins Stephen Soulsby was a Royal Naval College of Canada classmate.

H.M.C.S. CANADA AT DIGBY
MARCH 1916

14th Sailed from St. John at 6 A.M. with Capt. Pasco on board. Florence took station astern, carried out a few manoeuvres & also 12 pounder & rifle firing. Anchored at Digby about noon & Capt. Pasco left ship. Exercised abandon ship. Critchley & I exercising boat's crews in the afternoon.

15th WED. 9:10 weighed & proceeded down the coast towards Yarmouth. Got as far as Centreville when it came on thick so we did a sixteen-point turn shaping course for Digby anchoring at 1:0 P.M. Wind increasing & with snow. Officers keeping anchor watches.

16th High wind and sea. Officers keeping anchor watches. Let go second anchor. Seamanship class with the gunners at instruction.

17th FRIDAY Weather moderates. At 9 A.M. weighed and proceeded towards Yarmouth. Quite heavy sea against us and very cold. Arrived Yarmouth 4:00 P.M. and secured alongside in position for coaling. Rec'd one cruiser arc flashing lamp also mail. R.L.P. Of course Sankey rec'd much mail from Halifax.

H.M.C.S. CANADA AT YARMOUTH
MARCH 1916

18th SATURDAY Coaling ship, started at 7:30 AM & finished 12:45 PM. Took in 111 tons.

Used two broughs and we carried most of the coal aboard in baskets. Went skating in the evening & the ice was quite good.

[Quite an improvement signed C.J.S.]

19th SUNDAY Landed a church party under Mr. Critchley. Snowing very hard. Stayed on board in the afternoon. Arrived H.M.C.S. Starling.

20th MON. Rifle drill in the shed near jetty in the forenoon, transferred the 3 pounder we took from the S.S. Matatua at St. John to the H.M.C.S. Starling.

21st TUES. Rifle drill in the forenoon. Discharged Lieut. Julian to hospital. exercised out span lower anchor.

22nd WED. Drill in the forenoon, weather was quite mild in the middle part of the day & so we had an opportunity to wash decks and paintwork. Went to the moving pictures in the evening and had a game of bridge afterwards at the Janishes.

23rd THURS. Heavy wind from the East, with snow. Company drill in the forenoon the D.A.R. train snowed up and not expected in until Saturday as she only got as far as Kentville.

24th FRI. Company drill in forenoon and afternoon. Wind still blowing very hard. Played bridge at Miss Paterson's in the evening.

25th SAT. Rifle drill in the forenoon. Went ashore in afternoon to tea at the Janishes. Went skating in the evening.

H.M.C.S. CANADA AT HALIFAX
MARCH 1916

26th SUN. Cast off from the jetty at 6:15 A.M. but we were delayed an hour. Averaged about 14 knots on way up & arrived at Halifax 8 P.M. anchored near the "Coronia". Did some quite heavy rolling after leaving Yarmouth.

27th MON. Weighed and proceeded anchoring off the "Niobe". H.M.S. Carnarvon in port also transports "Baltic" and "Empress of Britain" in the basin. Had dinner at the Critchley's.

28th TUES. Splicing rope in the forenoon in the dockyard and had a signal exercise in Niobe after Church, went ashore later on to dinner & the Academy.

29th WED. Did some rifle drills & splicing during the forenoon, signal exercise in afternoon. Had a tea party onboard S.S. Olympic arrived & anchored in the stream.

30th THURS. Very fine day, same routine as Wed. in forenoon. The "Baltic" came out of the basin & went alongside. "Empress" sailed. "Calgarian" arrived.

H.M.C.S. CANADA AT HALIFAX
MARCH 1916

31st FRIDAY Rifle drill in the forenoon at 1 pm weighed & went alongside the "San Rito" at the drydock, had to shift further aft in order to take in water. Repairs being made on the boilers and boat deck.

APRIL

1st Saturday Alongside, S.S. Olympic went alongside No. 2. The "Baltic & Adriatic" sailed also H.M.S. Carnarvon and Empress of Britain. There are about 18000 troops in all going over in the above ships, the Olympic taking 6000.

2nd SUNDAY Raining in the forenoon, landed a church party under Mr. Critchley. The 64th regiment & 71st went aboard S.S. Olympic. I was on watch in the forenoon.

3rd MONDAY Fine and clear. Hands employed tarring[tearing] down the rigging. Dockyard parties working in the ship. Went to the Academy in the evening & saw "Bringing Up Father". Arrived H.M.S. Suffolk & went alongside No. 4.

4th TUESDAY Cast off at 1:10 P.M. anchored in the stream off No 4. Sent boats away sailing. Weighed at 6 P.M. & went alongside No. 3. Dad came off to tea.

5th WEDNESDAY Raining very hard all day so we did not get through much work on the upper deck. The "Olympic" sailed. H.M.C.S. Stadacona arrived. She tried to go alongside the Olympic outside the harbour and carried away one of her own & two of the Olympic's boats; she seems always in trouble. Went ashore in the afternoon.

6th THURSDAY Went to the rigging loft in the forenoon and did some splicing. In the afternoon played soccer against the R.N. College. We lost 2-3.

7th FRIDAY Did some splicing in the forenoon and also rifle drill. In the afternoon did some 12 pr. field fun drill & after that we had a tea party on board.

8th SATURDAY H.M.S. Suffolk sailed. Court of Inquiry in the Stadacona. Played the officers of the "Niobe" in soccer and got beaten 2-3. Tingley joined the Niobe as he takes his exam on Monday.

H.M.C.S. CANADA AT HALIFAX
APRIL 1916

9th SUNDAY Cast off from No. 3 at about 6:30 A.M. Heavy wind and sea outside and we rolled all over the place. Patrolled near the outer automatic buoy at about 5 knots we were going to sail to Yarmouth but it was too rough so we anchored inside Mayer's Reach Lighthouse.

10th MONDAY Weighed and proceeded about 9 A.M. for Yarmouth. Very heavy sea and we rolled quite a lot. Our cabin was wrecked and Critchley was very cheerful. Sea calmed down a bit in the evening. Made about 8 knots.

11th TUESDAY Anchored at Westport Brier Island. In the forenoon shifted berth. Went sailing in the afternoon and at 2:00 A.M. weighed and proceeded towards Yarmouth. Rec'd. a wireless to alter course for St. John. Arrived at St. John 10:30 P.M. Anchored. Very high tide & so we kept anchor watches. Rec'd. prisoner from "Florence".

H.M.C.S. CANADA AT ST. JOHN
APRIL 1916

12th WED. Weighed and proceeded at 6 A.M. Exercised man overboard. Last boat away in 3½ minutes. Arrived Yarmouth at 4:30 P.M. & went alongside Starling and Hochelaga here. Went to a bridge party at Mrs. Baker's in the evening.

13th THURS. Coaled ship in the forenoon, shoved off at Noon and shaped course for Halifax. Very fine day.

14th FRIDAY Arrived at Halifax ? P.M. and anchored off No. 4. H.M.S. Coronia here. Went sailing in the forenoon and in the afternoon landed and did some "field gun drill". Went ashore about 6 P.M. & S. met me in the Ford. Had dinner at the Critchley's.

15th SATURDAY Raining nearly all day. We thought that we were going to sea but didn't go. H.M.S. Drake arrived in the forenoon and anchored in the stream.

16th SUNDAY Blowing quite hard. Landed a church party. Critchley and I went to the Cathedral. I had lunch at Critchley's & we went out in the Ford in the afternoon.

17th Monday Drill in the forenoon with the ship's company of H.M.C.S. Stadacona. Somebody has been trying to christen this book. Went to the Strand in the evening.

18th TUES. Officers were drilling in the forenoon but A. & I weren't. Hands employed refitting the ship. But most of our boats on the jetty.

19th WED. Shifted from No. 4 to No. 3. Having a piece put on the keel of the dinghy. Had some leave.

H.M.C.S. CANADA AT HALIFAX

24th APRIL Returned. Small arms exercises in the forenoon. Went to a dance in the evening at the Queen Hotel.

25th TUESDAY Court of Inquiry on board. Capt. Grant president of the Court. Hands employed chipping and red leading the ship's sides.

26th WED. Usual routine. We take in a flag exercise every forenoon from the "Niobe" beginning at 9:10 & finishing at 10 A.M. Had dinner with Dad and Mr. MacMillan at the Halifax. I was going to the Academy but we decided not to go so P. & I stayed at home and talked.

27th THURS. Went for a walk in the afternoon. Met D. Angus an old St. Alban's boy. Walked around Pt. Pleasant with Polly[6] in the afternoon.

28th Friday Took in a flag exercise in the forenoon and also got the old bridge screen down. SS. Olympic went alongside. Critchley & I went ashore to have our uniforms tried on in the afternoon. We went to a show in the evening.

H.M.C.S. CANADA AT HALIFAX

29th SATURDAY Raining hard all day which made the roads rather rotten. Critchley and I were going to Londonderry in order to bring down the car. We decided to go by the late train but found out she wasn't running. Needless to say we did not go.

30th SUNDAY Aboard all day. Went ashore in the evening and had supper at the MacMechan's.

---

6 This would appear to Polly Easton. I was unable to find any information about her other than her name.

MAY 1916

1st MONDAY Shifted into white cap covers. Hands employed scraping and chipping paint. On Watch so did not go ashore. Heard that we are going to sea on Wed.

2nd TUESDAY Started painting ship, getting the bridge screen shifted. Had a tea party in the afternoon Mrs. Easton and Mrs. Critchley were the chaperones. Went to the Academy in the evening. The tea party was a great success after nearly everybody had cleared out except the chosen few. Polly & I went to Academy in evening but got fed up with the show so we went to Ackers.

3rd WED. Painting ship. "Grilse" arrived from Bermuda. The ships here now are the "Canada", "Stadacona", "Margaret", "Grilse". Went out to Critchley's for tea. Had a canoe on the "Arm" for the first time this year.

4th THURS. Cast off from No. 3 and anchored in the stream. Raining in the forenoon. Went to a boxing competition in the afternoon at the R.N. College gym & it was a very good show. Had dinner with Mr. Julian in the evening.

5th FRIDAY Painting ship. Launched the blue motor boat. Mr. Betts is going to take her to Sydney. Went in for a swim. Had a dinner party on board in the evening. Mrs. Easton & Polly came – great fun.

6th SATURDAY Hands painting ship. Went ashore in the afternoon and had a canoe on the Arm.

7th SUNDAY Church party in the forenoon Sub-lieut. Hibbard in charge. Had tea at Mrs. Easton's in the afternoon and went to church and afterwards went to supper at Mrs. MacMechan's.

8th MONDAY Ashore making a fender for the motor boat in the forenoon. Went to Niobe for signals P.M. Heard that Critchley was appointed to the Rainbow & leaves for Esquimalt tomorrow which is rotten luck for me. Went canoeing on the Arm in the afternoon with Polly.

9th Tuesday Critchley left by the Maritime Express and I went up to see him off. Went alongside & took in water. Stadacona & Margaret also alongside. Mr. Betts left for Sydney in the forenoon in Captain Pasco's motor boat, he took two men with him.

10th WED. Sailed from Halifax at 6:30 A.M. also Margaret & Stadacona. Carried out manoeuvres nearly all day. Capt. Pasco aboard Canada. We only had three ships so only did things such as 1 flag etc. Margaret uses too much helm & Stadacona does not use enough. Anchored at Whitehead about 7 P.M. which is quite a good anchorage.

11th Thursday Weighed and proceeded at 5 A.M. in formation single line ahead. Quite thick fog came on us & we started sounding machine.

Passed quite close to Scatarie & heard the fog horn. Fog lifted when we got close to Sydney and we anchored at about 6:30 P.M. opposite the yacht club.

12th Friday Hands employed cleaning ship. Went ashore in the afternoon & did some shopping. Margaret proceeded to sea at 10 A.M.

13th SATURDAY Cleaning ship. Make and Mend. On watch.

H.M.C.S. CANADA – AT SYDNEY

14th Sunday H.M.C.S. Hochelaga arrived. Sub-Lieut. Tingley joined the ship. Landed church parties from all the ships present. Had lunch with Lindsay in the Stadacona and went for a walk with Tingley into the country in the evening.

Monday 15th Sent all boats away and we anchored off Capt. Pasco's house and waited there for an hour. After that we went sailing. Went pulling in the whaler at 7 A.M. as the officers are practicing for a pulling race with the officers of H.M.C.S. Hochelaga.

Went ashore in the afternoon for a walk.

Tuesday 16th Hands employed chipping waterways, painting, etc. Rigged clothesline on fo'c'sle.

H.M.C.S. CANADA – AT SYDNEY
MAY 1916

Wed. 17th Ship's company employed painting ship.

THURS. 18th Went away pulling in the morning. "Margaret" arrived at 10:15 A.M. & Stadacona at noon. Went ashore in the afternoon.

Friday 19th In the forenoon the boats of the Canada and Stadacona went pulling and sailing. I was in the whaler. We came in first of the pulling and second in sailing. Soulsby in the "Stads" whaler won the sailing race. In the afternoon took Capt. Pasco's surveying instruments over to the Stadacona. Tingley & I joined the above ship at 11 P.M.

HMCS STADACONA

Sat 20th Weighed and proceeded at 5:00 A.M. with S. O. Patrols on board. Marked some lead lines in the forenoon and afternoon. The ship carried out target practice 4" & 12 pr. in the forenoon. Capt. Pasco gave us a dummy run with the theodolites.[7]

---

7 A theodolite is a precision instrument used for measuring angles both horizontally and vertically. Theodolites can rotate along their horizontal axis as well as their vertical axis. They were used for mapping in World War I.

H.M.C.S. STADACONA – MUTTON BAY, LABRADOR
MAY 1916

Sun. 21st Marked lead lines & took sights in the forenoon. Came in sight of Labrador coast about 11:50 A.M. Little Mekatina Lt. abeam about 1 P.M. I went up to masthead when entering harbour to watch for shoals & it was cold up there. Lindsay went ahead in the motor boat to take soundings. Passed three ice bergs outside the entrance. The inhabitants were all at church when we entered the harbour but they came out to see us. The village is small consisting of about 30 houses & a church, telegraph station, also lots of huskies. Quite a lot of snow here. In winter the mail is carried by dog teams. Provisions come twice a year. Very rocky ground. Fishing is the big industry also sealing.

Mon. 22nd Landed at 8:30 A.M. with whitewash, etc. to make white marks on the rocks and also to crest cairns, triangulation stations, etc. I, with two men, spent all the forenoon whitewashing. In the afternoon two parties went ashore with the theodolite to the main station & I took my sextant and went around taking sextant angles. Got back to ship about 6:45 P.M.

Surveying
H.M.C.S. STADACONA – MUTTON BAY LABRADOR
MAY 1916

Tues. 23rd Started out at 8:30 A.M. with my sextant to take angles of a new rock area near Seal Island. I went to prow first then harbour & afterwards climbed the mountain to Tingley. I have a beastly cold. In the afternoon Capt. Pasco and myself plotted the angles on the plotting sheet. Everything is taken very exact and the angles between distant objects are plotted by means of chords. We get the positions by working out triangles. Scale used 6"=1 mile. Went ashore at 6:30 to Goose to get some sextant angles. This cold of mine is hellish.

Wednes. 24 In the forenoon I worked with Capt. Pasco plotting positions on the plotting sheet. And in the afternoon I went over to Harbour Island to get some more sextant angles. I was there from 1:30 P.M. till 5 P.M. Two boats out sounding.

We sound in lines & plot the positions as we sound by Station Pointer fixes.
ROUGH POSITION OF MUTTON BAY LAT. 50 47 25 N
LONG 59 02 10 W

H.M.C.S. STADACONA – MUTTON BAY LABRADOR

MAY 25th Landed at 8:30 A.M. with Capt. Pasco & Mr. Osborne (Mate). Taking sextant angles to fill in the coast line. We use a ten foot pole & one person stands with it on a point or rock & the other takes the sextant angles between the two marks on the pole. RNR went out to Seal Isl. with the theodolite. Two ice bergs off the entrance.

H.M.C.S. CANADA AT SEA
MAY 1916

Monday 29th Weighed & proceeded to North Sydney at 8:30 A.M. Secured alongside coaling jetty. Took in 73 tons of coal. Started at 9 A.M. & finished 3:35 P.M. At 4:30 proceeded to sea and took up patrol on Cabot Strait speed 5 knots between Cape North and Cape Roy.

TUESDAY 30th Patrolling at 5 knots. In the afternoon carried out 1" aiming practice exercised sea boats crew.

Wed. 31st Raining nearly all day.

JUNE 1916

THURS. 1st June Steamed towards Sydney and picked up the "Margaret". We were joined at 9:30 by "Hochelaga", Stadacona & Florence. Captain Pasco in the Hochelaga. Carried out fleet manoeuvres such as 1 pt A, 2 flag B etc. Had the forenoon watch. Parted company at 3:30. Stadacona, Hochelaga and Canada on patrol. Rec'd. payment.

H.M.C.S. CANADA – ON PATROL
JUNE 1916

FRIDAY 2nd Took sights in the forenoon. Near Cape North. Had the afternoon watch. Passed two naval patrol motor boats who were on their way to Newfoundland. In the press news at 10 P.M. Learned that the "Queen Mary", "Invincible" & "Indefatigable" and cruisers "Defense", "Black Prince" and the destroyers "Turbulent", "Sparrowhawk", "Ardent" and "Tipperary" were sunk on Wednesday off the coast of Jutland. Also the cruiser "Warrior". The German ships "Pommern", "Weisbaden" and "Frauenlob" and several T.B.D.s.

H.M.C.S. CANADA – ON PATROL
JUNE 1916

SATURDAY 3rd Patrolling. Middle watch. Communicated with H.M.C.S. Hochelaga in the afternoon. At 4:30 P.M. Anchored in St. Lawrence Bay for two hours.

SUNDAY 4th On Patrol between St. Paul's Island and Cape Ray. Proceeded to go to assistance of stranded vessel.

Monday 5th Near Neil's Harbour. Found out at daylight that the vessel was not stranded. She was taken in tow by the "Aspy".

Tuesday 6th Anchored in St. Lawrence Bay at 4:05 P.M. and bought some fish. 6:30 weighed anchor and proceeded on patrol.

Wednesday (7th) Communicated with H.M.C.S. Hochelaga at 11:50 A.M. Hands at rifle drill. Very foggy. Doubled watches. Tingley & I had first & morning. Ship stopped about 5 miles off St. Paul's Is. Big schools of <u>mackerel</u>? around the ship. We tried to catch them. A big whale circled around the ship.

CANADA

THURSDAY 8th Communicated with the Margaret. Arrived at North Sydney about 3 P.M. and coaled. Took in 73 tons.

Friday 9th On watch. Cleaning ship, rec'd. some mail including a long letter from De toms which was mostly about getting across. Landed a patrol in the evening as we had the guard. War news better. Germans admit the loss of Lutzow battle cruiser and "Rostock" Lt. cr. "Karlsruhe" Class also a submarine and several more destroyers.

SATURDAY 10th Writing up of logs in the forenoon. Landed one fore derrick & spare gear at S.O.P.'s house. In the forenoon we had a photo taken of officer and ship's company. Went ashore to the tennis.

H.M.C.S. CANADA – AT SYDNEY, N.S.

SUNDAY 11th On watch. Landed church parties in the forenoon.

MONDAY 12th "Stadacona" sailed at 5 A.M. Photographer came off in the forenoon and took pictures of officer and ship's company. Went ashore in the afternoon. Sub. Lieut. Gauvreau joined the ship.

TUESDAY 13th H.M.S. Logota arrived at 7:00 A.M. and sailed at 10:30 A.M. On watch. Photographer again came off to take pictures as yesterday's weren't very successful.

Meeting onboard re regatta. Hands employed securing boats etc. for sea.

Wed. 14th Weighed and proceeded at 5 A.M. to take up patrol between Cape North and Cape Ray. Communicated with "Stadacona" 8:30 A.M. Communicated with H.M.C.S. "Margaret" in St. Lawrence Bay. Took sights. Weather fine.

THURSDAY 15th Had afternoon watch. Fine weather. S.S. "Gottland" (Belgian relief) passed outwards bound. Stopped off Port aux Basques about two cables from the light-house. Lowered the motor boat & Capt. & 1st Lt. went ashore. Bought some very good salmon at 6 ¢ per lb.

H.M.C.S. CANADA – AT SEA

FRIDAY 16th Fine and clear. Exercised general Quarters. Guns crews at 1" aiming and stokers at rifle firing. Fell in with a schooner flying white ensign and I went over away in the seaboat to tell him to take it down. Stopped for about 3 hours in St. Lawrence Bay.

SATURDAY 17th Patrolling near Cape North. Communicated with "Stadacona" and sent Sub-Lt. Kenworthy to "Stadacona" for passage to Sydney.

Sunday 18th Patrolling near St. Paul Island. Communicated with the Margaret in the afternoon.

Monday 19th Patrolling at 50 revs. About 2 P.M. shaped course to pass a mile to Northwards of Cape North.

H.M.C.S. CANADA – AT SEA

TUESDAY 20th Had morning watch. Shaped Co.[8] to pass 1 mile off Cape Egmont. 7:50 sighted Danish Barquentine Morgan. Closed her and 1st. Lieut. & myself boarded her.

She was Danish Barquentine Morgan. T.H. Christenson Capt. bound for Miramichi, N.B. 23 days out of Iceland. In ballast Crew 5. In the afternoon carried out 12 pr. & small arms drill. Thick fog and double watches at night. Hochelaga arrived with a little mail also Sub. Lt. Kenworthy joined ship.

WED. 21st Patrolling 50 revs. Shaped course to pass 2 miles off Port aux Basques. Thick fog nearly all day. Ran out to sea and doubled back on the course. Stopped part of the night in order to economise in coal so that we will be able to stay at sea for 14 days.

THURS. 22nd At 10:10 entered Port aux Basques harbour and secured along S.S. Lady Sybil in order to refill our fresh water tanks. Captain Stuart, O'Leary and myself went salmon fishing with the game warden up the river about two miles from the town. There are some very good pools & one is able to see the salmon but they would not rise for our flies. Returned to the ship at 5 P.M. in a drizzly rain and cast off, proceeding to sea. S.S. Lady Sybil proceeded at the same time.

FRIDAY 23rd "Stadacona" closed us in the forenoon and Tingley & I went aboard in order to return some cordite & also Fleet Signal book and Aux. code no. 2. Rec'd some more mail which included my laundry that had gone to the "Rainbow" in Critchley's bundle. Anchored in Aspy Bay late in the forenoon, the motor boat towed the dinghy ashore. We were going fishing but the natives said that the best time to go was with a rising tide. The channel at the entrance of the village is quite narrow and there is quite a swift tide race running through. Bought some fresh eggs and the 1st Lieut. got his bottle of cream—war in the Canadian Navy. Returned to the ship and hoisted the motor boat by hand, weighed and proceeded patrol 50 revs. Apparently we are not going to have any more fleet manoeuvres which seems rather a shame as they were good sport and gave the signalmen something to do, also practice in station-keeping.

SAT. 24th We were just entering Aspy Bay steering West when we sighted a big tramp on the Starboard bow. We increased to full speed closing her. She also started to close us. Cleared away foc's'le guns and the 1sr Lieut.

---

8 This is a short form of the word "course."

and I boarded her. She was the S.S. Cape Breton of Greenock, Lisle Steamship Company, 14 days out from Gibraltar via Marseilles in ballast bound for Montreal. Quite heavy sea for one boat alongside. The Capt. thought that Cape North was St. Pauls Island as it was quite foggy at the time and he could not hear Cape North fog signal. He was quite close to the beach when we sighted her and in another quarter of an hour would probably have piled up, when she saw us he a/a to get our masts in line knowing that we were on a course.

H.M.C.S. CANADA – AT SEA

Sat. 24th Anchored in Aspy Bay at about 1:15 P.M. Captain, O'Leary & myself went fishing for sea trout but did not catch any although we walked about 5 miles.

Sunday 25th Got under way at 8 A.M. Communicated with the Hochelaga. Patrolled near St. Pauls Island.

Monday 26th Relieved by the Margaret about 10 A.M. and proceeded to North Sydney where we are coaled. Took in 98 tons. Proceeded into Sydney harbour and anchored.

Tuesday 27th Saturday routine, cleaning ship. Kenworthy's people came off in the afternoon.

After lunch Capt. Pasco took galley's crew out for a pull as far as the second bridge.

The galley looks very nice now. Officer's crew out practicing in the early morning for our race with the officers of the Hochelaga. Heard that the Admiral is coming down about the end of next month. Hope it is true as I want to see him.

H.M.C.S. CANADA AT SYDNEY
JUNE 1916

Wed. 28th Landed ship's companies from "Canada" & "Stadacona" at the Bungalow and after a minutes drill went for a route march. It was quite warm.

Thurs. 29th Court of Inquiry aboard the Stadacona in the afternoon. Exercised galley's crew.

Went for quite a long pull with the rest of the officers' crew, after that went for a picnic up the river. Mrs. Stuart, Barber, Com. Barber and myself went in the motor boat. The remainder went in the motor cutter. Stadacona sailed. Raining nearly all day. Gauvreau and I went out to the Hollyers in the evening. I bought a canoe in the afternoon.

H.M.C.S. CANADA – AT SYDNEY
JUNE 1916

Friday 30th More or less raining all day. Went ashore in the afternoon and then called on the Kenworthy's. I was Officer of the Guard in the evening. H.M.C.S. Grilse arrived, Comm. White in command.

JULY 1916

Saturday July 1st Make & mend day, raining. Took Capt. Pasco's blue motor boat out in the forenoon. I was on watch all day. Getting ship ready for sea as we sail tomorrow at 3:45 A.M.

Sunday 2nd Weighed and proceeded at 3:45 A.M. to relieve the Hochelaga. Communicated with Margaret & Hochelaga and then took up patrol. Quite foggy weather.

H.M.C.S. CANADA – AT SEA
JULY 1916

MONDAY 3rd On patrol. Lots of fog and wind with quite heavy seas.

Tuesday 4th Foggy wind from East with high seas.

Wed. 5th Raining with fog but cleared up a little in the afternoon. 1st Lieut. & I boarded Danish Barquentine. Ludwig Bronsen from Cadiz to Gaspé, cargo, salt. Quite a heavy sea on alongside her.

Thurs. 6th Had morning watch, Outside Port Basque 1st Lieut. went in to the town in motor boat. Margaret arrived and communicated. Sent all boats away sailing except the galley. Proceeded at 100 revs (11 A.M.) to take up patrol between St. Pauls Island and Cape North.

H.M.C.S. CANADA – ON PATROL
JULY 1916

FRIDAY 7th Off St. Paul's Island. In the afternoon we stopped near the North end of island and sent boats along sailing. Whaler came in first, Cutter second, Galley (2) third star dinghy, Pat dinghy. About the first fine day that we have had this week.

SATURDAY 8th Anchored in Aspy Bay at 10:00 A.M. 1st. Lieut. and several officers went ashore.

Weighed & proceeded at noon. In the afternoon boarded the masted schooner "Arietis", Ireland to Miramichi in ballast 78 tons. Fine day.

Sunday 9th On Patrol. Shaped course for Sydney.

Monday 10th Went alongside at North Sydney and filled up with coal. Very fine day. Shoved off about 1 P.M. and shaped course for the patrol. Stopped near St. Paul's Island.

H.M.C.S. CANADA – ON PATROL
JULY 1916

TUESDAY 11th Anchored in Aspy Bay in the forenoon. Sent all boats away sailing-not much wind.

Weighed at noon.

Wed. 12th Usual thing – Patrolling at 50 revs.

Thurs. 13th Shaped course for Port aux Basques but it was quite foggy so we turned back and patrolled near St. Paul's Island.

Friday 14th Arrived at Port aux Basques around 9 A.M. and went inside and anchored. Took provisions on board. Proceeded at 12 knots for St. Paul's Island where the Hochelaga had caught an American fishing schooner J.J. Fallon trawling inside the three-mile limit. Sent Mr. Julian & 8 men to schooner and the Hochelaga took her in tow.

H.M.C.S. CANADA – AT SYDNEY
JULY 1916

Friday 15th Met the "Margaret" at 10 o'clock near Ingonish. She kept us waiting about half an hour. Made fast alongside the coaling pier ahead of two schooners. There was just room for us to squeeze in and then we had our ram in the mud. It is a good thing that the "Stadacona" doesn't have to coal there. Finished coaling about 3 P.M. and anchored one cable[9] from the "Grilse.

SAT. 16th Margaret arrived in forenoon but only stayed in for about half an hour. "Stadacona" arrived and anchored. On watch in forenoon. In the afternoon went on a picnic.

Sunday 17th Church party in the forenoon. I was in charge of the Wesl. party which consisted of four men. In the afternoon I kept watch in order to let Betts go ashore. In the evening I went ashore in the canoe to buy some tomatoes for the 1st Lieut. I also saw Amelia. It was quite rough returning to the ship and they sent out a boat to escort.

H.M.C.S. CANADA – AT SYDNEY
JULY 1916

I'm back.

Monday Same routine. Went ashore to pay the photographer. Met Amelia and we wandered around the town shopping. A & I went into town in the afternoon and in the evening I went to a dance at Mrs. Stuart's which I enjoyed very much indeed. Arrived after taking Agnew off to the Grilse in the canoe.

---

8 A cable length is the length of a ship's cable, about 600 feet.

TUESDAY 19th Kenworthy left for Halifax in the Grilse about 4 P.M. We celebrated Ken's departure in style.

Wed. 20th At about 2 P.M. rec'd a signal that I was appointed to "Berwick" and was to leave for Halifax that night. More celebrations. Got all my gear—at least all I could think of—safely aboard the train and finally left Sydney at about 10 P.M.

Thurs. 21st Arrived Truro at 6:20 A.M. and saw Mother, Harry, Muriel & Morris Lambe who motored up from Londonderry. Arrived Halifax somewhere about 9 A.M. and joined the Niobe. Heard I was to join Berwick tomorrow but of course they did not know anything about me on board. Saw Dad and in the evening went to the Orpheus. [10]

Fri. 22nd Berwick came alongside No. 4 and commenced coaling. Reported to Commander but he did not know anything regarding me. Saw Captain Martin & Captain Blunt in P.M. and they gave me leave until Aug. 4th.

Had a good time on leave. Fishing etc. came down to Halifax in the Ford. We had a fine run there and back.

H.M.S. BERWICK – AT HALIFAX
AUG. 1916

Aug. 3rd Left Londonderry at noon, arrived Halifax about 3 P.M. Went aboard Niobe. Lindsay and Soulsby were there. Rec'd. leave until A.M. 5th when we are to join Berwick. Amelia & I went to the Strand in the evening.

Fri. 4th Went to a celebration service at All Saints in morning.

SAT. 5th Lindsay, Soulsby and myself joined the Berwick at 9:30 A.M. Started the Gun-Room consisting of two R.N.R. Subs. Maillard & Barsbury, Clerk Rook and the three mids. Told off to our boats; mine is cutter. Went ashore in afternoon and saw a good show at the Strand.

Sunday 6th Running the cutter in the forenoon. Capt. Stuart had a tea party in the afternoon. I went ashore in the aft galley to bring off the guests which were Mr. & Mrs. & Miss Jack. Had a nice time.

H.M.S. BERWICK – AT HALIFAX
AUG. 1916

MON. 7th Running the 1st cutter. Stayed aboard all day. It was raining in the morning but turned out more or less fair. H.M.S. Drake arrived and went alongside No. 4 to coal. The Berwick is gradually getting clean. We are ashore once every three days which is rather rot. Rec'd a letter from Polly.

---

9 The Orpheus Theatre on Barrington Street was originally the Granville Street Baptist Church but was subsequently owned by the Orpheus Music Society. Later it became a movie theatre. The Orpheus was demolished during the summer of 1947; work began on the Paramount Theatre.

HMS Berwick

Tues. 8th The Canada arrived and anchored off the Niobe. Went aboard & saw the crowd, had a drink with Gauvreau and then went ashore. Amelia & I, Miss Fisher & Gauvreau went to the Strand and afterwards to supper at Green Lantern. Caught the 4 P.M. boat back to the ship.

Wed. 9th Aboard nearly all day running boats. Went ashore at 7 P.M. with rook. He & I, Miss Fisher & Amelia went to Orpheus which I enjoyed very much. Just caught the 10:30 boat back to the ship. Rec'd a letter from Polly.

H.M.S. BERWICK – AT HALIFAX AND CHESAPEAKE BAY
AUG 1916

Thurs. 10th At about 8 A.M. Transports "Scotian", "Cameronian", and "Scandinavia" sailed for England with troops. Carnarvon also sailed. We gave them three cheers as they passed. Went ashore in the cutter in forenoon; saw Dad, telephoned Amelia, sent some cigs. to Polly. Hands preparing ship for sea. Sailed at about 1 P.M. passing Empress of Britain on way out. Shaped course for New York.

Friday 11th Foggy. Told off to General Quarters stations. Mine is the fore top with the Gunnery Lieut. Mr. Russell) and Capt. of Marine (Yeo). The ship is simply covered with voice pipes. My job is asst. Navigator with Mr. Bennett. Soulsby & Lindsay keep OOW in day time.

Sat. 12th Took some sights in the forenoon. Met and communicated with the "Marseilles"[11] about 80 miles from Sandy Hook. Proceeded to Chesapeake as that is going to be our patrol.

---
11 The ship was actually called the S.S. *City of Marseilles*.

H.M.C.S. BERWICK – AT CHESAPEAKE BAY
AUG. 1916

Sunday 13th Went into full whites. Misty weather. Met and communicated with "Calgarian" at about 9:30 A.M. She is going to England & and is then going in the passenger service. Very hot. Took up our patrol steaming about 6 knots and going around the three buoys which are roughly 5-8 miles from Cape Henry. The coast is very low in the vicinity of Cape Henry and in misty weather it is quite hard to make a good landfall. There is also a bit of a current near here.

Monday 14th The Commander read an abandon ship stations after much cussing on the part of the skipper. After that we went away in the three cutters sailing. I was in the 2nd cutter. My station at abandon ship at present is in the Sailing Pinnacle. Corrected a few notices to Mariners.

H.M.S. BERWICK – CHESAPEAKE BAY
AUG. 16

TUES. 15th On patrol between the three buoys. Three American battleships passed us in the afternoon. Correcting Pilot Books. Not much doing on board. Rained in the evening. Italian battleship blown up.

Wed. 16th Raining in the morning. Cleared up a bit later on. Compass and wind chronometer every morning. In the forenoon I corrected the Pilot books. In the afternoon did 1" aiming. I was up in the fore top with the Gunnery Lieut. & Capt. of Marines.

The firing was fairly decent but a bit ragged. We did not see the rate clock as the ranges are small but we used an ordinary stop watch to give the range after we had got the rate from Dumaresque.

Rate	25 yards time	50 yards time
25	60 sec.	120 sec.
50	20 sec.	60 sec.
75	20 sec.	40 sec
100	15 sec.	30 sec.
etc.		

H.M.C.S. BERWICK CHESAPEAKE BAY–BERMUDA

SUNDAY 20th Co, S56E, Revs. 92. Put clocks on 80 min. during night. The sun came out for a little while in the forenoon & we were able to get sights. Altered Course in the forenoon to have a look at a steamer & in the afternoon turned back for an hour. Quite warm during the day.

MONDAY 21st Took some star sights in the early morning. Sighted Bermuda at about 2:30 P.M. and had some difficulty in making it out. A sail looked very much like North Rock Light. Entered the narrows at 14½ / Lots time taken 9 min. 33 sec. Did some torpedo

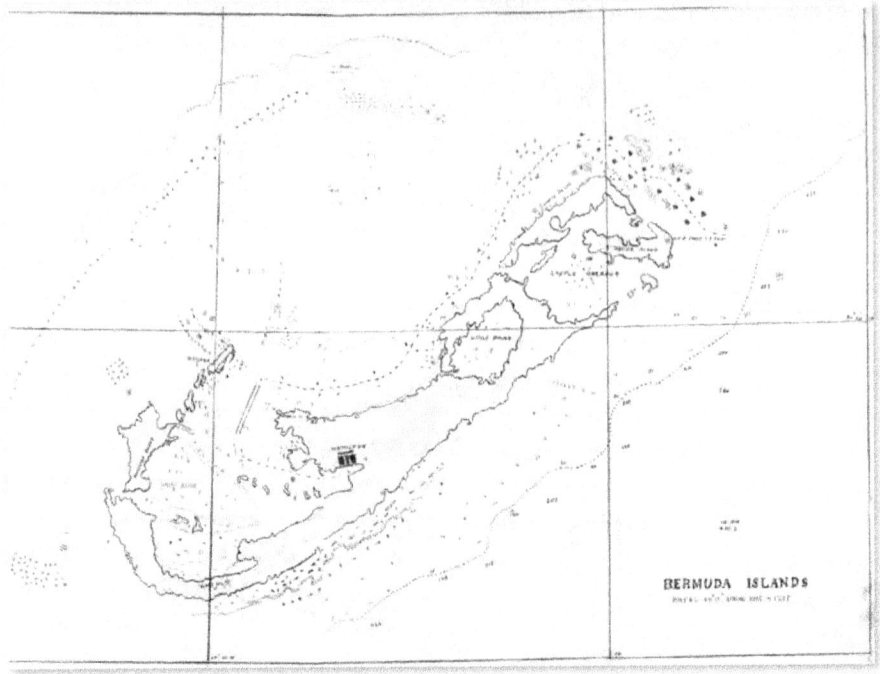

Hand-drawn map of the island of Bermuda

H.M.C.S. BERWICK – BERMUDA
AUGUST 1916

Wed. 23rd Went away sailing in the forenoon. I was in the Jolly-boat. Milliard & Banbury are told off for cutters and have to run duty trips. Heard that we are going to the West Indies which makes us fed up as we had planned to have a good time in Halifax.

Had to stay aboard all day as there is no leave.

Thurs. 24th Coaling ship. I did not coal as the Navigator gave me a job correcting chart lists.

We started at 5 A.M. and finished 11:30 A.M. took in 1270 tons. H.M.C.S. Highflyer entered harbour and went alongside.

Friday 25th Cleaning ship all day. Ran some cutters in the afternoon and finished my chart of channel. Lindsay's day ashore so I ran his picket boat for him. Did not have a swim. Very hot in the gunroom. We haven't had any wind scoops or a fan yet. All trips to the beach are done by pulling boats. And the Picket boat hasn't been to Hamilton yet and I don't expect she will do this trip. The ship is awfully mouldy.

H.M.C.S. BERWICK – AT BERMUDA
AUGUST 1916

SAT. 26th Still anchored in No. 3 berth. Hands employed getting in provisions and cleaning ship. We are provisioning for 6 months as we expect to go to the West Indies. Running a cutter in the afternoon.

Sunday 27th Very hot. Church on the Q.D. Running a cutter in the afternoon.

Monday 28th Went ashore in the afternoon with Maillard. Had a swim at "White's Island," dinner at the "American House", returned at 11 P.M. H.M.A.S. Melbourne sailed for Europe. Rec'd. mail. I had a camera from Joe, a photo from Sankey & a letter from home telling me of Nevill Fraser's death in Belgium which I was awfully sorry to hear.

Tues. 29th Running 2nd cutter. In the afternoon had a very nice game of tennis at the Lagoon Courts with the Captain of Marines, Albert Say, Lintrop & Pay Hodeler. Also had a fine swim.

H.M.S. BERWICK AT BERMUDA
AUGUST 1916

Wed. 30th Had a swim at the club. Carried out 1" aiming night firing. Steam Pinnace towing target range about 900 yards.

Thurs. 31st Running boats. In afternoon took the sailing Pinnace in for sand just the other side of the cut in a little bay. Commander Grayson went to hospital with appendicitis also Bronchitis. Had a good swim. August dist. run in Berwick 1909'

SEPTEMBER 1916

Friday 1st Sailed from Bermuda at 4 A.M. Anchored outside the entrance at 7:45. Carried out night firing with both 6" and 12 pr. guns; the shooting was quite good. At about 10:30 P.M. Shaped course S63W 62 revs for Nassau, New Providence Isl.

Sat. 2nd Fine day. Took sights. Had the swimming bath rigged in the afternoon. Wardroom officers came & had dinner in Gun Room, at least four of them did: Pilot, Crisp, Butler & Boyd.

H.M.S. BERWICK BERMUDA – NASSAU
SEPTEMBER 1916

Sunday 3rd Took star sights early in the morning. Same course and speed. Bath rigged.

Lindsay and Soulsby started a month's engineering.

Monday 4th Had a rotten night as it rained & my hammock got wet so shifted down to the chest-flat. Didn't get any stars in the early morning. Got a sight at about 5 P.M. We were set 10 miles to the Eastward. The Navigator got a star "Altair"[12]. We should sight Abaco Lt. at 1 A.M. Correcting charts in the afternoon and in the morning, took a bubble of oil of the Steam Purinace's compass (Chetywnd). Quite heavy sea and wind with much rain.

TUESDAY 5th At 8 A.M. anchored about ½ mile from Nassau Lt. Ho.[13] Raining all day. In the afternoon Anzac & I went ashore to the club and looked around a bit. Then we went up to the Governors, there were a whole bunch of N.O.s[14] there. We had afternoon tea. Returned to the ship at 6 P.M. and at 7 sailed for Jamaica.

H.M.S. BERWICK NASSAU – JAMAICA

Wed. 6th Passed Abaco Lt. on our course passing to the Eastward of Long Island. Rigged the bath in the afternoon, water is very warm. Painting party red-leading and painting the funnel.

Thurs. 7th Passed Great Ianagua about 12 miles on the star. beam. Sighted Cape Maysi in the afternoon. Same routine, correcting charts.

Fri. 8th Sighted Morant Pt. Lt. Hs. about 8 A.M. Entered the eastern channel at 11:38. Anchored off Leyland Wharf at 12:30 P.M. Went ashore at 3:45. Saw the MacCrindles. After that I had dinner at the Myrtle Beach Hotel and went to the movies. Jamaica is just the same as ever. They had a hurricane about two weeks ago which blew down trees, bananas and a few huts.

Sat. 9th Went ashore at 4 P.M. and had a couple of sets of tennis at the Jamaica club with P.M.O. Fleet Pay. Capt. of Marines & an RNUR chap called Maitland. It rained later on. I came aboard at 7 P.M. Danced on the Quarterdeck.

H.M.S. BERWICK

NEWSPAPER CLIPPINGS – *see pages 28-29 for original copies in Dutchy's journal.*

Unknown source, undated.

The Hamburg-American line steamer Spreewald has been captured by the British cruiser Berwick in the North Atlantic Ocean, according to an announcement by the admiralty tonight. It was stated that two colliers had been captured. The Spreewald was fitted out as an armed cruiser. The two colliers carried 2,600 tons of coals and 180 tons of provisions for the German cruisers in Atlantic waters. The Berwick is commanded by Captain Lewis C. Baker. The total number of German vessels which,

---

12 Altair, also designated as Aquilae, is the brightest star in the constellation of Aquila and the twelfth brightest star in the night sky.
13 This is an abbreviation for Lighthouse.
14 This is an abbreviation for Naval Officers.

according to latest reports, have been captured by British vessels at sea, or by British port authorities, is ninety-two. Ninety-five German vessels were detained in British ports at the outbreak of the war. Seventy British were held in German ports at the commencement of hostilities, and since then twelve British sea-going vessels, out of the upwards of four thousand carrying on over-sea trade, have been captured and sunk at sea. The Spreewald is a steamer of 2,214 tons. She was last reported as having sailed from Antwerp, July 12, for the West Indies, and to have arrived at St. Thomas, D.W.I., August 4.

Unknown source

U.S. STEAMER FIRED ON

Failed to Halt Quick Enough for H.M.S. Berwick

Panama, November 27.–The American steamship St. Helens, Captain Odland which sailed from New York November 17 for San Francisco, arrived at Colon today and reported that she had been fired on by the British cruiser Berwick. Captain Odland said that his ship was hailed but apparently failed to heave to as quickly as was expected, with the result that the British cruiser fired two shots across the stern of the American vessel. The incident occurred yesterday at a point 90 miles northwest of Colon.

An officer from the cruiser boarded the St. Helens and examined her papers and cargo and then the vessel was permitted to proceed on her voyage after a delay of three hours.

Halifax Herald, August 22, 1915

NEW YORK, August 22 —Two Germans, a third officer and a seaman of the crew of the Norwegian steamer Starkad, which arrived today from Bordeaux, were taken off just outside the harbor, near Fire Island, by the British cruiser Berwick. The Germans were transferred to the warship, after a boarding party came alongside in a small boat.

Unknown source

SWEEPING THE SEAS.

H.M.S. Berwick's Capture in the North Atlantic (Government Press Bureau)

London, Tuesday, 9:25 P.M.

The Secretary of the Admiralty communicates the following statement for publication:—

On September 12 H.M.S. Berwick (Captain Lewis. C. Baker), operating in North Atlantic waters, reported that she had captured the German Hamburg-America liner Spreewald. This vessel was known to be fitted as an armed merchant cruiser. At the same time, two colliers were captured

H.M.S. BERWICK

...o aboard.

* * * *

The Hamburg-American line steamer Spreewald has been captured by the British cruiser Berwick in the North Atlantic ocean, according to an announcement by the admiralty tonight. It was stated also that two colliers had been captured. The Spreewald was fitted out as an armed cruiser. The two colliers carried 2,600 tons of coal and 180 tons of provisions for the German cruisers in Atlantic waters. The Berwick is commanded by Captain Lewis G. Baker. The total number of German vessels which, according to latest reports, have been captured by British vessels at sea, or by British port authorities, is ninety-two. Ninety-five German vessels were detained in British ports at the outbreak of the war. Seventy British vessels were held in German ports at the commencement of hostilities, and since then twelve British sea-going vessels, out of the upwards of four thousand carrying on over-sea trade, have been captured and sunk at sea. The Spreebald is a steamer of 2,214 tons. She was last reported as having sailed from Antwerp, July 12, for the West Indies, and to have arrived at St. Thomas, D. W. I., August 4.

U.S. STEAMER FIRED ON

Failed to Halt Quick Enough for H.M.S. Berwick

Panama, November 27.—The American steamship St. Helens, Captain Odland, which sailed from New York November 17 for San Francisco, arrived at Colon today and reported that she had been fired on by the British cruiser Berwick. Captain Odland said that his ship was hailed, but apparently failed to heave to as quickly as was expected, with the result that the British cruiser fired two shots across the stern of the American vessel. The incident occurred yesterday at a point 90 miles northwest of Colon.

An officer from the cruiser boarded the St. Helens and examined her papers and cargo and then the vessel was permitted to proceed on her voyage after a delay of three hours.

Washington, November 27.—While no official report of the firing by the British cruiser Berwick toward the American steamer St. Helens off Panama had been received here tonight, State Department officials regarded the incident as not unusual in time of war.

Merchantmen, according to naval procedure, are expected to heave to immediately on demand of belligerent warships or promptly signal their intention of submitting to search. If there is any delay, the customary practice is to fire shot across the bow or stern of the merchantman as a warning. The right of search is generally recognized by neutrals and delays of three hours while cargo and papers are examined are not unusual. The belligerent is even authorized to use force in executing the right of search and is not held liable, according to International law authorities, for damages resulting from resistance by a neutral ship.

September 22.—It is reported that ... sunk by a mine in the North Sea. An... by. No official confirmation of the...

NEW YORK, August 22.—Two Germans, a third officer and a seaman, of the crew of the Norwegian steamer Starkad, which arrived today from Bordeaux, were taken off just outside the harbor, near Fire Island, by the British cruiser Berwick. The Germans were transferred to the warship, after a boarding party came alongside in a small boat.

Halifax Herald (1915)

German officer captured.

NEW YORK, Aug. 22—Two Germans, a third officer and a seaman, of the crew of the Norwegian steamer Starkard, which arrived today from Bordeaux, were taken off just outside the harbor near Fire Island by the British cruiser Berwick. The Germans were transferred to the warship, after a boarding party came alongside in a small boat.

H.M.S. BERWICK

SWEEPING THE SEAS.

H.M.S. BERWICK'S CAPTURE IN THE NORTH ATLANTIC.

(GOVERNMENT PRESS BUREAU.)

London, Tuesday, 9.25 p.m.

The Secretary of the Admiralty communicates the following statement for publication:—

On September 12th H.M.S. Berwick (Captain Lewis C. Baker), operating in North Atlantic waters, reported that she had captured the German Hamburg-American liner Spreewald. This vessel was known to be fitted as an armed merchant cruiser. At the same time two colliers were captured with coal for the German cruisers operating in Atlantic waters. The vessels had between them 6,000 tons of coal and 180 tons of provisions.

The total number of German vessels which, according to the latest reports, have been captured by British vessels at sea or by British port authorities now amounts to 92. In addition to this 95 German vessels were detained in British ports on the outbreak of war, making a total of 187 German vessels in our possession at present. As against this, 70 British vessels have been captured and sunk at sea out of upwards of 4,000 British vessels carrying on oversea trade.

PRIZES OF WAR.

The "Daily Chronicle" understands that the names of the two coal steamers in West Indian waters a little over a week ago are the Thor, a Norwegian vessel, and the Lorenzo, which was flying the American flag. The vessels had supplies for the German cruisers in these waters. The Berwick also captured the Hamburg-American Co's str. Spreewald. The three ships were rounded up within 24 hours. They were taken to Castries, St. Lucia, where they have since, it is reported, been condemned by a Prize Court. The Berwick is, as is well known, commanded by Capt. L. Clinton Baker, who is in the senior officer of a special British and French squadron in the Caribbean.

BERWICK SEIZES 3 SHIPS, 1 U.S., AS PRIZES OF WAR

Spreewald, Lorenzo and Thor Captured in Windward Isles—Crews of Two Latter Sent Here.

They told the first story of the work of the British cruiser Berwick, off the Windward Islands.

The crews of the Lorenzo, an American freight steamship, and the Thor, a Norwegian tramp, were brought to port yesterday afternoon by the Guiana, of the Quebec Steamship Company line from St. Lucia, one of the British islands of the West Indies.

Both steamships by the British are claimed as prizes of war, and in company with them is the 10,000-ton Spreewald, of the Hamburg-American Line, the richest prize of the lot.

Joachim Oleson, second mate of the Thor, said:

"Besides about 2,000 tons of coal we had a full cargo of engine oil, petroleum, flour and salt meats and other stores. We cleared for Frey Bentos, near Buenos Ayres. All on board knew we expected to pick up a German cruiser, but although we cruised up and down the Atlantic to the east and west side of Crooked Island, fifty miles off shore, we saw no warship flying the German flag.

"We cruised for three weeks off the Bahamas. The Neckar kept us supplied with provisions.

"One day the Berwick came up to us from the south. An officer with an armed crew came aboard, looked over our papers and put us under seizure.

"That night we headed for St. Lucia, the Berwick steaming ahead. During the night we saw lights astern of us, and turned about at full speed. We did not know what happened until three days later, when we saw her come in, bringing the Lorenzo and the Spreewald."

Newspaper clippings about the activities of HMS Berwick

with coal for the German cruisers operating in Atlantic waters. The vessels had between them 6,000 tons of coal and 180 tons of provisions.

The total number of German vessels which, according to latest reports, have been captured by British vessels at sea, or by British port authorities, now amounts to 92. In addition to this, 95 German vessels were detained in British ports at the outbreak of the war. Seventy British were held in German ports at the outbreak of war, making a total of 187 German vessels in our possession at present. As against this, 70 British vessels have been captured and sunk at sea out of upwards of 4,000 British vessels carrying on overseas trade.

Halifax Daily Chronicle, undated

PRIZES OF WAR

The "Daily Chronicle" understands that the names of the two coal steamers in West Indian waters a little over a week ago are the Thor, a Norwegian vessel, and the Lorenzo, which was flying the American flag. The vessels had supplies for the German cruisers in these waters. The Berwick also captured the Hamburg-American Co's str. Spreewald. The three ships were rounded up within 21 hours. They were taken to Castries, St. Lucia, where they have since, it is reported, been condemned by a Prize Court. The Berwick is as well known, commanded by Capt. L. Clinton Baker, who is the senior officer of a special British and French squadron in the Caribbean.

Unknown source, undated

BERWICK SEIZES 3 SHIPS, 1 U.S., AS PRIZES OF WAR

Spreewald, Lorenzo and Thor Captured in Windward Isles—Crews of Two Latter Sent Here.

They told the first story of the work of the British cruiser Berwick, off the Windward Islands.

The crews of the Lorenzo, an American freight steamship, and the Thor, a Norwegian tramp, were brought to port yesterday afternoon by the Guiana, of the Quebec Steamship Company line from St. Lucia, one of the British Islands of the West Indies.

Both steamships by the British are claimed as pries of war, in company with them is the 10,000-ton Spreewald, of the Hamburg-America Line, the richest prize of the lot.

Joachim Oleson, second mate of the Thor, said:

"Besides about 2,000 tons of coal, we had a full cargo of engine oil, petroleum, flour and salt meats and other stores. We cleared for Frey Bentos, near Buenos Ayres. All on board knew we expected to pick up

The Spreewald *(upper); German officers landing as prisoners at St. Lucia (lower)*

a German cruiser, but although we cruised up and down the Atlantic to the east and west side of Crooked Island, fifty miles off shore, we saw no warship flying the German flag.

"We cruised for three weeks off the Bahamas. The Neckar kept us supplied with provisions.

"One day the Berwick came up to us from the south. An officer with an armed crew came aboard, looked over our papers and put us under seizure.

"That night we headed for St. Lucia, the Berwick steaming ahead. During the night we saw lights astern, and turned about at full speed. We did not know what happened until three days later, when we saw her come in, bringing the Lorenzo and the Speedwald [Spreewald]."

CRUISER BERWICK DOING GOOD WORK

Three Steamers Supposed to be Supplying the Karlsruhe Tied up at St. Lucia.

New York, Nov. 21.—The captain and crews of the American steamer Lorenzo and the Norwegian steamer Thor, which were captured by a British war vessel in West India waters while alleged to have had on board coal for the German cruiser Karlsruhe, arrived here yesterday aboard the steamer Guiana from St. Lucia.

The Lorenzo and the Thor, together with the Spreewald of the Hamburg-American Line, are held as British prizes of war in the harbor of St. Lucia, whither they were taken by the prize crews after their capture by the British cruiser Berwick.

Captain Griffiths of the Lorenzo, and his American crew would not talk of the capture of their steamer; but the crew of the Norwegian steamer were not so reticent and Second Mate Glesen told of the seizure of the Thor.

The Thor cleared from Newport News on August 4 for Frey Bentos, near Buenos Aires, the mate said; but after leaving the Capes the course was laid for Crooked Island passage, in the Bahamas. There the Thor was joined by the Lorenzo, which appeared to be loaded with coal; the Neckar, of the North German Lloyd line, with a valuable cargo from Cuba; and the Spreewald. These vessels cruised about the Bahamas and the West Indies for several weeks, according to the mate of the Thor, who said the belief was they were seeking to pick up and provision German men-of-war.

On September 9, the Berwick came up from the south, Glesen said, and an officer with an armed crew went aboard the Thor, looked over her papers and put her under seizure. That night the Thor was taken by a prize crew to St. Lucia. The day after she reached St. Lucia harbor, the Berwick brought in the Lorenzo and the Spreewald, according to Glesen. He said that the crews were well treated.

Admiral von Spee.

BERWICK IS ACTIVE.

1914

NEW YORK, Nov. 21.—The first news of the activities of the British cruiser Berwick in capturing merchant vessels in the Caribbean Sea was brought to New York today by the Quebec steamship Guiana, which had on board the crews of the American steamer Lorenzo and the Norwegian steamer Thor, captured while waiting to coal the German cruiser Karlsruhe.

The junior officer told of the Thor's experiences. He said that both vessels were left under guard in the harbor of St. Lucia, and with them the ten-thousand-ton Hamburg-American liner Spreewald, which was the most valuable prize captured by the British cruiser in the West Indies.

"We left Newport News on August 4," said Olsen, "with 2,000 tons of coal and 200 tons of stores, of oil, salt beef, flour, and other articles. The Thor cleared for Fray Bentos, near Buenos Ayres, but after passing the Virginia Capes, we headed for the Crooked Island passage in the Bahamas, and we realized that our mission was to wait for one of the German cruisers.

SPREEWALD IN CHARGE.

"Shortly after our arrival there, we were joined by the Lorenzo and the Neckar, which was loaded with wines and delicacies of all kinds from Cuba. Finally the Spreewald steamed up and took charge of the small squadron.

"We cruised about the Bahamas for three weeks," Olsen went on, "and then sailed to the eastward and met at a rendezvous about 200 miles east of Trinidad.

"The Neckar supplied us with extra provisions, and we had to replenish the bunkers from the coal stowed in the forward hold. Finally the Neckar steamed back to Cuba for more stores, as none of the German warships had been sighted.

"On September 9, the Berwick came up from the south, fired a blank shot across our bows and sent a boat with an armed crew in charge of an officer, who examined the ship and her papers and put us under seizure. The prize crew was left on board and the Berwick crew saw the Thor well on her way to St. Lucia, and then went back to look for the Spreewald and the Lorenzo. These vessels she brought into the harbor three days later, with the British ensign flying at their mast heads."

GERMAN CRUISER CAPTURED.

H.M.S. Berwick Makes Big Haul In The North Atlantic.

The Secretary of the Admiralty announces that H.M.S. Berwick (Captain Lewis C. Baker) operating in the North Atlantic, reports that she has captured the German Hamburg-Amerika liner Spreewald. This vessel was known to be fitted as an armed merchant cruiser.

At the same time two colliers with coal for the German cruisers in the Atlantic were captured. They had between them 8,000 tons of coal and 180 tons of provisions.

The Spreewald is a steel screw steamer of 3,899 tons gross, built in 1897 by Furness, Withy and Co.

The Berwick is a cruiser of 9,800 tons, carrying 14 6-inch, eight 12-pounder, and three 3-pounder guns.

MEN TO APPLAUD.

Capt. Kennedy—(Crossed). Capt. L. C. Baker—(Round).

Captain Kennedy was in command of H.M.S. Lowestoft, which saved many lives when the three British cruisers were sunk in the North Sea. Captain Baker, of H.M.S. Berwick, has captured a Hamburg-Amerika liner converted into a cruiser.

More newspaper clippings about the activities of HMS Berwick, *from 1914*

H.M.S. BERWICK AT KINGSTON, JAMAICA
SEPT. 1916

Sept. 10th Sun. Church on board in the forenoon. In the afternoon had a fine swim at the Constant Spring Hotel[15] bath. Had afternoon tea with Miss Bonito. Met lots of girls, the three Miss Bells and some other girls.

Sept. 11th Mon. Correcting charts in the forenoon. Weighed at 2 P.M. and went alongside No. 3 pier. It took us about 90 min. to do it as the ship is very hard to handle when going astern in this shallow water. In the evening went out to Constant Spring hotel and then had a very enjoyable dance, walked back to the ship from the Cross Roads via East Street.

Tues. 12th At 5:00 went on a route march past the Cross Roads, Lieut. Godma in charge. I was a company commander. The other people had "Man and Arm Boat Exercise". The Niggers started coaling ship at 6:00 A.M. They put aboard about 60 tons an hour. Temp. 90 in Club. Soulsby, Millard and myself went out to the MacCrindles for tennis. Finished coaling at 10 P.M.

Green Very's Lights are all called in.

Dutchy as a midshipman at Kingston

H.M.S. BERWICK KINGSTON, JAMAICA
SEPT. 1916

Wed. 13th Had a tennis match against the St. Andrew Club. We had two Army officers playing for us, Nicholson & Link. Our team consisted of P.M.O. Capt. of Marines, Fleet Pay, and myself. We got beaten badly but we should do better if we have some more practice.

Thurs. 14th Correcting charts. Had some very good sets of tennis at the St. Andrews Club. Played with Captain of Marines P.M.O. & Mr. Pearce & Alexander. Returned to the ship at 7 P.M.

Friday 15th Cast off from No. 3 at 9:10 A.M. proceeded at 66 revs. Shaped course for Cartagena Colombia S12°E. Got sights in the afternoon and corrected a few charts.

SAT. 16th Got some sights. Between Noon and 5 P.M. we were set 15 miles to the Westward. The Brazil current runs along the coast here setting one to the Westward but inshore there is generally a counter current.

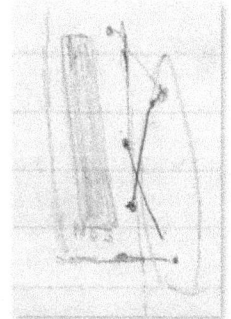

Sketch of how ship was moored at No. 3 berth

---

15 Built in preparation for the 1891 Exhibition when over 300,000 visitors were expected on the island, the Constant Spring Hotel was located at the end of an electric tram car line about six miles from the city of Kingston. It is credited with being the first building to have electricity and indoor plumbing. The Constant Spring Post Office was set up to facilitate hotel guests. By the mid-1890s it too had been taken over by the government.

Sunday 17th Arrived off the entrance to the harbour about 6:15 A.M. Very heavy rain so we could not enter for a little time. At 7 A.M proceeded. The channel is quite long and the buoys are out of place, also the light at Fort Fernando is obscured.

H.M.C.S. BERWICK CARTAGENA – CURACAO I.
SEPT. 1916

Monday 18th Usual routine, doing about 11 knots. Got sights. Chronometer working very well although the temp. in chron. room or rather Provision room is 90° F.

Tuesday 19th Arrived off the entrance to Wilhamstad [Willemstad], Curacao about 6:30 A.M. Waited outside for about 40 minutes while they moved the pontoon bridge which stretched across the channel (the signal for this being 3 blasts in the siren). Saluted the Dutch flag by firing 21 guns, also the Governor by 7 guns & the British consul with 11 (or something like that) guns. At 8:00 A.M. proceeded up the channel at 26 revs. It is only 50 yds. wide. There is a buoy at the entrance but there are no buoys in the channel. Anchored in St. Anna harbour. The Navigator made out some hydrographic notes. Went ashore in the afternoon. It was very hot & there was a tremendous sun glare on your eyes. The town is very neat and pretty. They have Naphtha trams. Weighed anchor at 5 P.M. and shaped course for La Guaira, Venezuela.

H.M.S. BERWICK AT LA GUAIRA VENEZ.

Wed. 20th Arrived off La Guaira about 6 A.M. The mountains are very high in the vicinity of the town, about 9,000 feet. At about 7 A.M. the Star.[16] H.P. Valve rod & guide suddenly went fut [phut] owing to priming of the star. engine. So we had to go into harbour using the Port engine only. Anchored just outside the Breakwater.

Went ashore for a walk. The town is much more modern & better laid out than Cartagena. They have street cars and lots of automobiles. Took in about 35 tons of water. Sailed at about 6:00 P.M. for Barbados 78 revs. on the port engine only which was 9.5 knots.

H.M.C.S. BERWICK LA GUAIRA, VEN. – BARBADOS
SEPTEMBER 1916

Thurs. 21st At sea usual routine. Doing 9.5 knots. Passed Orquilla Isl. & Pico Isl.

Fri. 22nd Passed through Martinique Channel, Grenadine Islands in the forenoon. Diamond Rock is quite conspicuous. Arrived at Barbados about 8 P.M. Had some difficulty in finding the anchorage nearly all

---

16 This is an abbreviation for starboard, i.e. the right side of the ship.

the small lights near the town are fixed lights and consequently are very hard to distinguish from the others.

Sat. 23rd Sighted St. Lucia at daylight (Northern part) we were set about 5 miles inside our course. Arrived off Fort-de-France about 9:30. A French naval officer and a nigger pilot also the Consul came onboard. Anchored in A Berth, Carenage[17] with both anchors and two or three wires out astern. "Descartes" here. Went ashore in the afternoon with Lindsay & saw Monsieur Dupont. Had a punk dinner at a hotel and afterwards went to a French moving picture show which was rather funny but the pictures were very old. It rains every night here and if one sleeps on deck you have to make a quick shift during the night. We expect to be here until Oct. 3rd as they are making a casting for us.

H.M.S. BERWICK AT FORT-DE-FRANCE, MARTINIQUE, F.W.I.
SEPTEMBER 1916

Sunday 24th Church on board in the forenoon. In the afternoon Mr. Dupont & two friends came off in the motor boat and six of us went over to the opposite shore and had a fine swim. The two friends had dinner on board.

Monday 25th Stayed aboard all day and corrected charts. Had a swim from the ship in the afternoon.

Tuesday 26th Left the ship at 10:00 A.M. Called at the "Descartes" for three officers and shaped course in Picket Boat for St. Pierre. Arrived off there at about 11:30 A.M. Had a fine swim and had lunch at the Hotel de Commerce. After that we all walked about the ruins of St. Pierre & they were very interesting. The city of about 30,000 was destroyed by Lava from Mount Pelee in 1902. Only 1 man was saved. We dug up some bones, etc. Niggers are at work excavating the ruins. Shoved off at 4:30 P.M. and called in at a village where we had another fine swim. Got back to the ship at 6:30 P.M.

H.M.S. BERWICK AT FORT-DE-FRANCE, MARTINIQUE, F.W.I.

Wed. 27th It rained on and off during the day. Went ashore at 8 P.M. with Lindsay and Milliard to the "Harts". From there we went out onto a French Family where we danced & tried to speak French. It was awfully funny. Shoved off at 2:30 A.M. and arrived back on board at about 3:00 A.M.

Thurs. 28th Stayed aboard all day. Went in for a swim in the afternoon. Hands employed scraping and painting ship. We are painting her a darker colour than before. Lt. Comm. Russell appointed Acting Commander & Lt. Bennet 1st (N).

---

17 The Carenage is the name of the harbour in St. George's, Grenada.

Fri. 29th Aboard all day. Correcting charts etc. We were going to take chronometer sights but it rained so much & that the sun is obscured most of the time.

Sat. 30th Went away in the cutter to replace a 2½" wire (which parted) with a 3½". In the afternoon went to a reception given by the Military Officers at Fort St. Louis & had a good time. After that Milliard, Lindsay and myself went to dinner at Mr. Harts & had a very good time.

H.M.S. BERWICK AT FORT DE FRANCE
OCTOBER 1916

Sunday 1st Went for a picnic across the harbour. Walked about 5 miles to see the tomb of Marie Antoinette. Picked some fine oranges and alligator pears. Had a fine swim. Mr. Hart also Denton & I off to dinner.

Monday 2nd Woke up with a raging headache and stomach trouble, evidentially been poisoned by some food. Proceeded to St. Lucia at 5 A.M. arriving there at 9:30 A.M. Went alongside & started coaling at once. There are about 300 soldiers stationed here.

Now there are two six inch and some French guns. Met a Lieut. in the R.C.G.A.[18] called "Bell" from Halifax. Could not go ashore.

H.M.S. BERWICK BARBADOS–ST. VINCENT ISL.
OCTOBER 1916

Thurs. 5th The Magdalena (troop ship) arrived in the forenoon with about 800 of the W.I.R. regiment on board. She is 30 years old & does a maximum speed of 10 knots. She coaled all day. Sailed at 5 P.M. in company with Magdalena for St. Vincent, Cape Verde Islands, speed about 9 knots. N84E (True). Set co.[19] by Mercator" Dist. of St. Vincent about 2090 miles.

Fri. 6th Head wind and a little bit of sea. Doing 8-8.5 knots. Engineering finished sketching the patch on H.P. sector. Good.

SAT. 7th Doing about 10 knots. Watch-keeping in the engine room 6-8 A.M. Sketching the forward lubrication system of the thrust blocks in the forenoon. Very hot down there. Franconia sunk.

Sun. 8t Rigged church in port battery.

Mon. 9th German submarines are reported to be in the Atlantic in the vicinity of Rhode Island, U.SA. Speed 10.2 knots. Sketching the forced lubrication system of thrust blocks. Finished reading the *Amateur Gentleman*. Darkened ship for the first time since we have been in the Tropics.

---

18 Royal Canadian Garrison Artillery.
19 Co. is an abbreviation for the word "compass."

H.M.S. BERWICK BARBADOS–ST VINCENT (CAPE VERDE ISL.)
OCTOBER 1916

Tuesday 10th Same routine as yesterday. A stoker died of phenomia [pneumonia] on board. Buried him in the afternoon. German submarines sank 5 ships off Nantucket Lt. Vessel.

Wed. 11th About 760 miles to go at noon. They buried three soldiers from the Magdalena. Burnt 89 tons of coal yesterday. Another solider died in the transport.

Thurs. 12th About 575 miles St. Vincent at noon. Exercised fire quarters in the afternoon. There have been 6 days in the "Magdalena" and there are 60 cases of pneumonia. The only exercise we get now is running around the Quarter-Deck.

FRIDAY 13th About 320 miles to St Vincent at noon. General Quarters in the forenoon. The "Magdalena" buried two more soldiers. Ran around the Q.D. 30 times around is nearly a mile.

SAT. 14th 98 miles to go at noon. We get the North Easterly Track winds but they are not of much force. Increased to 72 revs. at 6 A.M. but eased down to 48 at 3 P.M. as we are not allowed to enter St. Vincent after dark so we expect to get in at about 4:30 A.M. tomorrow morning.

H.M.S. BERWICK AT ST. VINCENT CAPE VERDE ISLANDS
OCTOBER 1916

Sunday 15th Anchored at St. Vincent at 6 A.M. "Highflyer" and "Donegal" here, two Portuguese gunboats and about 18 merchant ships including the "Medway" (Training ship). Collier "Gasconia" came alongside at 8 A.M. & shoved off at 1 P.M. Took in 200 tons of coal. "Highflyer" sailed at 3 P.M. for River Bras, Africa.

Soulsby & I went ashore a walked around the town. The island is volcanic & there are no trees. There is a big English cable station here employing about 200 people. There are two entrances to the harbour & there is always a big swell running. The ships on the station are "King Alfred", Flag, "Donegal", "Highflyer", "Swiftsure", "Sutlej", "Kent", "Essex". Reports that the German submarines are operating off South America & River Bass, Africa. A German submarine was seen off here ten days ago. Darkened ship.

Monday 16th Weighed and proceeded at 6:30 A.M. at 75 revs. 12½ knots. We have the current & wind with us as it gives us a speed of 18½ knots over the ground. There is a bit of a sea on the Quarter so had to keep Gun-Room scuttles closed. Exercised collision stations. We expect D.V. to make St. Lucia on Sunday night.

H.M.S. BERWICK ST. VINCENT–ST. LUCIA
OCTOBER 1916

Tuesd. 17th Sea on the quarter which gives us quite a roll. The grub is pretty fierce now; we haven't had any butter for two weeks. Did a mile run on the Quarter-Deck.

Wed. 18th Usual routine. Watch-keeping in the Engine Room from 6 to 8 A.M. Sketching the Capstan engine & gear in the forenoon & afternoon. Put clocks back 20 minutes. This is surely a monotonous life. This ship is supposed to have read more warrants in the last quarter than any other ship in the service.

Thurs. 19th Pretty hot. Sea has gone down a little so we are able to keep the Gun-Room ports open. Exercised fire stations.

Friday 20th Usual routine. Our run is about 312 miles per day. Did a mile run about the Q.D.

Sat. 21st On watch from 6-8 A.M. Sketching the controlling shafting in the forenoon & writing up engineering notes. Did a mile run around the Q.D. At 4 A.M. connected up 11 more boilers i.e. we have 27 altogether (steaming). Increased to 100 revs.

There is no wind & it is awfully hot down below, also there is nothing to eat. Talk about the trenches, I think that I would a hundred times be a soldier than a stoker.

Sunday 22nd Watch keeping from 6-8 A.M. Arrived at St. Lucia at 3:15 P.M. and spent an hour turning ship so as to point outwards. We have an anchor down and a wire out to a buoy astern. Very hot in the engine room, temp about 150°-180°. Had a big head of steam as we were steaming with 27 boilers.

H.M.S. BERWICK AT CASTRIES, ST. LUCIA
OCTOBER 1916

Rec'd. some much looked for mail. I rec'd. a letter from Mother, Joe. Heard that Mr. Allen N.I. has been appointed to the ship.

Mon. 23rd Lindsay and I had lunch at the R.C.G.A. mess with Lt. Bell and enjoyed ourselves. Met a Lieut. called Sharpe. We were going to a tea fight[20] at Government House but it rained very hard so we did not go. Remitted £6 13s. & 9d.[21] to Kirkwood, Halifax. Collier came alongside.

Tues. 24 Started coaling at 5 A.M. No. 3 hold has about 300 tons more than any of the other holds. We have to sweep the collier. Average per hour 80 tons. Heard at noon that we are going to Halifax & the "Chaleur" to take passage to England – oh joy. Coaled up until midnight then parts of the ship took on in two-hour watches until 6 A.M. when we all will start.

---

20 Tea fight was slang for a tea party.
21 British money at this time was in pounds sterling, shillings, and pence (pennies).

St. Lucia, part of the Caribbean patrol

Wed. 25th Started coaling at 6 A.M. It is either raining or very hot. Went to a tea fight at the Duff's in the afternoon.

Thurs. 26th They finished coaling at 2 A.M. and the collier shoved off. The ship played the R.C.G.A. but did not finish the game owing to rain, the score being 1-0 against us. Had a swim at Vigie beach in the rain.

Fri. 27th Had some mixed bathing at Vigie and tea afterwards. It did not rain quite so hard today 24 hours leave to Star Watch. We were all invited up to the Administration but no one turned up.

H.M.S. BERWICK AT PORT CASTRIES, ST. LUCIA
OCT. 1916

Saturday 28th GLOOM. Telegram from C in C Halifax cancelling our departure for the present. Just like them, they have to send about a dozen telegrams and cancel all sorts of things before they can do anything. Some of us in the Gunroom had to go & call on the Administrator & Mrs. Murray so Soulsby and I sweated up the hill and we got soaked coming back. H.M.T.B.D.[22] "Flirt" missing, "Nubian" down.

Sunday 29th Church on Q.D. Had a swim at Vigie beach in P.M.

---

22 This is the abbreviation for H.M. Torpedo Boat Destroyer. These vessels were introduced from the very late 19th century to ward off attacks on battleships etc. by torpedo boats, hence their name, of which only the 'destroyer' part has remained.

Monday 30th Engineering. Swim at Vigie beach in afternoon.

Tues. 31st Swim in afternoon. "Chignecto" arrived with mail in the evening. Rec'd. letters from Mother, Harry & Grace also Halifax papers from Dad containing news of the doings of U53 off the New England coast. Explosion in CO_2 machine.

Wed. 1st Nov. Went alongside in the afternoon. Anzac & I had a fine swim at Vigie and walked back to the ship.

Thurs. 2nd Nov. Coaling. Cast off from jetty at 1:30 P.M. and shaped course for Georgetown, Demerara. I am doing Gunnery this month. This is the day we would have sailed from St. Lucia to Halifax if our orders had not been cancelled. If they had not told us that we were going it would not have been so bad. U53 is supposed to have got back to Germany.

Friday 3rd Nov. At sea. General Quarters in forenoon working with training classes. Did usual run around the Q.D. in afternoon.

H.M.S. BERWICK AT GEORGETOWN, DEMERARA
NOV. 1916

Sat. 4th Arrived off Georgetown, Demerara in the early morning. Anchored 11 miles from the town as it was very shallow near here. Vessels of 20 feet draught can just cross the bar although it is deep enough inside the harbour. In hoisting out the pilot boat they damaged her so they hoisted out the Steam Pinnace but stove a good sized hole in her through a projection on X1 casemate. I went away in the 1st cutter and took the Skipper, P.M.O. and A.P. in to Georgetown. It was quite rough alongside & we had some difficulty in getting our masts up. It took us 2 hours to sail in (11 miles). Lindsay came along in the Picket Boat at noon & we bought fruit etc. in the market as we had no lunch with us & the skipper as usual did not say how long he was going to be so we had to stay with our boats & see that the crews did not get drunk. etc. The town is quite nice with lots of big shops & wide streets, heaps of coolies here. Very strong tide in the harbour about 4 knots with very dirty water. Shoved off at 5:15 P.M. Picket Boat towing the cutter parted our painter and the way back & shipped some water when we got alongside. There was no boat rope ready & falls are not manned but of course that is typical of this ship. Got quite sunburnt as it was awfully hot. A man got his leg broken by slinging his hammock to the capstan. The skipper is going ashore tomorrow to strafe the wireless propeller.

H.M.S. BERWICK
NOVEMBER 1916

Sunday 5th Church on Q.D. The P.B. went in to Georgetown but I did not go. Very hot here (alt. about 7°N).

Monday 6th Weighed and proceeded at 6 A.M.

Tuesday 7th At sea. Gunnery training classes passing out. Had our usual run around the Q.D. Anchored at Kingstown St. Vincent at 8:30 P.M.

Wed. 8th Exercising the 3rd cutter in the forenoon. Hands employed painting funnels & ship's side. In the afternoon went to tea and a dance at the Popham-Lobbs (Administrator) and had a very good time. German submarine reported in the Gulf of Mexico. The U20 blown up off the coast of Jutland.

Thurs. 9th Raining all day. They have had 15" of rainfall in 8 days here. In the afternoon went to tea and a dance at Government House. This is Sankey's birthday.

Fri. 10th Weighed & proceeded 75 revs. at 5 A.M. Arrived at St. Lucia at 9:30 A.M., turned around & went alongside stern first. The niggers commenced coaling & we took in 450 tons. Five men broke out of the ship & there were many drunks. Had a swim at Vigie, quite decent surf.

Sat. 11th Raining intermittently during the day. Had a very good swim at Vigie. Red Cross fete given by R.C.G.A. which was quite a good show.

Sun. 12th Went for a swim at Vigie. Very good surf. Weighed and proceeded at 9:30 P.M. for Martinique.

H.M.S. BERWICK
NOVEMBER 1916

Mond. 13th Arrived at Martinique at 1:00 A.M. and rec'd mail and stores from Jeanne d'Arc (French flagship) also a schoolmaster and a Gunnery Lieut. for passage to Jamaica. Sailed at 5:30 A.M. for Jamaica at 12½ knots at 10:00 A.M. Increased to 15 knots. As there are supposed to be submarines in the Gulf of Mexico I shouldn't be surprised if we are going there after Jamaica. Rec'd. a letter from Mother also one from Joe. The submarines have caused quite a scare in Halifax and it was reported there that 3 British cruisers were sunk. I heard from Lindsay that Ruth Bauld is engaged. The skipper read out 5 warrants today.

Tues. 14th Doing gunnery in the forenoon. Star. battery at control drill and P III gun's crew at first aid lecture. Did usual run about Q.D. in the P.M. The new dead light fitting for the scuttles at darken ship are very good as we get more air in the Gun-Room.

Wed. 15th Arrived off Port Royal at 7:30 P.M. and went alongside. Great excitement with the cutter getting the lines ashore as she got mixed up with a shore boat.

Thurs. 16th Niggers started coaling us at 7 A.M. & finished at 5 P.M, took in 500 tons. Shoved off at 5 P.M. and proceeded to Kingston ahead of the French cruiser "Montcalm". Rooke, Lindsay and myself had dinner at the Myrtlebank and went to the Palace afterwards. Rec'd. a letter from Polly.

Friday 17th Went ashore in the afternoon and had a very good swim at Constant Spring. Went to Palace in evening. Polly's birthday.

H.M.S. BERWICK KINGSTON, JAMAICA
NOVEMBER 1916

Sat. 18th Played tennis at St. Andrew's club but I couldn't hit a ball. Dinner at the Myrtle Bank & Rook and I & the MacCrindles went out to the Movies.

Sunday 19th Went out to Constant Spring and had a swim and tea. After that we danced for a little while.

Monday 20th Went to the "Descartes" at Port Royal at 6 A.M. in the cutter, we had to pull all the way over and back as there was no wind. Raining all day. Doc. Boyd & myself went to tea at the MacCrindles and in the evening went to the movies.

Tuesday 21st Went ashore in the afternoon with Lindsay and Rook and had a swim at Constant Spring. After that we danced. Rook was taken ill & we had to send for the MacCrindles. Doc Boyd came up later on in a car and we took the Clerk off to the ship.

Wednesday 22nd The Governor of Jamaica (Sir William Manning, KCB etc.) and his staff came on board at 8:30 A.M. and we proceeded to sea shaping course for Turk's Island, speed 14 knots. Hospital ship Britannic sunk (47500 tons) in Aegean Sea. Emperor Louis Joseph of Austria died.

Thursday 23rd Arrived at Turk's Island at 5 P.M. The Governor and his staff went ashore and we proceeded to Nassau at 80 revs. Did a mile run around the Q.D.

Friday 24th Usual sea routine. Doing gunnery training classes at maxim drill. General Quarters in forenoon. I have a new station now viz. P5 (or x.) which controls P4 & 5. Raining in the afternoon.

H.M.S. BERWICK
NOVEMBER 1916

SAT. 25th Arrived at Nassau, New Providence Island (5 A.M) and anchored just off the Lighthouse. Sailing the 1st cutter all day on duty trips so could not go ashore however Lindsay brought me some sponges from the beach. Picket boat with Depth Charge & a 3 pdr. went out patrolling between the black buoy & the island. Manning & Lindsay went out in her and I expect they will have a rotten night as there is a nasty sea running. Rig of the day – half whites.

Sunday 26th The Governor (Allardyce) & family came off for church. Took Doc. Boyd off in a cutter to a merchant ship which was in need of medical assistance. The cutter (1st) had a hole stove in the bottom by not having her oars boated when moving alongside the gangway. The block of one of the midship oars got underneath & gangway end as the boat came up on a swell, the oar went through. We passed in buckets & they kept busy bailing. The Picket boat towed her to the falls. The wind & sea suddenly increased at 2:30 so we hoisted the blue peler etc. & proceeded out from the land for about 2 miles where we hoisted the Picket boat. There was quite a nasty swell. A nigger came off to see the ship & could not get back to the beach again so we took him with us. Proceeded at 4 P.M. 72 revs.

Monday 27th Speed 80 revs. Wind on port beam with quite a big sea. Ship is very wet. Divisions on Main Deck. Had a run on the spotting table. Heard a buzz that there is a German submarine off Port Royal. The old bus has been rolling quite heavily today. We expect to go to Bermuda for stores etc. We have had no jam in the ship for a fortnight now.

H.M.S. BERWICK
NOVEMBER 1916

TUESDAY 28th Arrived at Turk's Island at 8:30 A.M. I had to go away in the 2nd cutter to bring off the Governor (of Jamaica). There was a heavy sea running and I had only one A.B. in the boats' crew so consequently it was hard to get alongside etc. Also the skipper always gets fearfully excited. Proceed at 18 knots for Jamaica. There is supposed to be a submarine off Port Royal waiting for us.

Wednesday 29th Arrived at Port Royal at 9:30 & went alongside. Niggers started coaling us. Went away for sand in Pinnace in forenoon & exercising cutter's crews in P.M. Rec'd. mail. Milliard and I went out in the P.B. (7 P.M.) patrolling off entrance to Port Royal. We had a 3 pr. & depth charge (T.NT.) Dashed about all over the place & nearly went aground in the one place. I did not get any sleep at all during the night. They really think that the battery did sink a submarine off here 3 night ago.

Thursday 30th Still coaling, finished at 5 A.M. Went for a swim in afternoon. Picket Boat and divers out searching for the sunken submarine off Port Royal.

1ST DECEMBER 1916

Friday 1st Went over to Constant Spring in afternoon and had a swim and danced. Anchored in Kingston harbour at 7 A.M. Divers out looking for submarine but the only thing they brought up was an old anchor.

Saturday 2nd I am doing assistant Navigator's job this month. Went out to Constant Spring and danced, also had a swim. Went out patrolling the channel in the Steam Pinnace all night. Mr. Manning was with us.

H.M.S. BERWICK
DECEMBER 1916

Sunday 3rd Swim at Constant Spring in the afternoon.

Monday 4th Went up to Constant Spring in the afternoon and had a swim and a one step. Took Agnes MacCrindle to the movies in the evening.

Tuesday 5th Stayed aboard all day and corrected charts. Went out in the Steam Pinnace patrolling the main channel to Kingston.

Wednesday 6th Rook & I went ashore and had tea with Mrs. Robins and Miss Roach. After that we went out to Constant Spring and had a small dance. There were about six girls there. After that we took the American girls out on the water and had a good time.

Thurs. 7th Lindsay and I went swimming at the Belmont Baths with Mrs. Robins and Miss Roach. After that I had tea at Constant Spring & another swim. Then I went to the movies to see the Battle of the Somme.

Fri. 8th Stayed aboard all day. Had tea with the Pilot & Mrs. Lee & Miss Hanley. Capt. of Marines and I had night patrol. Hazel & Catherine came along & visited us at about 1:30 A.M. At 2 A.M. a fishing boat came over to us with a dead nigger & so we took him to the Berwick. I only got two hours sleep tonight. Du Petit Thomas arrived.

Sat. 9th Went alongside No. 3 & took in 150 tons of coal. Anchored in the stream at 4 P.M. Lindsay & I had dinner at the Myrtle Beach with Hazel & Catherine. Later we went out in a motor boat & had a simply ripping time. And we were horribly fed up when we had to go onboard.

H.M.S. BERWICK
DECEMBER 1916

Sunday 10th H.M.S. Roxburgh arrived from Bermuda early in the morning with 41 bags of mail for us. We were (Lindsay, Soulsby & myself) promoted to acting subs. and when the ship reaches Bermuda we are going to England. Rec'd. about 40 German prisoners on board for passage to Bermuda. Weighed & proceeded at 10 A.M. but when we got outside Plum Point we had to turn back and wait at Port Royal while the "Roxburgh" sent out a P.B. & Steam Pinnace with mail which had got mixed up. Hazel & Cassie came out in a motor boat but could not stop the engine so did not have a chance to speak to them much. However, I dropped a letter into the boat which I had written to Hazel. At 2:30 P.M. proceeded at 66 revs. Du Petit Thomas also sailed. There is a German raider supposed to be in the Bahamas armed with 1-6", 4-4.1", 2-3" & 2 machine guns, also 4 torpedo tubes. All the ships on the station are closing on the Florida Strait as we think that we will get her there.

Monday 11th Passed Cape Maysi at noon and met several ships. We hope to see the raider in the vicinity of Florida Strait. We had rather a cheery night in the Gun Room last night. The Pilot, Godman, Woodward and the pay. came in and we had champs.[23] etc.

Tuesday 12th Correcting charts nearly all day. Passed Cat Island. Same speed i.e. 66 rev. We expect to be at sea until the 24th and the skipper says if we see a collier we will coal from her and will then be able to stay at sea longer in the hopes of finding the German raider.

H.M.S. BERWICK
DECEMBER 1916

Wed. 13th Arrived at patrol. Shifted into full blues. Corrected charts, slowed down at 6 P.M. to 42 revs.

Thurs. 14th On the patrol which is 135' long by 62' wide. We patrol at 66 revs. & slow down at night to 42 revs. Correcting charts in the P.M. I was very sorry to read in the press news that H.M.C.S. Grilse has foundered on the way down from Halifax to Bermuda. Lieut. Wingate is in command. I don't know whether Agnew is still in her or not.

Friday 15th We had more in the press about the Grilse. She is supposed to have gone down in a gale off Shelburne. Quite heavy wind from the South and S.W. Barometer dropped 23.95 to 29.10. Fairly high seas. 29° N, 70° 10' W.

Sat. 16th Heard in the press that the Grilse had arrived at Bermuda under her own steam. Storm carried her mainmast away wrecking her wireless. Still patrolling; got some good start sights today. The weather has moderated. It looks as we shall be out at sea until after Christmas arriving at Bermuda on the 26th. D.V.[24]

Sunday 17th There was a church stage on today. Skipper got quite wrathy because there weren't enough officers at church. Had dinner with Mr. Bennett.

Monday 18th Barometer dropped quite suddenly and we had a bit of a storm a/c[25] to S 73°E run out of it. There are hardly any provisions left in the ship now as when we left Jamaica we were going to Bermuda to fill up with stores and we didn't expect to be long at sea.

Tuesday 19th Fine weather today and quite cool. We are only allowed 1 potato per day now. Every one is fed up with this patrol. The "Drake" is off Trinidad, "Roxburgh" near Mona passage and "Devonshire" off New York. Ships company on biscuits & no spuds.

---

23 Champagne.
24 *Deo volente:* God willing; if nothing prevents it.
25 Altered course.

H.M.S. BERWICK
DECEMBER 1916

Wednesday 20th Went well down in the Gulf today and we were not very far from Jupiter Inlet. Carried out 1" aiming practice in forenoon. At 8 P.M. stopped a fruit steamer Esperanta & gave her some of our mails to post.

Thursday 21st Still patrolling. Correcting charts in afternoon. At 2:45 P.M. sighted 2 submarines on the horizon. Altered course for them and increased to full speed & went to General Quarters. Fore turret P. & S. loaded & all ready to fire, worked up to 18 knots in 35 minutes. The subs. turned out to be American ones L2 & L4 (41 & 93). The only thing that kept us from firing was the wireless signals they were making to one another. One of their signals was "The ship on the horizon is a three-stacked British cruiser". Our skipper sent "You can think yourselves lucky that we did not fire as you did not have an escorting cruiser". At 8:30 we were doing 112 revs.

29° 10' N
80° 03' W

Friday 22nd Heavy rainstorms & lightning last night with lots of wind & sea today. S.W. wind in forenoon steering to N.N.W. in P.M. They sounded of G.Q.s[26] by mistake today when we were closing a tramp. At 1L99 P.M. a/c to N 77° E (true), 66 revs. for Bermuda (thank heavens). We are all awfully fed up with this patrol. At this speed should get in on Xmas Day.

Saturday 23rd Quite fine weather. Got star sights. 475 miles to Gibbs' Hill Lt. at noon, Making good 10.5 knots.

Sunday 24th 234 Miles from Gibbs' Hill at noon. Sunday forenoon is the hardest forenoon of the week. Turn out at 5:30 A.M. to take star sights & write up log journal at 7:40. Compare chronometers at 8:40, take a sight & relieve O.O.W.[27] at 9:30 until 10:25. 10:30-11:30 Church. 11:30-12:30 work at sights & get mer. alt.[28] We should get in at 2:00 P.M. tomorrow & it will be a good thing as we are living on pressed beef biscuits. This is some Christmas eve – (I don't think). Making good ten knots. The deviation increases as we get near the island being 3° W at 4 P.M.

H.M.S. BERWICK
DECEMBER 1916

Hark the Berwick angels sing
Coaling ship is just the thing
Though provisions have run low

Monday 25th <u>Christmas day</u>. Turned out and took star sights. Got some soundings over the Angus Bank & sighted Gibb's Hill Lt. Ho.[29] at 8:20 P.M. Went to church in the forenoon. at 11:30 A.M. entered the

---

26 General Quarters.
27 Officer of the Watch.
28 Mercator alterations.
29 Light House.

Narrows and at 18:40 anchored in D berth, Grassy Bay. Leviathan here (FLAG), Carnarvon, Autumn, Caesar & "Weymouth" in dock. Had a dinner consisting of pressed beef and cold pancakes (nothing more). Went ashore and had tea in the Caesar, afterwards going over to Hamilton where I met MacRae and we had dinner at the Princess Hotel which I enjoyed very much. Arrived on board at 11:30 P.M. All the other ships have been in harbour for the last week – they have been expecting us in Bermuda for a week now.

Tuesday 26th Went alongside the dockyard between the Caesar and the drydock (at 8 A.M.). Admiral Browning came off to the ship. Hands employed provisioning ship and preparing for coaling. Went ashore to the club at 5 P.M. and saw Dand. We expect to start coaling at 4 A.M. if we finish provisioning in time but the hands are still working (9 P.M.). Manning got hurt, a guy carrying away & hitting him in the back.

Wednesday 27th Started coaling at 5 A.M. We averaged 85 tons per hour to begin but it slowed down until in the evening we were only doing 60. Knocked off at 10 P.M.

Thursday 28th Commenced coaling again at 6 A.M. finished at 8:30 P.M. having taken in 1600 tons. they are very short of coal here and these ships are going to stay in port until some more coal comes or else we get any definite word of the raider. The skipper won't let us use steam boats to run to Hamilton as they burn too much coal. Went ashore in the afternoon at 5:30 P.M. Harve, D and I came off to dinner.

Friday 29th Had a rugby game at 3 P.M, officers vs. Caesar, I played full back. The ground was wet & the ball slippery. We got beaten 6-5. Mr. Bennett, Lindsay & myself had dinner in the Caesar with Lowe & Mr. Stubbs. Afterwards we went to a concert given by the Caesar's ship's company (saw brother McCann) then to the club and ended up in the Caesar.

H.M.S. BERWICK
DECEMBER 1916

Saturday 30th Cast off from the jetty and anchored in "C" berth. Went ashore running the launch (under sail). We filled up with stores, brought off 12 drums of oil & lumber & the copper punt. I was in the dockyard about 2 or 3 hours. Lindsay had a tea fight on board, the Tuckers & Bluchs etc.

Sunday 31st Blew very strongly and the copper punt broke adrift. Navigator and I went away at 9 A.M. in the picket boat with the cutter in tow to look for the punt. We went down as far as the Flats and came up along the shore inside the reefs. got soaked to the skin as it was raining & blowing great guns. We had open house in the Gun Room and everyone came in a sweated up our wine bills. We sang Auld Lang Syne at midn.[30] but Suction Joe came out & stopped us.

---

30 Midnight.

JANUARY 1917

H.M.S. Berwick

Capt.	W. F. Blunt D.S.O.
Comm (act)	Russel
Lieut. (N)	Harry Bennet[t]
Lieut. R.N.R.	Godman Butler Ohlsnam
Eng. Comm.	H. Evans
Eng. Lieut.	R. K. Crisp Phillips
Sub Lieut.	Woodward
Fleet Pay.[31]	Hodder
Fleet Sng[32]	L. Lintrop
Fleet Sng.	Brander Boyd
Mate	Manning
Subs. (R.N.R.)[33]	T. Banbury
	G. Millard
Clerk	T. Rook
A.P.[34]	Vaughn (R.N.R.)
Gunner	Vugler Griffiths
Bosun	Swincock
Bosun	Bageley
Artif. Eng.[35]	Porteous Harris
	Morrison
	Halliday

H.M.S. BERWICK
JANUARY 1917

1st Monday Weighed and proceeded to Murray's Anchorage. Carried out .303 and 1 inch practice. "Bermudian" & "Chaudiere" arrived. Night firing.

2nd Tuesday Too rough to do any firing. Let go a 2nd ↓.[36] Lindsay went into Grassy Bay in picket boat and brought off the mail. I rec'd. a letter from Grace and Harry. Went out in the picket boat at night to tow targets.

3rd Wednesday Weighed and proceeded. Came to star ↓ about 5 cables. North (magnetic) from Ducking stool. Carried out 12 pr. practice and ran torpedoes. Antrim went to Murray's anchorage and Leviathan to Shelly Bay.

Running picket boat in evening, nearly everyone else in Gun room went ashore.

4th Thursday Weighed and proceeded outside the Narrows at 8 A.M. and

---

31 Fleet paymaster.
32 Fleet surgeon.
33 Sub-Lieutenant.
34 Assistant paymaster.
35 Artificer Engineer.
36 This down arrow is a short code for anchor or anchorage.

HMCS NIOBE AT CLARK'S HARBOUR

carried out sub calibre and 12 pr.[37] practice. I went away in the picket boat at noon towing targets. Got the wire fouled on the bottom when hauling in the target & it took us an hour to get it clear (parted it) as there was a good sea running. Proceeded up the Narrows at 6:30 P.M. [It was] very dark & it was quite a job to finding the buoys. Arrived back at the ship in Murray's ↓ at 7 P.M.

5th Friday Weighed at 1 P.M. & waited at entrance to Narrows while "Chaleur" entered.

Made a signal to her asking her when she was going to sail. She replied, "Today if I can." We went outside & carried out 6" practice & the C in C sent an urgent signal sang that we must catch the "Chaleur" so the skipper came into Murray's ↓ and we and all our gear got into Sailing Pinnace & were hoisted out by the main derrick after saying a hasty good bye to everyone & a tremendous rush to get all our gear. We left all our washing behind. I never left a ship in such a panic. I have only one shirt to last me until we get to Halifax. There are very few passengers on board mostly all NOs, Soulsby, Lindsay, myself, Hayes (mate), and a W.O.[38] from Carnarvon, and about 8 other passengers.

6th SATURDAY Wind from SW. Got veered to N.W. Our run to noon was 203. Nothing much doing.

---

37 Pounder.
38 Warrant Officer.

PASSAGE BERMUDA – HALIFAX IN R.M.S.P. CHALEUR
JANUARY 1917

7th Sunday Owing to bad weather we only did a sum of 197' but wind went down at noon Weather got colder.

8th Monday Weather very good. Sighted Seal Island Light at 5:30 P.M.

9th Tuesday Arrived at St. John at 8:30 A.M. Weather very mild. Caught the C.P.R. train at 1:30 P.M. for Halifax. Waited in Moncton for two hours for the Ocean Limited arriving in Halifax at 0:30 A.M. Was met by Harry & Francis in the new Ford.

10th Wednesday Saw Sankey in the afternoon & was awfully glad to know that he was here. Went to the Ackers in the evening after seeing Ruth off.

11th Thursday Raining all day. Sankey and I took Franny to tea at Tally Ho. Played bridge in the evening at the MacMechans with Polly and the Holloways.

12th Friday Went skating on Frog Pond with Sankey & had to go to the Armitages in the evening.

13th Saturday S & I invited Harold Higginson in the Mackay-Bennett & had dinner at the club with Dad.

14th Saturday Went to St. Paul's in the morning. S & I went to call on the Nixons & Mrs. Stuart but they were out. Had supper at Sankey's.

JANUARY 1917

Wed. 24th Rec'd. orders to join Niobe at 5 P.M. today. Very hurriedly packed my gear. Joined Niobe at 3 P.M. and then went down to Pier 2 and went aboard "Scandinavian". Critchley & I are in the same cabin. Got leave until 10 P.M. and went home & saw the people, said good bye to Polly & other people.

Thurs. 25th Went out in the stream & laid there all day. Quite cold.

Fri. 26th Sailed at about 4 P.M. also the "Canada", "Grampian", & Amiral Aube convoy. Snowing hard. We have a naval draft of R.N.C.V.R.[39] on board. Also the 118th Batt. & 197 & N.S. siege battery.

Sat. 27th Fine day making 12 knots. Loafed.

Sun. 28th Snow.

Mon. 29th Played bridge.

Tues. 30th Quite heavy wind and sea. Canada had to heave to. Wind about 8-12. Lost the other ships in the night.

---

[39] The Royal Naval Canadian Volunteer Reserve (RNCVR) was a naval reserve that was established in Canada in May 1914 and existed until 1923.

Wed. 31st Wind & sea went down in the afternoon. Picked up the Grampian in P.M.

Thurs. 1st Feb. Picked up Amiral Aube and "Canada" and proceeded at 12 knots.

Fri. 2nd 12 knots. Played bridge.

Sat. 3rd 12 knots. Played bridge.

Sunday 4th Destroyers came out to convoy us to Liverpool. Proceeded at full speed about 16 knots. Buried a soldier. Passed a sailing vessel on fire which had just been shelled by a submarine. Three ships sunk quite near us.

Monday 5th Arrived off Liverpool at 10 P.M. Thick fog. Went ashore on the bar and as the tide was falling, not much chance of getting her off before morning.

FEB. 1917

Tues. 6th We were all called at 3 A.M. as skipper thought the ship might break her back. Had a good game of bridge in the early hours of the morning. Two tugs came out from L'pool & Scandinavian got off the bar at about 11 A.M. Arrived at L'pool about 3 P.M. Caught the 5:30 train for London. Arrived there at about 10:30. Stayed at First Avenue Hotel, High Holburn [Holborn].

Wed. 7th Shifted my gear to Waldorf Hotel. Reported at Admiralty & they said we would have a Torpedo Control Course in Vernon & then go to Destroyers. We report at Portsmouth on Sunday P.M. Went to "Razzle-Dazzle" and "Under Cover". Both shows very good.

Thurs. 8th Saw Zig-Zag and Hoop La.

Fri. 9th Saw Theodore & Co in evening at Gaiety.

Sat. 10th Tea and dinner at cousin E. Saw Orchards in P.M.

Sun. 11th Caught 5:37 P.M. train for Portsmouth & reported at the barracks. Shifted to Navigation school.

Mon. 12th Started Torpedo Control Course in the "Vernon".

Tues. 13th Torpedo Control Course 9 A.M. – 3:30 P.M. Had tea at the "Dorothy", Swansea.

Wed. 14th Critchley & I had dinner with Tingley in the Melampus T.B.D. and had a very good time.

Thurs. 15th Same routine. Fog & misty weather.

Friday 16th Same routine. Fog & misty weather. Dummy runs with the directors. etc.

TORPEDO CONTROL COURSE H.M.S. VERNON
FEBRUARY 1917

Sat. 17th Caught the 3:40 train for Farnham, arrived there at 6 P.M. Cousin Katie met me at the station. Went to movies in the evening.

Sund. 18th Went to church in the morning. Caught the 4 P.M. train for Bentley & drove 3 miles to Froyle where I saw Cousin Will & Edith. Caught the 7:46 train back to Portsmouth.

Monday 19th Started Whitehead lectures. Lindsay & I went to the Mikado for tea.

Tuesday 20th Same sort of routine.

Wed. 21st Same sort of routine.

Thurs. 22nd Had tea and dinner with Tingley in the Melampus. Saw my appointment to the "Archer" in tonight's paper.

Friday 23rd Soulsby appointed to the "Jackal". He & I finished Torpedo Control Course. Torps gave us a dummy run in the afternoon which we did successfully.

Sat. 24th Taylor appointed to the Acheron & Reid to the Attack. I left Portsmouth by the 2:05 P.M. (just caught it) train, arrived Devonport at 8:30 P.M. Went to the Vivid.

Sunday 25th Reported to the Commander at 9 A.M. "Archer" is at sea and as the barracks are full up I had to lodge in Plymouth. Stopped at the Duke of Cornwallis Hotel which is just opposite Millbay station. Saw Pam Long also Doc. Carte.

Monday 26th Waiting for Archer to arrive which she did at about 8:30 P.M.

H.M.S. ARCHER 2ND FLOTILLA
MARCH 1917

Tues. 27th Got off to the Archer at about 11:00 A.M. after much trouble. I relieved Grabowsky as Sub. Stowed all my gear etc. She shoved off at about 3 P.M. I took over the charts etc. & wire books, log, and foremost four inch. Cast off from the trot[40] at 6 P.M. and anchored near Drake's Island.

Wed. 28th Weighed and proceeded with "Martin", "Brisk", "Lizard, "Lyra". Set and shaped course for V. Passed a boat of S.S. Normanna in afternoon.

---

40 "The Trot" was a type of mooring that was quite popular in the early twentieth century. Essentially the ship was secured to a mooring buoy fore and aft so that it wouldn't move around. When ships are at anchor there is just one point holding them to the sea bed and they will swing around their anchor cable based on wind and current. That is fine if you have a lot of rooms to give each ship a big circle and room to swing on their anchor, but in tight harbours or anchorages, they would install mooring buoys so that they could fit more ships in a tight space without the risk of them hitting each other. It's how they use to setup/organize the convoys in Halifax Harbour (which is narrower) before they departed.

HMS Archer

Thurs. 1st March 1917 Picked up our convoy about 8 P.M. Our ship is the "Themistocles" with troops (there are about 5 merchants ships altogether). Had afternoon & first.

Fri. 2nd Arrived off the breakwater about 9 P.M. and anchored just inside for the night.

Sat. 3rd Weighed at 6:30 A.M. and went alongside "Calcutta" oiler. Rec'd. mail. Shoved off at noon and proceeded for Queenstown convoying submarine H5. "Goshawk" went out ahead of us and picked up 22 survivors from a Greek steamer which had been shelled by a Hun submarine. Very heavy wind & sea & we rolled & pitched all over the place. Barometer dropped by middle with a bump.

Sunday 4th Arrived off Queenstown at about 9:30 A.M. Raining like the devil & cold. Went alongside the T.B.D. Parthian at the coaling jetty, dockyard. It certainly is a rotten day and thank heavens we are in harbour. Oiled from Haulbowline dockyard, and made fast to the No. 5 buoy in the harbour.

H.M.S. ARCHER 2ND FLOTILLA
MARCH 1917

Monday 5th Shipped from buoy at 9 A.M. and proceeded to sea in company with "Ruby" (who has rammed a derelict at night mistaking it for a submarine. We are going to convoy Ruby as far as Avonmouth where she is going to do a three weeks refit. At noon weather was bad, too much for Ruby so we turned 16 pts. and went back to Queenstown. Just as we were entering the harbour we had frantic message regarding mines off the entrance. We came right over the spot.

Tues. 6th Waiting for sea to go down.

Wed. 7th Went ashore in the afternoon for a walk. Very nice country around here.

Thurs. 8th Day on.

Fri. 9th Ariel, Brisk & Goshawk arrived from Devonport.

Sat. 10th Sailed at 1 P.M. in company with the above destroyers for R.V. where we meet convoy. The Berwick is expected to be in the convoy. Good sea.

Sun. 11th Arrived at R.V. and had a w/t that ships not expected until Tues. morning. As we haven't much oil, we all proceeded back to Queenstown to fill up. Speed 22 kn.[41]

Monday 12th Arrived at Queenstown at 7 A.M. and filled up with oil. There is a big merchant ship in here with her fore part blown away by a mine. Several ships torpedoed close to here.

Tues. 13th Picked up our convoy "Berwick", "Canada", "Ascania". We had the latter, she can only do 12 knots at her best.

Wed. 14th Arrived off Coningbeg Lt. V.[42] at 4 P.M. There had been all sorts of signals re huns in the vicinity and we were quite expecting one but nothing happened. Steering engine giving trouble.

H.M.S. ARCHER 2ND FLOTILLA
MARCH 1917

Thurs. 15th Arrived at Holyhead about 9 A.M. Went alongside and oiled & repaired our steering engine. Went ashore with first Lieut. Shoved off at 11:30 P.M. I had middle.

Fri. 16th Arrived at Devonport at 6 P.M. and oiled. There is a big transport which has been mined on the beach, also a Q boat.[43]

Sat. 17th Went out at 6 A.M. and fired a "mouldy"[44] which we could not find to pick up. Left the Tigress & our whaler out there. Archer proceeded into No. 2 basin and I went ashore to draw money. In the afternoon, I went out in the drifter "Morrison" with "Leader" to creep for torpedo. About 5 P.M. T.B. 074 came out & said mouldy was high and dry on the beach. Went in to shore in dinghy & secured her as we could not get it off. Got quite wet, finally arriving back at ship at 9 P.M.

---

41 Knots.
42 Light vessel.
43 Q ships were heavily armed merchant ships with concealed weaponry, designed to lure submarines into making surface attacks. This gave Q ships the chance to open fire and sink them. Dutchy told a tale of wearing women's clothing as part of the decoy.
44 Slang for torpedo.

Sunday 18th Same routine. I am the only one aboard.

Monday 19th Same routine. Captain went out with a party and tried to salve [salvage] torpedo. Great advance of the Allies on the Western Front.

Tues. 20th Same routine. Correcting charts. Brought mouldy in.

Wed. 21st Same routine. Saw Taylor & D for a few minutes. Attack and Acheron in harbour. Hospital ship torpedoed about 15 miles from here but got safely into harbour. Some nurses & soldiers killed. She was burning Navigation lights etc. and had red cross painted on side. The huns admit torpedoing her. A destroyer "Paragon" sunk and all officers lost and another T.B.D.[45] damaged.

Thurs. 22nd Still boiler cleaning.

Fri. 23rd Went ashore in forenoon to Plymouth and had lunch at the Royal. Did some shopping. Shoved off from basin at 4 P.M. and went alongside oiler. Steering gear jamming & we remained alongside all night. Had dinner with Reid in the Attack then saw Taylor in Acheron.

Sat. 24th Shoved off in forenoon, also Acheron, Attack, Goshawk, Ariel, Brisk, Lapwing Doing 20 knots when out to a R.V.

Sun. 25th Lyra, Goshawk, Acheron, Attack, Lizard, speed 20 knots. Sighted convoy, we had to go straight back to Plymouth as we haven't enough oil.

Monday 26th Ran into a gale & snowstorm in forenoon and it was pretty wet aboard. Arrived at Devonport about 8 P.M. and oiled at 6:45. Entered No. 2 basin.

Tues. 27th In the basin undergoing repairs to steering engine.

Wed. 28th In the basin undergoing repairs to steering engine. Taylor and Reid came onboard and we had dinner ashore.

Thurs. 29th At 2:30 P.M. proceeded. Met very heavy weather near the Lizard and put into Falmouth where we picked up S.S. Queen Louise who we are going to convoy to Cherbourg.

Fri. 30th Arrived off Cherbourg at 1:30 P.M. and turned SS. Queen Louise over to Froggies. Proceeded back to Devonport, arriving there are 11 P.M.

Sat. 31st At 0:10 Tigress & ourselves weighed & proceeded out to area C. Carried out 4" and 12 pr. & torpedo practice. Tried one torpedo H.S. setting 4000 yards and picked it up alongside target with a big dent in head; must have hit bottom in initial dive.

H.M.S. ARCHER 2ND FLOTILLA
APRIL 1917

April 1st Shipped at 7 A.M. from Gunboat moorings with Tigress & submarines D4 & D5, proceeded towards Queenstown. Had middle

---
45 Torpedo boat destroyer.

watch and about 2 A.M (2nd) ran into a regular blizzard so we rolled and threw ourselves about. Lost a sextant, range finder over board.

April 2nd Mon. Arrived at Queenstown at 8 A.M. & thawed ourselves out. Went for a walk with Taylor in P.M. and tea ashore.

3rd Tues. Still at Queenstown, raining and snowing.

4th Wed. Shoved off at 8 A.M. in company with other Destroyers went out to R.V.

5th Thurs. Met convoy "Calgarian", "Metagama", "Lapland", "Southland", "Missanabie", Saxonia". Ours was Lapland. Proceed back tods.[46] L'pool.

6th Fri. At about 10 P.M. South Stack abeam let Lapland proceed to L'pool as we did not have enough oil to get there ourselves. Put in to Holyhead and oiled.

7th Sat. Shoved off at 3:30 A.M. & proceeded. Heard that Lapland has struck a mine right inside the channel at Liverpool. Proceeded to Devonport where we arrived at 8 P.M.

8th Sun. Easter Sunday. At 2 P.M. shipped & proceeded, shaped course for R.V.

9th Mon. Joined by Canterbury & 7 other boats at 9 P.M. sighted convoy with Swiftsure. One ship S.S. Ayreshire 10-11 knots.

10th Tues. Zig-zagging.

11th Wed. Arrived at Devonport at 4 P.M. and made fast to a buoy.

12th Thurs. Rec'd. more mail including a parcel. Had dinner with skipper at his house.

H.M.S. ARCHER 2ND FLOTILLA
APRIL 1917

13th Friday On board all day. The Canadians are doing fine work in France at Vimy Ridge.

14th Sat. At 8 P.M. anchored in the Sound at 1½ hours notice.

15th Sunday Sankey in "Unity" is anchored close to us. Went over and saw him for a few minutes.

16th Monday Weighed & proceeded at 1 P.M., also Goshawk & Lizard. Very heavy weather, had to ease down from 20 to 12 knots. My middle.

17th Tues. Sighted convoy "Le Petit Thomas" and "Britain" in morning & took station.

18th Wed. My middle. Arrived "Brest" at 5 A.M. Shoved off. Ushant abeam at 8 A.M. Submarine stunt in forenoon. Arrived Plymouth in P.M. went into Mo. 2 basin for boiler cleaning.

---

46 Towards.

19th Thurs. Caught 1:27 P.M. for London. (Went to Defiance in A.M. about T.C.C also Reid unsuccessful). Arrived in town at 7 P.M. Went to Waldorf Hotel and saw "Chu Chin Chow" at His Majesty's and it was a very fine show.

20th Fri. Saw Mrs. Fraser in forenoon and had lunch at Pall Mall. Saw Hanky Panky in P.M. Tea at Piccadilly and dinner with Mrs. Fraser. Afterwards went to Gerald du Maurier in London Pride at Wyndham's & it was awfully good.

21st Sat. Caught 10 A.M. train from Liverpool station for Harwich, arrived at 12;15, met by Cousin Jack. Heard Sir Edward Carson speak to the submarine crews. Went out to Dovercourt & saw Cousin D.

22nd Sun. Dinner at Annesley, went to church with Cousin D. Larson came in to tea. Caught the 5 P.M. train, arrived in town at 7. Saw Cousin Bertie at British Empire Club, 12 St. James Square. He came & saw me off by 9:50 P.M. train.

23rd Mon. Arrived at Plymouth at 4:30 A.M. Dinner with Reid in Attack. On Sat. HMS Broke flotilla leader sank two German destroyers off Dover. She fired two torpedoes at first, rammed the second and struck the third a glancing blow.

24th Tues. Came out of basin at 8 P.M. & went straight to sea after oiling. 20 knots. Met "Marmora" aux. cruiser & convoyed her back.

25th Wed. Arrived Ply. at 3 P.M. Heard that one of the transports in our convoy, "Ballerat", was sunk either yesterday or today. Shoved off at midnight.

26th Thurs. Arrived off Falmouth at 3:30 A.M. and anchored. Picked up S.S. Colorado and convoyed her to Portland where we arrived at 8 P.M. Proceeded back to Ply. at 20 kn.

27th Fri. Arrived Ply. 2 A.M. anchored in sound. Went up harbour at 7 A.M.

28th Sat. At Plymouth.

29th Sun. Weighed and proceeded in company with Lapwing, Attack & Lizard. Speed 20 kn. At 4:15 sighted German submarine on horizon about 5½' distant. Went full speed and action stations. Submarine dove. Dropped depth charge on spot where we thought she dived. Got out Star. P.V. and steamed about, saw some oil & an oily track. Dropped 2nd depth charge. The depth charges are fine things and give a tremendous explosion sending up the whole surface of the sea. Pat.[47] about 200 yds. radius. Do not know whether or not we got a Fritz or not. Anyway we must have given him a nasty shake. He was too far away for the foremost 4".

---

47 Patrolled.

H.M.S. ARCHER 2ND FLOTILLA
APRIL 1917 & MAY

Monday 30th Picked up our convoy and shaped course for Plymouth, speed 10½ knots.

MAY 1917

Tues. 1st Same routine. Went to G.Q.s twice today, the second time when Lapwing opened fire on a derelict which a trawler was towing. She thought it was a Fritz.

Wed. 2nd Arrived & anchored in the sound at 3:30 A.M. My middle. Weighed and proceeded up harbour at 6 A.M. On board all day.

Thurs. 3rd Reid & I went ashore at 11 A.M. and went for a bike ride to Yelverton where we had tea. Returned at 6 P.M. Very fine ride, first exercise we have had for ages.

Fri. 4th Proceeded at 8 P.M. in company with 6 transports & 6 destroyers. There 11 Transports all told.

Sat. 5th Zig-zagging. Foggy.

Sun. 6th Arrived at R.V. at noon. Proceeded to Devonport. Gunner ill. In two watches. Very heavy weather in first watch. Had to ease down. I had first and 3 hours of middle. A/c [48] for Queenstown.

Mon. 7th Arrived at Queenstown in P.M. Oiled and proceeded for Belfast.

Tues. 8th Arrived Belfast at 11 A.M. Went alongside in Musgrave Channel & oiled. I went ashore for an hour in P.M. Liked the city very much. Shoved off about 7 P.M., proceeded to Lough Swilly, Rain and & fog arrived at 3 A.M. & anchored inside basin.

Wed. 9th At Lough Swilly. The wreck of Laurentic is just about 1 mile from Fanad Lt. Ho. She had about 10 million pounds (gold) when she went down. Shoved off at 10 P.M. in company with Lapwing, Tigress, Attack, Acheron, & Phoenix & proceeded to R.V.

Thurs. 10th Got a W/T to say convoy not expected till 5 A.M. (12th). Proceeded back to Lough

Fri. 11th Swilly & the Attack came alongside us & Phoenix came alongside her & we took in about 50 tons of oil (4 A.M.). This is second time we have gone out to a R.V.[49] ahead. Very extravagant & waste of oil blunder on part of V.A. Queenstown who thinks it only takes 7 days for convoy to cross Atlantic. They (convoy) left Halifax on the 3rd at 3 P.M. Weighed & proceeded in 1 pt. A.

Sat. 12th Picked up convoy at R.V. "Devonshire", "Antiyia", "Metagama", & Corsican. The latter is ours (speed 13 knots). The Gunner is off the sick

---
48 Altered course.
49 Rendezvous.

list which puts us back into three watches. Before I generally used to keep the first & middle & then up early all day. Key the forenoon or afternoon which was a bit strenuous.

Sun. 13th Had middle. Rain. Stopped south of Oversay Lt. owing to fog. Had W/T to say that Acheron and Attack had been in collision. It is a wonder that there are not more collisions etc. in these Durban fogs with lots of boats & transports moving about. Arrived off Liverpool about 7 P.M. & then proceeded to Holyhead. No. 1 and I went up to the hotel & had a glorious bath.

Monday 14th Proceeded at noon for Liverpool arriving there at about 5 P.M. Saw King George pass down harbour. Went alongside Woodside jetty. I went ashore in the evening and had dinner at the Adelphi.

Tues. 15th At 3:40 A.M. went into Alfred Locks & oiled then proceeded out and went alongside Olympic at 8 A.M. Went aboard Olympic in person & learnt that Cousin Bertie was O.C. troops. He gave me the awful news that Joe had been killed in action on April 29th at Arleux. I can hardly realize it to think that he has gone. It will seem awful without him and I can't realize it yet. Left Liverpool at 6 P.M. in company with Olympic, Phoenix and two other destroyers, doing about 22 knots.

Wed. 16th Turned back about 3 P.M. & proceeded to Belfast. Arrived there in middle (my) watch. Anchored outside channel. Went in & oiled about 7 A.M. 1 P.M. proceeded for Devonport. (17)th.

Thurs 17th Arrived Devonport about 1 P.M.

Fri. 18th At 5 P.M. proceeded, convoyed S.S. Madoupac to Portland. Arrived there at 6 A.M. Arrived back at Devonport noon 20th.

Mon. 21st Proceeded at 4 A.M. Met "Saxonia" 6 A.M. convoying her to Falmouth. She was bringing over medical corps from U.S. and was one of the first contingents.

Tues. 23rd (s.b. 22nd) Proceeded at 5 P.M. & with Highflyer, Ruby, Lizard, Durban, Castle & Ayreshire.

Wed. 24th (23rd) Zig-zagging. The Ayreshire only does about 11 knots.

Thurs. 25th (24th)

26th Fired a torpedo practice in morning. Secured to oiler. Hot. Went into No. 2 basin for boiler cleaning.

27th At boiler cleaning. The Doc and I are the only officers left onboard. I have a glorious night in.

H.M.S. ARCHER 2ND FLOTILLA
MAY 1917

28th Usual boiler cleaning routine.

29th Usual boiler cleaning routine.

30 Usual boiler cleaning routine.

31 Lieut. B.A. Taylor joined ship in command. Lieut. H.E. Horan D.S.C. has been appointed to Nereus 13th Flotilla. We were all very sorry to lose him.

JUNE 1917

1st Proceeded out of No. 2 basin complete with oil. 7 P.M. proceeded in company with Suffolk & other destroyers & transports out to usual R.V.

2nd At sea convoying – fine weather.

3rd At sea convoying – fine weather. Picked up convoy Australia & convoyed her to Falmouth.

4th Entered harbour 8 A.M., oiled. Badger secured alongside us at the trot. I had middle watch this morning & saw a rocket go up. We looked around but could not see anything. Q ship had been torpedoed & had fired this rocket. The Christopher (4th Flotilla) went up to her and took off survivors & a Fritz fired a mouldy which hit her & did not explode. Some time afterwards the Christopher dropped 2 depth charges which did not explode – a case of mutual luck. The Badger's people had a lot of yarns to spin about Portsmouth convoying. They were escorting hospital ship Highland Corrie when she was torpedoed & it was quite interesting learning their yarns.

W/T transmission regarding location of possible torpedo, June 6, 1917

5th In harbour. Funny we should get a night in like this.

7th Proceeded at 2 P.M. in company Ariel, Brisk, Hope, Ruby, Jackal, Brisk, Lizard. Archer, ? out to R.V.

8th Picked up convoy about 4 P.M. Eight transports.

9th Fritz is evidently waiting for us as Medina saw one & dropped 8 D.C.s & Lapwing also saw. Medina also came across two abandoned ships. Our division altered course as the Badger who was ahead of us had a torpedo fired at her which luckily missed.

10th Arrived at Devonport at 2 P.M. with all our convoy safe & sound.

June 11th Went outside to pump out water in oil fuel tanks. Carried out 1" aiming & .303, also ran P.Y. Proceeded to Falmouth & escorted S.S. "Ascania" to Portland.

June 12th Arrived Ply. in forenoon. Got a 2½ inch wire around star. propeller – cleared. At 40 min. not.

June 13th At 3 A.M. shipped & proceeded to meet SS Baron Juding & escort her to Falmouth. Could not find her but in my watch forenoon saw a Fritz & dropped D.C. & lowered P.V. Lost star. P.V. & 1 main ankle broken when P.V. winch took charge. Fritz was about 5-6 miles away. Arrived in Ply.[50] about 8 P.M. Big aeroplane raid over London, 50 killed.

June 15th At Ply. Proceeded into Sound at 8 P.M. We were to take S.S. Madusa [Medusa] Portland but it was cancelled. Proceeded at 11 P.M. to south of Lizard to pick up a ship but did not find her.

June 16th Arrived at Devonport at 2 P.M. Went ashore for a couple of hours.

June 17th At Plymouth all day. 40 min. notice.

June 18th Proceeded at 1 P.M. (max. speed 20 knots as Dckyd.[51] won't repair fans in E.R.) to convoy S.S. "Rathlamba" [Kathlamba] to Falmouth. She was attacked at 9:30 & 12:30 by Fritz and torpedo hit her. We picked her up at 8 P.M. she was escorted by Victor. Had a big list to star. & after holds full of water. Arrived at Swillys 1 A.M. and as she had no charts I was going over to pilot her in, but an officer came off & did the job.

June 19th Arrived D'port in forenoon. Went ashore with Doc. in P.M. Came on board about 7 P.M.

June 20th Heard we were going into No. 2 basin to fix fans. Went up to oiler to pump out tanks, just missed the gate. Saw Sankey.

June 21st At the trot. Doc & I pulled up to Saltash in the skiff and saw Sankey & Lenn in "Unity". Went into No. 2 basin to repair fans and to clean boilers.

June 22nd Went ashore with the Doc & walked to Cawsand.

---

50 Plymouth.
51 Dockyard.

H.M.S. ARCHER 2ND FLOTILLA
JUNE 1917

June 23rd Stayed on board nearly all day. We expect to go to Newport on the 26th to refit. Our wrapper plates are also supposed to be in a rather bad state.

June 24th Went to Presbyterian church in morning at St. Andrews in evening with the Doc. Raining all day. Laverock (Hibbard) came into the basin.

June 25th Went up to Defiance for instruction in torpedo control & as they have no attacks table rigged, got fed up. Walked from Defiance to Saltash & from there took motor to Devonport. Went ashore with the Doc. & Hibbard. Had tea at Goodbody's & then loafed on the Hoe.

June 26th Proceeded to Newport 4 P.M.

June 27th Arrived off Newport about 8 A.M. Pilot came off and we went into dock at Morley & Carney. Raining, went ashore in evening with skipper & No. 1.

June 28th Left Newport at 9 A.M. Arrived reading about 11:30. Had lunch there & caught S.E. & C. train to Ash. Changed there & at Aldershot. Finally arrived Farnham 4 P.M. Dorothy and Mary there. Had tea at Cooper Kings.

June 29th Raining all day.

June 30th Fine day. Marked out Chrissus' tennis court. Frances Gore arrived from Winchester. Picked cherries.

July 1st Went to church in A.M. Did some work to tennis court in P.M. & played some Badminton.

July 2nd Played tennis in afternoon also badminton. Frances & I went to Aldershot & saw a show at the Hippodrome which was quite good.

July 3rd Frances left in A.M. Played tennis in afternoon at Cooper Kings. Picked some more cherries.

July 4th Raining. In afternoon I biked to Froyle and saw them all there. Had two functions on way back. I left Froyle at 5:30 & arrived Eastleigh 7:30 P.M. in the rain.

July 5th My birthday. Left Farnham at 9 A.M., arrived in London 10:30. Had lunch at Harrods. Looked up Mrs. Fraser who was out. Went to Garricks and saw "Smile". Met Ned Reynolds & we had dinner together at Georgian Court Hotel. Saw "High Jinks" in evening & it was very good.

July 6th Left Paddington 9 A.M., arrived Newport at 12:30 P.M.

July 7th Went to Golf Links.

July 8th Raining nearly all day. Went to St Paul's church in morning. In evening No. 1 & I went to St Wollos [Woolos]. It is a very old church founded in about 650 and it is quite interesting.

Mond. 9th Went out & played golf. Had tea at the Dutch café & then bought a motor bike for £12 12s. A 1 cyl. 3¼ H.P. Quadrant.

Tues. 10th Went out on the bike to the golf links (Ladyhill).

Wed. 11th Rode about 5 miles out towards Chapstone. Very pretty and quite good road.

Th. 12th Repairing bike. Nothing much doing.

13th Watch returned from leave. Had tea at Dutch café.

14th Skipper & Doc. returned.

15th Went for a walk into the park and then went to church at St Wollos [Woolos].

16th Stayed aboard all day repairing clutch of motor bike.

H.M.S. ARCHER

July 17th Took motor bike to garage. Played tennis at Newport Athletic Club with Doc.

July 18th Raining all day. My day on. Ladies of office staff Morley & Carney came off to tea.

July 19th Doc. & I went out to Caerleon and saw King Arthur's round table which was also an old Roman arena. Also saw the museum there. Caerleon was an old Roman city about 400 A.D. In the afternoon, I motor biked to Cardiff & met the Doc. at the Dorothy. Had tea at the Louis Café (very nice place). Cardiff is a very nice place at least what we saw was. Left there at 7 P.M. & arrived back about 7:45 the distance is 12 miles. The road is quite good but a little bit bumpy in places for a motor bike.

July 20th My day on. Nothing much doing.

July 21st Played tennis with Doc. at Newport Athletic club in afternoon.

July 22nd Went to church early & also 11 A.M. at St. Wollos [Woolos]. Went for a ride on motor bike in afternoon. Got too much oil in engine and so emitted dense clouds of smoke.

July 23rd Shifted from Morley & Carneys to Alexandra Dock. In afternoon I motor biked to Chefstone and had tea with the Doc. who went out by train. We walked 3 miles to Wyndecliff and had a most excellent view. It was awfully petty. Biked back arriving at 9:15 P.M.

July 24th Stayed aboard all day.

July 25th Doc & I went to Caerphilly as they had a flower show at the castle there. Met some V.A.D.s & had tea. The castle is very old, about 1400. Cromwell blew it up about 2 or three hundred years after this date.

H.M.S. ARCHER

July 26th My day on. Painting ship and trying fans, etc.

July 27th Went to Hospital with the Doc & had dinner there.

July 28th Proceeded from Newport in forenoon & ran trials. Arrived at Avonmouth about 2 P.M. & oiled. Went into Bristol. It is a very nice place, lots of classy kids. It is about 8 miles from Avonmouth to Bristol by Motor bus; had tea at Bonnets. Left Avonmouth at midnight & anchored outside.

July 29th Sun. Swang compasses in early morning & then proceeded at 24 knots to Devonport, arrived there at 8 P.M. & went alongside & took in our ammunition & stores. Got sailing orders to proceed to Brest and then to Gibraltar at 6 A.M. Monday. They do believe in short notice. Everyone very fed up with the idea of going to Mediterranean.

July 30th Proceeded 6 A.M. 22 knots. Arrived at Brest about 4 P.M. Went ashore in dchyd & tried to find out about oil (Marjou) some job. They are the most casual blighters I ever met. We had oil with our nose up against a jetty & they didn't have enough hose to reach to after tank until they had a good look around & discovered some. No. 1, Doc and myself had dinner ashore.

July 31st Sailed at 8 P.M. in company with Phoenix & transports Inventor & Bellerophon. doing about 27 knots. Arrived back in harbour about 9 P.M. and oiled ship.

H.M.S. ARCHER DARDANELLES

Aug. 11th Returned my home set of charges and pilot books to Dckyd. Shipped & proceeded at 6 P.M. for Suda Bay, Candia or Crete. One would get soon fed up with Malta as it is very hot. There are some interesting places about including the chapel of bones which I did not see as I was kept rather busy.

12th Donned my khaki uniform today.

13th Arrived at Suda Bay 9 A.M. Anchored near Pelorus. Quite a decent harbour but not much doing ashore. Very hot. Did not go ashore. Weighed and proceeded at 2 P.M. for Mudros.

14th Arrived at the famous "Mudros" Lemnos Island about 9 A.M. Discharged mails to "Europa" & then oiled & came to port ↓ at 5th Destroyer anchorage. Went ashore in P.M. & had a swim. Very hot & this certainly isn't much of a place. Lots of fruit but a shortage of other things like matches, butter etc. and we only have one tin of cond. milk between ten of us. Went to dinner in the Harpy. We have no awnings as yet.

15th We were all inoculated this morning. Went for a sail in whaler P.M.

16th "Grasshopper" & "Archer" proceeded out of harbour at 9 A.M. We got out our mine sweep & towed it for a bit. Seaplane reported a submarine a few miles from us so we searched for it but saw nothing. Saw a mine in afternoon. Proceeded to our patrol which is from Cape Niger (Imbros) to Tenedos. I think that we are in range of the forts as they hit some of our boats in this patrol a short time ago. There are heaps of mines knocking about so they say. The Bulldog had her stern blown off a short time ago.

H.M.S. ARCHER DARDANELLES PATROL
AUGUST 1917

Aug. 17th On patrol, anchored for an hour near Cape Aliki. At 6 P.M. took up northern patrol which is north of Zusu Pt. and about 6-7 miles from Suvla. My middle and I was nearly gassed.

Aug. 18th On northern patrol. Pretty hot. Changed to southern patrol at 6 P.M. At about 7:20 as we were all in the ward-room having dinner a mine was sighted. It just missed hitting us at Wardroom by about 3 feet. Grasshopper sunk it with one round of 12 pr. Quite a good explosion.

Aug. 19th Sunday. Arrived off Mudros at 9 A/M/ Got out mine sweep and swept. Lost Tadpole and searched for it until 3 P.M. then went in and oiled after which we ran both Torpedoes. Anchored ab[o]ut 7:30 P.M. ahead of Phoenix.

Aug. 20th Commenced our boiler cleaning. Never saw so much paper work as we have to do this flotilla. It is about 6 times as much as we had at Devonport.

Aug. 21st Landed at 8:30 with some other officers & walked 4 miles over to Kanbra where we went to Hydrophone station to attend a lecture but as wind was high we didn't hear much. Had lunch in Osiris II & walked back. "Fury" towed us alongside Blenheim at 6:30 P.M.

Aug. 22nd Boiler cleaning routine. Went ashore for swim in afternoon and we were all inoculated again. Still no mail, we haven't had any since we left Newport.

Aug. 23rd Felt pretty mouldy from the effects of inoculation. Spent all day on board trying to compete with some of the paper work which they throw at us here. Tug towed us out to an anchorage.

Aug 24th Sailed at 9 A.M. in company with "Basili[s]k". Took up main patrol.

Aug 25th One of the T.B.D.s brought out our mail which has at last arrived. Took Wear and Ribble's mail to Zusu Bay, then anchored in Aliki Bay until 6 P.M. when we proceeded to northern patrol.

H.M.S. ARCHER 5TH FLOTILLA
DARDANELLES PATROL

Aug. 26th Patrolling. Aeroplane report that Turkish destroyers in Narrows with steam up. We wonder if they are coming out.

Aug. 27th Proced. to Mudros at 8 A.M. and anchored after oiling & coaling etc.

Aug. 28th Still busy with paper work. Had a good swim & in P.M. Doc, No. 1 & myself went away in dinghy to Mudros & then went & made tea on the rocks. We are now rationed on jam. We should be in good training after some time of this as our rations are: ½ oz. milk, no butter, no spuds, about 2 oz. jam per day. In fact, everything which is tinned. Still we are not rationed on bully beef & bread.

Aug. 29th Weighed at 9 A.M. and proceeded to Dardanelles patrol in company with "Basili[s]k". On main patrol.

Aug. 30th On main patrol anchored in Aliki Bay in afternoon for a few hours.

Aug. 31st On main patrol anchored in Zusu Bay.

SEPTEMBER 1917

Sept. 1st Returned to Mudros. Went for swim in P.M.

Sept. 2nd Sunday At 6 A.M. there was an air raid over Mudros. 6 German machines all the guns loosed off at them. They dropped bombs not far from us, quite a good show as it is the first one I have seen. Sub.-Lt. of Harpy came off to dinner. Mail arrived. At about 11 P.M. another air raid over Mudros. Darkened ship & all the A.A. guns commenced firing. We couldn't get the machines but heard them. Firing kept up intermittently until after midnight.

Sept. 3rd Weighed & proced. at 9 A.M. with Capt. D. on board. Carried out 4" & 12 pr. practice firing. I am control officer and didn't do badly. The idea is to get as many as poss. in shortest time. Range 2000. Got 6 hits. Speed of target 8 kn. Speed of ship 20 kn. 12 prs. shot well.

Sept. 4th On patrol, moderate sea.

Sept. 5th Proceeded to Kephalo Bay[52] & embarked Brig. Gen. Grey & staff. Proceeded to Teredos [Tenedos] where we ↓ed. Waited for them & took them back to Aliki. Proced. to Mudros 20 kn. Bit of a sea —saw a mine but lost it. Anch. Mudros 7:30 P.M. Stayed alongside oiler for night.

Sept. 6th Came to port ↓ Mudros at 7 A.M. Sailed for Falmouth at 7 P.M. in company with Basilisk as we are joining the 1st Detached Squadron.

Sept. 7th Arrived Salonika at 8 A.M. and anchored. Went ashore in P.M. Never saw so many different uniforms in my life. Lots of soldiers here of all nations. Big fire recently which burnt out half the place. Had tea at white

---

52 Name is now spelled Kefalos Bay.

tower. Another good place is the French military club. The city is awfully dirty & lots of things are dear & scarce. The front (Stammos?) [Stamos] is about 40 miles from here.

Sept. 8th My day on. Pretty hot. Had a swim.

Sept. 9th Sunday. Small mail arrived but no letters for me. The last letters from home are dated Halifax July 12th. Weighed at 10 P.M. & proceeded in company with Basilisk & "Angora" (HMT). Shaped course for Alexandria. 19 knots. Salonika – Alex. is about 700 miles.

Sept. 10th At sea.

Sept. 11th Arrived at entrance to Swept Channel 3:30 P.M. Secured to Vacuum oil jetty & oiled. Went ashore & had dinner at the Majestic (quite a swank place), This seems to be a very nice place & is cleaner than most of these places. Once can buy fruit & there are some quite decent shops.

H.M.S. ARCHER 1ST D.S 5TH FLOTILLA
SEPTEMBER 1917

Sept. 12th Went ashore in P.M. to do some shopping & have a hair cut.

Sept. 13th In the A.M. the Doc & myself to see the catacombs which are only two or three miles from the "Majestic Hotel". They are about 2000 years old but were only discovered about 20 years ago. Came off to ship at 2 P.M. as I thought that we were sailing at 4 but we are due to sail tomorrow. I was going to meet No. 1 and the Doc. at the "Star of Italy" but went for a swim instead. 2 Jap. destroyers arrived & anchored quite close to us.

Sept. 14th Sailed from Alex. at 4 P.M. in company with "Volumnia" (9½ knots).

Sept. 15th At sea. Quite fine weather.

Sept. 16th (Sun.) Quite heavy wind from NW with fairly heavy sea.

Sept. 17th Anchored in Port Trebuki. Skyros Is. at 6 A.M. Quite a good ↓ge. Phoenix & Fury arrived with transport on the way to Alex. Weighed at 4 P.M. Had good swim in early morning; water was cool.

Sept. 18th Arrived Salonika at 11 P.M. went alongside oiler. Rec'd. mail. I had letters from Grace & parcels from home, Frances & Chrissie Cooper-King. The two latter ones had been travelling for nearly two months & cakes & apples were all bad – worse luck so I am sure the cake from Frances was a corker. We are due to sail at 5 P.M. with Aragon for Alex. She has 2700 troops on board and is she is torpedoed we are to take the 1700 troops aboard & the "Wear" 1800—some job. They are evidently taking nearly all the troops from the Struma Front to Palestine or Mesopotamia. Heard that Taylor (Archer) has arrived out here. Proceeded at 5 P.M. in company with "Wear" & "Aragon".

Sept. 19th Aragon anchored at Port Trebuki & we went alongside here. Lots of military officers came aboard. I met two or three very nice ones. One was Hyland Smith, Captain in M———. Some of them are quite fed up as the[y] have been in quite heavy fighting at Salonika and nothing has been said about it at home. In fact the people at home think they are having an awfully slack time of it. Proceeded at 5:30 P.M. for Alex.

Sept. 20th At sea – fine weather.

Sept. 21st Arrived at Alex. about 4 P.M. & anchored near Hannibal. Went ashore with No. 1 and the Doc. & had dinner at the Star of Italy. No oiler in yet and we are waiting for one to round from Port Said. The Phoenix and Fury went to Port Said to oil which is a distance of about 140 miles. Tube in one boiler leaking.

Sept. 22nd My day on. Still waiting for the oiler to arrive, no one seems to know definitely when she is due.

Sept. 23rd Went to church in P.M. with No. 1 & Doc. & enjoyed the service.

Sept. 24th Oiler arrived & we oiled. Sailed at 4 P.M. in company with Wear & Louvain for Sula Bay.

Sept. 25th Quite heavy sea & it is washing down.

Sept. 26th Arrived at Souda Bay about 8 A.M. Oiled. Had a swim. Hydra arrived. Heard that the Japs are taking over the oil boats i.e. they have already taken over "Rifleman", "Minstrel" and another. War news seems very good at present & we have had a big success on Western Front.

Sept. 27th Sailed at 8 A.M. for Salonika in company with "Wear". Very heavy sea—foc's'le matting torn up & all "wears" howsers unshipped & reels broken up. It eased down in the evening.

Sept. 28th Air raid here this morning. Arrived at Salonika and oiled. Rec'd. a big mail. I got letter from home dated Aug. 11th, pretty quick. Also from Mrs. Diggan & others. Our Yarrow-Terry fans are giving trouble again.

H.M.S. ARCHER 5TH FLOTILLA – 1ST. D.S.

Sept. 29th Sailed at 4. At sea Salonika-Alex. In company with "Wear" and "Bohemian".

Sept. 30th At sea.

OCTOBER 1917

Oct. 1st At sea.

2nd Arrived at Alex. about 9 A.M. Oiled & anchored at destroyer anchorage. My day on.

3rd Oct. Went ashore in forenoon and did some shopping. We have given the Turks an awful hammering in Mesopotamia. Sailed at 4 P.M. in company with Sloop Anenome, Wear, Transport for Suda Bay. Fritzys are very active off Alex. & Port Said. Transport only does about 8½ knots.

4th October At sea, fine weather, making good 8½ knots.

5th Oct. Arrived at Suda Bay 9 P.M. Rec'd. mail.

6th Oct. At Suda Bay. Blowing quite hard. Skipper capsized the whaler when away sailing.

7th Oct. Rec'd. another mail. Sailed at 6 P.M. in company with H.M.T. Briton for Navarin Bay (Albania).

8th Oct. Arrived Navarin Bay & ↓d. Sailed at 6 P.M. for Corfu.

9th Oct. Arrived Corfu at 9 A.M. & anchored. The Kaiser has a place here (or had). We did not go right up to Corfu Town. Had tea in the Briton. Proceeded at 6 P.M. for Taranto.

10th Oct. Arrived at Taranto about 10 A.M. in company with Briton & 6 Australian destroyers. Went right inside to the inner harbour where all the Italian fleet is; they never got to sea. Lots of cruisers & other craft here. It is reported that the fleet did not go as far as the outer harbour since the war started. We oiled at the most awful place with one 2" hose. The "Bristol" was in dock so I aboard and saw Tim Bartlett (Eng. comm.). He was as cheery as ever. Proceeded at 6 P.M. in company with a sloop & "Aragon" to Corfu.

11th Oct. Arrived Corfu 11 A.M. Went alongside "Aragon". Lots of Military officers onboard. Proceeded at 5 P.M. for Navarin Bay.

12th Oct. Arrived Navarin Bay at 10 A.M. Went alongside Aragon. Had lunch aboard her. Proceeded at 5 A.M. for Suda Bay.

13th Oct. Arrived Sud[a] Bay 10 A.M., oiled & proceeded to Mudros.

14th Oct. Arrived Mudros 11 A.M. Went alongside Blenheim to boiler clean.

15th Oct. I have taken over Captain's Secretary job & have an awful lot of paper work. There is such a tremendous amount of unnecessary paperwork in 'this' flotilla & the number of reports one has to send in is legion.

17th Oct. Capt. D. Chetwoode came on board & walked around & asked a lot of questions.

18th Oct. Still boiler cleaning & making good defects.

19th Oct. Still boiler cleaning & making good defects. Kept pretty busy writing all day.

20th Oct. Went for a swim & picnic in whaler near one of the villages. Went for a walk into one of the villages. It is funny to see their way of irrigation. The method is to harness a donkey to a pole which heaves round & is connected by wooden dog wheels to a drum over which an endless chain runs into the well. On the chain there are empty standard oil tins nailed which scoop up the water. When the water gets to the top it falls into a trough & so runs over the ground.

21st October Shifted astern of Blenheim.

22nd Oct. Proceeded at 6 A.M. to Dardanelles patrol. Quite cool weather with lots of wind. Shifted into blue clothing.

23rd Oct. Dardanelles patrol —exploded a mine.

24th Oct. Submarine panic on patrol. Towed out P.V.s & exploded one by mistake by an S.T putting home the firing switch. Jackal relieved us & we proceeded to Mudros where we arrived at 6 P.M. Oiled & at 11:30 P.M. proceeded & escorted "Triad" (R.A.) to Port Trebuki.

25th Oct. Arrived Mudros noon. Oiled & ↓ed. At ½ hrs notice.

26th Oct. Proceeded to Dardanelles patrol at 9 A.M. and relieved Jed. Nasty weather.

27th Oct. Dardanelles patrol.

28th Oct. Relieved by Jed, proceeded to Mudros.

29th Oct. At Mudros. Ship's company had soccer match. I am secretary of the team. Proceeded at midnight for Suda Bay.

30th Oct. Arrived at Suda Bay 6 P.M.

31st Oct. At Suda Bay. Rec'd. 282 bags of mail for pass. to Mudros. Sailed at noon in company with Triad for Mudros. Lovely day, my afternoon & first. Passed the Doro Channel at midnight.

November 1st Arrived Mudros 2 P.M. Oiled and came to ↓. Blowing quite hard.

November 2nd We were going to do firing but it was cancelled. I have been writing steadily from 9:15 A.M. up till now which is 7 P.M. reports, returns etc.

H.M.S. ARCHER

November 3rd 1917 9 A.M. Proceeded in company with Fury to Dardanelles Patrol. Blowing quite hard from N.E.

Nov. 4th Sunday – On Patrol

Nov. 5th Relieved by "Chelmer". Arrived Mudros about 3 P.M.

Nov. 6th Had a game of Soccer in P.M. "Jackal" arrived and I saw Soulsby. Heard that "Bush" and "Drake" had been sunk.

Nov 7th Proceeded to Dardanelles patrol in company Hydra. Lovely day. Hun airplanes bombed the Abercrombie at Tenedos.

Nov 8th Two Turkish planes over Mavros, they did not come close enough for us to fire. The Canadians have made another big advance of the western front.

Nov 9th   Relieved by Redpole, proceeded to Mudros.

Nov 10th   At Mudros. Went to dinner in Jackal with Soulsby. In evening was discharged to Blenheim (sick) as my ankles and legs were quite swollen. Sub Lt. White R.N.R. relieved me in Archer.

Nov 11th   Turned in all day. Fine sleep.

Nov 12th   Turned in all day. Heard that "Staunch" and Monitor were sunk at or near Gaza.

Nov 13th   Got up today. Archer returned from patrol. Rec'd. my mail.

Nov 14th   Went back to Archer. New gunner Mr. Burns joined ship, Mr. Pollard disc. to Blen.[53]

Nov 15th   At Mudros. Soulsby came off to dinner.

Nov 16th   Raining and blowing from NE.

Nov 17th   At hours notice. Came on to rain and blow very hard from the N.E. Keeping anchor watches.

H.M.S. ARCHER 5TH FLOTILLA

Nov. 18th Sunday – At Mudros keeping ↓ watch. Still blowing hard from N.E. Anchored quite close to Jackal.

Nov 19th   Weighed and proceeded to oiler at 7 A.M. then to Dardanelles patrol. Weather eased up slightly.

Nov 20th   On Patrol.

Nov 21st   Arrived Mudros. Ran Torpedoes & went along side Blenheim.

Nov 22nd   Boiler cleaning, went ashore shooting in P.M.

Nov 23rd   Mail arrived – a good big one.

Nov 24th   Doc rec'd notice of his demobilization. Went ashore shooting with No. 1 & the chief, walking about 10 miles, but didn't get any birds.

Nov 25th   Doc and Mr. Pollard sailed in Louvain. Had dinner in the "Pincher" with Beard.

Nov 26th   Sailed for Patrol at 7 A.M. & relieved Hydra.

Nov 27th   On Patrol.

Nov 28th   Arrived Mudros after running paravanes.

Nov 29th   Thursday. Proceeded at 9 A.M. in company with Ruby to carry out C firing. It was very foggy in forenoon & we did not get outside until about 1 P.M. Ruby fired first. We opened fire at about 2400 yards, my first

---

53 Abbreviation for Blenheim.

spotting correction down 800 was bad, however after the first round it was much better. I did not get any hits but Captain D seemed to be quite pleased. My rate corrections were too small.

H.M.S. ARCHER 5TH FLOTILLA

Nov 30th At 9 AM proceeded in company with "Ruby" for Dardanelles patrol.

December 1st On Dardanelles patrol.

December 2nd Relieved by Jackal – proceeded to Mudros. Anchored at 3 P.M. AT 6 P.M. weighed and proceeded out on Submarine Hunt near Cape Castro. blowing quite hard from N.E.

December 3rd On Submarine Hunt – towing paravanes, etc.

December 4th On Submarine Hunt – Closed Ruby who had sighted periscope & dropped depth charges, she must have given Fritz a bad shake up. One of D.C.s exploded under P.V. and crushed it like a concertina.

December 5th Arrived Mudros 8 A.M. and oiled. We were going to sea in the afternoon but some of our boiler tubes split & so we will get a night.

December 6th At 5 P.M. proceeded to Syra [Syros]. Blowing hard with quite a sea.

When I came off watch at midnight, I found my cabin flooded.

Snowing quite hard.

December 7th Arrived at Syra [Syros] 8 A.M. & discharged the officers taking passage. – Proceeded to Milo arriving about 2 P.M. – oiled and proceeded at 5 P.M. for Port Said.

December 8th At Sea. Milo – Port Said.

December 9th Arrived off Port Said at 8 A.M. Had some difficulty in finding the entrance & we experienced a considerable set to the Eastward.

Went alongside oiling jetty at noon. Lots of ships although the pilot told us that the harbour was practically empty. Just managed to land the steward for an hour. Shoved off at 3 P.M. escorting S. S. "Pacuare" to Salonika via Milo.

December 10th At sea quite fine weather, got quite decent sun sights.

December 11th Arrived at Milo 6 P.M. and oiled – Joy, a night in.

MUTUAL LUCK

June 8th 1917 [No entry entered on this page for this date: see later entry]

[The rest of the page continues the Dardanelles story.]

Dec. 12th Proceeded to Salonika via Doro Channel.

Dec. 13th Arrived Salonika 10 A.M. & anchored. The Purser and Chief Officer of "Briton" came off to tea.

Dec. 14th Went off to lunch in the Britain and a most excellent one. Afterwards No. 1 & I were just having dinner in the S. S. Pacuare, the meat ship which we brought up from Port Said, when we had a message to return onboard as we were sailing at 8 P.M. for Milo. I thought it was rather suspicious having two nights in. Fouled the nets going out of harbour. Heard that there has been a big disaster at Halifax when two ships with T.N.T. collided – Heavy loss of life about 2000. I am most anxious for news but cannot obtain any.

Dec. 15th Arrived at Milo about 8 P.M. & saw the old Bermudian anchored in the harbour. No 1 & I went over in P.M. & saw the Chief Officer who is a Chinese from Pictou (Carmichael). The war news lately hasn't been very optimistic. Romania signing an Armistice & fighting in Russia (internally).

Dec. 16th Sunday. About 10 nurses from the Bermudian came over in A.M. to see ship. Sailed at 2 P.M. for Port Said in company with Verbena and Bermudian. It is about time we had some fresh meat as we have been on bully beef & no veg. for about two weeks now.

Dec. 17th At Sea Milos – Port Said very heavy weather and we were rolling all over the place.

Dec. 18th Arrived Port Said about noon after quite a bad night. Raining – No 1 & I went ashore & had dinner at the Mariana Hotel which is quite a decent place. It was a great change after the everlasting bully. I see that we have lost another destroyer.

H.M.S. ARCHER 5TH FLOTILLA

Dec. 19th My day on but went ashore in afternoon & did some shopping.

No. 1 of "Lizard" was over to dinner, they have been up at Gaza bombarding. They landed 50 000 camels a short time ago.

Dec. 20th Sailed from Port Said for Salonika conveying a frozen meat ship S.S. "San Rito".

Dec. 21st At sea making about 10 knots.

Dec. 22nd It came to blow hard from the S.E. with rain.

Dec. 23rd Wind backed to N.E. very heavy weather & sea. Doing speed for 10 knots but only making about 3 good. It took us all day to clear Skyros Island. At one time we lost suction in the circulator. Raining. We thought at one time that we would have to run for shelter but towards evening we got up in the lee of the land.

Dec. 24th Arrived Salonika at 11 AM & oiled – proceeded alongside collier at 2 P.M. & then anchored. Raining & no mail for us.

December 25th – Christmas Day

Went to communion in St Margaret of Scotland at 7 AM. Had our goose for Xmas dinner & proceeded to sea at 4 P.M. We were kept rather on the jump all day over our sailing orders. Had an excellent dinner of goose – rice, corn, cauliflower, some Plum Pudding & mince pies. Proceeded to Milo at 4 P.M. in company with El Kharia. My middle watch.

Dec. 26th Arrived Milo about 5 P.M. & rec'd about two letters.

Dec. 27th 3 P.M. proceeded as far as Kasos with convoy El Kaharia. Rec'd some letters and heaps of official correspondence which keeps me up to my ears in work. No parcels as yet & lots of our mail must be adrift.

H.M.S. ARCHER 5TH FLOTILLA

December 28th Arrived out at position by Kaso[s] at 10 AM & then proceeded back to Milo arriving at 8 P.M.

Dec. 29th [no entry]

Jan. 10th – 1918 At Port Said. At 4:30 P.M, French ship Tibor, loaded with Benzine, exploded just off us. Away all boats & picked up mate and a stoker. Slipped one cable 5 skls (buoyed) & Japanese destroyer towed us clear. Tug towed us up canal at 8 P.M. Secured to canal bank at 10 P.M. Big explosion on board burning ship at about 11 P.M. when 100-millimetre shells exploded causing quite a lot of damage in the Town – 5 men killed.

Jan. 11th – 1918 At Port Said. Secured to bank in Suez Canal. No. 1 & I went & tried to shoot some duck in forenoon but nothing doing. Proceeded down to Port Said at 2 P.M. Chief & I went ashore for a walk in P.M.

Jan 12th At Port Said.

Jan. 13 Sailed from Port Said at 9 A.M. in company convoy San Rito. Blowing quite hard – making 9 km.

Jan. 14th At Sea. Port Said – Salonika.

Jan. 15th At. Sea. Port Said – Salonika.

Jan. 16th Arrived Salonika about 6 P.M. Quite cold.

Jan. 17th Sailed for Milo at 5 P.M. At 6 got W/T to proceed to Mudros.

Jan. 18th Arrived Mudros 7 A.M. Oiled. My day on.

Jan. 19th Proceeded at noon in company "Renaud"[Reynard] to Port Trebuki & pick up S.S. "Mexican Prince" & escort her to Mudros. Arrived there at 7 P.M. & convey not here – Proceeded at 9:30 P.M. to pick her up.

Jan. 20th Sunday Got a W/T/ from "Lizard" at 8 A.M. – Goeben and Breslau & destroyers coming out. Took convoy to Kondia & were proceeding to Dardanelles when we were recalled to Mudros. Escorted "Aggie" out in company with Renaud & Shirmisher. Was then ordered to meet Lord Nelson and escort her to Dard. Were recalled & proceeded back to Mudros, thereby missing the show. Arrived Mudros 10 P.M. Apparently Goeben, Breslau & some destroyers came out and sank two monitors in Kusu Bay—Raglan & M29. Breslau sunk & Goeben reported badly damaged & had to be beached inside Dard. Lizard arrived with 14 Off. survived from Breslau & another ship brought in 120 other survivors.

Jan. 21st Monday Sailed for Dardanelles patrol at 7 A.M. in company Arno. Took Northern Patrol of Kusu & saw tops of masts and funnel of Monitor Raglan which was sunk yesterday in Kusu Bay. Went to act[ion] stations 10 P.M. and nearly fired on Kennet.

H.M.S. ARCHER 5TH FLOTILLA
JAN. 1918

Jan. 22th 1918 Tues. On Dardanelles patrol – picked up some bits of wreckage from Monitor. Our airplanes bombing Goeben who has been beached inside Dards. Anti-aircraft firing continued all first watch.

Jan. 23rd 1918 On Dards patrol in company "Renaud". We are going to screen M17 – who is going to bombard Goeben at 8 P.M. from a pos. 3' distance Gale Tep. We got to action stations at 8 P.M. & as it is my middle I don't expect much sleep tonight.

Later – Went to action stations at 8-10 & cruised about in company Renaud and Monitor over numerous minefields. Kephalo Lt. was off & so the shelling was abandoned. Anti-aircraft guns very busy near Suvla.

Jan. 24th Hostile aircraft dropped bomb not far from us at Kastro. Relieved from patrol & proceeded to Mudros. Rec'd. part of our six weeks mail. I was awfully relieved to hear from Mother saying that they were all uninjured at home, after the recent Halifax explosion. Rec'd. numerous letters & Xmas parcels & a whole bag of official correspondence. Heard that the Louvain has been torpedoed quite close to Mudros, with quite a large loss of life. Also most of our Xmas parcels. The "Colne" is pretty sure she got the Fritz who loosed off a mouldy[54] & only missed by three feet. The latter streamed up the track of torpedo & dropped depth charges.

It is fine getting some of our mail although I think that a lot of my parcels have gone down.

Jan. 25th At Mudros. Some of the Lizard's people came over and told us all about the Goeben Breslau stunt. They sighted the Goeben & Breslau at about 7:30 A.M. in company with Turkish destroyers coming of out of the Dards. Lizard and Tigress immediately attacked. After the first rounds the enemy destroyers turned and returned to Dards. Goeben and Breslau were firing at Liz. and Tig. the shells passing all round them. The former after coming out of t Dards. Steamed towards Kusu and as they opened the two monitors Raglan and M28 they commenced firing, sinking them in a few minutes, with great loss of life.

---

54 This term is slang for a torpedo.

Jan. 26th Proceeded at 7 A.M. in company "Comet" to Dardanelles patrol. Attack by aeroplanes still continues on "Goeben", they are rigging up depth charges. – I hear that the Raccoon has been wrecked on Rathlin Island with great loss of life. That makes the 9th destroyer which we have lost this month.

Jan. 27th On Dardanelles patrol.

Jan. 28th Returned to Mudros at noon owing to a defect in evaps.

Jan. 29th At Mudros. Fine day. I hear that E14 has gone up the Dards to finish off Goeben and has been lost. Goeben seems to have disappeared & we are sending seaplanes up to Constantinople to see if she is there.

Jan. 30th Went shooting with No. 1 in whaler, we shot one shag.[55] Mail arrived & I rec'd. many letters and parcels, wonders will never cease. The people are awfully good in the way of sending me things.

Jan. 31st Sailed for patrol at 7 A.M. in company "Colne".

Feb. 1st On patrol, blowing hard from N.E. We were ordered back to Mudros about 2 P.M. – Arrived Mudros about 7 P.M., oiled and ↓d. Anchor watches.

Feb. 2nd Sailed at 6 P.M. in company Foresight (with C in C) for Piraeus – Athens. Blowing great guns & we had a pretty rough night. We have a lot of ratings aboard for Malta. We expect to go to Taranto after Athens & then to Malta, for our refit —perhaps to England. Doing 17 knots, sea on beam.

H.M.S. ARCHER
1918

Feb. 3rd Sunday Arrived Pireaus at 8 A.M. & came to port ↓ 5 shls, stern secured to wall. Went ashore at 4 P.M. & took train to Athens where I met No. 1 & Surg. Prob. – walked out to stadium where the Olympic games are held. Fine place & also saw various other places of interest. Quite a nice place but is quiet on Sunday. Some parts are quite modern. Lots of fruit, currants, etc. Had dinner at the Grand Hotel D'Angleterre. Returned to ship at 9 P.M. It is about 7 miles from Pireaus to Athens by electric railway.

Feb. 4th 1918 Sailed at 8 A.M. in company "Foresight". Passed through the famous Corinth Canal at noon. The canal is 3 miles long.

Feb. 5th Arrived Taranto at 9 A.M., oiled & secured to dockyard. Went ashore with Davies No. 1 of Chelmer & a French chap. Had dinner at the Europa. Taranto is not much of a place.

Feb. 6th My day on. Nereide arrived.

---

55 The European shag is a species of cormorant that is found around the rocky coasts of western and southern Europe, southwest Asia and north Africa.

Feb. 7th Had dinner in the "Nereide" with Trefry (Surg. Prob.) who comes from Halifax & Sitwell the sub.

Feb. 8th Went ashore with "Trefry" in the afternoon.

Feb. 9th Stillwell & Trefry had dinner with in the evening.

Feb. 10th Had dinner in Nereide.

Feb. 11th Shoved off at 4 P.M. in company "Foresight" with C in C for Malta. We have two more officers for passage making a total of 4. I have an awful cold & feel pretty mouldy.[56]

H.M.S. ARCHER

Feb. 12th Arrived at Malta about 2:30 P.M. & were immediately ordered out to bring in a convoy from Comino Sound. We arrived back in harbour about 7 P.M. for our long looked forward to refit. We don't know whether they are going to England or not, as I think that we will need new wrapper plates. Phoenix, Ruby, Rifleman, Chelmer, Jed, Cameleon here.

Feb. 13th My day on. Stayed aboard.

Feb. 14th Went ashore in P.M. with Davis (No. 1 Chelmer) & visited Saccone's & various other places. In the evening went to Rigoletto opera which was very good although in Italian.

Feb. 15th Day on – Rotten cold, feeling pretty mouldy.

Feb. 16th Stayed aboard all day.

Feb. 17th Went to St. Paul's Church — very nice church but a poor service.

Feb. 18th Went ashore in P.M. had tea with Shaw (late clerk in Suffolk), returned aboard to dinner.

Feb. 19th Tuesday.

Feb. 20th Played a rugby match at Marsa against E.T.C. & lost. I played back. Ground very hard & I got lots of cuts and bruises. When I got back on board found that I had to join H.M.S. Lychnis.

Feb. 21st Joined Lychnis in forenoon, also a R.N.R. sub from Foresight called Pemberton in place of two officers who went sick. This ship is a Q boat & only commissioned in October. Sailed at 3 P.M. for Port Said.

Feb. 22nd At Sea Malta – Port Said

Feb. 23 At Sea Malta – Port Said

Feb. 24 At Sea Malta – Port Said

Feb. 25 Arrived P. Said

Feb. 26th 1918 Went to Cairo. Left P. Said & arrived in Cairo about 11:30 P.M. With Ray and May. Stopped at Hotel Continental.

---

56 Here, mouldy is used to describe a feeling of illness.

Feb. 28th 1918 At Port Said, went ashore in afternoon.

March 1st At Port Said, went ashore in afternoon.

March 2nd Sailed for Malta in A.M. in company convoy of 14 ships.

3rd At Sea.

4th At Sea.

5th Very heavy sea & rain.

6th Arrived at Malta.

7th At Malta.

8th Sailed for Corfu in company with Heroic.

9th At Sea Malta-Corfu

10th Arrived Corfu 10 A.M. – Proceeded at 10 P.M. for Milo.

11th Went through Gulf of Patras and Corinth Canal.

12th Arrived Milo-coaled ship-Proceeded to Malta 3 P.M. with survivors of Chagres on board.

13th At Sea Milo-Malta

14th Arrived at Malta.

15th At Malta.

16th At Malta.

17th Returned to Archer.

18th Malta.

19th Malta.

20 Went to Hydrophone lecture – Ricasoli camp[57] in P.M.

21 Hydrophone lec.

22 [no entry]

23 [no entry]

24 [no entry]

March 25 Went to Royal Hotel as they are painting out our cabins.

March 26 Hydrophone Lecture in A.M. I am taking the Fish Course.

March 27 Hydrophone Lecture in A.M.

March 28

March 29

March 30

---

57 RNRR Ricasoli Camp was a training centre on Malta.

H.M.S. ARCHER

April 20th Lieut. Taylor went to hosp.

April 21st There has been a scrap up on the Brindisi Barrage—our destroyers & the Austrians. No authentic news yet but the buzz is that "Hornet" has been sunk & Jackal (Soulsby) has been badly damaged. Fine naval stunt off Bruges, in blocking up the port by sinking of old cruisers, etc.

April 24th Went ashore in afternoon. Went to "Beaver" in evening & saw Grant.

April 25 [no entry for this date]

April 26 Met Grant ashore & he came onboard to dinner. Afterwards we went to a dance in Sliema & had a good time.

April 27th Went out 9 A.M. for the Fish Hydrophone trials which proved quite successful although there was a heavy swell.

April 28th Played tennis Marsa with Jack Grant, dinner in the Beaver.

April 29 Day on.

April 30 Went swimming at Tirage. Shaw & Grant dined aboard.

May 1st Went swimming at Tirage & had dinner with Shaw at Sliema.

May 2nd [no entry for this date]

May 3rd .303 in forenoon, did some shopping in P.M.

May 4th Sailed at 8 A.M. & proceeded about 140° NW of Malta to aid SS. Pancras -torpedoed. Arrived by her at 3:30 P.M. A Jap. Destroyer Momo here. She took her in tow & we formed submarine screen. Proceeded back to Malta.

H.M.S. ARCHER

May 5th At Sea in company with S.S. Pancras & Jap. dest. Tug came out from Malta & took the former in tow.

May 6th Met and escorted S.S. Chile into harbour. Secured alongside "Nereide", 5 P.M.

May 7th Sailed from Malta at 5 P.M. in company Ceanothus, some sloops, Nereide & anchored at Marsa Scirocco.

May 8th Sailed at 1 A.M. & met convoy at dawn (18 ships). At 11:30 A.M. Wallflower (sloop) sighted a sub. 500 yards ahead & they tried to ram it, dropped 2 depth charges & am sure did it in. We were passed too soon over the spot to see any wreckage.

May 9th At 2:30 P.M. Atlantic a big French ship, was torpedoed quite close to us. She was hit in the bow; several boats were lowered evidently panic ones. We dashed about over the spot & dropped a depth charge. Quite a big sea running & we all got nearly drowned dashing about at full speed.

The Atlantic proceeded to Bisenta. Very heavy sea & wind got up & we had a rotten night. Gunner is sick with very bad neuralgia etc. & poor old doc has mal de mer. In the middle (hrs.) wind went down a bit.

May 10th At sea, weather moderated.

May 11th Arrived at Marseilles at noon. Convoy proceeded inside. Usk & ourselves proceeded to Toulon at 3:30 P.M. and secured to a buoy with our stern to a jetty. Went ashore at 7 P.M. & had a look round, visited a movie show etc. Not a bad place with quite a number of big hotels, but most of the streets are very narrow and not very clean.

May 12th 1918 At Toulon. Went ashore in afternoon with the chief.

May 13th 1918 Sailed for Messina at 9 A.M. 20 knots.

May 14th Arrived Messina at 5 P.M. & as usual could not find a billet. Finally came to port ↓ & secured stem to wall. Quite interesting place.

15th Sailed for Brindisi at 6 P.M. No. 1 & Doc. are down with fever so skipper & I are in two watches.

16th Arrived Brindisi about noon & went alongside oiling jetty. As soon as we were secured there was an air raid but not much damage done. Secured to Hospital trot. Lots of destroyers here, simply crowds of Italians who do nothing. Very unhealthy place, 3 Officers & 40 men of Goshawk down with this fever & in one of the Lt. cruisers there are 350. Phoenix was torpedoed two days ago on the Barrage. Am kept pretty busy No. 1 being sick & having no Gunner.

17th At Hospital trot. We were going to do "C" firing but it was cancelled.

18th At Hospital trot.

19th Weighed & proceeded at 6 A.M. to pump out bad oil & water which we took in at Messina. Returned to harbour about 11 A.M. & went alongside "Beaver". Saw Grant. Soulsby came off to lunch. He was in the scrap here about two weeks ago when Jackal & Hornet fought the Austrian destroyers. The former was hit in 4 places.

20 At 7 A.M. proceeded out of harbour & took up Barrage Patrol with "Forrester". There are 2 destroyers out. No. 1 & I are in two watches, pretty strenuous when there are stunts as well. A submarine was sighted a few miles from us & we got out P.V.s etc. but no luck.

May 21st 1918 On Adriatic Barrage.

May 22nd 1918 Proceeded into harbour at 7 A.M. after carrying out .303". Oiled & went alongside Blenheim for boiler cleaning.

May 23rd Boiler cleaning. Went off to Jackal for dinner but there was sudden panic & everyone except us & Forester raised steam.

May 24th Friday – Boiler cleaning. H4 torpedoed & sank a German submarine just outside. She brought in 2 prisoners. The Fritz had been out for 6 weeks.

May 25th Saturday. Captain D. came on board and walked round the ship in the forenoon. They take out our Fish Hydrophone. Martin & Beaver secured alongside. I see that the Huns have taken to bombing hospitals in France. Went ashore in afternoon for a walk, but this is certainly not much of a place.

May 26th Sunday. Saw Jack Grant in the forenoon. Shifted to trot at 1 P.M.

May 27th Went to spotting table in forenoon in Blenheim.

May 28th Tuesday. Sailed at 8 A.M. in company Forester, Lapwing, Alarm, Forester & 2 French TBDs for patrol.

May 29th Wed. – On patrol. No. 1 & myself both feeling pretty seedy, we are still in two watches, which is rather strenuous.

May 30th Returned to Brindisi for oil & went straight back again on patrol. Feeling a bit better today. 2 tubes in no. 3 boiler went this P.M.

May 31st Fri. Returned to Brindisi.

June 1st At Brindisi.

June 2nd Sunday – At Brindisi. Went for a walk with the Doc out into country in P.M.

H.M.S. ARCHER

June 3rd Went alongside oiler at 5:30 A.M. & completed with oil. Embarked 3 U.S. naval officers + 11 ratings. Proceeded to Corfu. Landed one Fish Hydrophone & then proceeded on patrol.

June 4th TUESDAY. On patrol.

June 5th Wed. On patrol.

June 6th Arrived at Corfu 6 A.M. & ↓e.d Very fine day in A.M. Commodore Kelly came onboard at 12:30 & we proceeded to Brindisi at 23 knots, arriving at 7 P.M.

June 7th Went out torpedo running with Forester, "D" came onboard. Both Mouldies ran well but we closed to too small a range before firing. Returned to harbour and oiled. Brindisi certainly isn't much of a place & there is nothing to do, it isn't very clean, & one cannot swim in the harbour.

June 8th Went out "C' firing with Forester. Very good. We took 3½ minutes & and we had a hang up in the orders through the T.S. We were well on the target with the 1st salvo.—Got a hit, Forester didn't score any.

June 9th I was awakened about 5 A.M. by A.A. guns[58]. Austrian aeroplanes dropping bombs all over the place & bits of shrapnel kept falling on deck & made quite a row. Could see aeroplanes very plainly. Sailed for barrage at 7 A.M.

---

58 This is a short code for anti-aircraft guns.

June 10th Proceeded to Brindisi & oiled. Austrians fleet reported out & Lt. Cruisers Gloucester, Lowenstoft, Weymouth, Dartmouth went out & all the destroyers.

We were at action stations all afternoon & steamed up near Danazo but did not see anything. Returned to patrol in evening.

June 11th Returned to Brindisi. Spent all day at oil jetty. Very hot. Chief & I went over to Defender in evening and had a game of bridge with Hibbard and their chief.

June 12th Went ashore in P.M. with Hibbard.

June 13th Sailed for barrage at 7 A.M. with Lt. Cruisers who we located to Vallema.

H.M.S. ARCHER – JUNE 1918 – ADRIATIC BARRAGE

June 14th On patrol.

June 15th Returned to Brindisi and oiled.

June 16th Returned to Brindisi and oiled.

June 17th At Brindisi. Went for a swim in P.M. near kite balloon station, which is about 2 miles from trot.

June 18th Sailed for Barrage at 7 A.M. in company Hydra, Bisson, Cimitene, Defender & Nymphe.

June 19th Proceeded at 5 A.M. to entrance to Vallona. Swept channel to meet Lt. Cruisers then we steamed with them up to ab[o]ut 10-15 miles from Durazzo, while Capt. D. & other part of flotilla went up close to the place to see what was doing. Nothing happened except some aeroplanes dropped bombs. Returned to Brindisi in P.M.

June 20th Control drill in Blenheim in A.M. – swim in P.M.

June 21st At hospital trot. Hot & swarms of flies. Soulsby & I went for a walk into the town. He has just got his 2nd stripe & he dined with me. Mr. Burns returned to ship from Malta. Heard that the Lichnys bagged a Fritz off Marseilles & got 5 prisoners.

June 22nd Soulsby & I went for a swim. Dined with him in Jackal.

June 23rd Sailed for patrol at 7 A.M.

June 24th On patrol – heavy sea all day.

June 25th [no entry for this date]

June 26th Proceeded to Vallona to bring General Wake to Brindisi but when we got there found he had left. Returned to Brindisi.

June 27th Started boiler cleaning. Alongside Blenheim. Had dinner with Grant, Hibbard, Soulsby & Capt. of Beaver (Tollumache) at Europa hotel. Went to Italian officers' club & had a game of bridge about midnight.

H.M.S. ARCHER

June 28th Went for a swim in P.M. Afterwards I went with a funeral party to cemetery. Divers went down & find a lot of wear in one shaft, which will necessitate docking. Dined with Soulsby, Hibbard & Grant & Capt. of Beaver at Europa hotel.

June 29th Dined with Soulsby in evening.

June 30th Sunday. Waiting to hear where we are going to dock, wrote out my application for C.M.B.S. Shifted from alongside Blenheim to trot. Went for a swim in evening.

July 1st Went for a swim with Ewart of Hydra. My day on.

July 2nd Nothing much doing raining all day. Still waiting for orders about our refit.

July 3rd Played tennis in afternoon. No. 1 went to the Beaver in command temporarily.

July 4th At Brindisi.

July 5th Went for a walk. Played bridge with Hibbard in evening.

July 6th Sailed at 6 A.M. for Taranto, arrived at 4:30 P.M. Had dinner ashore with Captain & Lieut. Comm. Turner.

July 7th Sailed at 6:30 P.M. for Leghorn.

July 8th At sea in two watches. G. Q.s at 3 A.M.

July 9th Arrived at Leghorn about 10 A.M. and ↓ed with stern to wall. Seems a very nice place. We are going to go on the ship to have our A frame brushes refitted. I am kept quite busy getting ammunition ready to go out of ship etc.

July 10th Shifted ship. Went ashore in P.M. & had a look around. Fine baths here, skipper & I had dinner there & went to a show afterwards.

July 11th Still waiting for them to shift ammunition lighters. Skipper, Doc and myself went to tea at the Consuls (Carmichael). Met some people called the Roes.—Very nice time. The firm here have to send to Genoa for metal for one of our brushes, so I expect we shall be here a month.

H.M.S. ARCHER

July 12th Doc & I went ashore & had a fine swim & dinner at the baths. Met some Ital. naval cadets who are coming off to see the ship tomorrow. The baths are fine with a restaurant attached.

July 13th At Livorno. Ital. naval cadets came off to see the ship in forenoon. Went to tea at the Roe's in P.M. & had a good time.

July 14th The big French day. Left the ship at 7 A.M. in charge of rifle & cutlass party & marched down to race course, and some medals etc. presented

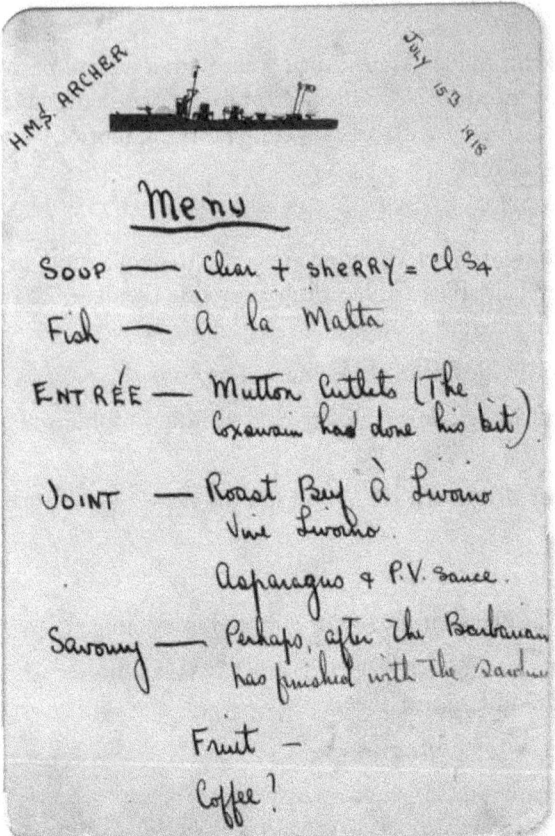

Menu from special meal on July 15, 1918

& then marched back to the ship. Captain and I went to the dinner given by municipality of Livorno which lasted from 1:30 until 3:30 & included many speeches in Italian. At 5 P.M. went to French mission & reception afterwards went to Consuls to clap hands etc. for the march past. Some day.

July 15th   Decorated the Q.D. with bunting etc. & had a dinner party. The guests were Consul & Wife (Carmichael), Mr. & Mrs. Roe and two Miss Roes. Had a good time.

July 16th   My day on.

July 17th   Went on a picnic with the Roes in the motor boat up the canal. We started with the idea of reaching Pisa but did not go the whole distance. When getting close to Leghorn we were stopped by Ital. sentry who would not let us proceed. We waited in boat until 3 P.M. when he finally let us get out & walk. We arrived back at 4 P.M. The M.B. returned to slip at 9 A.M. next morning. It was a very amusing stunt.

July 18th   Day on. Got my second stripe.

END OF JOURNAL ONE

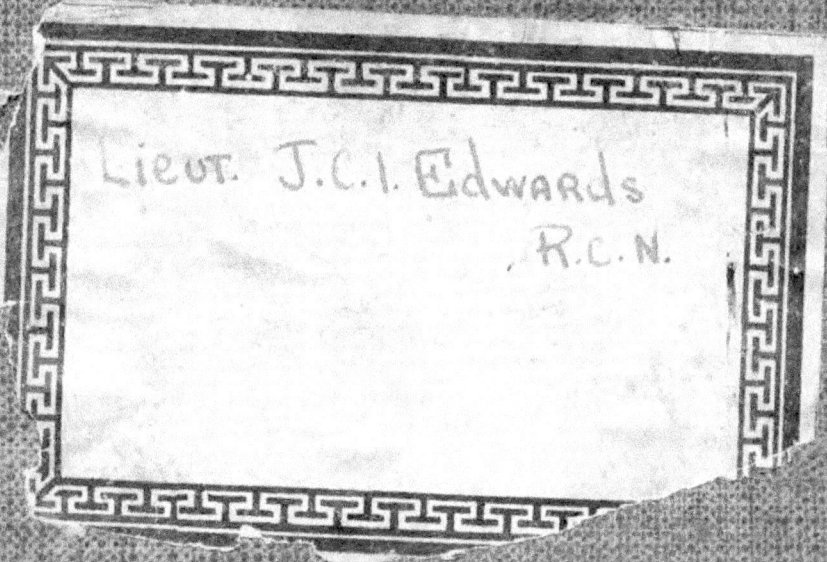

JOURNAL TWO
July 19, 1918 – November 14, 1920

The port of Livorno, Italy

JOURNAL TWO
July 19, 1918 – November 14, 1920

In which Dutchy Edwards continues the Dardanelles patrol in HMS Archer, an armistice ends hostilities, he transfers to HMS Cameleon based in Malta, travels to England to serve in HMS Galatea patrolling northern waters for German ships leaving ports illegally, visits his brother's grave in France, testifies at the Hebburn salvage hearing, patrols the Caribbean on HMS Calliope and joins the Royal Naval College at Esquimalt as instructor.

H.M.S ARCHER 1918 AT LEGHORN (LIVORNO)

July 19th Friday – Missed the early morning train to Florence (Firenza). Caught the 11:15 and arrived there at 2:30 P.M. Saw the leaning Tower of Pisa en route. Stopped at Hotel Minerva & in afternoon went and saw some of the sights include Chapel of Medicine, Cathedral & walked around the town. Did not feel well so turned in early.

July 20th Met a R.F.A.[59] Major at the hotel & went along to Allied Officers club where we met Mr. Scott who took us around. We saw the Bargello, museum, Dante's House, etc. which were very fine. This is certainly a very interesting place. Met Mr. Proctor at Jockquins & went to lunch with him. Caught the 3:30 P.M. train back & arrived Leghorn 7:30 P.M.

July 21st My day on.

July 22nd My day on.

July 23rd Went out sailing in the whaler with Mrs. Rae, Dolly & the Doc. We are still waiting for new of metal for our bushes.

July 24th Went to a tea fight at Mrs. Vespunies. Very hot.

July 25th Started to go up on the ship but the cradle wouldn't fit. Had another try in the afternoon, but nothing doing. Very hot.

July 26th Had another try at the ship. In the afternoon went to the Rae's for tea.

July 27th Finally got up on the ship. The Rae's came off to dinner in the evening,

July 28th Sunday. Played tennis at the Rae's. Went to Puncaldis in the evening with the chief and gunner. The metal for our bushes finally has arrived.

29th Went for a swim about 6 P.M. & after dinner went out to . . . . with Rae's.

---

[59] Royal Field Artillery.

July 30th Day on.

July 31st Number one rejoined ship.

August 1st The Rae's gave a garden party for the ship's company. We had races, etc. & it was as big success.

August 2nd Went up to station at 2:10 A.M. to catch the train for Rome, missed it however and so caught the 4:50 one which left Livorno at 5:30. I waited at the station all this time. Arrived Rome about 11:0 A.M. & stopped at Grand Continental Hotel which is just opposite the station. In the afternoon took a guide and visited Forum, Capitol, Coliseum, Bridge of Horatius etc.

Saturday Aug. 3rd Went out with guide at about 9:30 A.M. and visited Pantheon & saw various other famous things. Went to St. Peter's & spent about two hours inside, climbed up to the top, it is over 400 feet high. In P.M. walked out to Borghese garden.

Sunday 4th Aug. 1918 We played a football match against an Italian team, which was a tie 3-3. The referee was pretty awful & had a game leg which prevented him from moving about very much. After the match we took the Rae's for Puncaldis for dinner.

Aug. 5th Went for a picnic up the canal in the motor boat with the Rae's. Landed at quite a decent spot & made tea, arrived back at the ship about 8:45 & had supper aboard.

Aug. 6th [No entry]

Aug. 7th Went to tea & the Rae's & Ward A.P. (R.N.R.)[60] came off to dinner with me.

Aug. 8th Dined at Puncaldis with No. 1 Cilree & Ward. We haven't had any mail now for over two weeks.

Aug. 9th Went to Montenero with Mrs. Rae, Kather, Dolly, Skipper & myself. Left about 5:30 & went out by tram, took the rly[61] up to the top & had tea there. Returned about 10:30 P.M.

Aug. 10th Our troops on the Western front capturing about 10000 prisoners & 150 guns. Went to the Venetian glass factory in the forenoon with Mrs. Rae & Dolly. It was very interesting to see what fine things they do with such crude tools & the way they blow it etc. Had a swim & went to the Rae's for dinner. We were to come off the slip today but as usual it is "tomorrow".

Aug. 11th Football match against Italians, we lost 3-0. Out troops are still advancing on the western front. We aren't coming off the slip until tomorrow.

---

60 Royal Naval Reserve.
61 Railway.

Aug. 12th Still waiting to come off the slip. Had a swim in the afternoon & went to the theatre with the Rae's in the evening.

Aug. 13th We expect to go off the slip today. While at lunch there was a terrific explosion & on going on deck we learnt that some ammunition of ours which was in the lighter alongside the Italian cruiser "Etruria" had exploded. People were swimming in all directions, windows broken. Our sentry arrived back but was more or less unconscious. A tug was sunk, also Italian cruiser & French T.B.D.[62] badly damaged. 4 men were killed & about 40 badly injured. Bits of gun 4" & 12 pr. shell were found all over the town. The story of the sentry was that he first heard a small expl.[63] from lighter as he went aboard "Etruria" & gave alarm but they thought he was mad.

Aug. 14th We went off the slip at 12:30 & spent all afternoon picking up anchors. At 6:15 Gunner & I landed in charge of funeral party to attend funeral of people killed by explosion. We marched with reversed arms for about 1 hour. Went out to the Rae's in evening.

Aug. 15th Secured alongside Custom House jetty in forenoon & oiled. I expect that we will be kept here a few days while a court of inquiry is being held. We have now no ammunition but as soon as Ital. auth. will let us we will proceed to Genoa & take in ¼ of Beaver's.

Aug. 16th Comm. Goddard & Capt. of Beaver arrived from Genoa & held a small court of inquiry. Another officer is coming up from Malta on Monday. Had a session in P.M. & went out to the Rae's. We are all ready to sail but Italian authorities are keeping us here.

Aug. 17th Still at Livorno.

Aug. 18th Still at Livorno.

Aug. 19th A commander from Malta is coming up, so the inquiry is waiting for him. Rec'd. two parcels from home (via Malta) containing most excellent eats, cake & real chocolate which are very welcome in this butterless & black bread land. Ward came off to lunch. Had a swim at Puncaldis in P.M.

Aug. 20th H.M.A.S. Yarra arrived. She has been in collision with Hun. Court of Inquiry on all day. Dinner at Puncaldis with Skipper, Ward, Lt. Comm. Bowles & Comm. Tindal.

Aug. 21st My day on.

Aug. 22nd Went up to the station to see Mrs. Rae off. Afterwards went to Puncaldis for a swim. The water was fine. Had dinner there with Ward & Cousins. The Beaver arrived from Genoa & we took some of her ammunition. She sailed for Brindisi at 7 P.M. Court of Inquiry finished

---

62 Torpedo boat destroyer.
63 Explosion.

this afternoon, but I don't know the finding of the court. It is awfully hot where we are lying & the smell of hides which they are loading is pretty bad. I expect that we shall shove off for Brindisi tomorrow.

Aug. 23rd Sailed at about 6 P.M. for Messina.

Aug. 24th Had an excellent view of Stromboli (Volcano) as we passed very close to it. We passed between it & Strombolenza. Arrived Messina at about 5 P.M. and sailed for Brindisi at 8:30 P.M.

Aug. 25th Sunday. Arrived Brindisi at noon and went alongside oil jetty. Newman has been appointed to the Welland & H.P. Chubb is coming here as 1st Lieut. My application for C.M.B.s has been forward & I got a chit from Admiralty saying my name had been noted. We received our six weeks mail & I got heaps of letters. We expect to sail for Mudros on Tuesday.

Aug. 26th Very busy all day getting in provisions & ammunition etc. Dined in Blenheim.

Aug. 27th Sailed at 9 A.M. for Corfu where we arrived at 5 P.M. Sailed at 7 P.M. for Piraeus.

Aug. 28th Passed through Corinth Canal at about 10 A.M. & arrived at Piraeus at noon. Weighed & proceeded at 5 P.M. & picked up convoy at Corinth. Proceeded to Mudros.

Aug. 29th Arrived at Mudros at about 10 P.M.& anchored.

Aug. 30th Rear Adm. Cecil Lambert inspected us at 2 P.M. It only lasted about ¾ of an hour. No. 1 & I went over to the Agamemnon & saw Sitwell.

Aug. 31st Weighed & proceeded at 8 A.M. in company with "Hope" & French T.B.D. to Dardanelles patrol. Jove, I never thought I would see old Imbros, Tenedos, Samothraki, etc. again, & Suvla Pt. bores me stiff.

Sept. 1st 1918 Anchored at Py[rg]os about 8 A.M. No. 1 & I went ashore in afternoon with a shot gun & tried to bag some partridges. Saw quite a number but did not shoot any. Weighed at 5 P.M. & proceeded on patrol.

Sept. 2nd On patrol.

Sept. 3rd On patrol. Anchored at Pyrgos. Skipper shot four partridges.

Sept. 4th Returned to Mudros, oiled & went alongside Agam.[64] No. 1, O'Leary & myself dined with Sitwell in the Gun Room of the Aggie.

Sept. 5th Sailed down to the bathing place in the whaler.

Sept. 6th Went for swim & dined with Heasley in the Aggie.

Sept. 7th We were to have gone to sea at 6 A.M. but owing to a gland. going in E.R, did not sail until noon. Procd. At noon in comp. Larne to

---

64 *Agamemnon.*

H.M.S. ARCHER SEPT. 1918

Stavros (speed 29 kn.). Arrived at 7 P.M. & proceeded to convoy Endymion (Blister ship who had been torpedoed) back to Mudros.

Sept. 8th Arrived Mudros at about 10 A.M. Went for a swim with "Lapwing" crowd in afternoon. Heasley from the "Aggie" dined with me.

Sept. 9th Sailed at 6 A.M. for Kastro & brought Capt. Lecky back to Mudros, then proceeded onto Dardanelles patrol.

Sept. 10th On Dards. Patrol. Anchored in Pyrgos in afternoon.

Sept. 11th Anchored in Pyrgos. Skipper shot some partridges as there are quite a number on Imbros Island, also lots of grapes. Weighed at 6 P.M. & proceeded on patrol.

Sept. 12th Relieved on patrol about noon, returned to Mudros & anchored.

Sept. 13th Rear Admiral Lambert inspected T.B.D.s Larne, Lapwing, Hope & Archer. We came last on the list so he only spent about twenty minutes on board.

Sept. 14th Went for a swim in afternoon, in the evening it commenced blowing the usual Mudros style & we let go another anchor—kept anchor watches.

Sept. 15th High wind still continues. Keeping anchor watched.

Sept. 16th Wind still blowing hard from N.E. Steam for slow speed.

Sept. 17th Wind still blowing hard from N.E. but went down in evening.

Sept. 18th The long expected mail arrived but there were only two small bags for us & I only rec'd. 2 letters. This a second mail we have had in two months. I am waiting to hear about my relief in this ship. Went swimming in the afternoon. Heasley dined with me in evening & O'Leary from Triad with Chubb. Redpole arrived from Brindisi, she relieves the Lapwing who sailed yesterday.

Sept. 19th Sailed for patrol with Larne & Hope. Anchored in Pyrgos, skipper shot two partridges. Fine day.

Sept. 20th Patrolling all day —fine weather.

Sept. 21 Patrolling all day. Arrived at Pyrgos in P.M.

Sept. 22 Relieved by French destroyers, sank two mines on way back to Mudros. Anchored at about 5 P.M.

EDITOR'S NOTE: INSERTED THROUGHOUT THE JOURNALS ARE RANDOM THOUGHTS NOT RELEVANT TO THE MAIN JOURNAL.

How can one expect to be original or to have original ideas about a thing which you know little about. Therefore the first thing to do is to "understand" the fact; this is accomplished by Analysis. Analysis is taking things to pieces, resolving facts. Synthesis is the art of building up anew—creating a unit out of the results of analysis.

Sept. 23rd   Went swimming in P.M. Dined with Doc McClelland in the Aggie. The Turks or Huns (airmen) raided this place at 3 & 5 A.M. this morning. Dropped bombs on the air station, huts, etc. 5000 g.[65] of petrol destroyed.

Sept. 24th   Swim in P.M. Heasley dined with me. Heard that we are going to take the Prince Edward (a netlayer)[66] down to Port Said. After that we expect to go to Brindisi or perhaps go to Palestine coast. Our troops are chasing the Turks there. 25000 prisoners taken was in today's press news.

Sept. 25th   At 10 minutes notice. Hornet arrived from Brindisi. Sailed at 7 P.M. & waited outside the boom until 9:30 P.M. for the Prince Edward. Shaped course for Port Said, speed 13 knots. We may be sent to Haifa with the P.E.

Sept. 26th   At sea. Mudros-Port Said in company Net Layer Prince Edward. Quite a fine day with a bit of wind from N.E.

Sept. 27th   At Sea. Mudros-Port Said.

Sept. 28th   Arrived Port Said at 9 A.M. Oiled. We are going to have six days to boiler clean. Doc McClelland & I went for a swim & had dinner at the Eastern Exchange Hotel. We are planning to go to Cairo tomorrow. Our troops in Palestine have captured 50000 & have practically wiped out the Turks. Forester & Druid arrived. They have been up at Haifa & around the shooting at the Turks.

Sept. 29th   Chubb, McClelland, Bearblock & myself caught the 6:15 P.M. train to Cairo & arrived at 11:30 P.M. Stopped at Continental Hotel. Good journey down.

Sept. 30th   We all went to the Egypt. native bazaars in forenoon, after a most excellent breakfast. In the afternoon Chubb & I called on Judge Amos at Zamank,[67] took tea at the sports club with Mts. Algood & Lady Oakes. Dinner at Continental. War news is very good. Bulgaria has surrendered & we have captured practically all the Turks in Palestine. In fact Cairo & all along the line is full of them especially at Kantara.

Oct. 1st   Chubb & I Museum in forenoon. Went to lunch with Judge Amos. Met Archibauld from Montreal (son of Judge Archibauld). On our way out in taxi we knocked down a negress which caused a good deal of excitement. The 2 doc. & skipper went out to the pyramids.

Oct. 2nd   Caught the 11 A.M. train back to P. Said.

October 3rd   Went ashore in forenoon.

---

65 Gallons.
66 A net laying ship, also known as a net layer, net tender, gate ship or boom defence vessel, was a type of small auxiliary ship. A net layer's primary function was to lay and maintain steel anti-torpedo or anti-submarine nets. Nets could be laid around an individual ship at anchor, or around harbours or other anchorages. Net laying was potentially dangerous work, and net laying seamen were experts at dealing with blocks, tackles, knots and splicing.
67 This is likely a reference to Zamalek, a suburb of Cairo.

MEDITERRANEAN TEMPORARY MEMORANDUM No. 9.

The following copies of telegrams which have passed between the Commander-in-Chief, Allied Fleets, and the British Commander-in-Chief, Mediterranean, are promulgated for general information :—

From...COMMANDER-IN-CHIEF, ALLIED FLEETS.
To.......BRITISH COMMANDER-IN-CHIEF, MEDITERRANEAN.
Date....3rd OCTOBER, 1918.

On the occasion of the capitulation of the Bulgarian Army, the Commander-in-Chief of the Allied Fleets in the Mediterranean expresses his satisfaction and thanks to all Allied ships, battleships, cruisers, transports, merchant ships, flotillas of destroyers, torpedo boats, trawlers, patrol ships, sweepers, tugs, etc., aerial patrols and bases, who by their energy, devotion, zeal, and their fine patriotic qualities have assured for more than three years the transport and protection at sea of Allied armies and their supplies of all kinds under specially difficult conditions.

From...BRITISH COMMANDER-IN-CHIEF, MEDITERRANEAN.
To.......COMMANDER-IN-CHIEF, ALLIED FLEETS.
Date....3rd OCTOBER, 1918.

The British Naval Forces in the Mediterranean send their thanks for your very kind message on the occasion of the capitulation of the Bulgarian Army. They regard an expression of satisfaction and thanks from the Allied Commander-in-Chief as a great honour.

A. CALTHORPE,
Vice-Admiral,
British Commander-in-Chief,
Mediterranean Station.

9th October, 1918.

M.N.P. 1,013. 1,200. 10/18.

Memorandum from Vice-Admiral A. Calthorpe (Sir Somerset Arthur Gough-Calthorpe), Chief, Mediterranean Station, October 9, 1918

October 4th Still boiler cleaning, finished in the evening. We have got the Turks on the move in Palestine & have taken Damascus. Altogether the prisoners amount to 70000. We are advancing on the Western front & the surrender of Bulgaria will mean that the Austrians will have to withdraw from Albania.

Oct. 5th Still at Port Said, waiting for orders. Played tennis.

Oct. 6th Still at Port Said.

Oct. 7th Chubb & I went to tea at Col. Ellgoods.

Oct. 8th Weighed & proceeded at 4 P.M. for Milos (15 knots). We have 11 of the ship's company down with the flu.

Oct. 9th At Sea. Port Said to Milos.

Oct. 10th Arrived Milos about 7 A.M. & oiled. Sold some of our 1700 eggs to Theseus. Proceeded at 10 A.M., entered Corinth Channel at 5 P.M. War news today is very good. We have taken Cambrai & are advancing all along the front.

Oct. 11th Arrived at Brindisi at 6 P.M. Stopped at oil jetty all night.

Oct. 12th Had a signal from Blenheim that I was to join Cameleon as No. 1 & relieve Clarke who has been appointed to the "Ribble." Saw Grant. There has been a lot of flu here and quite a number of deaths. Dined in Blenheim.

Oct. 13th Had a signal to join Cameleon this morning but it was cancelled a short time afterwards. Then another to say join her forthwith, so I went on board and immediately after we slipped so I left a lot of my gear behind in Archer.

HMS Cameleon

We proceeded in company with Jackal & Tigress for Gib. Calling at Biserta for oil. Pretty bad weather.

Oct. 14th Passed through Strait of Messina at about 1 A.M. Very nasty weather. Arrived Biserta at 5 P.M. and oiled.

Oct. 15th Sailed at 4 A.M. for Gib. Doing 22 knots into a big sea. Carried away all foc'sle matting, broke two ventilators and tore up shell racks etc. Had to ease down to 20 knots.

Oct. 16th Still a heavy sea which went down in afternoon. Arrived at Gib. About 10 P.M.

Oct. 17th Went ashore with Soulsby & had tea, dined at hotel Cecil.

Oct. 18 Went ashore with Soulsby. Proceeded at midnight to meet the Temeraire.

Oct. 19 Met the Temeraire at 6:30 A.M. and returned to Gib. with her. Soulsby, Sub & myself went to theatre, which was quite amazing.

Oct. 20 Sailed at noon in company Temeraire, Jackal, Tigress. Heavy swell running.

Oct 21st At sea.

Oct. 22 At sea, bad weather.

Oct 23 Arrived at Malta. Caesar here. I went aboard & saw Low. Soulsby & I went ashore afterwards. They are getting ready here for a landing at Mudros i.e. the common buzz.

Oct. 24 At Malta. Very busy all day getting in stores etc. McCrae came off in the afternoon. Soulsby, Low & two lads from Tigress had dinner together at the Westminster.

Oct. 25th Sailed at 9 A.M. for Mudros in company Temeraire, Lord Nelson, Tigress, Jackal. Doing 15½ knots.

Oct. 26th At sea.

Oct. 27th Arrived at Mudros 3:30 P.M. but did not finish oiling until midnight. All the destroyers are at Dedeagatch, having landed about 5000 there which they embarked at Stavros. It must have been quite a crush.

October 28th Started boiler cleaning. The remainder if the destroyers arrived from Dedeagatch. Went aboard the Archer. My relief hasn't arrived yet.

Oct. 29th Towed alongside Blenheim at 7 A.M. by Tribune and secured alongside Tigress. Larne also alongside.

Oct. 30th Boiler cleaning.

Oct. 31st Boiler cleaning.

Nov. 1st Boiler cleaning. Played rugby.

Nov. 2nd Boiler cleaning.

Nov. 3rd Heard that we were going to refit in Malta in lieu of Lapwing. Everyone is very fed up as we are not due for our annual refit to another month, & we will miss the Dardanelles stunt, which should take place within the next week, in fact as soon as they sweep the mines up. Turkey has chucked her hand in and the Goeben has been interned, the former is allowing us free passage up the Dardanelles & the occupation of the forts. The Turkish delegates have been at Mudros in the Agamemnon for the last four or five days. Austria is on the verge of surrendering. There are 25 destroyers here.

Nov. 4th At Mudros. 10 minutes notice.

Nov. 5th Sailed at 1 A.M. for Dedeagatch where we arrived 7:30 A.M. Embarked Gen. Wilson & his staff (part) of six, also Tommies[68] and much gear. Proceeded to Stavros. Arrived at Stavros at 2 P.M. & waited there for a couple of hours, after which we proceeded to Mudros, where we arrived at 10 P.M. Had a great time sorting out gear etc. Oiled ship.

Nov. 6th Anchored at 6 A.M. & at 11 A.M. went out & joined division who were torpedo firing. Apparently we should have gone to sea at 8 A.M. Returned to harbour 1 P.M. & anchored. Dined in Jackal with Soulsby. War news very good; negotiations for Armistice with Germany are in progress & on Western front they are retreating full speed. The Italians have occupied Pola. We are all waiting to go up to the Dardanelles.

Nov. 7th Blowing quite hard all day. Went off to "Liverpool" in evening and saw Acheron's concert.

Nov. 8th Weighed. Sailed from Salonika at 2 P.M. in company Grafton, Bermudian, etc. for Kephalo.

Nov. 9th Had an awful morning with the mine sweeps as they got foul owing to Tadpole breaking surface We worked from 6 until 10 A.M. Arrived & anchored in Kephalo Bay. "Alarm" came alongside at 6 P.M. with new mine sweep P.V.s.

Nov. 10th Sailed at 7 A.M. for Ismid. Arrived off Cape Helles 9:30 & had a look at the famous place. River Clyde, etc. still here. There are crowds of ships & troops going up to Ismid & heaps of minesweepers about. There are still lots of mines about which haven't been swept up yet. Stopped at Chinak, Liman Pasha to deliver despatches. Arrived at Ismid about 11 P.M. & anchored near "Acheron".

Nov. 11th Weighed at 6 A.M. & in company with Acheron began sweeping the channel inside the nets which the Prince Edward & Queen Victoria have been laying. One of our mine sweeps collapsed. Anchored at 5:30 P.M. outside the nets. Sub, Gunner, cox, etc & myself went away in the dinghy & blew up a 2¼ lb. charge. Got 4 large Golden Bream fish weighing about 24 lbs. each & any number of small fish.

---

68 Slang for a common soldier in the British Army.

Nov. 12th Went away at 6 A.M. & blew up another 2¼ charge but no fish. Proceeded into Ismid and ↓ed. Heard that an **ARMISTICE SIGNED WITH GERMANY** . . . We only got a bit of the press.

HORSEA PRESS – 13 November 1918

The Prime Minister the House of Commons read the terms of the armistice. The terms include immediate evacuation of Belgium, Alsace Lorraine and Luxemburg. Evacuation by the enemy to be completed within three days. Railway of Alsace Lorraine to be handed over. All troops in Rumania and Russia to be withdrawn. Complete abandonment of the treaties of Bucharest and Brest Litovsk. Immediate cessation of all hostilities at sea. Handing over to Allies and United States of all Submarines. Duration of the Armistice to be 6 days. 5,000 guns (2500 heavy and 2500 field guns), 13,000 machine guns to be handed over. Germans are to retire beyond the Rhine. Rhine strategical bridges to be occupied as well as German territory west of the Rhine. 5,000 locomotives and 50,000 waggons in good working order shall be delivered to the Associate Powers. Repatriation without reciprocity within one month of all civilians interned. Freedom of, and access to the Baltic. Allies and United States to be empowered to occupy old German Ports and defence works in the entrance to HI-CHIEGUT and to sweep up mines. All the Black Sea Ports to be evacuated by the Germans. All the Russian warships seized by Germany in the Black Sea are to be handed over and all neutral ships seized by Germany to be released. All materials seized by Germany are to be abandoned and all Allied ships seized by Germany are to be returned.

SECOND PRESS MESSAGE

[?] were suspended at 11 a.m. this morning. At that hour our troops have breached the following general line Franco Belgian frontier east of Avesnes Jeromont Givry 4 miles east of MONS, CHIEVRES, Lessene Grammont. It is reported on 10th November our squadrons continue their work in fine weather actively co-operating in general advance and vigorously bombing the enemy's troops and transport. Over 2,000 photographs were taken and a great deal of valuable information was brought in by our reconnaissance machines. More than 19 tons of bombs were dropped during the day; the enemy did not show great activity in air fighting. 16 hostile machines were shot down and 1 driven down out of control in addition to German machines standing on an aerodrome were destroyed by bombs dropped from lo[w] altitude; 9 of our machines are missing. At night our bombing operations were continued. Louvain, Numur, Charleroi and many other important railway centres were attacked with excellent results. In one case an ammunition train was blown up and fires and explosions were caused on the siding in which it was standing. In all 20 tons of bombs were dropped; all our machines have returned. H.M. S. "Britannia", Capt. Francis Coalfield, was torpedoed morning 9th of November in western entrance of Gibraltar straits, sank 3½ hours later. 99 officers, 673 men were saved.

1st Lieut.

3571–3572

FOR OFFICIAL USE ONLY.

Not to be communicated to anyone outside H.M. Naval Service.

ADMIRALTY WEEKLY ORDERS.

ADMIRALTY, S.W.,
13th November, 1918.

The following Orders having been approved by my Lords Commissioners of the Admiralty are hereby promulgated for information and guidance and necessary action.

A list of these Orders is attached.

By Command of Their Lordships.

O. Murray

To all Commanders-in-Chief, Flag Officers, Senior Naval Officers, Captains, and Commanding Officers of H.M. Ships and Vessels, Superintendents or Officers in Charge of H.M. Civil Establishments, and Admiralty Overseers concerned.

Distribution.

The distribution is to be made upon the following basis:—

	Number of Copies
Flag Officers and Staffs	6
Commodores and Staffs	3
Battleships, Battle Cruisers, Cruisers, Light Cruisers and Depôts for Destroyers or Submarines	6
Submarine Depôt Ships—Additional for each Submarine	1
Armed Merchant Cruisers	4
Armed Boarding Steamers, Monitors (Large) and Commissioned Mercantile Fleet Auxiliaries	4
Destroyers, T.Bs., Monitors (Small), Sloops and Registered R.F.A.'s	2
Naval Establishments, Dockyards, Victualling Yards, &c.	(as requisite)

(B2894) Wt. 44—88 Pds. 8750. 11/18. Sir J. C. & S. **Gp. 48**

Admiralty Weekly Orders, November 13, 1918

3   3571

Orders marked * *have been issued to Hospital Ships.*
            ,,   ,, † ,,   ,, *included in the " Auxiliary Patrol Issue."*

*†3571.—THE KING'S MESSAGE TO THE FLEET.

(11th November 1918.)

Now that the last and most formidable of our enemies has acknowledged the triumph of the Allied Arms on behalf of Right and Justice, I wish to express my praise and thankfulness to the Officers, men and women of the Royal Navy and Marines, with their comrades of the Fleet Auxiliaries and Mercantile Marine, who for more than four years have kept open the seas, protected our shores, and given us safety.

Ever since that fateful Fourth of August 1914, I have remained stedfast in my confidence that, whether fortune frowned or smiled, the Royal Navy would once more prove the sure shield of the British Empire in the hour of trial.

Never in its history has the Royal Navy, with God's help, done greater things for us, nor better sustained its old glories and the chivalry of the Seas.

With full and grateful hearts the Peoples of the British Empire salute the White, the Red and the Blue Ensigns, and those who have given their lives for the Flag.

I am proud to have served in the Navy. I am prouder still to be its head on this memorable day.

(Signed) GEORGE R.I.

The King's Message to the Fleet, November 13, 1918

*†3571a.—Parliamentary Elections—Position of Naval Officers and Men in Relation to.

(Sec.—13.11.1918.)

In view of the possibility of an early General Election, the Board have had under their consideration the question of the extent to which Officers and Men of the Royal Navy can be granted facilities to stand as Parliamentary Candidates or can be permitted to take an active part in the Election in support of Candidates whose views they share.

They have decided that the following rules shall be strictly adhered to:—

(1) Officers and Men invited to stand as Parliamentary Candidates must obtain the permission of the Admiralty to do so through the usual Service channel. The granting of such permission must depend upon the exigencies of the Service.

(2) In cases in which such permission has been granted to an Officer or man, he is to be granted leave of absence to appear before the duly accredited Committee or Association of the recognised Party, or any other body of persons proposing to adopt him. The leave should commence 8 days before the issue of the Writs. A public announcement as to the date on which Writs will be issued will in all probability be made in advance of the Proclamation, but in any case, notification regarding this date will be issued by the Admiralty. Should the Candidate be adopted, this 8 days will be extended so as to cover the additional 9 days of the Election, plus a period of 7 to 10 days representing the period which must elapse between the opening and declaration of the poll.

(3) Leave is similarly to be granted, subject to the exigencies of the Service, to Officers or men who were in the service of the respective Political Parties prior to the War as Constituency Agents or in a like capacity, and who have joined the Naval Service for the period of hostilities or have been mobilised with the Reserves. In their cases the leave may be extended until six weeks after the polling. The names of such Agents, &c., should be forwarded by an Official of the Party concerned to the Admiralty, who will communicate with the Fleet or Unit in which the Officer or man is serving.

(4) An Officer on full pay or a man who has been given permission as above to stand as a Parliamentary Candidate may during the period above-mentioned address meetings and otherwise prosecute his own candidature but may not wear uniform when doing so. Similarly an Officer on full pay or a man who has been granted leave as a Constituency Agent or in a like capacity may not wear uniform whilst acting as such.

(5) An Officer on full pay or a man who, having received permission to stand, is elected to Parliament will not during the continuance of the War be placed on half-pay or otherwise affected as regards his active service employment merely by reason of his election, but his attendance to his Parliamentary duties must be subject to the exigencies of the Service. At the end of the War, however, any such Officer will be placed on the half-pay list and will be subject to the ordinary rules of retirement for non-service. In the case of a man, however, he will be given the option of taking a free discharge or of being transferred to the Royal Fleet Reserve for a period not exceeding two years, during which he may elect to take his discharge or may, subject to the permission of the Admiralty, revert to the active service to complete his engagement.

(6) No Officer on full pay or man except those referred to above in paragraph 4 can be permitted to speak, whether in uniform or in plain clothes, at any political meeting, nor to serve on an election committee or other body formed to promote a Parliamentary candidature, nor to canvass or take any other active part in support of any candidate.

(M.O. 1375/18 is cancelled.)

(This Order will be included in the December M.O.'s.)

*†3572.—Demobilisation of Personnel—Registration and Release of "Demobilisers" and "Pivotal" Men.

(D.M.D.—13.11.1918.)

REGISTRATION.

Certain Officers and ratings will be registered by the Admiralty for release from Naval Service prior to general demobilisation. These Officers and men are

Post-war election procedures with regard to Royal Navy personnel being candidates for political office, November 13, 1918

C O P Y

ADMIRALTY to CAPTAIN COMMANDING
MALTA BASE.

The Board of Admiralty desire to express to the Officers and Men of the Royal Navy and Royal Marines on the completion of their great work their congratulations on a triumph to which History knows no parallel.

The Surrender of the German Fleet accomplished without shock of Battle will remain for all time the example of the wonderful silence and sureness with which sea power attains its ends. The world recognises that this consumation is due to the steadfastness with which the Navy has maintained its pressure on the enemy through more than four years of war, a pressure exerted no less insistently during the long monotony of waiting than in the rare opportunities of attack.

Congratulations to Captain Commanding, Malta Base from Admiralty on the success of naval action in the region

H.M.S. CAMELEON – AT ISMID TURKEY

Nov. 13th Proced. in company Acheron Hydra Jackal Beaver at 2 A.M. & met the fleet English & French with the remainder of the flotilla & proceeded to Constantinople where we anchored, while the big ships went inside. The ships included Temeraire, Superb, Lord Nelson, Agamemnon, Liverpool, Canterbury, Forward, Skirmisher etc. & practically all the I & H destroyers & Australian destroyers, the French fleet & some Greek ships. Weighed at 12:30 P.M. & proceeded to Ismid where we anchored. Acheron & Cameleon are sailing tomorrow for Malta.

Nov 14th At Ismid. Oiled & secured alongside Hind. Dined with Milbourn in the Hind. Sailed at 9:30 P.M. for Mudros in company Acheron, Jackal & Hornet.

Nov. 15th Arrived Mudros at noon. Sailed for Malta 5 P.M.

Nov. 16th At sea Mudros – Malta.

Nov. 17th Arrived off Malta 10 A.M. Secured alongside wharf at noon.

Nov. 18th At Malta.

Nov. 19th [No entry]

HORSEA PRESS NEWS – 13 NOV. '18

Mr. Bonar Law moved a new vote of credit for Seven hundred million in House of Commons. He said he believed there would be a reduction in expenditure owing to the change in the Military situation. Greater expenditures might be incurred owing to the Allies having made preparation for getting food supplies to Europe. He predicted plenty of work to replace the countries ravaged by the War. The future prosperity and well-being of the Country depended on harmonious co-operation, capital and labour. The British Empire has played a greater part in the War than any other Country in the world. The down-fall of the military colossus was due to blockade which handicapped whole foundation of Germany both in military and civil life. We had won a victory at great pain and we must never forget that. It is stated that the Dutch Government allowed Kaiser to remain in Holland on terms similar to those of the internment of high Officers. Kaiser accepted terms on parole with probably state in Holland and settle there indefinitely. Kaiser assumed & name of Count Wilhelm Hohengar. President Poincare replied to King George's message "I warmly thank your Majesty for your cordial message which will be read with deep gratitude by France and her Army. The brave British troops which have played such a brilliant part in securing common victory are united to their French brothers-in-arms by bands which peace will cement still further". President refers kindly feelings shown by British troops to French civilian population which has been reported by Municipal Authorities in terms of warmest gratitude. "Both our countries which suffered together may now rejoice

BRITISH AEGEAN SQUADRON.

The following wireless message, dated 14th November, 1918, has been received from the Lords Commissioners of the Admiralty. It is to be read to the Ship's Company on the Quarter-Deck and placed on the notice board.

"The Lords Commissioners of the Admiralty desire heartly to congratulate the Officers and Men of the Royal Navy and Royal Marines upon the triumph(?) of the true Allied cause in the realization of which they have played so splendid a part, adding lustre throughout to the great traditions of the service to which they belong.

Their Lordships feel that after four years of ceaseless vigilance, a relaxation of war conditions cannot but be eagerly desired by Officers and Men, and they may be relied upon to grant leave and modify war routine immediately when circumstances permit.

For the present, however, with German submarines possibly still at sea and ignorant of the armistice, with the work of the escorting ships to be surrended or interned devolving largely on the British Navy, and with the full capacity of the measures required for clearing the seas, it is plain that no Officers and Men can be spared from their duties until the safety of the Country at sea is assured.

The Navy had in time of peace to be ready for war in a sense in which land forces cannot be. Now that peace is again in prospect, it may prove that even after the troops in the field are enjoying a relief from tension, the Navy must for a time continue its war routine. If so, their Lordships are confident that this will be cheerfully accepted as being at once the burden and the privilege of the Empire's first line of defence."

M. CULME-SEYMOUR,
REAR-ADMIRAL.

"TRIAD,"
16TH NOVEMBER, 1918.

Message from Rear Admiral Michael Culme-Seymour that was to be read to the ship's company and then posted on the notice board

at the thought that their sacrifices have not been in vain, and that they both served the cause of humanity. I beg your Majesty to convey my admiration to the British people, Army and Navy". Lord Northcliffe resigned directorship of propaganda in enemy country upon conclusion of the armistice; Premier accepted on conclusion of the armistice. Premier accepted the resignation expressing his gratitude for the great services Lord Northcliffe rendered to the Allied cause—"I have had many direct evidences of the success of your invaluable work and of the extent to which it has contributed to the dramatic collapse of the enemy's strength in Austria and Germany".

Nov 24th I was Officer of the Guard & had to board the Jap. destroyers Momo & Kashi.

Nov. 25 Played tennis at Marsa with Clark, Taylor, Doc.

Nov. 26th On board.

Nov. 27th Went ashore & met Shaw. Dined in Acheron.

Nov. 28th Dined at Club in the evening with Shaw and Taylor. In the afternoon Taylor & I went for a long walk, about the only thing there is to do here in the way of amusement as it has rained every day since we arrived.

Nov. 29th The Huns are busy handing over their fleet to us at Scapa Flow.

Nov. 30th Still in dock, ship is in an awful mess. They are cutting up all the engine room casing, preparatory to lifting the turbines, they haven't given us a date of completion yet, but it looks as if we should be here for about two more months. Taylor & I had a little dinner at the club.

Dec. 1st Raining again. Had tea in Acheron with some W.R.N.S.s.[69] From all appearances it doesn't look as if peace will be signed for about three or four months. Some of our flotilla & a couple of Light cruisers have gone up to Savastapool [Sevastapol]. Home destroyers have gone to Kiel & Copenhagen. Rec'd. mail about 5 or 6 letters. Bad epidemic of Spanish Flu[70] in Canada.

Dec. 2nd Rec'd. pay & back pay 43s one sure does need it here. Raining very hard all day. Sent half of our ship's company on 4 days leave.

Dec. 3rd In afternoon played golf with Taylor at the Marsa. Dined at Club.

Dec. 5th Played golf at the Marsa.

Dec. 6th Went to races with Taylor at the Marsa. Dined in "Acheron" 9 of the W.R.N.S. off.[71]

---

69 The Women's Royal Naval Service (WRNS; popularly and officially known as the Wrens) was the women's branch of the United Kingdom's Royal Navy. First formed in 1917 for the First World War, it was disbanded in 1919, then revived in 1939 at the beginning of the Second World War, remaining active until integrated into the Royal Navy in 1993. WRNs included cooks, clerks, wireless telegraphists, radar plotters, weapons analysts, range assessors, electricians and air mechanics.
70 The Spanish flu of 1918-19 killed between 20 and 40 million people worldwide. It is one of the largest outbreaks of disease in recorded history.
71 Officers.

Dec. 7th Sat. O. O. Guard.

Dec. 8th Sunday. Still in dock, we should undock Tuesday. Had a tea party onboard.

Dec. 9th Went for a walk in P.M. Two men discharged to hospital.

Dec. 10th Undocked at 9:30 A.M. & went alongside "Colne". All River class destroyers are going home to pay off, also H class submarines. We have no date of completion yet. Taylor & I dined at the club in the evening.

Dec. 11th My day on.

Dec. 12th

Dec. 13th Lapwing, Tilbury, Hope, Parthian arrived.

Dec. 14th Taylor, Chief of Acheron and myself walked out to Curta Veichio 7 miles. Dined at the club in the evening with Taylor, Shaw & Spiller.

Dec. 15th

Dec. 23rd

Dec. 24th Went ashore in P.M. with Taylor & bought Xmas things.

Dec. 25th Church in forenoon & walked around the ship, wacked out beer. Xmas dinner aboard at 1:30 which was very cheery. Slept all afternoon. Went ashore in the evening for an hour or so but the place was pretty well deserted.

Dec. 26th Dined at the club with Taylor & Grant. Went to J.O.C. afterwards & finished up on the Parthian. I am trying to get 14 days leave in England but it doesn't seem to be much use.

Dec. 27th In the evening went to a dance at the Palace—pretty dud affair.

Dec. 28th Saw C.C.M.B. about my leave. I can't work it.

Dec. 29 Tea fight on board.

Dec. 30th Went up to the W.R.N.S.s.

Jan. 1st Very quiet day.

Jan. 2nd

Jan. 3rd Rugger match against the E.T.C.

Jan. 4th Boxing competition at Corradino Canteen, quite a good stunt.

Jan. 5th Sunday. Tea fight in "Acheron".

H.M.S. CAMELEON – AT MALTA

Jan. 6th Monday—Went for walk with Grant & Taylor

Jan. 7 I gave a dinner party onboard. Miss Short, Howell & Horan, Taylor, Thistlewaite, Had a good time. Had a cable from the skipper. He is leaving England on the 9th. The rumour here is that 20 S Class destroyers are coming out, and the Hs & I class are going home. In the latest A.W.O.s, I see that we get 15 days leave for every six months of foreign service. So that I will do quite well. Our date of completion is the 22nd of this month & things are getting cleared up a bit.

Jan. 8th

Jan. 9th Taylor gave a dinner party in the Acheron as he joins the Druid tomorrow. I was O.O. Guard.

Jan. 10th Went out to watch the rugger match, & had tea with WRNS.

Jan. 11th Sat. Bad cold.

Jan. 12th Tea fight on board.

Jan. 13th Bad fight—Peace conference meets today. Skipper returned from leave in England.

Jan. 14th Dined with Taylor in the Druid.

Jan. 15th Went ashore at 6, dined at club and met WRNS after at Camarata. We are getting ready for sea now. Jack Grant is going home to Canada as his eyesight has given out.

Jan. 16 Agamemnon arrived. Went for a walk to Sliema with Miss H. Shaw & Taylor dined with me. Heard that all the H. class destroyers are going to England when the S class come out to relieve us, which will probably be sometime in March.

Jan. 17th Took in ammunition.

Jan. 18th Taylor gave a dinner party in the "Druid" which was very good fun. Gwen & Mab.

Jan. 19th Tea fight on board.

Jan 20 —

Jan 21st

Jan. 22nd Completed refit. At Portaton wharf.

Jan.

Jan. 25 We were going out on full speed trials but weather was bad.

Jan. 26th Picnic out near Tigne. Good fun. Taylor Mabel, Gwen & I. Did full speed trials in forenoon. Painted ship in autumn.

Jan 27th Went ashore & had tea with G. Dined with Taylor?

Jan. 28th Did shopping in person. Sailed at 8 P.M for Mudros at 17 knots.

Jan. 29th At Sea. Malta-Mudros.

Jan. 30th Arrived Mudros at 9 A.M., oiled & proceeded to Ismid. Entered Dardanelles about 3 P.M. Raining hard.

SAILING ORDERS.

"BLENHEIM" – 3rd.February.1919.

MEMORANDUM.
No.108/149.

H.M.Ship under your command being in all respects ready for sea, you are to sail at 1500, Monday, 3rd. February,for Mudros, via Constantinople.
  (ii) You are to arrive Constantinople at 1800 3rd.February and report to the British Commander-in-Chief ("SUPERB") that you have arrived for duty in accordance with his W/T signal 0841 of 2nd.February.

2. You are to request permission to sail for Mudros at 2000, Monday, 3rd.February, and adjust speed so that you arrive at the Northern entrance to the Dardanelles by daylight 4th.February.
  (ii) After passing through the Dardanelles you are to proceed Northabout of Imbros and Westabout of Lemnos, speed being adjusted to enable you to arrive Mudros 1400,Tuesday 4th.February, at which time the Commodore Commanding British Aegean Squadron has been informed you will arrive.

3. At Mudros you should report to the Commodore Commanding British Aegean Squadron ("EUROPA"), and to the Commanding Officer, H.M.S "ACORN", that you have arrived for duty with the Destroyer Division attached to the Aegean Squadron as relief for "HIND".

4. All mails carried by you are to be transferred to "HIND" immediately on arrival.
  (ii) An envelope numbered 108/150 addressed to Lieutenant.D.J.R.Simson, R.N, H.M.S "HIND", which will be sent to you before sailing today, is to be delivered by you to Lieutenant Simson personally.

5. Receipt of this memorandum is to be acknowledged by signal "108/149 received".

6. Your mails have been ordered to Mudros.

George Chetwode
CAPTAIN (D),
FIFTH DESTROYER FLOTILLA.

Lieutenant-in-Command,
GERALD MORRELL McKENNA, Royal Navy,

  H.M.Ship "CAMELEON".

Orders for HMS Cameleon *to sail to Mudros, February 3, 1919*

Jan. 31   Arrived at Ismid about 9 A.M. and anchored. Goeben is here also Volaya who is alongside Blenheim. 2 Russian destroyers & submarines. Saw Soulsby & had lunch with him. Jackal & Goshawk left for England to pay off. Archer arrived.

Feb. 1st   Had the duty trip to Constantinople. Left Ismid 7 A.M. & arrived Constant. 10 A.M. Had lunch with McCrae ashore. Raining hard & the streets were inches deep in mud. Most awfully dirty place but interesting.

Feb. 2nd   Started at 7 A.M. shifting ships alongside oiler etc. also Russian destroyers which have been taken over by us. Tried to weigh one Russ. destr. ↓ but broke all capstan bars in the attempt. Finally we had to slip it. Finished at 5 P.M. & anchored. Capt. D. is going to inspect the ship tomorrow.

Feb. 3rd   Waiting for Captain D's inspection which should come off at 10 A.M. but owing to rain it was postponed until 2 P.M. Rain still continuing, he washed it out. Druid arrived & I saw Taylor. Sailed at 4 P.M. for Constantinople where we arrived at 7 P.M. Embarked Comm. Strang & two other N.O.s & proceeded to Mudros.

Feb. 4th   Arrived Mudros at 2:30 P.M. and relieved the Hind.

H.M.S. CAMELEON

Feb. 11th   Went alongside St. George at 7 A.M. completing defects. Snowing all day and quite cold.

Feb. 12   At Mudros, Fine day. Caught my usual cold.

Feb. 13th   At Mudros.

Feb. 14th   Went fishing.

Feb. 15th

Feb. 16th   Blew quite hard from S.W. 11 of ships company discharged to Europa (ship men). Went off in P.M. & exploded a 2¼ lb. charge. Got some fish.

Feb. 17th   Proceeded to patrol at 7 A.M. & relieved Rifleman. Stopped near Zuafa Rock. Gunner in whaler & myself went away & exploded a 16¼ lb. charge. Got hundreds of fish. Anchored in Kusu Bay in afternoon.

Feb. 18th   Blowing from S. W. & rain. Escorting ships between Kusu & Dardanelles. Anchored in Kusu.

Feb. 19th   At Kusu most of the day. Had two fish bombing expeditions with 16½ lb. charges. Got about 100 lbs. of fish. We had a fire in the gunner's cabin today which was quickly extinguished.

Feb. 20th   Did some more fish bombing; got a rock cod weighing 30 lb.

Feb. 21st Escorted Malwa to Helles at 7 A.M. relieved by "Ruby" at 10 A.M. who told us that we sail tomorrow for Malta and then to England. Arrived Mudros 1 P.M. Parthian, Tribune & Shark arrived from Malta. They are our reliefs. Hoisted our paying off pendant.

Feb. 22nd Sailed for Malta at 1 P.M. Rec'd. mails & passengers for Malta.

Feb. 23rd At Sea Mudros – Malta.

Feb. 24th Arrived Malta at 7 A.M. & finally secured to magazine trot at 10 A.M. Blowing fairly hard here. Went ashore in P.M. and had tea with Gwen. Dined with Hibbard & an R.N.R. Lieut. at Great Britain Hotel. Am thinking of volunteering for mine sweeping.

H.M.S. CAMELEON

Feb. 25th At Malta.

Feb. 26th At Malta.

Feb. 27th At Malta. Had to see Capt. D. this morning as the C in C made a signal asking whether Bain (No. 1 of Acorn) & myself volunteered for further service in the Mediterranean. However, D saw C in C & made a signal saying that we need no longer volunteer. Went ashore in the afternoon for a walk. The war gratuity has come out. A Lieut. gets £45 & £1 add. for each month at sea.

Feb. 28th The Sub & I dined with the skipper at the club. The Maltese carnival is on now & is the big stunt here. A fancy dress ball at the Opera House is the big attraction

March 1st Bain, Eveleigh, French & myself (No. 1s of Acorn, Rifleman, Hope & Cameleon) had to see Captain D. this morning as one of us has to do to the "Superb"; of course none of us wanted it so we cut (three). Eveleigh was lucked. Went over to Bighi in P.M. and G. & M. Dined in the Rifleman with Eveleigh. Capt. D. is going to attend divisions tomorrow at 10 A.M.

March 2nd Capt. D. came onboard for divisions & walked around the ship. He gave us a little speech afterwards & said that he has inspected a good many destroyers; but he has never found one as clean, efficient & as well kept as the Cameleon in every department.

March 3rd Had a farewell dance in Blenheim, adjourned to the J.O.C. afterwards.

March 4th Shipped & proceeded at 5 P.M. in company Acorn, Rifleman, Redpole for Gib. Plymouth. We got a decent number of cheers as we steamed out with paying off pendants flying., We have 22 ratings onboard for passage & 3 officers.

March 5th At sea Malta-Gib. Fine weather.

SAILING ORDERS.

"Blenheim" – 4th. March. 1919.

MEMORANDUM.
No. 106/159.

H.M. Ship under your command being in all respects ready for sea, you are to take "RIFLEMAN", "REDPOLE" and "CAMELEON" under your orders and sail at 1600 GMT to-day Tuesday 4th. March, and proceed to Plymouth.

(ii) You are to proceed at economical speed throughout the whole of the passage, calling at Gibraltar en route to oil.

2. Arrangements are to be made for the return of any documents and charts required to be surrendered before leaving the station; and if this has not been done at Malta, the necessary action should be taken upon arrival at Gibraltar.

(ii) Your Home Chart Sets, if deposited at Malta, are to be drawn before sailing.

3. Upon arrival at your Home Port, your crew will be reduced and leave given, "ACORN", "REDPOLE" and "CAMELEON" will be transferred to "VIVID", and "RIFLEMAN" to "VICTORY" from p.m 3rd. March. 1919.

4. Receipt of this memorandum is to be acknowledged by signal quoting "No. 106/159".

George Chetwode
CAPTAIN (D),
SIXTH DESTROYER FLOTILLA.

Commander WILLIAM BOWEN MACKENZIE,
Royal Navy,
His Majesty's Ship "ACORN".
Copies to Commanding Officers, H.M.S "RIFLEMAN", "REDPOLE", "CAMELEON"

Orders for HMS Cameleon *to sail to Plymouth, England, March 4, 1919*

H.M.S. CAMELEON

March 6th 1919 At sea. Malta – Gib. Fine weather.

March 7 Arrived Gib. 7 A.M. & secured alongside Acorn. S class destroyers here viz. Stuart, Spear, Swallow, Speedy, Sportive, Torch, Tumult, Tryphon. An awful day as it rained & blew hard.

March 8th Saturday. Fine day. Went ashore in afternoon with Fullida & did some more shopping. Tea at Bristol. Walked out to Linea which is just outside Gib.

March 9 The S class proceeded to Malta at 10 A.M. Acorn, Rifleman, Cameleon & Redpole proceeded at 11 A.M. for England, speed 18 knots. Passed Australian destroyers & Light cruisers at entrance to the harbour. Proceeded at 11 A.M. with Acorn, Rifleman & Redpole.

March 10th At sea. Gib.-Plymouth.

March 11th At sea. Gib-Plymouth. Quite a heavy following sea.

March 12th Arrived at Devonport 7:30 A.M. Blowing hard & pretty cold for us after Malta. Secured to oiler then alongside "Mischief" above the bridge at Saltach. Collingwood, Benbow, Marlborough, Centurion, etc. and crowds of destroyers here. All the M class etc, destroyers with only a few men onboard. "Acorn" secured alongside us. Went ashore with Bain. Dined at the Globe. Met Ossie, Critchley, Hibbard, Brodeur and lots of people I knew. Seems very funny to be in England again.

March 13 At Devonport.

March 14 The Gunner and I caught the 4 P.M. train to London. Arrived London 10:30 P.M. & stopped at Overseas Club (R.A.C.), Pall Mall.

March 15th Went to the Admiralty in forenoon but could not see Commander Merrick. Saw Tails Up in P.M. which was very good. Went to Soldier Boy in evening. Supper at Troc.

March 16th Went to Westminster Abbey in morning. Caught the 2:30 train from Waterloo for Farnham where I arrived at 4:00 P.M.

March 17th At Farnham.

March 18th At Farnham.

March 19th Wednesday. Dorothy D. & myself caught 8:55 train to town. Met Jack there. Lunched at Bankers. Went to Hullo America with Katie & Willie; a very good show. Elsie James is awfully good. Returned to Farnham by 5 P.M. train.

March 20th Thursday.

March 21st Went to Aldershot.

March 22nd Sat. Went to town by 10:30 train. Stopped at R.A.C. Saw the Guards procession in afternoon. Went to the Boy in P.M.

23rd Met Dicky Bugno. We went out to zoo in the afternoon. In evening met Mr. Camm and we dined together at R.A.C. Some dinner.

24th Lunched with Mr. Camm (30 Onslow Gardens) at the Orleans Club which is the smallest and one of the best clubs in London. Went to play "In the Night Watch". Had tea at the Ritz. Went out to the Frasers in evening & caught the midnight train to Plymouth.

25th Arrived Ply. 7:30 after a most cold journey. I couldn't get a sleeper. Went on board.

26th The Sub went on leave. We dined at the Globe.

27th At Plymouth.

28th Dined with Critchley at the Barracks. I am the only officer onboard & live a sort of bachelor existence.

29 Met Rook.

30 Rook & Vaughan dined onboard.

31

APRIL 1919 — H.M.S. CAMELEON AT DEVONPORT

April 1st Went to Centurion in evening and dined with Rook. Slept aboard her.

April 2nd My day on.

April 3rd Thursday. Lunched in Carnarvon with Vaughan. Afterwards went to "Going Up" at the Royal. I haven't had any reply to my application for leave to Canada which I put in for on March 27th.

April 4th Aboard all day. Took over S.O. group from Lt. Comm. Maxwell.

April 5th Saturday. Went out for a walk out Saltash way.

April 6th Sunday. Fine day.

April 7th

April 8th Went ashore. Saw "Nurse Benson" at the Royal, a good show.

9 On board.

10 Day on.

11 Call on Gauvreau.

12 Dinner at Jones' with Worth.

13 Lunched with Worth in "Spendrift". Tea at Gauvreau's.

17th Caught the 2:28 train. Arrived Farnham 11:30 P.M.

18th Good Friday. Awfully fine weather now. Saw Jack & D. Annesley also Richard Annesley.

19 Walked over to Froyle in P.M.

20 Easter Sunday.

21

22 Left Farnham 9:00 A.M., arrived London 10:10. Arrived Plymouth at 5 P.M. No news of my leave. Lt. Comm. Nevill has joined "Acorn".

23 Went ashore to do some shopping but stores closed.

24 Down to South Yard to Apollo to see about demobilising some of the ship's company, then to Luscomb to order a lounge suit (7 guineas). Peace has not been signed yet. The Italians are trying to get hold of Fuime & Orlando is very fed up that we won't give it to them. Had a long letter from Taylor who is still in the Black Sea (Druid). (Try on suit May 2nd).

April 25th

April 26th Ainslie & I caught the 2:34 P.M. train for Tavistock where we arrived at 3 P.M. Walked from Tavistock to Two Bridges, distance 8 miles. Over the moors, quite steep hills but very fine view from the top. Two Bridges is about 12 miles from Princetown. Stopped the night at the Two Bridges Hotel which is very good.

April 27th Sunday. Walked back from Two Bridges to Tavistock in the afternoon. Very bad day, snow, rain. etc. and the wind against us all the way. Arrived Tavistock 4:45 P.M. & had an excellent tea with real D. cream. Dined at Bedford Hotel & caught the 8:00 train to St. Budeaux & after waiting at Saltash about an hour arrived on board 10:30 P.M. Snowing hard.

April 28th

April 30

May 1st Dined with Hacket & went to the Palace afterwards.

2nd On board.

3rd Got 10 days leave. Left Plymouth for Jersey at 4 P.M. Arrived at Weymouth at 10 P.M. having changed at Yeovil. Shoved off 1:30 A.M.

4th Arrived St. Helier 9 A.M. Sunday morning. Francis Gore met me & went up to the Gores (Fontille Mount Leland). Went to tea at the Coxes P.M.

May 13th Left St. Helier at 7:30, arrived Weymouth 3:15 P.M. (Stopped Guernsey). Caught 4:15 train to Yeovil where I changed, arrived Taunton at 9:15 P.M. where I stopped the night at G. W. Hotel.

May 14th Left Taunton 8 A.M., arrived Ply. 10. I have got seven weeks leave for Canada & am now waiting for my passage.

May 15th Thursday. At Plymouth.

May 16th At Plymouth. Had tea with Brodeur. Saw Bing Boys at Royal.

May 17th Got all my gear packed up & landed it. Had dinner with Hacket & Stapleton at Jones. Did order a suit 10 guineas.

May 18th Sunday. Dined with Hacket in the Indus.

19th Went ashore in forenoon to see about some clothes. Received my passage to Canada. I sail in the Adriatic from Liverpool May 28th.

20 Tuesday

21 Wednesday

22 Thursday. Got my gear ashore. Dined with Rook at Jones.

23rd Friday. Left Cameleon at 8 A.M. Did some shopping in Plymouth. Caught the 11:20 train from Millbay. Had to check all my gear again at North Road. Arrived Basin[g]stoke about 5:30 P.M. Changed trains and went on to Brookwood where I changed again. Finally arrived at Farnham 8 P.M. Willie & Katie were at Aldershot.

No date recorded In town. Saw Joy Bells. Russian Ballet at Alhambra & Buzz Buzz. Dined at Purvis, Troc. etc. Good time.

May 30th Did some shopping during the day. Shoved from Euston Station at 11:45 P.M. for Liverpool. Did not draw a horse in R.A.C. duchy sweep.

May 31st Arrived Liverpool 6:30 A.M. Had breakfast at G.N. Hotel & the went to White Star office to see about ticket etc. & my gear. Could not find any trace of my gear having arrived in Liverpool & so spent the whole morning chasing around about it. Went on board "Adriatic" at noon & we went out into the stream at 1:30 P.M. 85th N.S. regiment onboard & some of the 78th. Shoved off from Liverpool at about 8:30 P.M. Fine weather.

June 1st Sunday. Fine weather. Passed Queenstown about noon.

June 2nd Fine weather. Very comfortable ship.

June 21st Polly & I motored up to Windsor. Left Halifax at 10:30 A.M. Stopped the night at the MacMechan's.

June 22 Left Windsor at 2:30 P.M. arrived Halifax 7 P.M.

June 23 Mond.

24 Tues.

25 Wed.

26 Ths.

27 Fri. P & I went to Davie [?].

28 Sat.

Aug. 23rd 1919 Sailed from Montreal in Megantic for Liverpool. Brodeur, Grant, Hart, Donald, Gow – onboard. Good passage down St. Lawrence. Arrived Quebec. 10 P.M. "Renown & Dragon" there with Prince of Wales.

Aug. 24 In Gulf of St. Lawrence – Fog.

Aug. 25 Foggy & ice. Stopped.

By Command of the Commissioners for Executing the Office of Lord High Admiral of the United Kingdom of Great Britain and Ireland, &c.

C.W.

To Lieutenant John C. I. Edwards, R.C.N.

The Lords Commissioners of the Admiralty hereby appoint you *Lieutenant* of His Majesty's Ship "*Galatea*"

and direct you to repair on board that Ship at *Rosyth*

Your appointment is to take effect from the 3rd September 1919.

You are to acknowlege the receipt of this Appointment forthwith, addressing your letter to taking care to furnish your address.

By Command of Their Lordships.

O. Murray

Admiralty, S.W. 1.
3 Sept 1919.

Vice Hanson (RNR)

Dutchy's orders to join HMS Galatea as Lieutenant, September 3, 1919

Aug. 26 Stopped. Saw ice bergs.

Aug. 27 Stopped. Fog cleared in evening. Proceeded.

Aug. 28 Clear of ice but still in dense fog.

Sept. 2nd Arrived Liverpool & docked 7 A.M. Caught 11:00 A.M boat train to London. Arrived there at 4 P.M. Had a job getting a hotel. Finally got in at Wigmore in Lower Seymour St. Went to Maid of Mountains in evening.

Sept. 3rd Reported at Admiralty in forenoon & was appointed to the "Galatea" Light cruiser. Had to leave London (King's Cross) 10:30 P.M. for Rosyth as they thought the Galatea was sailing for Baltic on the 4th. Could not get a sleeper.

Sept. 4th Arrived Edinburgh 9:00 & caught next train to Inverkeithing. Joined Galatea at Rosyth Dockyard. Not sailing for Baltic until Monday. went to Edinburgh in P.M. & did some shopping.

Sept. 5th Stopped on board.

Sept. 6th Saturday. Went into Edinburgh & did some shopping.

Sept 7 Bradshaw, Gow & myself walked into Dumferry [Dunfermline]. Had tea there.

Sept 8 No news of General Goff. Had a telegram from him saying that he was not leaving until the week end.

H.M.S. GALATEA AT ROSYTH
SEPTEMBER 1919

9th Sept. My day on.

10th Sept. Played tennis at Officers' Recreation Club. (Cheque to Luscombe Plymouth for £8 10s 0d.)

11 Sept. Murphy & I went to Edinburgh.

12 Sept. My day on. Shifted out to buoy & back again to alongside dockyard.

13th Went in to Edinburgh.

14th Sunday. Aboard all day.

15 Day on. Rec'd. telegram from Admiralty giving Officers & ship's company 10 days leave.

16th Ship's company & officers left ship on 10 days leave. Gow & myself are the unfortunates who have to stop behind.

17th - - -

18

19 Shifted into Basin alongside Neptune.

20 Went to Edinburgh in morning to meet Taylor.

21 Sunday. Aboard all day.

22 Taylor & I went to Dunfermline.

23 Went to Edinburgh. Dined at North British with Taylor.

24 On board all day.

25 Went to Edinburgh.

26 Railway strike. Our people who were returning from leave hung up all over the country.

27 Saturday. Officers and ship's company should have returned today from leave but only a few arrived owing to the strike. There are 150 ratings & 4 officers at Grantham.

28 No. 1, Bradshaw & Murphy arrived having motored from Dumfries.

29 Raining hard all day.

30th Walked to Dunfermline.

OCTOBER 1919

1st Went to thé Dansant[72] at Dunfermline.

2 Walk.

3 Day on.

4 Walked to Dunfermline.

5 (**Sunday**) Rec'd. cheque for $368 W.S.G. (3 mos. instalment). Strike settled.

6 Day on.

7 Routine as for 4th.

8 Went for walk at S. Queensferry.

9 Shifted from basin to No. 27 buoy. Forwarded cheque for $368.00 to Dad. Mess bill £8 4s. 3d.

10 **Friday.** Went to Edinburgh with Murphy & Bradshaw. Saw Brewster's Millions. Dined at N.B.

11th Received a signal at 1 P.M. telling us to sail for Copenhagen as soon as possible. Recalled all our people on shore & sailed at 4 P.M. 13 knots.

12 **Sunday** At Sea. Rosyth-Copenhagen. Intercepted message that all German steamers at sea in the Baltic are liable to capture by us.

13 **Mon.** Blowing hard. Rain & pretty cold. Arrived Copenhagen at 2:30 P.M. Discharged some ammunition to Sandhurst & proceeded at 4 P.M. for Libau.

---

[72] A tea dance, also called a thé dansant (French for "dancing tea"), was historically a dance held on a summer or autumn afternoon or early evening, from 4 to 7 p.m. In the English countryside, a garden party sometimes preceded the dance.

14 Tues. Arrived Libau 2:30 P.M. & ↓ed. Phaeton S.N.O. Kept regular sea watches & guns crews closed up as Germans are about 20 away. They fired on ships at Riga.

15th At Libau.

16th Thurs. Proceeded at 10 A.M. R.V. with destroyers off Memel. Our job is to not let any German ships leave German ports. Examined all ships.

17th Fri. Took up patrol between Jerkof & Bornholm Island. Examining ships.

18 On patrol near Bornholm Isl. & Sandhammaren Lt. Captured a German Schooner[73] in P.M. Sent her for Libau with Armed guard.

19 Captured another German schooner Johan. Sent Sub Lt. Murphy & armed guard onboard. Falls & I are practically in two watches. Examined about 20 ships.

20 At sea, patrolling. Met T.B.D.s Winchester & Whitley.

21 At 8:00 A.M. met German sailing vessel "Neptune" lat. 55°37'N 16° 55'E). Falls & I boarded her. I was onboard her all forenoon looking thru passes etc. Finally took her as prize. "Valorous" sent a prize crew & she proceeded to Libau. Barquentine.

22nd Went alongside at 10 A.M. Dined with Pilot, Falls & Trotter (A.D.C. to General Gugh) at Wivels. Went to Palais de Dance afterwards. Had a very amusing evening.

23rd Went ashore with Bradshaw & had tea with some Danish people (Cuffs) at Hotel D'Angleterre. Very nice girls. Dined onboard. We are taking General Haking[74] and staff to Björkö on Monday. I like Copenhagen very much; it is quite clean & has very good shops although things are more expensive than in England; some fine buildings, modern hotels & restaurants. Heaps of bicycles.

24th Falls, Bradshaw and myself dined the Cuffs at Hotel D'Angleterre & we danced afterwards there.

25th

26th Sunday.

27th Sailed at 10:00 A.M. with General Haking and his staff for Reval & Björkö.

---

73 This was the Frida of Gotenburg per the ship's log found at https://www.naval-history.net/OWShips-WW1-06-HMS_Galatea.htm.
74 Sir Richard Haking.

28th Arrived at Reval at 5 P.M. Went alongside oiler.

29th Sailed for Helsingfors[75] at 5 P.M. Arrived Helsingfors 9:30 A.M. General Marsh came off to see Gen. Haking. Went ashore for an hour in P.M. Rate of exchange 102 for £1.

30th Arrived at Björkö (which is about 30' from Kronsadt) about 3 P.M. Delhi (Flag Read. Adm. Cowan). Lots of light cruisers & destroyers here. Gen. Haking saw the Admiral. Later on the former read us the telegram which he is sending to War Office re Russian situation Baltic etc. H.M.S. Erebus monitor is employed shelling the forts & there is a destroyer patrol of 6 boats, outside Björkö which has net defence. We are leaving tomorrow for Narva and Reval. We disembark the General at the former place & proceed to Reval to wait for him as he is going by train between the two places. I spent an hour on foc'sle hoisting out our "Camel". It was very cold & we have no winter clothing. The situation here is that Gen. Haking suggests 3 things.

To land an expeditionary force of 2 divisions etc. combined with naval force.

Loan of £15 million to Finland

[no entry here]

31st Sailed from Björkö at 7 A.M. Arrived Narva noon. Disembarked General Haking and staff; he is meeting Eugenic & is coming on to Reval by train. Arrive Reval at 8:30 P.M.

November 1st Went alongside at 9 A.M. Snowing hard all day and quite cold. Pilot & I went ashore and bought stamps. Reval is not much of a place. The exchange is down to about 250 marks to the pound so things are fairly cheap.

Nov 2nd My day on.

November 3rd Temp. 26°F.

4th At Reval.

5th Sailed for Helsingfors at 9 A.M. & arrived noon, Bradshaw & I went ashore. Went to Fenni Cabaret after dinner.

6th Sailed at 9 A.M. & arrived Reval noon.

7th At Reval. Dined at British Embassy with Dewel & Foster. First sleigh drive this year.

8th Dined with Oland in Maidstone.

9 At Reval.

10th At Reval. Temp. about 17°F., very cold.

11

---

75 Helsingfors was the Swedish name for what is now Helsinki, the capital of Finland.

12 Mail arrived.

13

14th Sailed at 6 A.M. with Gen. Haking for Chatham. Got W/T message from S.N.O. Libau to turn over our ammunition to ships bombarding. Arrived Libau 10 P.M. "Valorous" came alongside also lighters for amm. Ships here (Erebus, Phaeton, etc.) have been bombarding Germans who are trying to capture the town from the Letts. Ships practically run out of ammunition. There are about 5000 Huns attacking about 1000 Letts defending.

15th Sailed at 4 A.M. for Copenhagen. Arrived 8 P.M.

16 Oiled & sailed at 2 A.M. for Chatham.

17 At sea. In first watch got in amongst fishing fleet which was unfortunate for their nets. Raining hard.

18 Arrived at Sheerness 7 A.M. Disembarked General Haking. Proceeded to Portsmouth. Anchored at Spithead.

19 Proceeded up harbour at 9:30 A.M. and secured to No. 4 buoy.

20 At Portsmouth.

21 Ship's company —one watch went on 9 days leave. No. 1, myself & Murphy are stopping on board for the first nine days.

22 At Portsmouth.

23 At Portsmouth.

24 At Portsmouth. Murphy & I went ashore.

25 At Portsmouth.

26

27

28 Dined with Taylor at Tots.

29 Saw rugger game U.S. vs. Devonport.

30

1st December Raining. H.M.S. Renown arrived with the Prince of Wales from Halifax. Gallo & Gleed came back so I caught the 4 P.M. train to Guildford. Arrived Farnham at 6:30. Katie & Willie well.

2nd At Farnham.

3rd At Farnham.

4th At Farnham.

5th Went up to Town at 12:49. Caught the 3:25 from Victoria for Sittingbourne. Walked from station to Jack & Dorothy's which is about 3½ miles by the way I went.

6th Saturday @ Church House.

7th Sunday.

8th Monday.

9th Tues. Went up to Town with Edith Leckie. She & Mary Henderson lunched with me at Pall Mall. Transferred $130 from Halifax to London as Canadian exchange is up to $4.07. Went down to Farnham. Willie, Katie & myself saw "General Post" at Aldershot theatre—very good.

10 Left Farnham 4:43, arrived Portsm. 7:28. No news.

11th At Portsmouth.

12 At Portsmouth. Queen Elizabeth, Royal Sovereign, Canada arrived.

13 No Christmas leave for us.

14th

15

16 Went to Hippodrome.

17 Practiced rugger at United Service ground.

18 Practiced rugger at United Service ground. No. 1 and myself dined ashore & went to Kings theatre.

19 At Portsmouth.

20 At Portsmouth. Saw U.S. play Blackheath 11-15.

23rd Left Portsmouth at 9 A.M. with McCubbin & party for Portland to bring Drifter "Flat Calm" back to Portsmouth. Arrived Portland at 4 P.M. & found that the Drifter would not be ready for about 5 days as the engines were in bits.

24 Tried to return to Portsmouth but S.N.O. wouldn't let me.

25 Went off to "Monarch" in forenoon (Christmas Day) and had lunch. Met Crisp (Eng. Lieut.). Went ashore for a walk in Weymouth. Fed up with the idea of not being in Galatea for Xmas or on leave.

26 Getting Drifter ready for sea.

27 Getting Drifter ready for sea.

28 Getting Drifter ready for sea.

29 Coaled at 8 A.M. and proceeded for Portsmouth at 10:30 A.M. Blowing quite hard off St. Alban's Head. Thick fog which was a nuisance when making the Needles as we were about ½ mile off course when I picked up the buoys. Arrived Portsmouth at 8 P.M. and went alongside Galatea.

30th At Portsmouth. Went ashore with Morris & Murphy. Dined at Toots.

31st Aboard all day. Saw the New Year in onboard.

JANUARY 1920 – H.M.S. GALATEA PORTSMOUTH

Jan 1st At Portsmouth.

2nd Rec'd. pay for quarter. £32.0.0. Mess 6.0.0. Went ashore with No. 1 Sub. dined with Falls & went on to Kings. A very good show. Gleed appointed to Dyad. Elbrow appoint. Galatea.

3rd Went out to Spithead at 8 AM. We stay out here until 15th. Blowing hard.

4th At Spithead.

5th At Spithead.

6th At Spithead. Falls appointed to President for I.D. Course.

7th Went ashore with Murphy. Elbrow joined ship.

8th On board. Blowing hard.

9th Day on.

10th Still blowing hard. Went ashore in Drifter with No. 1 & Murphy. Saw Sleeping Beauty at Hippodrome.

11th Blowing hard all day.

12th Blowing hard all day. Anchor watches.

13th Blowing hard all day. Saw McKenna in Barham re salvage claims. Had evolutions this morning. Farce. We are due to go up harbour on the 17th. Saw Lt. Comm Boles in Barham re specializing in Torpedo. He advises me to wait as the subject is under revision.

14 Had tea at Gow's relations. Still humming & hawing about the Canadian Navy.

15th One watch went on 14 days Christmas leave. Raining.

16 At Spithead. Today's news in the papers is that the Bolsheviks are overrunning Europe (East) and threaten India, China. etc.. We are due to go up harbour tomorrow which will be a blessing.

Jan. 17th Went up harbour at 9:30 A.M. Bradshaw returned from hospital.

18th At Portsmouth.

19 At Portsmouth.

20 At Portsmouth.

21 At Portsmouth.

Jan. 22nd At Portsmouth.

23rd At Portsmouth.

24 At Portsmouth.

25 At Portsmouth.

26

27

28

29

30 Went on Xmas leave. Arrived Farnham 6:30 P.M.

31 At Farnham.

Feb. 1 At Farnham.

2 At Farnham.

3 At Farnham.

4 At Farnham. Went up to Town to see about passport.

5 Left Victoria 8 A.M. Arrived Folk[e]stone 10. Arrived Boulogne about 12:15. Lunch at Hotel de London. Caught the 2:30 P.M. train for Arras. Arrived Arras 6:50 P.M. Hotels Commercial & Strassburg full up. Finally got a room at the "England & Dominions", a little place run by an ex R.E. corporal.

6th Walked to Mont St. Eloi and Ecoivres where I visited Joe's grave in the military cemetery. It is about 5 miles from Ecoivres to Arras. I walked out past La Targette to Vimy. Saw Vimy Ridge. The country looks very desolate and is full of ruins. From Vimy I got a lift back to Arras. Saw Arras Cathedral which is in ruins. Most of Arras is in ruins but the French people are busy at work rebuilding. The cemetery at Ecroivres is a very peaceful spot. There are a number of Canadians buried there also English and French.

Feb. 7th Caught the 10 A.M. train to Amiens. Passed thru Albert etc. which is in ruins. Caught the 12:45 train for Boulogne. Arrived Boulogne at 3 P.M. Arrived Folkestone 5:30, caught 6 P.M. for Dover & the 7:45 train for Sittingbourne where I arrived at 9:15 P.M.

Feb. 8th At Roamersham. Drill Hall

Feb. 9th At Roamersham.

10 At Roamersham.

11 At Roamersham.

12 At Roamersham. Caught the 8 A.M. train for Town. Met No. 1 & Murphy at Adelphi Hotel. Called on Botterell & Rocke re Hebburn Salvage. Tea at Waldorf with Mary Henderson. Saw Joy Bells at Hippodrome.

13th Lunched at Queens. Br. Museum in P.M. Dined at Romanos and saw "Who's Hooper" at Adelphi theatre.

14th Left Waterloo 9:50, arrived Pompey 11:50. Got a signal in P.M. that Galatea is going to reduce and go into reserve fleet.

15th On board.

The position of the "Hebburn" was in was an extremely nasty one, her head to the shore and about 1½ lengths distant, she was lying heading about E.N.E. and it was a dangerous business going alongside her, we had to keep the lead going the whole time, and were afraid of striking some of the submerged wreckage. The depth of water round the "Cameleon" was 12 to 20 fathoms.

A heaving line was thrown on board the "Hebburn" which was secured by those on the "Hebburn". To a hawser, made fast to the hawser was an 8" manilla which was hauled onboard the "Cameleon" and connected to our cable. The manilla belonged to the "Hebburn".

Lt. McKenna ordered the trawler to make fast alongside the port quarter of the "Hebburn" heading the same way as the Hebburn. The Cameleon lay off her starboard quarter with her stern out with a scope of about 60 fathoms of tow rope and when all was ready a signal was passed to the trawler and our engines, and engines of "Hebburn" and "Faraday" were put to slow astern and the power was gradually increased.

After straining for about ten minutes the rope parted. Lt. McKenna then told the Captain of the "Hebburn" that he was going to try and come alongside and make fast on the starboard side in a similar manner to the trawler. This was risky work, but it is much more satisfactory if you get a vessel of the type of the "Cameleon" made fast alongside the ship you wish to tow. This is partly owing to the very large power of the engines of these vessels, and also because they do not carry very heavy tackle.

The sea was rough & there was a nasty short swell. In coming alongside the "Hebburn" a certain amount of damage was done to the "Cameleon". After about an hour we eventually made fast with all available wires that we had and the "Hebburn" had.

All three vessels engines were put astern and after about an hour as the Hebburn did not move, the attempt was given up in order to make further arrangements.

I suggested to Lieut McKenna that if we turned our vessel round and

Dutchy's written testimony before the Hebburn Salvage Arbitration, page 1

and went ahead our engines would exert more power.

This manoeuvre of turning round was carried out by means of leading wires out as springs and turning around on them as owing to the limited space in which it was safe to manoeuvre the "Cameleon". This was a very ticklish job.

We then made fast again, our starboard side lying alongside the starboard quarter of the "Hebburn", with bows pointing in the opposite way to the "Hebburn".

As soon as all was made fast, our engines were put slow ahead, and the engines of the other vessels were put astern, and our engines were gradually worked up to full power. This operation was repeated three or four times, and after about half an hour, the Hebburn finally moved and came off into deep water where she anchored. The Captain of the Hebburn was very apprehensive that his ship was damaged. She was in fact making water, he therefore asked us to "stand by". We stood by for an hour, and we then proceeded to Mudros and the "Hebburn" went to Constantinople under her own power. At this time there were few ships in the neighbourhood with the exception of H.M.S. "Pelorus" a cruiser which would have been no good at rendering services such as the "Hebburn" required, and who also I think, did not have steam raised. There was a Sig. station at Cape Helles but I do not think it was in touch by telephone or wire with any W.T. station, so it was extremely fortunate for the Hebburn that the "Cameleon" and "Faraday" were handy.

By the promptitude with which the services were rendered the "Hebburn" was only on the wreckage of the "Majestic" about twenty hours. Time was extremely important to the "Hebburn" as, of course, the longer she remained on the wreckage the greater damage she would have received, and in that part of the globe the wind is very shifty, and squalls are continually coming on. In my opinion a destroyer was one of the best instruments of salvage that the "Hebburn" could have possibly had, as the "Cameleon" had very large horse power, and light draft and if she could be made fast to a vessel such as the Hebburn with a sufficient number of ropes which would hold, an enormous power could be exerted by her engines. An ordinary steamer or a tug cannot exert this power and I consider Lt. McKenna showed great skill in handling the "Cameleon" under the circumstances and I think it was largely due to this and our perseverance that the Hebburn was got off, as before we secured alongside the 2nd time it did not seem likely

Dutchy's written testimony before the Hebburn Salvage Arbitration, page 2

that we should salve the 'Hebburn' and her captain was extremely doubtful if we should be able to accomplish it and was very apprehensive as to the fate of the Hebburn.

A copy of the signals from the signal log of the Cameleon is produced which show all the signals passing, and the times.

J. Edwards
1st Lieut H.M.S. Cameleon
Feb 10th 1919.

Dutchy's written testimony before the Hebburn Salvage Arbitration, page 3

16th Monday. Bradshaw & I went to a dance at Fareham with the Cades at a Connaught Drill Hall. Arrived onboard at 3 A.M.

17 On board. Went to tea at Mrs. Cooks.

18th Our date of going into reserve fleet is March 1st.

19th Salvage case of Hebburn come off on Feb. 25th.

20th Went up to Town & went to Admiralty re appointment. Asked for Lt. cruiser on N.A. & W.I.[76] Arrived back on board at 9:30. Went to Palais de Danse on P.M.

21st At Portsmouth.

22 At Portsmouth.

23 At Portsmouth.

24 At Portsmouth.

25 Went up to Town with Murphy. Attended the "Hebburn Salvage" Arbitration before Mr, J. Butler Aspinal, 2 Paper Buildings Temple. Botterell & Roche are our solicitors. I think our salvage claim will stand and we should get something, but will not know for about two weeks. Returned to Portsmouth at 10 P.M.

26 Went to a dance at Branchmere Hall, Kent Road.

---

[76] North America and West Indies.

> **CANADIAN NAVAL SURPRISE.**
>
> **DRASTIC DEMOBILIZATION ORDER.**
>
> (FROM OUR OWN CORRESPONDENT.)
>
> OTTAWA, MARCH 22.
>
> Extreme surprise has been created by the news that Mr. Ballantyne, the Minister of Naval Service, has ordered the demobilization of the Canadian naval organization. The naval dockyards at Esquimalt and Halifax are to be dismantled, the Niobe and Rainbow to be sold, and all officers in charge of them to be disbanded.
>
> The reason for this apparently extraordinary order has so far not been disclosed, as Mr. Ballantyne is out of the city, and other Ministers refuse to talk, although the officials of the Department admit that the orders are correct. The action is considered strange in view of the recent report of Lord Jellicoe, even if the Government caucus had decided for the present not to proceed with any naval programme. The question will be brought up in the House of Commons, when an explanation is expected.

March 22, 1919

27 On board.

28

1st March Galatea reduced & went into reserve fleet. I reported at Barracks & was told to go on leave. Dined with Morris & Murphy. Stopped at Totts.

2nd Caught the 7:48 A.M. train, arrived Farnham about 10 A.M.

3 At Farnham.

15th Went to London. Met Gleed and Morris at Trocadero. Dined at Café Royal. Stopped at Adelphi.

March 25th Joined H.M.S. Calliope at Devonport. She commissioned today.

March 26th On board. Went to a dance at R.N.B.

27th Went into 4 watches which seems unnecessary as we are in the basin.

28 Our date of departure is April 10th Azores & Trinidad.

29th See all sorts of things in the paper re demobilizing Canadian Navy.

30

31

April 1st Went to Mount Gold with Edith Leckie & had tea there.

April 2nd Lunched with Grant in the Warwick.

3 At Devonport.

4 At Devonport.

5 At Devonport.

6 At Devonport.

7

8

9 Went out to Sound, carried out basin trials. Oil fuel pipes leaking.

10 In Sound. We should have sailed today but owing to repairs we will do trials on Monday. Went ashore.

11 Day on.

12 Went out for steam trials, blowing quite hard. Anchored at 3 P.M. Rec'd. mail. A Sub. Brass has been appointed here, vice myself. I don't know what they are doing. The skipper has signalled to C in C re appointment.

H.M.S. CALLIOPE

PLYMOUTH – AZORES & TRINIDAD

April 13 Waiting in the Sound until weather moderates. Heard nothing more about my appointment although my relief's app. to Calliope is in the papers.

14th Sailed at 6:30 A.M. for the Azores. Weather quite bad. Had to reduce speed in evening & everything battened down. One Co. S68½ W. Sea wind about W'S. Heaps of seasick people all over the place. My forenoon at first. Alleyne & I keep forenoon, afternoon, first & middle between us.

16th Weather improved at noon, went on to 16 knots.

17th At sea. Plymouth-Azores.

18th Sunday. Arrived Azores 10:30 A.M. & anchored. Fired salute. No leave.

19th Sailed at 4 P.M. for Trinidad – Co. S50W (True) 15 knots. Fine weather.

20th My middle & forenoon. Fine weather, put clocks back 15 min.

21st At Sea. 15 knots S50W. Noon pos. 30° 44' N, 35° 52' W.

22nd At Sea.

23rd Whites. Increased to 16 knots. Watching keeping & general drill. Nothing exciting doing.

25th Sighted Ragged Lt., Barbados in middle watch (26th).

26 Arrived at Port of Spain, Trinidad, B.W.I. at 4 P.M. Anchored about 2' off the town. Did not go ashore. Quite hot. The last time I was here was Aug. 1914 with the Good Hope & Bristol.

27 Weighed at 6 A.M. & proceeded to Point a Rene to oil. Trinidad Leaseholds Oil Company.

28th Went ashore with Pearce, Soldier, Sub. In evening went to Harlequins; revue at Prince's building in Governor's box. Dance afterwards which was a fine show. Heaps of girls. Unfortunately, had to get back on board at 1:30 A.M.

H.M.S. CALLIOPE 8TH LIGHT CRUISER SQUADRON
N. AMERICA & WEST INDIES

April 29th My day on.

April 30th Played tennis at Tranquility courts with P.M.O. & Major Waldegrave & Capt. Lannigan. Danced at St. Clair Club.

May 1st Played tennis at Government House with the Captain, P.M.O., Pearce, Dewhurst. Swim afterwards. Dined at Union Club & went to Harlequins afterwards. After the show we danced until 3 A.M. Met lots of people. Mr. Baker the American consul took us in his box at show.

2nd My day on. Mangot came on board to tea.

3rd

4th Played tennis & dined at Government House. Went to a dance given for Miss Turgueson by the Hutchinsons, 16 Queens Park West. It was an awfully good show & the organization was most excellent; danced until about 2:30 A.M. Got back to the ship at 3 A.M.

5th My day on.

6th Played tennis at St. Clair club with Barnes. Dined at Union Club with Dewhurst, Barnes & P.M.O. Miss Robinson & Pradda picked us up in the car at 9 P.M. Went to St. James Barracks where we joined the picnic party, 5 cars full. Went out to ??? about 12' from Port of Spain Had an awfully good time but unfortunately fell into the ditch & had to come back in wet clothes as we had a race around a pole which was sticking out on the water. Danced at the Waldegraves & finally got back to the ship at 3 A.M. An awfully good show.

7th Went ashore with Dewhurst in afternoon. Rec'd. a signal from C. in C. that my relief sails from England on the 12th May.

H.M.S. CALLIOPE 8TH LIGHT CRUISER SQUADRON
NORTH AMERICAN & WEST INDIES STATION

8th Day on.

9th Dewhurst, Barnes & myself landed at noon & went off to Manzanillo Bay in Major DePasse's car. Had a most excellent day. Driving back through some village we knocked a nigger over, took him to the hospital & he had a couple of stitches put in.

10th Proceeded to Cheramas Bay at 9 A.M. The Bay is about 10 miles from Port of Spain & is very pretty. Went swimming in P.M. Good fun, got quite number of fish. Lots of summer places here.

11th My day on & "Soldiers". Skipper had luncheon party to Robinson & Miss Turgueson. Rec'd. orders at noon to proceed to Jamaica. Sailed at 5 P.M. 14 knots. We shall probably go on to Mexico as the usual American/Mexican fuss is happening there. Left some washing ashore. Dewhurst is learning to keep Officer of the Day as Skipper thinks he goes ashore too much so he keeps a day on with me.

12th At Sea. Trinidad–Jamaica. 4 knots.

13th At Sea. Trinidad–Jamaica.

14th Arrived at Kingston, Jamaica at 1 P.M. Went alongside oiler.

15th Went ashore with Dewhurst. Called at St. Andrews Club & MacCrindles; then went on to Constant Spring Hotel where we dined. Saw the Miss Bonitoes.

16th **Sunday.** My day on. Lot of troubles between a P.O. & C.P.O. etc.

17th Went into 4 watches. My second day on.

18th Played tennis at MacCrindles. Went to a dance at the Johnson in the evening, "The Priory" Hope Road.

19 Went to call on the Governor but he was asleep so we put our names in the visitors book & shoved off. Had tea at Constant Spring Hotel & I dined at the MacCrindles. Went to a garrison dance which was an awfully good show.

H.M.S. CALLIOPE 8TH LIGHT CRUISER SQUADRON
NORTH AMERICAN & WEST INDIES STATION
AT KINGSTON JAMAICA

I am trying to find out when to expect my relief in Jamaica. He is due at Trinidad on the 27th but there is practically no communication between Trinidad & Jamaica. In fact, I should think an inter Island steamship line would pay very well.

20th Forenoon, 1st dog & first.

21st Afternoon etc.

22 Went to Constant Spring. Tea with Miss Bonito. Dined with the Soldier at the Jamaica Club.

23rd Played tennis at Colonel Pomeroy's WI.R South Park Camp. S.S. "Corilla" arrived.

24th Empire Day. May 2nd day one. Went to P.O. for stamps but no luck.

25th Went to a dance at the MacCrindles, a very good show. Barnes, Dewhurst & myself were the only representatives from the ship.

26th Raining hard all day so did not go ashore. This is the rainy season.

27th Went ashore in afternoon with Pearce and the soldier. Tea at Constant Spring. Six officers of W1.R. dined onboard.

28th Day on.

29th Saturday – Day on.

30th Went for a picnic in the Naval Agent's steamboat to a Cay outside Port Royal. Had an awfully good time & a good swim.

June 1st Tuesday. Day on Dined with the Captain. Col. & Mrs. Glasgow & Miss Bradford & Miss Burberry also dined with him.

June 2nd Waiting for the mail steamer to arrive before we push off. Went out to Constant Spring.

H.M.S. CALLIOPE

June 3rd King's birthday. Mail steamer arrived at noon. We sailed for Bermuda. Speed 15 knots. Did not get any mail from steamer. Fired royal salute at noon.

June 4th At Sea. Passed Cape Maysi (Cuba) 8 A.M. Crooked Isl. about 4 P.M.

June 5th At Sea. Thought we might have to tow the S.S. Holstein to Bermuda, as her tug is short of coal; but they are sending out another tug from Bermuda.

June 6th At Sea.

June 7th Arrived Bermuda 3 P.M. Went alongside Camber in the dockyard. Swim at the club. Received a letter from the Sec. Naval Depart. Ottawa to say that I have been appointed to the R.C.N. College at Esquimalt. H.M.S. Constance in dock.

June 8th Day on.

June 9th Day on. Raining hard.

June 10th Raining.

June 11th Swim.

June 12th Played tennis at Admiralty House. C. in C. Sir ----Napier. Barnes is going to the "Constance" and a mate is coming here.

13 At Bermuda.

14 At Bermuda.

15 At Bermuda.

16 At Bermuda.

17 My relief arrived from Trinidad. I embarked in Oiler "Cherryleaf" for passage to Halifax. Bottomley the Flag Lieut. of the Calcutta is also taking passage. Barnes & Dewhurst saw me off.

18th At Sea. Bermuda–Halifax.

19th Arrived Halifax 11:55 P.M.

20 Went ashore to dockyard & was met by Harry.

July 13th Left Halifax in the O.L.[77]

14 Arrived Montreal 9 A.M. Caught 10 A.M. rain for Toronto. Arrived Toronto 5:30 P.M. Saw the Annesley's. Left Toronto 11 P.M. by C.N.R.[78]

15

16 Arrived Winnipeg 6 P.M. Uncle Frank, Aunt Gertrude & Clara met me at station. Went to their house for dinner. Left Winnipeg 10:30 P.M.

17 Arrived Biggar 3 P.M. Aunt Clara & Doctor met me.

18 Met Clara at 1 P.M. train & went up to Edmonton with her. I arrived Edmonton 10:30 P.M. Arthur was at station. Left at midnight.

19 Went through the Rockies. A Very fine view. Mt. Robson.

20 Arrived Vancouver 9 A.M. Caught 10:30 boat to Victoria. Joined the R.N. College. Went to a dance at the Sayward's.

21st Played tennis at the Oliver's.

22nd Grant went on leave to Halifax.

26 Bought a Dodge Coupe 4 cyl, from Plimley's. $1400.00.

27th Tennis at Sayward's in afternoon. Took Robinson out to the Alder's where we danced in the evening. A very good show. Arrived back at 3 A.M.

28 Went out to the Haddon's in Saanich.

29 Watched the tennis.

30 Played tennis at the Peas. Bought Overland 4, $1485, run 22 miles.

31 Watched the tennis finals. Awfully good games in the singles. Near beat Milne. Grace & Edgar arrived from New Westminster & I saw them in the evening.

August 1st Took Grace & Edgar out for a drive in the forenoon & showed them the college, etc. Lunched at the Empress; they left at 2:15 P.M. Had dinner with Robinson.

Aug. 2nd Played tennis at Vict. with Miss Sayward & Miss Carey. Dance at Mrs. Luxton's (Rockland Avenue).

---

77 The Ocean, previously known as the Ocean Limited, is a passenger train operated by Via Rail in Canada between Montreal, Quebec and Halifax, Nova Scotia. It is the oldest continuously operated named passenger train in North America.
78 Canadian National Railway Company.

Aug. 3rd Played tennis at Vict. with 3 others. Went out to the Wolverton's.

4th Tennis in P.M. at College. Went out to McClure's in P.M.

5th Thursday. Played tennis. Dinner with Robinson and went to a dance at the Matthews. A very good show.

6th Went out to the Deans in the afternoon. Was going to a dance at the Montizambert's but had engine trouble. The Wood brothers arrived from Duncan.

7th Tennis at the Wolfenden's. Dinner at Robinsons.

8th Called on Hartley's.

9th Played tennis at Victoria courts.

10th Tuesday. Wilson & his W. came in to tennis.

11 Was Officer of Guard and had to call on American destroyer which arrived with Admiral Rodman. Tennis at the Scott's in afternoon.

ROYAL NAVAL COLLEGE ESQUIMALT, BC

12th Thursday. Tennis at Wolfenden's. Dinner at Haywards.

13th Friday Played tennis.

14th Bill Higgs & I left Victoria for South Pender Island at 8 A.M. where we arrived 10:30 A.M. went to the Higgs' house. Awfully beautiful spot, with wonderful flowers & fruit.

15th Went for a picnic in motor boat to North Pender Isl. & at 6 P.M. left for Sidney where we arrived at 8:30. Caught the motor bus back to Esquimalt.

16 Monday. Went out to the Jones at Metchosin.

17 Tues. Played tennis with Grant.

18 Wed. Called on Pemberton's at Finnerty. Tennis at Pooley's. Danced at Mrs. Crofts. Took Naden round to Victoria Machinery Depot in forenoon.

19 Thurs. Played tennis. Steamed Naden round to Esquimalt in forenoon.

20th Fri. Went out to Sidney in afternoon. Nix. took me up to the top of the Malahat in the forenoon, awfully pretty drive.

21 Sat. Tennis at Mrs. Crofts. Had very good games.

22nd Sunday. Went out to the Pemberton's at Finnerty Bay. Played tennis.

23rd Monday. Had some people to tennis in P.M. Terry & Mrs. Maxwell, Carmichael, Shellback, etc. Hon. C.W. Ballantyne inspected the college in the forenoon. He stayed two hours; it is the first time that he has been over the place and seemed very surprised to find that it was so well equipped. The Aurora is the new cruiser for Canada. She leaves England in October. The Canadian Navy is going to be wet.

24th Tuesday. Tennis at Carmichaels, Oak Bay. Dinner at the Maunsell's.

25th Played tennis at College courts. Dinner at the Matson's and Vivien, Jack M. & myself went on the McCallum's—a dance, rather a dud show.

ROYAL NAVAL COLLEGE ESQUIMALT. B.C.

Aug. 26th Gen. & Mrs. Maunsell, Winn & Terry & myself went out to Deep Cove. A lovely spot about 20 miles from Victoria; fished all afternoon but didn't catch any salmon.

Aug. 27th Rained all morning. Dance at Matson's.

Aug. 28th Sat. Played tennis & danced at college. Mr. & Mrs. Morton, Cicely,[79] Dave. Went to Criterion in the evening with Terry & Win.

29 Sun. Lunched at the Maunsell's. Took Robbie out to Metchosin. Supper with the Jones.

30th Monday.

31st Tuesday. Cicely, Tommy Scott & Wilson played tennis here. Went to the dentist in forenoon. Dr. Tanner.

September 1st Wednesday. Went out to Metchosin.

2nd Grant arrived from Halifax. Played tennis at Sayward's.

3rd

4th Went to Salt Spring Island with Grant. Supper at the Bridgeman's.

5. Terry Maunsell and I left at 8 A.M. for Duncan. Arrived at Wood's house at 11 A.M. Awfully fine view of Malahat. Car ran very well. Rupert & Maurine Wood at home. Went out to their camp at Maple Bay on P.M. A lovely spot. Fishing in P.M.

Sept. 6th At "Lukammon" Maple Bay. Fishing, etc.

Sept. 7th At "Lukammon" Maple Bay.

Sept. 8th Left at 8 A.M. for Victoria, arrived about 11 A.M. Went out to Haddon's in the afternoon. Dined at Pemberton's in the evening, Trinity Bay. Got back to College at 3:30 A.M.

Sept. 9th Wood lunched with me. Went to Criterion in evening with Terry & Mrs. Wood & Miss S, Cicely & myself. Very amusing show as we brought a bottle with us.

Sept. 10th The Cadets returned from leave. Raining all day. Went to the Nimeses in evening.

Sept. 11 Day on.

Sept. 12 Church, in forenoon. Lunch at the Maunsell's. Went down to the boat to meet Uncle Frank but he didn't arrive.

---

79 This is Cecily Simonds. She worked as a stenographer and lived at the Alexandra Club. She married Herbert Turner Matson in Vancouver on August 7, 1922.

ROYAL NAVAL COLLEGE ESQUIMALT, B.C.

Sept. 13th Monday. Raining. Dined with Uncle Frank & Aunt Gertrude, Mr. & Mrs. Wilson, Mr. Rowley at the Empress.

Sept. 14th Raining. Took cadets out in the cutters.

Sept 15th Picnic at Metchosin. Grant & I had tea at the Jones—Dentist—in forenoon.

Sept. 16th Tennis on hard courts, raining in forenoon.

Sept. 17th

Sept. 18th Grant took the Naden out with some of the cadets. Tennis and blue boats in P.M.

Sept. 19th Sunday. The Maunsell's came to the college for tea. Supper at the Nixon's. I towed his car as it wouldn't start.

Sept. 20th Started the tennis tournament on the hard court.

Sept. 21st Played our first game of rugby on canteen ground. We play the Wanderers on Saturday.

Sept. 22 Wed. Rugby. Dance at Streatfield.

Sept. 23 Thurs. Rugby.

Sept. 24 Fri. Rugby. Dance at the barracks Work Point 9–2 A.M.

Sept. 25 Saturday. Played the Wanderers at rugby. Very good game indeed. We were beaten 15-13. I played back. Crandell was hurt at the end of the first half.

Sept. 26 Sunday. Church. I intended playing golf but it rained hard in the afternoon.

Sept. 27 Monday. Rugby. Dinner at the Wolfenden's. In the forenoon about 12 members of the opposition including McKenzie-King [Mackenzie King], Duff, etc. visited the college. A funny crowd of stiffs.

Sept. 28 Played rugby.

Sept. 29 Lunch at Robinson's. Took the cadets for a picnic in the cutters in P.M.

Sept. 30 Fine day.

ROYAL NAVAL COLLEGE OF CANADA ESQUIMALT, BC

October 1st 1920 Raining.

October 2nd Raining. Went to thé Dansant at Empress with Terry & Wife. Supper at Jefferson's.

October 3rd Sunday. Raining.

October 4th Raining. Went to funeral at Naval Cemetery. Rugby, hurt knee.

October 5th Rain, rugger.

October 6th Dance at Alexander Hall. I took Cicely.

October 7th Dinner at the Maunsell's.

October 8th Played golf at Esquimalt Links with the Maunsell's. Went to Matson's in the evening.

October 9th Went out in the "Naden" with cadets. Anchored at William Head. Dinner with the Jones'.

October 10th Drifted about off William Head as there was no wind. Returned to the college 6:30 P.M.

October 11 Monday. Raining. Rugby.

October 12 Played golf at Esquimalt Links with Cicely. Good game. Went to Pemberton's in evening. Rugby.

October 13 Day on. Rugby.

October 14th Thurs.

October 15 Fri. Dinner at Mattson's. Went to a dance at the Matthews'.

October 16 Sat. Took Vivien & Cicely to rugger match Oak Bay. Rain.

October 17 Sun. Cicely, Vivien, Tim & myself played golf at Colwood. Very good time. Supper at the Matson's.

October 18 Thanksgiving Day. Played golf at Esquimalt with Tim. Matson in afternoon. Went to movie in evening. "Naden" returned from Salt Spring Island.

October 19 Took the car into Plimley. Rugger in P.M. Day on.

October 20 Brought car back. Rugger.

October 21 Raining. Played rugger.

October 22 Raining. Our 2nd team played the Victoria High School and beat them 3-0.

23rd Day on.

24th Sun.

25th Started winter routine.

26th Rugger.

27th Played Victoria High School—the college won 6-0.

28th Thurs. Rugger. Dined at Robinson's and went to a concert given by Yarrows.

29th Rugger. Rec'd. prize money. £37 10.

30th Sat. Day on.

31st Church. Bad cold. Tea and Maunsell's. Supper at Robinson's.

NOVEMBER

1st Mon. Cold. V.B.

2nd Tues. Muriel Galt & I myself motored to Shawnigan Lake in Overland. Arrived there at 1 P.M. Had lunch at the Mones. Got back at 6 P.M. raining in P.M. Our second team played V.H.S. 2nd I won 6-0. Taylor had his rib broken.

3rd

5

6

7

8 Played rugger, sprained my foot. Skating club opened today. I can't skate.

9 Went to Sick Quarters.

10 Still at Sick Quarters but watched the match against University Military School we won 3-0.

11 Commander Nixon left for Ottawa at 2:15 P.M. to attend conference.

12 **Friday.** In bed all day.

13 **Sat.** Grant broke his shoulder blade playing rugger.

14 **Sun.** Wolfenden was found in the harbour at 8:25 A.M. Just rescued in time. We think it is a case of attempted suicide. Returned to College in P.M. Drove Mrs. Nixon & Mones to the Haddan's.

END OF JOURNAL TWO

Postcard from the Constant Spring Hotel, Kingston, Jamaica

JOURNAL THREE

December 21, 1920 – November 25, 1925

DAILY JOURNAL
1921

Lieut. J.C.I. Edwards R.C.N.
Royal Naval College
Esquimalt
B.C.

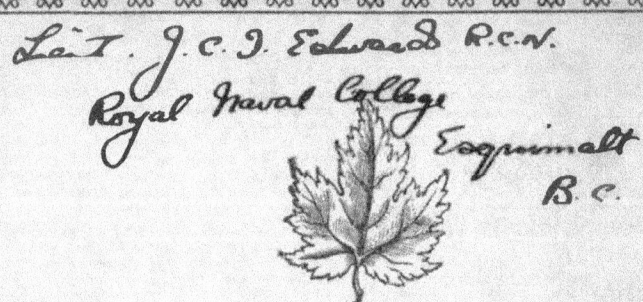

DAILY

JOURNAL

FOR

1921

TORONTO:
PUBLISHED BY
THE BROWN BROTHERS, LIMITED
MANUFACTURING STATIONERS
Cor. Simcoe, Pearl and Adelaide Sts.

JOURNAL THREE
December 21, 1920 – November 25, 1925

In which Dutchy Edwards continues at the Royal Naval College in Esquimalt as an instructor, travels across Canada via train when the College is closed, almost quits the Royal Canadian Navy, meets his future wife, takes a Physical and Recreational Training (P. & R.T.) course at Portsmouth England, returns to Halifax as Commanding Officer of HCMS Festubert, and patrols the east coast of North America.

Dec. 21st 1920 Cadet dance – very good show.

Dec. 22 1920 Cadets went on leave.

Dec 23 1920

Dec 24 1920 Played golf with Grant and Monty B. Dinner at B's. Went to a dance at Pemberton's. Returned 3 A.M.

Dec. 25 Church in early morning. Called on Commander with Grant. Called on Commander Holme & Robinsons. Saw hockey match in afternoon. Seattle vs. Victoria. Dinner at the Boak's—very good time.

26 Went to (Grace's) New Westminster where I arrived 8 P.M.

27 At New Westminster.

28 Dinner at Gillies, Vancouver. Bertie & J. Leckie there.

29 Arrived Victoria 7 A.M. Lunch with Dr. Orchard at Empress. Dance at R.N.C. in evening. Very good indeed.

30.

31 Dinner in Naden & Dance at Yacht club. V.G. I. Got back at 4:30 A.M. Haddon & Mrs. Boak and Mrs. Miss Haddon, Misses G & J Bridgman. Monty B., Cicely.

Jan 7th Rugger practice. Saw hockey match in P.M. Seattle vs. Victoria. Victoria won 2-0. V.G. Game. Fredrickson is wonderful player. Dinner with Robbie & Bun Hobday.

Jan 8th SAT. Raining. We were going to play Old Boys team in rugger, but cancelled the match.

Jan. 9th Very fine day & cold. Went for a walk in P.M. Tea at the Maunsell's. Went to Matson's in the evening.

Jan 10th Walk.

Jan. 11th Walk. Landed opposite college. Went to hockey meeting. Victoria Lawn Tennis Dance at Alexandra Club 9-2. V.G.1.

Jan. 12 Wed.

Jan. 13 Practiced with Garrison. I played badly.

Jan. 14 Officers played Cadets.

Ryall	Goal	Hatcher
DeWolf	R.D.	Allan
Kingsmill	L.D.	Edwards
Mitchell	Rover	Penny
Bearment	Centre	Richardson
Porteous	Centre	Grant
Knowlton	Wing	Robinson
Lay	Utility	Napier Henry

The cadets won 6-0. Quite a good game. I must remember to shoot more & get control of puck.

Jan. 15th Sat. Day on.

Jan. 16th Sun. Went for a walk in P.M. Tea at Dean's. Snowing quite hard all day.

Jan. 17th Skating club. Hockey meeting.

Jan. 18th Hockey practice from 2-3 P.M. Went to a hockey match Colonist vs. Old Boys. Quite amusing.

Jan. 19 Spent the forenoon in taking the engine of Chalmers down; found a broken wrist pin. It has made a groove in one cylinder. Rugby 2-3. Hockey practice with the garrison from 7:15-8:15. Very good one.

Jan. 20th Thurs. Rugby practice.

Jan. 21 Fri. Cadets had team at the Arena.

22 Sat. Lunch at Matson's. Saw the rugby match Vancouver vs. Victoria; the latter won 6-3. Went to a thé Dansant at the Innes's.

23 Sun. Tim, Vivian, Cicely & I played golf at Colwood. Supper at the Matson's.

24 Took the engine out of the Chalmers. New piston etc. $5.50. Played rugger – very fine day.

18th Hockey practice.

Roper	Ryall
Burpee	Kingsmill
Lt. Edwards	DeWolf
Mitchell	Jay
Beament	Loosemore
Porteous Curry	Cundill Knowlton

21st Hockey practice

    Parker   Holman
    Adams   Hope
    Price
    MacDonald
    J.B. Kid[ston]   Roberts   J.R. Kid[ston]   Pullen Monis

January 25th Played rugby.

January 26th Played Victoria High School in rugby & we won 17-3. A very good game. Bought my 1921 Motor license & registration $30.40. Quite a mild day.

January 27th Played rugger. Dinner at the Matson's. Skated at arena.

Jan. 28th Fri. Off. vs Cadets.

Richardson	Goal	Ryall	
Allin	Def	Ketchum	Ref. Tim Matson
Robinson	Def	DeWolf	
Penny	Rover	Mitchell	
Edwards	Centre	Beaument	
Grant	Wing	Porteous	
Henry	Wing	Knowlton	

The Officers won 7-6, quite a good game. I scored 5 goals. Saw hockey match in evening, Seattle vs. Victoria. Victoria won 5-3. Good game. Dinner with Bun Hobday.

Jan. 29th Sat. Day on.

Jan. 30th Played golf at Colwood with Vivian & Cicely. Raining in P.M. Supper at the Bridgman's.

Jan. 31st Skating club. Rugby.

Feb. 1st Tuesday. Day on.

Feb. 2nd R.N.C. played U.M.S. Jr. at Mount Tolmie; we won 3-0. Dinner at the Matson's. Watched a hockey match at the Arena.

3rd

4th Dinner at Robbie's. Hockey match in evening, Vancouver vs. Victoria. Van won 4-3, good game.

5th Took Cicely to thé Dansant at the Streatfield's. Hockey practice at Garrison at 7:15 P.M. Freidrickson coached. Went to Robbie's in P.M.

Feb. 6th Sunday. Day on.

Feb. 7th Rugby in P.M. Skating club. Dinner at the Pemberton's.

Feb. 8th Went to the opening of Parliament by Lieut. Governor Nicol. Dinner at McCallum's. Took B.M. Pemb. to dance at Empress.

9th Wed.

10th Thurs. Rugby. Hockey practice with Garrison.

11th Fri. Dinner at Commander Noble's. John Grant & Marty B. saw hockey match Victoria v. Seattle, Victoria won 3-1. hockey practice.

12 Sat. Day on. Played tennis with Tim Matson.

13 Sun. Played golf at Colwood. Cicely, Vivian, Tommy Tomalin played in forenoon and P.M. Supper at Matson's.

14th Monday.

15th Tues. Lieut. Governor & Admiral Pears inspected College at 11 A.M. Cadets a half holiday. At Sick Quarters in P.M. with cut leg.

Feb. 16th Went to Sick Quarters in P.M. Returned after dinner.

STARTED SUMMER ROUTINE.

Feb. 17th Thurs. At Sick Quarters A.M.

Feb. 18th Dinner at Bridgman's. Went to hockey match with Monty. Vancouver vs. Victoria; very good game, Vancouver won 2-0.

Feb. 19th Day on. Raining.

Feb. 20th Lunched at Maunsell's. Tea fight in P.M. at College. Supper at Matson's.

Feb. 22nd Monday. Day on. Took Chalmers engine down again. Pistons are worn.

Feb. 22 –

Feb. 23

Feb. 24 Supper at Robbie's.

Feb. 25 Friday. Junior rugby match against O.B.H.S.[80] We won 12-0, quite a good game.

Our 2nd XV
J.B. Kidston

Dalton	Mitchell	Brock	Holman
Merry	J.R. Kidston		
MacDonald	Taylor II	Woolcombe	
Curry	Kelly		
Packer	Roper		

March 9th The "Aurora", "Patriot" & "Patrician" arrived at 2:30 P.M. I boarded Patriot. Beard (Patriot), Jones (Patrician), Agnew, Grant & Barnes dined at the College. Captain Hose arrived from Ottawa.

March 10th Thursday. Rugger practice, 5-6. Played hockey in evening 6:25-7:15. United Press vs. Sprott Shaw. We won 4-3. Hurt my shoulder playing rugger. Barnes & I went to the Bridgman's in evening.

---

80 Oak Bay High School.

March 11th "Aurora", "Patriot" & "Patrician" sailed at 10 A.M. for Vancouver. Saw the hockey match in evening Vancouver vs. Victoria; Victoria won 11-8. Dinner at the Matson's. Captain Hose is going to inspect the college sometime but don't know when. There is a buzz that Lindsay is coming here vice, Grant—I don't go much on the change.

March 12th Tea at Muriel Galt's.

March 13th Sunday. Played golf in afternoon with Tim, Vivian, & Cicely. Heard that Lindsay has been appointed to College. The Commander & I are going to see Captain Hose about it.

March 14th Monday –

March 15th Tuesday. Captain Hose, Director of Naval Service, inspected the college at 10:30 A.M. -12:00. He seemed very pleased with what he saw. I saw him about staying at the College for another year. Said I wanted to specialize as I considered it a dud job if I am kept on for two years here not as 1st Lieut. He said that the college job was a picked one and that I should finish my two years here and then specialize. The Commander want me to stay on for another year. He has asked for Beech to come here. John Grant is leaving at the end of the term, & will leave the R.C.N. altogether. He will be a great loss to the service.

March 16th 1921 Wed.

March 17

March 18 Went ashore with Grant & Moffat.

March 19 Played the "Aurora", "Patriot" & "Patrician" in rugby & beat them 19-0.

Our team R.N.C.
Lt. Edwards

DeWolf	Porteous	Ryall	Ketchum
Lt. Grant	Knowlton		
Loosemore	Kingsmill	Cunhill	
Lay	Burpee		
Adams	McKinch	Jeckell	

March 20th Played golf at Colwood with Harold Grant, Vivian & Cicely, good game. Supper at the Matson's.

March 21st Dance at Government House 9-4. Very good show. John & I both went.

March 22nd

March 23

March 24 Proceeded to Fulford in the Naden with twelve cadets for their Easter leave. Fair wind & left Esquimalt at noon & anchored Fulford 5 P.M.

March 25th Good Friday. Stern gland leaking so could not use the engines. Sailed to Cowichan Bay and anchored there.

March 26th At Cowichan. Walked to Duncan in the evening.

March 27th

Easter Sunday Walked to Quamichan church with the cadets. 6½ miles. Left Naden at 9:45 and returned at 3:30 P.M.

March 28th Sailed to Fulford.

March 29th Returned to Esquimalt under sail. Navy league dance at the Empress. Jack B., Vivian, Cicely, John, Harold & I had dinner at the Oak Bay Hotel first.

March 30th

March 31st

April 1

April 2nd Played tennis.

April 3rd Played golf with Cicely. Tea & supper at the Inneses.

April 4th Traded in the Chalmers & got a Chev.

Dance at the Boaks. Very good party.

April 5th

April 6th

April 7th Harold Grant, Vivian & myself played golf at Colwood in the afternoon.

April 8th Dance at college for Officers of Squadron. Very good show.

April 9th Cicely & I went to the Haddon's for tea.

April 10th Sunday. My day on.

11th Started the boxing tournament. Played tennis.

12th Tuesday. Boxing tournament. Banquet. Gave cadets a lecture on gunnery in the evening. I went to a dance at the Sailor's Rest. All the girls from the Cabaret which was put on for Navy League were there.

13th Wednesday. Sailing in cutter in P.M.

14th The finals of the boxing tournament.

> J.R. Kidston – featherweight
> Holman – Lt.
> Porteous – midd
> Knowlton & Jackal did not box.

15th Friday. Signal exam.

16th Sat. Wake, Robbie & myself played tennis. Dinner at the Matson's. Jock Innes, Viv., Cicely, John M. & Wake & myself went to Pantages[81] & Criterion[82] afterwards.

Sun. 17th Day on.

Mon. 18th Proceeded in the "Naden" at 9 A.M. Anchored at Ganges Harbour at 5 P.M. Went to the Scott's.

Tuesday 19th Weighed at 9 A.M. Passed to the Northwards of Salt Spring Island. Anchored at Chemainus.

Wed. 20th Securing ship. Weighed at 9 A.M. Sailing all day. Anchored at Maple Bay 5 P.M.

Thurs. 21st Weighed at 9 A.M. Passed down Sansum Narrows. Anchored Ganges at 1 P.M. Dinner at the Scott's.

Friday 22nd Weighed & proceeded at 9 A.M. Blowing very hard. Could not get through Trial Island so anchored at Cordova Bay.

Sat. 23rd Arrived Esquimalt 11 A.M. Played golf in P.M. with Cicely, Vivian, Wake.

APRIL 1921–MAY 1921

Sun. 24th Day on.

Mon. 25th Went for a picnic at Shawnigan Lake, 6 car loads. Distance 35 miles. Played baseball. Returned at 6 P.M. No functions. Did the 35 miles back in 1 hours & 30 minutes.

Tuesday 26 "Naden" shoved off at 8 A.M. Sailing in the afternoon.

Wednesday 27 Landed at Metchosin Beach in afternoon with the cadets. Tea at the Jones'.

Thursday 28 Sailing.

Friday 29 "Naden" returned. Went to "Arts & Crafts" dance at Alexandra Club.

Saturday 30th Cadets had a cross country run. Porteous 1st.

Sunday May 1st Day on. Played tennis.

Mon. May 2nd Proceeded at 9 A.M. in "Naden" with 7 cadets. Heavy swell off Trial Island. Anchored at Fulford Harbour 8 P.M.

May 3rd Proceeded through Sansum Narrows. Anchored off Crofton. Allan & I went ashore for a walk.

Cadets in Naden May 2-6.

Hope	Parker
J.B. Kidston	Loosemore

---

81 The Pantages was a movie theatre located at 1609 Government Street, Victoria.
82 The Criterion was a cabaret located in the Belmont House at 805 Government Street, Victoria.

J.R Kidston
Roper
Roberts

May 4th Proceeded to Thetis Island, anchored in Preedy harbour. Went for a walk.

May 5th Proceeded to Bedwell Harbour, Pender Isl. Very fine day.

May 6th Proceeded to Esquimalt. Heavy wind and tide off Discovery Island. 3 hours making good 1 mile. Very heavy sea. Arrived Esquimalt 8:45 P.M.

May 7th Day on. Played tennis on the grass courts.

May 8th Cadets in quarantine for chicken pox. Went out to the Matson's Farm[83] at Saanich. Tea at Col. Grant's. Out in boat with V. & Hugh, got wet.

May 9th John Grant proceeded in the "Naden" at 9 A.M.

May 10th Tuesday. Surprise party at the Streatfield's. Danced.

May 11th Cadets sailing race in the afternoon. Played tennis. "Naden" touched on a sandbank at Preedy Harbour, Thetis Island, but Grant got her off all right at High Water.

May 12th A class at rifle range, Clover Point,[84] 9 A.M. Played tennis in the afternoon. Aurora, Patriot & Patrician arrived. The Patriot went on the slip.

May 13th "Naden" returned. Tim dined with me. Went to Winter G. in evening, after spending some time in Aurora & Patrician.

May 14th Jumping competition for the cadets. Picnic in the afternoon.

May 15 Played tennis with Grant, Basanquet, Jones, Capt. Adams. Supper at the Gault's.

May 16 Proceeded in the "Naden" at 9 A.M. with C class cadets. Anchored at Ganges Harbour at 5 P.M. A fine day.

May 17th Proceeded to Vesuvius Bay, anchored at 4 P.M. Allin & I went fishing in St. Mary's Lake but did not catch anything.

May 18th Sailing off Sansum Narrows, proceeded to Cowichan Bay. Saw Capt. Arthur Lane.

May 19th Proceeded to Ganges & anchored at 4:30 P.M. Raining hard. Allin & I went fishing in Cusheon Lake but did not catch anything.

---

83 The Matson Farm was located at what is now 1805 Glamorgan Rd, North Saanich, BC. It was originally part of a 500-acre farm which was purchased by Richard John who named it for the county in Wales where he was born. In 1919, Glamorgan was purchased by Sam Matson, a Victoria businessman who developed an excellent dairy herd of Jersey cattle. The farm was restored and brought back to life by Anny Scoones who bought it in 2000. The farm is now run as a petting farm with an adoption option. Glamorgan is recognized as a national historic site in Canada.

84 A rifle range had been constructed about 1900 and was used extensively during World War I. The range was still used up until 1931 when the trenches were filled in.

May 20th Weighed & Proceeded at 6:15 for Esquimalt. C. very good at reefing (2m 45 s) one reef in all. Secured alongside at 5 P.M. Dance in the Aurora.

May 21st Day On. Long jump. DeWolf 19' 3½".

May 22nd Cicely, Viv. Harold Grant & myself went off to Aldermere. Good picnic, fishing. Supper at the Matson's.

May 23rd John Grant proceeded in the "Naden" at 9 A.M. with C2 class. Tennis in P.M.

May 24th Holiday. Small tennis tournament in the forenoon. I took the senior term up the Gorge in the motor boat in the afternoon to watch the regatta. Whaler races etc. between Aurora, Patriot & Patrician. Good war canoe races. Towed Aurora's motor boat back. Dinner in the Aurora.

May 25th Playing tennis. Tea party in Patrician. Vivian, Cicely, Jones & myself.

May 26th Dinner at Union Club. Surprise party at the Matson's. Danced until 2:00 A.M. I took Jones & Cicely.

May 27th Friday. Naden returned.

May 28th Cutter race. Cadets vs. Ex-Cadets. Cadets won by about 5 lengths.

Our crew: Mancy, Pressy, Moffat, Jones, Edwards, Godfrey, Grant, Hibbard, Grant, Wurtele, Cox. Hart. Played tennis in P.M.

May 29th Cicely, Vivian Tm, G.C. Jones & myself went for a picnic at "Aldermere". Good swim. Went to Matson's in the evening.

May 30th Cutter competition in P.M. Started the cadets singles tournament.

May 31st Cutter competition. Tennis tournament. Played tennis at Victoria Lawn Tennis Club. Supper at the Matson's.

June 1st Cutter competition. Cundills won by 1 sec. from Knowlton. Tennis Tournament, Ryall beat Knowlton.

June 2nd Peter Grant had a tea party in the Aurora. Vivian, Cicely, & Gwen Bridgman. Dinner with Harold.

June 3rd The Aurora & Patrician sailed on return journey to Halifax. Took the cadets to Shawnigan on a picnic. 7 cars. Played baseball & had a very good swim. Returned 7 P.M.

June 4th Saturday. Tennis.

June 5th Sun. Went to Memorial service at the Cathedral in the afternoon.

June 6th Raining. Went to Matson's in evening.

June 7th Patriot sailed in early A.M. Tennis.

June 8th Tennis finals. Singles, Ryall won. Dinner at the Matson's.

June 9th Played tennis with Cicely in forenoon. Finals of the doubles in P.M. Ryall & Cundill won.

Passing out term
  Knowlton
  Beament
  DeWolf
  Cundill
  Burpee
  Porteous
  Ryall
  Ketchum
  Winfield
  Lay
  Kingsmill

June 10th Fri. Raining. Dinner at Matson's. Dance at Streatfield's.

June 11th Tennis.

June 12th Sunday. Day on.

June 13th Monday.

June 14th Tues. Tennis. Dinner at Commander Nixon's.

June 15th Wednesday. Tennis. Grant & I played Ryall & Cundill in the finals of the handicap doubles. We lost. Dance for the senior term passing out 9-1. Very good show.

June 16th Thursday. Cadets left on 3:15 boat for their homes. Played tennis with Tim. Dinner at the Matson's.

June 17th Grant & Commander went up the Island. Vivian, Cicely, Tim played tennis here. Supper at College.

June 18th Lunch at Md [?]. Cicely & I went out to the courts to play our tennis tournament off but in the end did not play. Dinner at the Matson's.

June 19th Went out to Sooke with Mrs. Tomalin, Tommy, Vivian & Cicely. Lunch at Sooke Hotel. Played tennis in the wooden court. O.K. Returned 9 P.M.

June 20th Rain. Could not play off tennis tournament. Dinner at the Maunsell's.

June 21st Tournament at Victoria Lawn Tennis Club. I beat Hewnel 6-1, 6-1. Cicely & I beat Mr. & Mrs. Vickery 6-4, 7-5.

June 22nd T. Matson & myself were beaten by Leeming & Idiens 6-4, 7-5.

June 23rd Cicely & I were beaten by Miss Hodgins & brother 6-4, 7-5.

June 24

June 25 Henry's wedding in P.M. Played Beatty in tennis tournament & won 6-2, 6-0. Took C. to Saanich. Dinner at the Haddon's.

June 26th Played tennis at the college. Went out the Ineses in the evening.

June 28th Played Jack Matson at 5:15 P.M. and won 6-1, 6-4. Went to Dance in the evening.

June 29th

June 30

July 1st Went to Cowichan by Island Princess. Joined the "Naden" there. Regatta. Naden's propeller loose. Lieu. Governor off for lunch. Rained.

2nd Went down to the Haddon's by motor boat. Played Vickery in the finals of the singles handicap and beat him 6-2, 6-3, 6-4.

3rd Took Mr. Kelly up to Cowichan in my car with tools etc. Secured Naden alongside wharf & put new nut on. Naden proceeded at 3 A.M. next morning for Victoria.

4th

5

6

7

8. Shaw Ross & I caught the late boat for Vancouver.

9. Went out to New Westminster. Caught 5:30 train for Agassiz. Arrived at 9:30 P.M. Camped.

10. Bad cold. Woke up at 5 A.M.

11 At Agassiz. Mosquitoes bad.

12 Did a 10 mile walk with 60 lb. pack. Very hot and the mosquitoes hellish. Caught evening train back to Vancouver where we arrived at 11:15 P.M. Slept on Veranda at the Gillies'.

Tennis by E. Gordon Lowe

Rules for good strokes

Keep the eye on the ball as long as possible before impact.

Let your follow-through be unchecked, finishing with your racket pointing to where your racket has been directed.

Do not swing the racket far back before striking.

Hit the ball at the top of the bound or before.

Keep the head of the racket above the wrist or, at any rate, never much below it.

Remember that it is not strength but perfect timing body swing, & follow through that produces pace.

FOOTWORK

Unless the feet take the body into the correct position to strike the ball, it is impossible to bring your stroke into execution, no matter how good it is.

JULY

13th Tennis at Jericho club with Miss Roberts & Armour. Dined at Jericho.

14th Lunch with Jack Leckie at Club. Tennis at Jericho.

15th

16th Tennis at the Hamilton's.

17th Went to New Westminster.

18th Mainland tennis tournament started. I played Carmichael at 10 A.M. & beat him 6-2, 6-3. Shawcross was beaten. We played a doubles match and were beaten 7-5, 6-4. Some very good players including Marshall Allen, Ingraham, Beltons, etc.

19 Played Maw & was beaten 6-4, 6-1.

20 Rain. Tennis dance.

21 Miss Roberts & I played Flake & Miss Bloomfield and were beaten 4-6, 6-2, 6-3.

22nd Caught morning boat to Victoria.

23rd Tennis.

24th Tennis. Tea at Wolfenden's.

25th B.C. Tennis championship started at The Willows. I was down to play Hill from N. Vancouver at 6 P.M. but did not play.

26th Mr. Ryall & I played Bettens & Suhr & were beaten 3-6, 6-3, 6-4. Good game, Miss Barton & I beat Lee & Miss Teague 6-2, 6-2. Beech arrived from Salt Spring Island.

July 27th Wed. Miss Barton & I beat Dixon (Vanc.) & Miss Teague 6-2, 8-6. Flye beat me 6-2, 6-2. A Good game. He is in the Pac. N.W. doubles & is very good. Saw some V.G. Tennis. Marshall Allen beat Verlequin P.N.W. finals & Allen & Taylor beat Scott & Flye. Grant went on leave.

28 Played H. Jones of Vancouver & beat him 6-2, 6-2. Miss Barton & I beat Miss McNeil & McDonnel. Tennis club dance. Dinner at Nairn Robertson's.

29th Played Mr. & Mrs. Grant in mixed doubles, beaten 7-5, 6-3. Played Idiens at 4 & beat him. Played Ryall at 5 and beat him & had to play McDonnel straight after that. Was beaten 9-7, 6-3 (cross court, backhand drives, lobs, overhead work).

30th Sat. Lunch with the Commander. Watched tennis in P.M. Dinner at Robbie's.

31st Tennis in A.M. Lunch at Nairn Robertson's, sailing in afternoon.

Aug. 1st Tennis at the Wolfenden's.

2nd Tennis at the Wolfenden's. Dinner at Croft's.

3rd Working on car, battery dud.

4th Working on car.

5th Went to Shawnigan Lake with Commander.

6. Working on car and tennis.

August 7th Played tennis in morning. Lunch at Commander's. Went out to Haddon's. Excellent swim.

August 8th Went for a swim in P.M. Tennis at MacDonald's. Shawcross & I went out to the Ineses in the evening.

August 9th Tennis at the MacDonald's. Dinner Mrs. Crofts.

August 10th Played Cowichan at tennis. I played Stepney in the singles & won 6-4, 6-2. Idiens & I played Knox & Stepney in doubles & won 7-5, 6-3. Miss Pegg & I beat Stepney & Miss Wally 6-0, 6-2. Dinner at the Maunsell's.

11 Tennis. Went off to the Jones in the evening.

12 Ruth, Ticky & Tom Jones played tennis at the college. Dentist 11:30 Tuesday & 10:00 Wednesday.

13th Went out to the Haddon's in the afternoon.

14th At the Haddon's.

15th Returned to the College. Went out to the Matthews in the evening with Shawcross. Stayed the night.

16th Dentist in the morning. Beech arrived. Tennis in the afternoon.

17th Wed.

18th Thurs. Tennis.

19th Tennis in the afternoon. Dinner at the Matson's. Went to the Yacht club dance. Vivian, Jock, Jack Matson—good.

20th Went out to the tennis courts but it rained all day.

21st Working on the car. Played tennis in P.M. Unsettled weather.

August 22nd Raining. Took the Maunsell's in to Town. They are leaving for France. Made up a party & we went to the Movies.

23rd Raining.

24th Played tennis in the rain. Tea at the Carmichael's.

25th Fine day, tennis.

26th

27th Fine day. Lunch at the Matson's. Tennis.

28th Tennis. Jack Matson, Mill Wilson & myself went out to the Ineses in the evening.

29th Tennis at the Croft's. Dinner at the Matson's.

30th John Grant returned from Salt Spring Island. Went out to Inneses in evening.

31st Showers. Played tennis against Kingston Street Club. I won all my matches. Beech bought a Dodge.

September 1st Thurs. Raining.

2nd Tennis. Dinner at Matson's. Bridge in evening.

3rd Tennis. Dinner at Matson's. Left my car at Tait's to be sold.

4th Sunday. Cicely, Vivian, & I went up to Aldermere bridge in evening. Tea.

5th Tennis at Pemberton's. Surprise party at MacDonald's.

6th Went up to the Bridgman's at Salt Spring Island. Monty, John Grant & I left at 6 P.M. Arrived 9 P.M.

7th At the Bridgman's.

Sept. 8th At the Bridgman's.

Sept. 9th Left at 9 A.M. Returned to College. Cadets returned from leave.

Sept. 10th Cadet picnic in afternoon at Lagoon beach. There are 10 new cadets, 2 more are coming later.

11th Day on. Tennis. Matson's in evening.

12th Weight 165 pounds. Started another routine in morning. Tennis in afternoon. Fine weather.

13. Same routine. Put in my application to specialize in Navigation. New cadets this term: McLaren, Tisdall, Tam, Mitchell, Curtis, Wright, McAvity, Hemming, Spencer, Coyle.

14th Wednesday. Tennis & boats. Fine day.

15th John Grant left for Halifax. Went down to the boat to see him off. Went

Receipt for purchase of Gordon Setter puppy, September 16, 1921

out to the Jones' in the evening. Bought a Gordon Setter pup age 9 weeks. Tennis S. at R.

17th Beech went out in the "Naden". I took the remainder of the cadets for a picnic at Metchosin.

18th Rain. "Naden" returned in P.M. Day on.

19th Took the 1st XV to rugger practice at 7 A.M. Went to the Inneses in P.M. The Hudson Bay shop opened.[85]

Sept. 20th Raining. Gym in P.M.

Sept. 21st Took the junior team to Y.M.C.A. swimming bath. Went to races after. Lost.

Sept. 22nd Cadets played soccer.

Sept 23rd Officers played Cadets in soccer. Officers won 2-0.

Haddon				
Penny	McCallum			
Edwards	Krich	Robinson		
Hatcher	Styles	Alliston	Beech	Richardson

Cicely & I went to yacht club dance in the evening—a good show.

24th Went to the races at the exhibition. Big crowd. Lost.

25th Sunday. Day on. Raining.

26th Started rugger. We play the Wanderers on Saturday. Ground fairly soft.

27th Rugby practice.

28th Rugby practice. Wank's game. Bridge at the Matson's in the evening.

29th Rec'd. reply from Ottawa re specializing in Navigation. My name has been noted but at present time, full number of Officers have either qualified in Navigation or are now qualifying to fill anticipated requirements. A Dud Show.

Sept. 30th Rugby practice. Fine day. Bought Victory bond (1934). Clocks go back an hour at midnight. Ed. Stewart came over from New Westminster.

October 1st Fine day. Played the Wanderers in Rugby at 8 A.M. at Oak Bay. Ground very hard and has not been marked. Fast & good game although we had the better of the play & would have scored many more tries if the ground had been marked. Won 8-0. Went to a dance at Government House in evening.

Oct. 2nd Commander & I went out to Colwood to see Kirkwood the Australian trick player. Fine day & quite warm.

---

85 Victoria's new landmark at 1701 Douglas Street at Fisgard was designed by architects Burke, Horwood, and White. The construction was halted in 1914 due to the continuing economic depression and the labour shortage caused by the outbreak of World War I. The store was finally opened September 19, 1921, an occasion marked by day-long celebrations. Guests included the Lieutenant-Governor, Premier, CPR President, and other heads of major department stores.

Oct. 3rd Played soccer. Dinner at Tommy Tomalin's. Fine day.

Oct. 4th Fine day. Rugger. I did not play.

Oct. 5th Played tennis. Saw Commander Moues. He said that Kingscote & party had returned and Gold mine came up to more than expectation.

Oct. 6th Soccer. Ground is too hard for rugger. Went to take the M's in the evening.

October 7th Played soccer. Rugger practice in early morning. Fine day.

Oct. 8th Fine day. Day on.

Oct 9th Went on a picnic with the Inneses, Esquimalt Harbour.

Oct. 10th We are entering a rugby team in the senior league, as there are only three teams in it at present and they want a fourth. Rugby practice. Party at the MacDonald's for Jack Matson.

Oct. 11th Rugger work out. Dinner with party (Miss Wigley) at Angela— danced at the Alexandria Club afterwards. I took Vivian.

Oct. 12th Rugger work out. Ground too hard to play.

Oct. 13th Raining hard. Went for a run about 6'.

Oct. 14th Agnew arrived. Played a practice game of rugger. Creery came down to the college.

Oct. 15th Agnew & Tommy Monteith married at 2 P.M., St. Mary's Church, Oak Bay. Went to reception at the Gore's afterwards.

Oct. 16th Day on. Raining. Shawcross came to supper.

Oct 17th Rugger practice.

Oct. 18th Examined for civil service life insurance $5000.00. Rugby practice. Went to the Matson's in the evening. Jack left for England.

October 19th Rugger practice. Dinner at the Luxton's. Went to Jubilee Hospital Ball afterwards, Empress. Quite good dance.

October 20th Lunch at the Bridgman's. Fine day.

Oct. 21st Fine day. Rugger workout.

Oct. 22nd Fine day. Played our first match in the senior league against the University Old Boys. We were beaten 4-3. Quite a good game although the referee spoilt it for us. I scored the lone try. Nairn Robertson kicked a goal for them. Went to the Inneses in P.M. Took Jock to a show & "Criterion".

Oct. 23rd Went to the Davies in evening.

Oct. 24 Rugger practice. Took car in to be overhauled.

Oct. 25th Gym. Shawcross dined with me.

Oct 26th The Cadets senior team played Victoria High School at Cranmore

Road. Result—a draw. Our forwards played a very good game. Roberts had a rib broken. Played bridge at the Matson's in the evening.

Oct. 27th Raining. Gym.

Oct 28th Raining. Gym.

October 29th Played the Wanderers at University School grounds. Result—draw. Awfully good game & our team played a wonderful game. We had 75% of the game & in the last half were on their line the whole time although we could not score. Our passing was O.K. The Wanderers play an awfully nice game.

Cicely & I went to the Movies in the evening. J.B.A.A.[86] beat V.O.B. 14-0 at Oak Bay.

Oct. 30th Sunday. Day on. Played tennis.

Oct. 31st The Commander & I went to watch Oak Bay High School & V.M.S.—latter won 6-3. Dinner at the Matson's. Surprise party at Dennison's.

November 1st Rugby practice.

Nov. 2nd Rugby match 2nd XV vs. U.M.S. 2nd. Thick fog. could not see more than 30 yards. We won 6-0. Dance at Mrs. Burke-Boche. Tim M. & I went.

Nov. 3rd Rugby practice.

Nov 4th Cadets went on Week end Thanksgiving leave.

November 5th Ruth, Ticky, Jones & myself watched rugby at Oak Bay. Wanderers beat Old Boys 3-0. Tea at Aclands.

Nov. 6th Peter Bangs[87] & myself went out to the Haddon's in the morning. The Jones' came over from Metchosin in the afternoon.

Nov. 7th Thanksgiving Day. Returned to the college in the evening.

Nov. 8th Friday. Rugger practice.

Nov. 9th Wed. Our senior cadets team played the University School in rugger at Mt. Tolmie. Result a draw. Good game. One of the cadets hurt in first 5 minutes (Merry) so we were one short.

Nov. 10th Played golf with Beamy at Colwood in the forenoon Rugger practice in the P.M.

Nov. 11th Armistice Day. 2 minute silence at 11 A.M. Rugger practice. Union Club dance in the evening. Good show; dinner at the Carey's. Went with Miss Sayward & Cicely.

Nov. 12th Played the J.B.A.A. at Oak Bay & were beaten 31-0. They have a very fast team, especially their ¾s. We did not get the ball very often.

---

86 James Bay Athletic Association.
87 This is the name that he gave to his puppy.

Have been chosen to play outside ¾ on the Victoria Rep. team.

Nov. 13th Went to the Inneses in afternoon.

Nov. 14th Rugby practice. Saw Marie Lohr at Royal Victoria. Went with Ticky Jones & Mrs. Falls—Good show.

Nov. 15th Tues. Rugger & practice for Rep. team at J.B.A.A. Went to tennis club danced afterwards.

Nov. 16th Golf in morning. Rugger practice. Some of rep. team came down to the college.

Nov. 17th Thursday. Rugger practice in the afternoon. Work out at the J.B.A.A.

Nov. 18th I have a cold & sore knee. Went to Sick Quarters. Went to a dance at Alexandra in evening with the Haddon's & Ticky Jones. Left on the night boat for Vancouver with the Rep. team.

Nov. 19th Arrived Vancouver 7 AM. after a cold night in which no one slept very much. Went to Elaine Hotel, Pender Street. Lunch at the Gillies. Played Vancouver rep. team 3 P.M. Brockton Point. We were beaten 20-6. Ground hard. I scored a try. Vancouver's forwards were better than ours. One of our ¾ Heyland was hurt in the first half so we played one man short. Went to the Bell-Irving's in the evening to dinner. Left for Victoria on the night boat.

Nov. 20th Sunday. Arrived back at the college 9 A.M.

Nov. 21st Snowing all day. Went to a rugby meeting in the afternoon

Nov. 22nd Rain & snow. Gym. Bad cold. "Raleigh", "Calcutta", "Cambrian" & "Constantine" expected Dec. 14th.

Nov. 23rd Raining. Dinner at the Matson's. Gym.

Nov. 24th Went to S.Q.[88] in the morning. Boils.

Nov. 25th S.Q.'s

Nov. 26th Raining hard. Went into Town in morning. Played the Wanderers at Oak Bay in the rain; ground was in awful condition, lakes all over it. Was a forwards' game and just suited the Wanderers. They won 11-6. I got a try. Very cold & miserable.

Nov 27th Memorial service at the Cathedral in memory of University Old Boys. Lunch at Bridgman's. Supper at the Wolfenden's. Very cheesy party.

Nov. 28th Wedding at noon. I was best man. Miss Sherman & Burchett. Lunch at the Commander's afterwards. Skating club. Rain.

Nov. 29th Rain. Rugger practice.

Nov. 30th 2nd XV vs. O.B.H.S. 2nd and Cranmore Road. Won 6-0. I refereed. Dinner at the Matson's, went to the Inneses in the evening.

---

88 Sick Quarters.

December 1st Rugger practice in the rain.

Dec. 2nd Senior cadets played O.B.H.S. and won 24-0. The team played very well together. D. at M's.[89] Skating at Arena.

Dec. 3rd Sat. Took Cicely, Beamy & Jock to rugger match at Oak Bay. Wanderers vs. J.B.A.A. which was pretty rotten & was very dirty. Rugger meeting at Oak Bay Hotel for Rep. Team. I'm playing. D. at M's. Movie in the evening.

Dec. 4th Day on.

Dec. 5th Rugger practice. Skating club. Dinner at Robbie's.

Tues. 6th Hockey practice at the Arena. Rep. team rugger practice at J.B.A.A. in evening.

Wed. 7th Rugger practice. Watched Old Bays & Gyros play hockey with Cicely & Beamy. Show.

Dec. 8th Rep. rugger practice at J.B.A.A.

Dec. 9th Pro. hockey match Seattle v. Victoria. Tie—good game.

Dec. 10th Rep. rugby match. Vancouver v. Victoria. Victoria won 3-0. Pretty good game. I missed a kick at goal. Victoria forwards played a very good game but ¾ did not get the ball often.

Victoria team
Boss Johnson[90]

McInnes	Edwards	Heyland	Webster
Lumsden ⅝			
MacNaught	Anderson		
Brynjolfson	Sanson	Pendray	
McRae	Tolmie	Robinson	
Herman[91]			

Tea at Denniston's after the match.

Dec. 11th Went to Memorial service at Quamichan Church near Duncan. Left college at 8 A.M. in Beech's car. Had a breakdown & puncture. Arrived at 11:30. Lunch at Maitland-Dougall's. Arrived back at college 5:30 P.M.

Dec. 12th Dinner at the Matson's. Dance at the Nash's.

Dec. 13th Rugger practice. H.M.S. Raleigh Vice Admiral Sir William Packenham arrived & anchored.

Dec. 14th Rugger practice. Some of Raleigh's played. Dinner with Bearcroft in Raleigh.

---

89 Dinner at Matson's.
90 This is undoubtedly Byron Ingemar "Boss" Johnson (December 10, 1890–January 12, 1964) who served as the 24th Premier of British Columbia from 1947 to 1952. He was well known for his sporting prowess having played three seasons of professional lacrosse in Vancouver from 1913-1915.
91 Spelling of names confirmed by an article in *The Daily Colonist*, December 10, 1921, page 10.

Dec. 15th Played Officers of Raleigh in rugger and were beaten 16-4. Quite a good game. Navy League dance but I cannot go as I have day on.

Dec. 16th Dinner at the Matson's. Went to hockey match Vancouver vs. Victoria; Victoria won 4-3. Good game.

Dec. 17th Vice Admiral Sir William Packenham inspected the college at 10:30 A.M. and seemed well pleased with everything. Gave us a little speech at the end.

Mrs. Matson, Beamy & Tim left for California by the afternoon boat & Cicely & I went down to see them off.

18th Sunday. Tea at the Foreman's. Supper at the Haddon's. Very cold day.

19th Mon. Very cold. Skating club. Dance at the Pemberton's. I took Gwen & Cicely.

20th Tuesday.

21st Wed. Gave our dance, about 300 people. Good show.

22nd Cadets went on leave. Back on b???. Took Cicely to Hullo Canada. Good show.

23rd Went to hockey match Seattle vs. Victoria. The former won 3-2.

24th Party at the Pemberton's.

25th Christmas; church in morning. Christmas lunch in the Raleigh. Took Pay comm. Pellew & Reed out to the Jones'. Car broke down i.e. only firing on 2 cylinders.

26th The Commander took me out to the Jones' in morning & I brought my car back. Dinner at the Boak's. V.G.I. dance at Government House. Very good show. Packed up at 4 A.M.

27th Lunch with Cicely.

Dec. 28th

Dec. 29th Beech returned from leave. Dinner at the Inneses.

Dec. 30 Went out to Metchosin to stay overnight with the Jones'.

Dec. 31 Came into town for a rep. rugby practice. Beech & I gave a dinner in the "Naden". Mr. & Mrs. Haddon, Ruth Jones, Mrs. Henry & Bea, Cicely, Roddy Mathews, Shawcross, Beech & myself. Went on to dance at Armouries. Went out to Metchosin afterwards.

Jan. 1st Sunday.

Jan. 2nd Rep. rugby practice. Skating club. Calling, Beech had an auto crash. Went to Vancouver by night boat.

Jan. 3rd Lunch at Grace's. Dinner at Nora Bell-Irving's.

Jan. 4 At Grace's. Lunch at Magaret. Went to dance at Jericho with Ticky Jones. V. Good show.

Jan. 5 Dinner at Bell-Irving's. Caught night boat back to Victoria.

6th Went out to Metchosin. Cadets returned from leave.

Jan. 7th Victoria rep vs. U.B.C. U.BC. won 5-3. Fairly good game, although not very good for ¾s; forward's game.

Jan. 8th WT. 168. Day on.

Jan 9th Rugby practice. Skating club. Car license $28.80.

Jan. 10th Rugger practice. Fine day.

Jan. 11th Cadets played Victoria High School at Cranmore Road ground and won 11-0. V.G. game.

Jan. 12th Gym. Dinner at the Inneses.

Jan. 13th Rugger practice. Robbie & I watched the hockey match. Seattle v. Victoria; Victoria own 5-2.

Jan. 14th Played J.B.A.A. at Oak Bay—result a 3-3 draw. Good game, Cadets played very well. Mitchell scored our try on a good ¾ run. The result of the game was a surprise as in our last game with the Bays we were badly beaten. The Cadets played a very hard game.

Jan. 15th 1922 Sunday. Went to the B.'s[92] to tea.

Jan. 16th Rain & snow. Gym. Skating club.

Jan. 17th Officers played the Cadets at hockey. Officers won 6-5.

Jan. 18th Cold weather. No rugby. Supper at Robinson's. Took battery in to Weiler's. Gas 5 gall.[93]

Jan. 19th Basketball in the gym. Snow. Dinner at the Wolfenden's. Coasting.

Jan 20th Basketball in gym. Got my battery.

Jan. 21st Played the V.O.B. at Oak Bay. Ground very hard as frost was still in it, also very muddy. We won 29-0. The college played a very good game, the three-quarter work was very good.

  Our tries: MacDonald 1, Adams 1, Dalton 1, Dawson 1, Loosemore 1, Edwards 2, & a drop goal.

Jan. 22nd Supper at the Haddon's.

Jan. 23rd Ground too hard for rugger. Walk, skating club.

1922

Jan. 24th Basketball in gym.

Jan. 25th 2nd XV beat V.H.S. II at Cranmore Road 8-5.

Jan. 26th Rugger practice. Dinner and dance at the Jones'. Road very bad out to Metchosin.

---
92 Bridgman's.
93 Gallons.

Jan. 27th Went to hockey match, Victoria vs. Seattle which was pretty dud.

Jan. 28th About four inches of snow so could not play rugger against the Wanderers. Day on. Varsity won the McKechnie cup in Vancouver by beating the Vancouver Rep. team 10-3.

Jan. 29th Lunch at Matson's. Mrs. M, Cicely and I went out to Saanich. Cold day. Temp. 18°F. at night.

Jan 30th The Commander & I took cadets out to Colwood to skate; ice quite good. Skating club. Rep. team selected. I am playing ¾. 5 gall. of gas, tank empty.

Jan. 31st Walk. Rugby practice at J.B.A.A. for rep. team.

Feb. 1st Weather still cold. Cadets went skating at Colwood. Took Cicely to a fancy dress dance at the Alexandria club.

Feb. 2nd 1922 Cold. Basketball. Inspection by Brig-gen Ross.

Feb. 3rd The rep. team is not going to Vancouver tonight owing to the state of the grounds. Dinner at the Haddon's.

Feb. 4th The college played the Wanderers at Oak Bay & won 17-0. Ground very wet & ball heavy. We had much the better of the game though. Our ¾ played very well.

Feb. 5th Day on.

Feb. 6th Skating club. Bridge at the Inneses in P.M.

Feb. 7th Rugby work out. Dinner at Dr. McCallum's.

Feb. 8th 2nd XV beat V.M.S. 2nd XV at Mount Tolmie 3-0. Quite a good game.

Feb. 9th Rugby practice.

Feb. 10th Rugby work out.

Feb. 11th Played the J.B.A.A. at Oak Bay and we won 11-6 (2 tries & 1 goal). A great victory as we were not expected to win. Everyone played a very good game. We had much the better of the 1st half & score was 8-0 at half time.

Feb. 12th Went out to the Jones at Metchosin. Awful roads.

Feb. 13th Basketball. Skating club. (About 2" of snow).

Feb. 14th Tuesday. Hockey practice at the Arena.

Feb. 15th Refereed a game R.N.C. 2nd XV vs. O.B.H.S. 2nd XV. We won 5-3. Dinner at the Bridgman's.

Feb. 16th Rain. Rugby practice.

Feb. 17th Friday. Basketball. Rain.

Feb. 18th Played the Old Boys at Mt. Tolmie We won 11-0. Ground in an awful condition, regular quagmire in places. Pretty dud game. J.B.A.A. won Barnard cup by beating Wanderers. Robbie's in P.M.

Feb. 19th Sunday. Day on.

Feb. 20th Skating club.

Feb. 21st Rugger. Wanderers dance at Alexandria Club. Cicely, Miss Ware, Randell, Matthews.

Feb. 22nd Senior cadets team vs. U.M.S.[94] at Mt. Tolmie. We won 8-0. V.G. game. Our forwards played splendidly. MacDonald 2 tries, 1 convert J.R. Kidston. Many cadets in S.Q.'s.

Feb. 23rd Thursday. Many cadets in S.Q. with flu. Played hockey at Arena. Union Club vs. Civil Services. I played for the former. We won 4-3.

Feb. 24th Went sick with flu. About 30 cadets have it. Turned a dormitory into a ward.

25th Flu.

26th Flu.

27th Flu.

28th Flu.

March 1st

March 2nd

March 3rd Got up for an hour.

March 4th Up.

March 5th Cadets in Quarantine for Flu. Supper at the Boak's.

March 6th Took car in to garage to have gear repaired. Rain. Day on.

March 7th Fetched my car back. Went to Sick Quarters with a touch of pleurisy.

March 8th At S.Q.'s.

March 9th At S.Q.'s.

March 10th At S.Q.'s. Went to the Commander's House in the evening. Am staying the week end there.

March 11th At the Commander's.

March 12th Sunday. At the Commander's.

March 13th Returned to the college in the A.M. Rugby meeting.

March 14th Still on light duty. Rugger work out.

March 15th Cadets senior team played Oak Bay High School at Cranmore Road. We won 27-0. Dinner at the Ineses.

---

94 University Military School. The name was changed around 1924 to University School. This school merged with St. Michael's School in 1971 to form St. Michael's University School (SMU).

March 16th Dramatic club dance at the Alexandria Club. I took Ticky. V.G. show.

March 17th Played soccer. Dinner at Robbie's.

March 18th Watched the rugger match Vancouver intermediate vs. Victoria 2nd rep. team. We had seven from the College playing. The result was a draw. Dinner at the Matson's. Beamy & I went out to the Pemberton's afterwards.

March 19th 1923 Tea at the Bridgman's. Supper at Wolfenden's.

March 20th Rain. Started the group competition with a rugger match. Snowed hard in evening.

March 21st Robbie dined with me. Group rugger in afternoon.

March 22nd Rugger teams had their photos taken. Robbie & I went out to the Jones' (Metchosin).

March 23rd Thurs. Group rugger. Bridge at the Matson's in the evening.

24th

25th Left Victoria at 9 A.M. with the Wanderers to play rugby against Cowichan. Arrive 11 A.M. Played at 2:00. We won 18-0. Good game. Dinner at the Bevan's. Cheery party. In morning's paper that the Can. Naval estimates are going to be reduced by a million.

26th Left Duncan at 3:30 P.M. & arrived Esquimalt 5:30 P.M.

27th Group soccer. Dinner at the Matson's. Went to the Inneses in the evening.

28th Group soccer.

29th Group boxing. Very good bouts.

30th Group soccer. Went to the Bridgman's in the evening.

March 31st Group soccer. Dinner at the Matson's. Dance at the Pemberton's. The Comm. received a telegram from the Naval Dept. It is very possible that the college may be closed down. Gloom.

April 1st Played rugby for the Wanderers against Cowichan. Were beaten 4-3. Dance at Nairn Robertson's. Very good party. Dinner at Matson's.

April 2nd Sunday. Day on.

April 3rd Group soccer. Dinner at the George Galt's.

April 4th Dance at the MacCulloch's. Very good party.

April 5th Preliminary round of the boxing competition. 3 knock outs. Very fine day.

Took car into Tait & Mackie.

April 6th Tennis. Dinner at the Denniston's.

April 7th Rain. Boxing competition. Some V.G. scraps.

April 8th Played tennis at the club on the hard courts. V.G. games. Dinner at the M's. Took Beamy to supper dance at the Empress.

April 9th Day on.

April 10th Semi-finals and finals of the boxing competition.

> Loosemore
> Mitchell
> Price
> Groves

> Dinner at Robbie's.

APRIL 1922

11th Tennis on hard court. We haven't heard anything more re the college closing. Lots or rumours about it.

12th Wed. Cross country run. 1st Hodgins 16.37, 2nd Loosemore.

13th Cadets went on leave at noon. Ticky, Ruth Jones & Susi McCallum played tennis in dockyard.

14th Played tennis at club. Tea at Sue McCallum's. Naden returned to Esquimalt for the night owing to engine trouble.

15th Sat. Lunch at Nairn Robertson's. Tennis. Thé Dansant at the Empress. Dinner at the Galt's. Naden broke her propeller shaft & is at Deep Cove.

16th Sun. Went to the Jones' Metchosin.

17th Mon. Naden returned. Took Jocky B. to movies and Westholme.

18th Tues. Traded my Overland for a 1917 Chev. no. 11462. $200.00 cash. Went to a bridge and dance at the George Galt's. Beached the "Naden" alongside Jettys.

19th Rec'd. another memo from Ottawa saying it was very probable that the College would close, and giving instructions for disposal of officers & men. Tennis and Boats. Dance at the Pitts'.

20th Tennis. Day on. Hauled the Naden off at midnight.

APRIL 1922

April 21st Dinner at M's. Went to Movies in P.M.

April 22nd Lunch at M's. Group wrestling in the afternoon. Dog show in evening. Peter Bangs won blue ribbon in Gordon Setter puppies class.

April 23rd Tea & supper at the Haddon's.

April 24th Proceeded in the Naden at 9 A.M. Celars & Allison. Anchored Fulford Harbour 6 P.M. Good passage.

April 25th Engines failed to start, no wind. Played a soccer match against a team from Fulford—great fun. Warm day. Cadets went in swimming.

April 26th Proceeded at 9 A.M. Sailed and carried out evolutions. Anchored at Ganges Harbour. Dinner with Hotham.

April 27th Proceeded at 9 A.M. . . . Cowichan Bay & anchored at Fulford Harbour.

April 28th Proceeded at 5 A.M. so as to make Baynes Channel on ebb tide. Anchored William Head 3:45 P.M. Tennis at Dr. Nelson's.

April 29th Proceeded 9 A.M. Secured alongside Esquimalt 11:30. No news re college closing. Tennis with Nairn Robertson. Dinner with Robbie.

April 30th Picnic at Aldermere.

May 1st, 1922 Beech proceeded in the Naden at 9 A.M. Commander & I went out with her to swing ship. Muriel Galt down to see college. Rain.

May 2nd Tues. Tennis.

May 3rd V.G. cutter races in P.M. Rain in forenoon.

May 4th Thursday. Beamy & I went to matinée.

May 5th Fri. News in the paper that the whole Canadian Navy would probably be packed up, gratuities are under consideration. Dinner at the Commander's.

May 6th "Naden" returned. High jump in afternoon. Dinner at Robbie's. Went to Community dance with Beamy, Cicely & Tim.

May 7th Sunday. Command & I went to the Highland Lakes in eh Chev. Fishing.

May 8th Proceeded at 9 A.M. in the Naden with B2 Class. Dawson, Johnson, Pullen, Hodgins, Holman & Robbie. Anchored Fulford 5 P.M.

May 9th Proceeded to Chemainus. Fine weather.

10th Proceeded to Ganges. Fishing Blackburn Lake.

11th Proceeded to Fulford. Fishing Weston's Lake.

12th Proceeded to William Head. Tennis at Dr. Nelson's. Jones' in the evening.

13th Arrived Esquimalt 11:30 A.M. In the morning's paper, news about the closing up of the Canadian Navy & only keeping 233 officers & men. Laying up of Aurora, Patriot, Patrician & two submarines. Fed up. Tennis & went to the Matson's in the evening.

14th Sunday. Day on. Trench came down to play tennis.

15th Mon. Beech proceeded in the Naden at 9 A.M. with a1 class. Tennis & boats.

16th Tennis & boats. Naval questions up for debate in House of Commons. They now say they are going to keep Patriot & Patrician running. Dinner at the Galt's.

17th Tennis. No further news from Ottawa.

Exn. 18.

CLAIM BY AN OFFICER OF H.M. NAVY OR ROYAL INDIAN MARINE
FOR A
MASTER'S OR ENGINEER'S CERTIFICATE OF SERVICE.

77118

(A.) PARTICULARS, &c., OF APPLICANT.

Name in full		When Born		Where Born	
Christian Name	Surname	Date	Year	Town	County
John Crispo Inglis	Edwards	July 5th	1896	Londonderry	Nova Scotia Canada

PRESENT RESIDENCE

No. of House	Name of Street	Town	County
78	Seymour St	Halifax	Nova Scotia

(B.) PARTICULARS OF SERVICE.

SHIPS' NAMES (H.M. NAVY OR ROYAL INDIAN MARINE)	STATIONS	Capacity	Date of Service		REMARKS
			From	To	
R.N.C. College	Halifax	Naval Cadet			
H.M.S. Berwick	North America & West Indies	Midshipman	Feb 1914	Sept 1915	
H.M.S. Caesar	" "	"	Sept 1915	Jan 1916	
H.M.C.S. Canada	North Atlantic	"	Feb 1916	July 1916	
H.M.S. Berwick	N.A. & West Indies	Sub Lt	July 1916	Jan 1917	
H.M.S. Archer	Channel	Sub Lt & Lieut	Feb 1917	July 1918	lent to "Lychnis" as Navigator for two months
H.M.S. Cameleon	Med.	Lieut	July 1918	March 1919	
H.M.S. Galatea	Baltic	"	Sept 1919	March 1920	
H.M.S. Calliope	West Indies	"	March 1920	June 1920	
H.M.C.S. Naden for R.N.C. College	Pacific	"	July 1920	July 1922	

Application for Master's Certificate, 1922

18th Dentist in morning. Some good tennis with Beament.

19th Tennis & boats. Went to the Ineses in the evening.

20th In hand in pocket book $52.00.

21st Played tennis with Beament. Supper at the Galt's.

22nd Proceeded at 9 A.M. in the Naden with A2 class. Adams, J.R. Kidston, Hyndman, Creery, Wolfenden, Loosemore, Roper. Anchored at Fulford 6 P.M.

23rd Proceeded 9 A.M. Anchored Ganges 6 P.M.

24th Proceeded 7 A.M. Anchored Fulford. Played tennis at the Pollock's. Played Fulford at soccer lost 1-4. Played Fulford at Baseball 3-3. Sports. I won long jump & Adams & I came second in 3-legged race—good fun. Heard yesterday that the Parliament had passed the estimates for the Navy 1½ million. They are abolishing the college; Capt. Hose was against it.

25. Sailing outside Fulford, anchored there in the afternoon. I played tennis at the Pollock's.

26. Proceeded at 5 A.M. & anchored at William Head 3:30 P.M. Tennis at Dr. Nelson's. Saw the Jones' in the evening.

27 Returned to Esquimalt. Tennis match Officers V. cadets. Officers won. Dinner at the Matson's. Went to a dud show.

28th The Jones' played tennis here in afternoon.

29th Started the Cadets singles tournament. Dinner at the M.'s. Beamy & I went to a dance in "Princess Louise" given by Captain Troop. Very good party.

30th Tues. Tennis Tournament.

31st Tennis Tournament. Boxing Adams v. Jeckel boxing, the former won. Dinner at Robbie's. Applied for a Masters Certificate Board of Trade.

JUNE 1922

June 1st Lunch at the Matson's. Played Tennis with Tim. Shelf competition. Now news from Ottawa re gratuities.

June 2nd The Commander, Robbie, Hatcher & myself left college at 1:15 P.M. in the former's car. Arrived Qualicum Beach Hotel at 6:30 (110 miles). A V.G. run up. This is a lovely spot & hotel is very nice. Swimming, water warm.

June 3rd Played golf. Swim. Went to Cameron Lake after dinner. Scenery is wonderful & roads good. In forenoon went up in the car to Little Qualicum river.

June 4th Golf in A.M. Left Qualicum 3:00 P.M. I drove as far as Nanaimo. Arrived Victoria 8 P.M. Malahat roads not V.G. Very pretty drive down.

Should like to have a lot at Qualicum. They are quite expensive, about $500.00. Stephens heard from Jones that the R.C.N. is going to keep its officers, 26 appointments in Canada & the remainder abroad. Gratuity a month's pay for each year's service dating from time of first commission.

June 5th Tennis. No official news from Ottawa.

June 6th Cutter race. News in tonight's paper re gratuities. 1 Month pay for every year & 3 months for 7 years service. Letter from Mother saying that Dad was leaving for the coast on June 3rd. Dinner at the Wolfenden's.

June 7th Semi-finals of the Tennis tournament. Robbie dined with me.

June 8th Mrs. Matson came down to see the college in the afternoon. Dinner there. Went to a dance at Government House for the golfers. V.G. party.

June 9th Fri. Tennis.

June 10th Commander & I went out to Colwood to watch the finals of the golf tournament. Von Stearn & Von Elor. V.G. Still no news from Ottawa.

June 11th Church at the Cathedral. Tennis at the "Crofts". Supper at the Matson's. Ruth, Ticky Jones, Rodney, Beamy.

Jun. 12th Mon. Seamanship Exam. Tennis.

Jun. 13th Seamanship papers. Dinner at Robbie's. No news from Ottawa.

Jun. 14th Cadets finished the exams. Final Cadet's dance. Very good party.

Jun. 15th Some cadets left. Bridge at the Inneses. Party at the Wolfenden's for the senior term

Jun. 16th Dance at the MacDowell's. I expected Dad to arrive today but he missed the boat.

Jun. 17th Sat. Played tennis at the club. Canoeing on the Gorge. Stopping at the Matson's.

Jun. 18th Sunday. Played tennis at the Pemberton's.

Jun. 19th Tennis.

Jun. 20th Dad arrived on afternoon boat. Dinner at Robbie's.

21st Wed. Went up the Malahat & later out the Saanich Road. Dinner at the Matson's.

22nd Went out to Butchart's Gardens. Provincial library. Dad left on afternoon boat for Seattle. Tennis & supper at the MacDonald's.

July 4th Out to the Jones'.

July 5th Went to Chemainus. Mrs. Arthur Coles.

6 Played in Duncan tournament. Was beaten by Westwood. Tim & I were beaten by Corfield & Christmas.

7 Vivian & I played Marjorie Leeming & J.G. Brown & were beaten.

8 At Chemainus.

9 Picnic down river. Returned to Victoria.

10th Monday At Victoria.

11 Tues.

Sat. July 29 Rec'd. telegram from Ottawa giving me approval to go to Halifax. Beamy & I went to the courts in P.M.

Sunday July 30 The Matson's left at 7 A.M. for Campbell River. Good bye to Beamy in morning. Packing. Tea at Nairn Robertson's. Went to Boak's in evening with John Grant and Jock.

Monday July 31st Left Victoria on afternoon boat 3:15 P.M. for Ottawa & Halifax. Peter Bangs missed the boat as Mr. Day arrived too late. Saw Grace in Vancouver. Caught the National leaving Vancouver at 7:45 P.M.

Aug. 1st Very hot & dusty.

Aug. 2nd Arrived Biggar at 2:40 P.M. Stopped off for a day with Aunt Clara & Dr. Shaw.

Aug. 3 Left Biggar at 2:50 P.M.

Aug. 4 Arrived Winnipeg at 10 A.M. Uncle Frank met me at the station, family all away. Saw Mrs. Galt. Dinner with Rupert Carr. Left at 7:30 P.M. for Port Arthur.

Aug. 5 Arrived Port Arthur at 10 A.M. Sailed in "Harmonic" 1 P.M. for Sault Ste. Marie. Very comfortable packet. Dance.

Aug. 6 Arrived at the Sault at 7:30 A.M. Frank me at the boat.

7. At the Soo.

8. Sailed at 10 A.M. for Sarnia.

9. Arrived Sarnia 9 A.M. Toronto 3:30 P.M. Dinner at the Annesley's. Left at 11:30 for Ottawa.

10. Arrived at Ottawa. Saw Terry Mansell then went to the Naval Dept. where I saw Capt. Hose. Told him I didn't see many prospects in the R.C.N. & was thinking of leaving the service. He told me that he was sorry to say that his advice was that if any one had a good job to go to he would advise the to take the offer. Said that I could probably specialize in P.T. & R. if I wanted to. Went to Terry Maunsell.

11th Lunch with Nelles.

12 Went fishing.

13 At Terry's.

14. Left Ottawa 1 P.M. Met by Arthur.

16. Tennis with Harry.

17. Lunch with Wood.
18. Harry & I went down to Chester in the morning to play tennis but tournament was off. Saw a moose on the road. Rain.
19. Rain. Sent in travelling expense sheet to Ottawa.

J.C.I.E. AUGUST 1922 AT HALIFAX

Aug. 20th Rain.

Aug. 21st Rain. Jefferson arrived with letter from Ottawa, asking me if I would like to accept appointment to the "Vancouver". I replied no.

Aug. 22nd Mother, Muriel, Arthur & myself went to Grand Pré in the car. Two blowouts.

Aug. 23rd Sports at Wanderer's ground. Tennis.

Aug. 24th Sent $154.00 to Dr. Shaw for half share of house. Mother the other half.

Aug. 25th Tennis at South End.

Aug. 27th Rained hard. Church in morning. Called on Commander Jermain & Woods, dockyard.

Aug. 28th Tennis. Dance at the Mitchell's. V.G. party.

Aug. 29th Rained in the morning but played tennis in P.M.

HMC Dockyard, Halifax, NS

Aug. 30th Tennis, had some very good games.

31. Thurs. Went down to Surfdale[95] in A.M. I played tennis in the afternoon.

September 1st 1922 Played tennis at the South End. Went down to see Taylor in the "Patriot".

Sept. 2nd Played tennis. Bad cold.

Sept. 3rd Went down to Surfdale. Taylor came out in P.M.

Sept. 4th Out to Surfdale in A.M. Played tennis in P.M.

Sept. 5th

Sept. 6 Joined the barracks at 9 A.M. Mother had operation on hand. Dance at the Dree[?] Tower Road.

Sept. 7th Played tennis.

Sept. 8th Day on at Barracks. O.O.G. "Cape Town" arrived.

Sept. 9th Prize money $130.00. Tennis.

Sept. 10th Sunday. Preary, Creery & myself sailed around to Surfdale. Dinner in the Patrician.

Sept. 11th Day on.

Sept. 12th Tennis.

Sept. 13th Rain. Wanderers meeting. Joined the club. $7.50.

Sept. 14 Day on. Lunch with G.C. Jones.

Sept. 15th Running & lunch at Wanderers. W'T. with clothes 164 lb.

Sept. 16th Sat. Rain. Played with G.C. Jones.

Sept. 17th Sunday. Day on.

Sept. 18 Rec'd. travel expenses cheque $54.00. Played tennis.

Sept. 19 Played tennis. Destroyers sailed for Lunenburg.

Sept. 20th Day on.

Sept. 21st Thursday. Donald left for England. Destroyers arrived. Patriot alongside with bearings run. Day on.

Sept. 22nd Run at Wanderers. Comm. rec'd. letter from Ottawa re my P. & R.T.[96] course. Lieut. J.C.I. Edwards' name has been noted and will be forwarded in due course for submission to the Admiralty for next P. & R.T. course.

23rd Saturday. Played tennis.

24 Sunday. Creery & I went to Surfdale in afternoon.

25 Monday. Rugger and Warders.

---

95 This was a property at Purcell's Cove that the family purchased with the insurance received when Joe died in 1917.
96 Physical and Recreational Training course.

Dutchy's dog, Peter Bangs

26

27

28 Day on. Peter Bangs arrived from Victoria.

29 Tea & dinner with John Grant. Hilliard resigned.

30 Rugger practice at Wanderers. Pretty strenuous. Dinner with Creery. Patrician sailed at midnight for Esquimalt.

Oct. 1st Day on.

Oct. 2nd Monday. Practice at Wanderers.

Oct. 3rd Tues. The Doc's (McCallum) and Miss MacKenzie wedding at 1 P.M. I was best man. Reception at his house. Went out to Wayside Inn. Miss MacKenzie's bridesmaid.

Oct. 4 Day on. Bidwell joined the barracks.

Oct. 5 Rugger practice in evening. Took W. McF. to movies.

Oct. 6 Day on. Rugger practice.

Oct. 7th Schooner elimination race. Went out to see the start. "Bluenose",

"Canadia," "Mahaska", Margaret K. Smith. 39 mile course time 4:35. Bluenose won.

Oct. 8th Sunday. Rain.

Oct. 9th Went out in the "Bluenose" in Schooner race. Capt. Angus Walters. Race started at 10 A.M. We finished 1st at about 7 P.M. No race as time limit is 6½ hours. Not enough wind. Heavy swell outside. Dist. 39.85'.

Oct. 10th Rugger practice.

Oct. 11th Rugger practice.

Oct. 12th Rugger practice.

Oct. 13th Rugger practice.

October 14 Wanderers played Dalhousie at 4 P.M. V.G game We led 8-0 until about 15 minutes before time. I scored a try & got my wind knocked out. John had his collar bone broken on a foul. Final score – a draw 8-8.

Wanderers line up

H. Edwards
F. Lane   J. Edwards   A. Lilley
T. Hunter
R. McCoy   J. Grant
Holmes
Stack   Hattie   Schwartz   Hoskings
Atkins   Studd   Younge

Wanderers' Squad Working Hard

WANDERERS football squad of 50 players is working out daily. Some of the newcomers are showing ability. The work of Edwards, a brother of Harry Edwards, the fullback, has been conspicuous. Edwards is a halfliner and he should catch a regular position. Fred Lane is also showing rare form on the backfield and is much faster than he was two years ago when he played on the Wanderers. Norm Sutcliffe, who is out of the city most of the time, was out for practice Saturday, but it is not likely that he will play this year. George Hattie, former Dalhousie star, looks good enough to catch a place on the forward line if he continues to star. Jack Usher, Art Phillips and N. E. McKay are coaching the Wanderers.

Coverage of Halifax Wanderers rugby team, October 24, 1922

Oct. 15th Day on.

Oct. 16 Rugger practice at Wanderers.

Oct. 17 Rugger practice. Took Mother to see movies of the Navy.

Oct. 18th

Oct. 19 Rugger practice.

Oct. 20 Snow about 3". Quite cold.

Oct. 21 Sat. Wanderers played Dalhousie at Wanderer's grounds & won 11-10. Lane had collar bone broken in first half. MacCoy hurt. We scored in the last few minutes. Very exciting and hard game.

Oct. 22nd Day on.

Halifax Wanderers rugby team, 1922 – Dutchy, fourth from the left, back row

Oct. 28 Wanderers played Dalhousie at Studley. Result a draw 3-3. Not a very good game and I did not enjoy it very much as I was a bit stale. Haslam scored for Dalhousie and Lilley for us, both penalty goals. Dancing at Auditorium in evening with Dorothy Campbell.

Sunday Oct. 29th Tea party at Barracks.

Oct. 30 Rugger practice.

31 Rugger practice.

Nov. 1st

Nov. 2nd Rugger practice.

Nov. 3rd

Nov. 4th Wanderers v. Dalhousie. Wanderers won 6-0. Quite good game. Wanderers played and better game and halves were working very well.

5 Tea party at Barracks.

6 Thanksgiving day. Wanderers beat Acadia College 13-8. Quite good game. I scored a try. Bidwell left for England.

7 Tuesday.

8 Wed. Day on.

9 Thurs. Day on. Rugger practice.

10 Friday. I intended going to a dance at Armouries but had a bad cold.

11 Played Caledonia for the rugger championship of Nova Scotia. We won 24-0. I scored a try. The Wanderers played a very good game and the half line was playing the best game of the season. Dinner with G.C. Jones in the "Patriot".

12th Sunday. Day on. Tea party at barracks and in Patriot.

13 Mon. Went out to Surfdale with D.S. At Bannantyne's in evening.

14 Tues. Day on.

15 Dance at the MacDonald's in evening. Rugger practice as the Wanderers may play Montreal here on Saturday.

16 Rugger practice. Went out to Bedford. Aud in evening.

17 Day on.

18 Played Montreal at 3 P.M. on Wanderers ground. Very muddy & heavy ground. We won 8-0. I scored a try they played a V.G. game especially the forwards. T. Lane got other try. Ritch McCoy played a star game.

19 Taylor & I had tea at D.S. Went to Bannantyne's in the evening.

20 Monday

21

22 Day on.

23 Went to Dumbells with Taylor. D.C. & D S. Very good show.

24

NOVEMBER 1922

Nov 25th Sat. Thé Dansant at yacht club in afternoon. Went to John Grant's in evening.

Nov 26 Day on. Light tea party.

Nov. 27 Skating in afternoon at Pt. Pleasant. Tea at Philpot's.

Nov. 30th

Dec. 1st At home.

Dec. 2nd Sat. Day on.

Dec. 3rd Sunday. Tea at D.S. Bannantyne's in evening.

Dec. 4th Ashore with Mull in afternoon. Strand in evening with Mainguy, D.C. & D. Banks.

Dec. 5th Snow. Day on. 4 years seniority as Lieut. today.

Dec. 6th About a foot of snow. We were going to shift the Aurora in the morning but orders were cancelled. Went for a walk with John Grant & dogs.

Dec. 7 Taylor & I went for a walk.

Dec. 8 Mooring up the Aurora all day. Dinner party in the "Patriot" for Ruth & Ticky Jones, the MacKeens & John Grant.

Dec. 9th Sat. Thé Dansant at Yacht Squadron. D.S. Went out to Bannantyne's (Bedford) in evening.

Dec. 10th Went to see Jones off in the Regina. Skating at Chocolate Lake.

Dec. 11 Day on.

Dec. 12.

Dec. 13 Party at Inspector Le Nauge.

Dec. 14 Day on.

Dec. 15 Hockey practice at Arena with Wanderers.

Dec. 16 Skating Frog Pond. V.G. Aud. in evening.

Dec. 17 Day on.

Dec. 18

Dec. 19

Dec. 20 Rec'd. a telegram from Ottawa saying that I was to take next P.&R.T. course commencing Jan. 3rd. Day on.

Dec. 21 Thurs. Shopping, bridge.

Dec. 22

Dec. 23

Dec. 24 Sunday. Tea at Dot's.[97] Supper with John Grant. Went down to Patriot in evening.

Dec. 25th CHRISTMAS DAY. Church at St. Pauls'—dedicated a tablet to Joe. Went out to Bedford & had Christmas dinner with the Bannantyne's. Drove Dot & Marge in & had dinner at home. Later went down to Patriot with D. & M.S. Very cheery party.

Dec. 26th Packing. Said good bye in dockyard. Tea with D. Left on 8 P.M. train for St. John. Art Philips, Roy Studd, Dad, Harry, Art, P. Bangs, J. Grant saw me off.

Dec. 27 Arrived St. John[Saint John] at 9 A.M. & went on board Minnedosa ay 10:30 A.M. Sailed at 5 P.M.

Dec. 28 Fog. Not very exciting crowd on board.

Dec. 29 Played bridge all day with "Auld", "Hoey" & Sera. Foggy.

Dec. 30

> LIEUT. J. C. I. Edwards, R. C. N. son of Mr. and Mrs. J. P. Edwards, 78 Seymour street, left today for Portsmouth, England, on the steamer Minnedosa, to take a long course on physical training at the Royal Naval Barracks. During the Rugby football season just closed, he made a brilliant record as a three-quarter back in the senior fifteen of the Wanderers, and will be much missed in sporting circles.

December 26, 1922 clipping from a Halifax newspaper

---

97 This is Dorothy Elizabeth Symons whom Dutchy met on a tennis court and subsequently married on April 26, 1926 in Halifax. Her sister, Marjorie, is listed in the journals as M. or Marge.

Jan. 1st

Jan. 2nd

Jan. 3rd Quite heavy sea.

Jan. 4th Fine day. Arrived Cherbourg 10 P.M.

Fri. Jan. 5th Arrived Southampton 2 P.M.—Portsmouth 4 P.M. Beech & Reid at Barracks. At The Barracks.

Jan. 6th Saturday. Went down to P.&R.T. School in forenoon. Saw Blackheath beat U.S. 8-0. Tea at Dorothy. Saw "Sally" at hippodrome. V.G.

Jan. 7th Sunday. Started short P.&R.T. course. There are 5 of us doing course viz. Chappel, Harrison, Bucher, Sitwell. Fairly strenuous. Activity exercise, P.&R.T. games, sabre. Weight 11 st. 5 lb.[98] Ht. 5'9½"

Jan. 9th Swedish, medical lecture, boxing lecture. "Kings" with Reid & Beech.

Jan. 10th Med. lec. Swimming. P.&R.T. games, apparatus, etc.

Jan. 11

Jan. 12 Chappel took me to Farnham in his car in P.M.

Jan. 13 At Farnham. Katie, Willie & myself went to Aldershot. Show at Hippodrome. V.G.

Jan. 14th Left Farnham 6:40 P.M. Arrived Pompey at 10:00 P.M. V. bad cold.

Jan. 15th Monday. Boxing lecture, etc.

Jan. 16th Tuesday. Cold still very bad.

Jan. 17th Wed. Tea at Sam Worth's with Reid. Foil, epée & bayonet. RN v. RAF at P.&R.T. School. V. good.

Jan. 18 Thurs.

Jan. 19 Fri. Shopping after P.&R.T. Saw H.T. Grant in Ramillies.

Jan. 20 Sat. Caught the 8 o'clock to London. Arrive 10:00. Reid & I went out to Twickenham to see England v. Wales. 40,000 people. V.G. game. England won 7-3. Drop goal by Smallwood & try by Price. Forwards good but was a little disappointed in ¾. Returned to Portsmouth ay 9.M. Saw Hoey & Sera.

Jan. 21 Sun. Reid & I listened band S. Parade Royal Artill. V.G. tea at the Queen's.

Jan. 22 PT. Practical soccer in forenoon.

Jan. 23rd Tues. P.&R.T. all day.

Jan 24th Wed. Prac. soccer etc.

Jan. 25th Thurs.

---

98 The British measured weight in stones and pounds. One stone is equal to 14 pounds.

Jan. 26th Fri.

Jan. 27th Sat. Saw the U.S. best Cardiff in a v. good game. at U.S. grounds. Shopping in forenoon.

Jan. 28th Sun. Week end on.

Jan. 29th Mon. Trapeze. 1st Lord of Admiralty Mr. Amery inspected the barracks & P.&R.T. School.

Jan. 30th Water polo. Tea at Watson's.

Jan. 31st Kicking prac. V.S. ground.

Feb. 1st Thursday.

Feb. 2nd

Feb. 3rd Went up to Basin[g]stoke. Tony Shawcross met me & motored me up to Town. Saw the "Colonial Girl" at Winter Gardens. V.G. show. Leslie Hewson. Stopped at Waldorf.

Feb. 4th David came around at eleven & we motored to Puttenham where we had a round of golf. Lovely day. Tea at Milford. Got back Barracks 6:30 P.M.

Feb. 5 P.&R.T. boxing, etc. Mess president.

Feb. 6 P.&R.T. Prac. soccer, boxing, etc. Mess president. (Rec'd. letter Beamy)

Feb. 7 P.&R.T.

Feb. 8 Meet Tickie Jones & Jock B. Dance at R.N.B. 9-3 A.M. Very cheery. Rickie, Jock, Harold Grant, Reid, Mrs. Davies, Radell.

Feb. 9 Water polo, etc. Harold & I dined Torts.

Feb. 10 Saturday. Raining. Movies.

Feb. 11 Sun. Supper at Watson's.

Feb. 12 Mon. Trapeze. P.T. etc.

Tues. 13th

Wed. 14 R.A.F. beat Navy 3-0.

Thurs. 15th Saw U.S. draw with Leicester 3-3.

Fri. 16 Caught 4:50 Train to Town. Arrived Sittingbourne 9:10, Rodmersham about 10:00 P.M. Jack, Dorothy & all family very well.

Sat. 17 At Rodmersham.

Sun. 18 Church. Left 4 P.M. Arrived Barracks 10 P.M.

Mon. 19 P.&R.T. Run at U.S ground.

Tues. 20 Judging boxing in Fisgard. U.S. in P.M.

Wed. 21

Thurs. 22 Left at 8 A.M. for Marefield in char-a-banc.[99] Arrived 12:00 (75 miles). Rugger at 2:15 P.M. Awful day & ground, raining hard. We won 4-3. Boxing, soccer, etc. Dined in Royal Corps of Signals' mess. Left at midnight, arrived Barracks 5 A.M.

Fri. 23rd Our course ends March 9th, not 3rd.

Sat. 24th Watched rugger match U.S. v. Chatham U.S.

Sun. 25th Played golf with Reid at Haslar. 36 holes.

Mon. 26

Tues. 27

Wed. 28

Thurs. 1st March Inoculated against colds.

Fri. 2nd March Chappel took me to Farnham in his car. Puncture and had to ship spare wheel in rain, very wet.

Sat. 3rd Arrived Waterloo 12:40. Reid, Ridell & I went to Twickenham. Navy v. Army rugger. Navy won 16-11. The best game I have ever seen. Wonderful day. Went back to Farnham.

Sun. 4th Left Farnham 6:40 P.M. Arrived Ponfey 9:45 motor bus.

Monday March 5th Medical exam.

Tues. March 6 General knowledge exam.

Wed. March 7 Apparatus exam. Hor. & par. bar,[100] box horse, I came second.

Thurs. March 8 Trapeze, water polo. Class taking exam. Dinner.

Fri. March 9 Finished short course.

March 10 Up to Town. Met Jock Bridgman at Waterloo. Saw "Marriage of Kitty" at Duke of Yorks.

March 11 Walk.

March 12 Tues.

March 13 Wed. Up to Town & came down to Rodmersham.

March 14 Lunch with Jack at the Barracks.

March 15 Fri.

March 16 Sat.

March 17 Sun.

March 18 Mon. To Maidstone with Dorothy. Looked at cars at Chaldecott. Went to Faversham to look at Chev.

---

99 A charabanc or "char-à-banc" is a type of horse-drawn vehicle or early motor coach, usually open-topped, common in Britain during the early part of the 20th century. It has "benched seats arranged in rows, looking forward, commonly used for large parties, whether as public conveyances or for excursions."

100 Horizontal and parallel bar.

> B.—162. (Revised—March, 1908.)   Number
>
> ### CLASS CERTIFICATE.
>
> This is to certify that *Lieutenant John C. J. Edwards, R.C.N.* passed through a *Short's* course at the Naval School of Physical Training, Portsmouth, and is qualified to act as an Instructor in Physical Training.
>
> Naval School of Physical Training,
> Portsmouth.
>
> *TmBarrett*
> Commander
> Superintendent of Physical & Recreational Training.
>
> (Date) *9th March 1923.*
> Sta. 1425/08

Certificate presented to Dutchy on completion of a short course at the Naval School of Physical Training, March 9, 1923

March 19 Tues.

March 20 D. J. & myself went to Ideal Home exhibition at Olympia. Teas at the Parker's.

March 21 Thurs. Went into Maidstone & bought Chevrolet. K.N. 9181 1920 Model £75:0:0. Owned by Dr. Bird, Faversham.

March 22 Fri.

March 23 Went to Maidstone to bring back Chev. Off to London to see Oxford & Cambridge boat race. Oxford won. I saw it from near Turnham Green. Returned to Maidstone, picked up car & back to Rodmersham.

25 Sunday Jack, John & myself set out at 10 A.M. for Farnham by Chev. Arrived 2 P.M. dist. 80 miles. Left at 3:45 and arrived back about 6 P.M. V.G. trip.

26 Mon.

27 Tues. To Maidstone to have brakes attended to.

28 Wed. Dorothy & I went to the Point to Point Races.

29 Thursday.

30 Good Friday.

31 Sat. Left for Farnham at 10 A.M. in the Chev. Jack, Dorothy, Dot & John. Lunch near Red Hill. Arrived about 2:30 P.M.

April 1st Easter Sunday. Took Katie, Jack etc. to Froyle – church.

April 2nd Left at about 2:30 P.M. for Rodmersham. Heaps of cars & cyclists on roads. Arrive at 8 P.M. Good run.

April 3rd Tues.

April 4th Played tennis at the Bull H.C. Gasgorines, Dr. Penney, Miss Grant.

April 5th Thur.

6 Fri.

7 Went to Margate in car. Stopped at Canterbury.

8 Sun.

9 Mon.

10 Tues.

11 Wed. Went to Town 10:50 train. Queens club saw covered court tournament. Wheatley playing Sheila Barton. Ret'd. 8:30 P.M. train.

12 Thurs.

13 Fri. Transfer of £83 15 rec'd. London C.B. of C. from Halifax.

14. Sat. Played tennis at Gasgorines.

15. Sunday. Jack, Dorothy, Dot, Robert Orchard & I motored to Canterbury to cathedral for church. Very fine music. Went to Whitestable picnic on beach.

16 Mon.

17 Tues.

18 Wed. Up to Town to see Reid & Beech.

19 Thurs. Went to Cobham saw "Leather Bottle" where Dickens wrote, also "Bleak House" where Charles Dickens lived at Gads Hill.

20

21

22

23 Went to Town. Saw Tickie Jones married to Surg. Lt. Comm. Quinton, St. Stephen's Church.

24 T

25 W

26 T

27 F. Tennis at Bull. Mrs. Earle, Miss Nash, Beech, Dr. Pas.

28 S. Went to Chatham to see R.N. & R.M.L.T.A v. Chatham U.S.

30 Mon. Went up to London. Entered in North London Tennis Tournament at Highbury. Met Seth.

Tues. 1st Left at 12:15 P.M. for Portsmouth.

Went to Farnham on way. Arrived Barracks at 8 P.M. Dist. about 115 miles.

May 2nd Joined up with short course P.T. at school.

May 3rd Thurs. Tennis.

4 Fri.

5 Sat. Tennis at U.S.

6 Sun. Took Watson out to see Elgar. Tennis in P.M. on Ramillies with H.T. Grant.

7 Mon. Played tennis with Buggard. H.T. Grant had dinner with me, we went to a show afterwards.

8 Tues. Tennis.

9 Wed.

10 Thurs. Day on at P.T. School.

11 Fri. Went to a display at Whale Island. H. Grant had dinner with me. Show afterwards, dancing at Assembly Rooms.

12 Sat. Played tennis in a match at U.S.

13 Sun. Tennis.

14 Mon.

15 Tues.

16 Wed.

17 Thurs. Tennis.

18 Fri. Ashore with H. T. Grant in evening. Watson left.

19 Sat. Tennis at U.S.

20 Sun. Went to Farnham in car. Church at Froyle.

21 Mon. Holiday. Returned to Barracks. Tennis at U.S. with Newman. Letter from Beamy.

22 Tues.

23 Wed. Tennis, rain.

24 Thurs.

25 Friday. Tennis at U.S. Capt. Sidebottom.

26 Saturday. Tennis at U.S. Miss Bowling & Humphries.

27 Sunday. Tennis at Barracks.

Dutchy was a world-ranked tennis player and won championships in Canada and internationally

28 Mon. Rain.

29 Tues. Rain.

30 Wed. Tennis & show.

31 Thurs. Hit my head on bottom of swimming bath during forward dive from Trapeze. Tennis.

JUNE 1 1923 Tennis at U.S. Dinner with Dewhurst in Malaya.

June 2nd Went up to Guildford. Met Monty Bridgman,[101] sold him the Chevrolet for £80.0.0.

3rd Sunday.

4 Was Officer of Guard. Had to board a Dutch Yacht complete in cooked hat, etc.

5 Tues.

6 Wed.

---

101 This is Montague Bridgman after whom a famous china shop in Victoria was named. The store carried the finest china in town with more than 100 open stock patterns of Minton, Wedgwood, Royal Doulton, and North America's largest selection of Wedgwood.

7 Thurs. Tennis, show.

8 Fri. End of P.&R.T. short course.

9 Sat. Played tennis against Worthing. I played with Martyr P. of W. Volunteers.

10 Sun.

11 Mon. Bought 4 h.p. Triumph combination from Mundell £50.0.0. Left for Farnham 3 P.M. Belt broke. Arrived 7 P.M.

12 Tues. Called on Mr. Steele, Highways.

13 Wed. Went to Beckenham to see the Kent championship. Saw W.M. Johnson, Misher, Mrs. Mallory, Miss McKane play. Arrived back at about 9:30 P.M.

14 Thurs. Tennis at Pompey with Martyr, Stow, Buzzard.

15 Fri. Making hay. Started for Beckenham but it rained. Slipping belt.

16 Sat. Tennis at Portsmouth. Had a crash in Triumph. Went up to Town with D. Shawcross, 77 Hamilton Terrace.

17 Sun. Tennis at Shirley Preston's. Dressing gown. Watch.

JULY 1923

July 2nd Hurt my knee jumping (high jump) at P.&R.T. School. Taken over to Haslar in ambulance. Had to scratch US. tournament. Fed up. Back splint.

3rd X-ray, nothing broken. Water on knee.

4 Haslar.

5,6,7,8,9, —

17 Allowed to walk.

18 Ashore for couple of hours.

19 & 20 Ashore for couple of hours.

22 Tea at Vive Rowling.

23 Discharged from hospital. Had to scratch in Havant tournament.

24 Took Vive to Havant. Massage at Haslar.

25th Demonstration at P.&R.T. School for the British Medical Association which is having a conference in Portsmouth. Very good show. Went out to Havant. It will be a month or so before my knee is all right again. Meanwhile I can't play tennis or do anything at all strenuous.

26th Havant with V.B. Massage.

27 Havant with V.B.

28 Saturday. Massage, Haslar. Tea at Shaw's. Called on J. Annesley (not in). Dinner with Hope in "Malaya".

AUGUST 1923

1st

2nd

3rd Started at 1 P.M. for Babbacombe, S. Devon. Arrived Teignmouth 9:30 P.M. Difficulty with my lights. Finally arrived at Links Hotel. St. Mary's Church at midnight.

4th Went to "Glen" in morning where Hope, Grant, Geo. Mitchell, McInnes were. Awfully pretty place. Torquay in evening.

5th Sun. Bathing etc.

6th Mon. Bathing etc.

7th Tues. Bathing etc.

8th Wed. Bathing etc. Picnic with the Trontors & Jockey (Nugs). Took Jocky to movie.

9 Thurs. H. Grant & myself started on bike at 11:30 A.M. Went well until about 2 P.M. when we began to have puncture Very hilly near Lyme Regis & Bridport. Dinner at Dorchester. Arrived Ringwood at 11:30 P.M. where we had beer and cheese & repaired our lights. Finally arrived Pompey at 4:30 A.M.

10 Long P.&R.T. course started. Tennis & party with H. Grant. Weight 11 st. 3 lb.

11th Sat. Massage in forenoon. Went to Southampton to see John Grant, Jock & Harold off in the Pittsburgh for Canada.

12th Sunday. Played tennis with Bartley.

13th Monday. Haslar in A.M. Tennis P.M. after P.T.

14th Tues. Haslam in A.M. Tennis P.M. after P.R. (Live saving boxing, etc.)

AUGUST 1923 P.&R.T. SCHOOL PORTSMOUTH

15th Wednesday. P.T. Haslar in morning. Beat Allen in Barracks tennis tournament. My handicap is owe 30.

16th Thurs. Haslar. P.T. Day on at Barracks.

17th Fri. Haslar. P.T. Day on at Barracks. P.T. School.

18th Sat. Haslar. R. leg ¾" smaller than left. Played Lt. Comm. Morgan in handicap singles. Won 3-6, 6-3, 6-4.

19th SUNDAY. Played tennis with Bartley.

20 Mon. Haslar. P.T. Tennis (Kennedy £1).

21 Tues. Haslar. P.T. Tennis. Played Digby-Bell & beat him 7-5, 6-2. Nonweiler & I went to see "Sally" in the evening.

22 Wed. Nonweiler & I dancing at Assembly Rooms.

23 Thurs. Dinner with Hope at Whaley.

24 Fri.

25 Sat. Haslar. Tennis with Bartley & at U.S. Ashore with Chappel.

26 Sunday. Day on.

27 Mon.

28 Tues.

29 W

30 T. Dancing with Vive. Bowling at Assembly Rooms.

31 Fri. Went to Southampton with Nonweiler. Dance at the Picture House given by Sally C. 11-4 A.M.

Sat. 1st Arrived back in Portsmouth 1 P.M. Played Percival in U.S. handicap singles, was beaten 6-2, 6-4. My handicap -4/6

2nd Sun. Went to Southampton in forenoon. Tennis with Bartley & tea with the Bowlings'.

3rd Mon. Played Tate in U.S. tournament & won 6-0, 6-4.

4th Tues. Bartley & I played Ryan & Newman & beat them 6-2, 6-3.

5th Day on Barracks.

6th Thurs. Played J.L. Robinson and won 8-10, 6-4, 6-4. Bartley & I beat Gugson & King 6-4, 7-9, 6-4. Dawson dropped a beam on me at P.T. School.

7 Fri. Bartley & I played Knox & Davies & were just beaten 7-5, 2-6, 6-4. I played Bartley afterwards but was very tired.

8 Sat. Bartley was beaten by Hunter 7-5, 2-6, 6-4. Played Bower in semi-finals of Barracks tournament & won 7-5, 6-4.

9 Sunday. Tennis at the Barracks.

10 Monday. Playing Commander Barrett in finals of Barracks handicap tournament – did not finish.

11 P.T. Beat Comm. Barrett & won handicap singles. Lent Hacket £2.0.0.

12 Wed.

13 Thurs.

14 Fri. Water polo. Caught a cold.

15. Sat. Watched the U.S. rugger trials.

16th Sunday. Went up to Farnham in forenoon & returned in afternoon.

17th Mon. Tennis & run about at U.S.

18th Tues. Played back for U.S. until half time v. W.5.A, Davies team.

19 Wed. Examined for Life saving bronze medals at swimming bath. Very cold—I got the proficiency certificate.

SEPT. 1923 R.N.B. PORTSMOUTH

20 Thurs. Rugger trial practice at U.S. Davies & Kershaw playing.

21 Fri. Tennis at U.S. v. Gugson's Team. I was playing with Sidebottom. Saw Beggar's Opera.

22nd Sat. Played U.S. against Bath. Ground very slippery & ball hard to hold. Bath won 5-0. I played full back. Hippodrome in evening.

23rd Sun. Called on David Lambert.

24th Mon. Kicking about at U.S.

25 Tues.

26 Wed. Strenuous day. Soccer, water polo, etc.

27 Thurs. Fencing port.

28 Fri.

29. Sat. Played rugger for U.S. "C" v. Selsey. Won 28-13. Good fun but not much of a match.

30 Sun. Played a little tennis.

OCTOBER

1st Mon. P.T. School.

2nd Tu. P.T. School.

3rd W. P.T. School.

4th Thurs. Passed out as soccer referees. R.N. & R.M.

5th Fri. Dinner with J. Annesley. Show at the Kings "The sign on the door".

6th Sat. Went to Southampton vs. B.V. Trojans A. We won 50-12. Not much of a field. Saw "Battling Butler" in evening.

OCTOBER 1923 R.N. BARRACKS PORTSMOUTH

7th Sun.

8th Mon. Wrote to Brodeur.

9th Tues.

10th Wed. Rugger practice.

11th Thurs.

12th Fri.

13th Sat. Played in A team v. Old Paulines. Won.

14th Sun. Played golf. Hope & Mainguy at Lee.

15 Mon.

16 Tues. Passed out as water polo referee.

17 Wed.

18 Thurs. Passed out as Diving & Trapeze 42/50

19 Fri.

20 Sat. Played in A team v. Wasps. Won 20-0. Caught 4:50 train to Town. Arrived 6:50 P.M. Met Jackie & saw the "Beauty Prize" at Winter Garden. Very good show. Stopped at Waldorf.

21 Sun. Jackie had lunch with me at Troc. Albert Hall in P.M. Very Good concert. Frieda Hempel singing. Caught the 9:30 P.M. to Portsmouth.

22 Mon.

23 Tues.

24 Wed.

25 Thurs.

26 Fri.

27 Sat. Played on B team v. USC & won 16-3. Good game. Oxford beat U.S. 30-3. Party with Mainguy. Letter from Brodeur.

Oct. 28th Sunday.

29

30

31

November 1st Fri. [actually Thurs.] Supper at the Grove White's.

2nd Sat. [actually Fri.] B. Team v. London Irish. Lost 18-6. Very fast game. Mikado with Chappel.

  Kitwood 2/6. Chappel 8/-, Oliver 22/11.

3rd Sun. [actually Sat.]

5th Mon.

6 Tues.

7 Wed. Party with Chappel. at Mikado.

8 Thurs. The P.T. School went to Aldershot to play rugger v. Army P.T. School. They won 16-0. V.G. game., I went up in Wallace's car.

9 Fri. Caught 8:45 to Town. Lunch with Chappel & Nonweiler. Went to motor show afterwards. Saw Nairn Robertson in the evening. Stayed at Charing Cross Hotel.

10 Sat. Caught 11:45 to Pompey, arrived 1:45. Played R.A.F. at Fort Grange; we won 42-0. U.S.I beat London Scottish. All five US teams won. Dinner at barracks for London Scottish.

11 Played golf with Mainguy & Sharp at Hayling Island.

12

13 Dance at the Pinchard's. Went with Steve. Very good party.

14 Display at the P.T. School which was very good. The heads of all various P.T. Schools came down to see it. Danced at Assembly Rooms with Miss Pease.

15th Thursday Display at P.T. School.

16th Fri.

17th Sat. Played for U.S. B at East Croydon v. Old. Very cold day. Arrived back at 9 A.M. Assembly Rooms.

18 Sun. Tea at Pinchard's.

19 Mon. Rugger dance at Assembly Rooms. Took Vive Bowling.

20 Tues.

21 Wed.

22 Thurs. Time keeping at Marathon race.

23 Fri. Dancing at Assembly Rooms with the Wallace's.

24 Sat. U.S. beat Cambridge 18-13. Played for B team v. Air Services, beaten 5-4. Assembly Rooms with Dot Pease.

25th Sun. Foggy all day.

26 Mon.

27 Tues.

28 Wed.

29 Thurs.

30 Fri. Judging at the boxing.

1 Played v. London Dental hospital, 11-11. Dancing in evening with Mainguy, Evie & Olive Fenton at Assembly Rooms.

2 Sun. Tea at Pinchard's.

3 Mon. Started exams—Medical.

4 Tues. Swimming exam.

5 Wed. Exams.

6 Thurs. Exams. Danced at barracks in evening, Dinner at Corner House. Mainguy, Brut, Chappel, Wallace, Evie Fenton, Marg, Mrs. W., Miss Pitcher.

Officers' long course August–December 1923 – Dutchy second from right, seated

DECEMBER 1923

Friday 7th Exams. Window Ladder, Shelf, Rope climbing, etc.

8 Sat. Played ¾ v. Trojans, Southampton. Beaten 14-8. Assembly Rooms in evening with Mainguy, Brett, Lawson, Evie & Olive, etc.

9th Sunday

10th Mon. Exams.

11th Tues. Exams.

13th Wed. [Thurs.] Exams.

14th Thurs. [Fri.] Finished exams. P.T dinner at barracks.

15 Fri. [Sat.] Heard results of exams. All passed. Watched a hurdling etc. display. In evening Chappel & I took Evie & Olive to Assembly Rooms.

16 Sat. [Sun.] Billy and Leake took me in car to Winchester to play R.A.F. We arrived at half time, beaten 11-5. Dancing at Assembly Rooms. Mainguy, Eve Fenton, & Dot Bailey.

17 Sun. [Mon.]

18 Mon. [Tues.]

19 Tues. [Wed.]

20 W. [Thurs.]

21. Th. [Fri.] Went to Town. Stayed with Brett.

22. Fri. [Sat.] Betly. Met G.C. Jones, stopped at Regent's Palace.

23. Sat. [Sun.] Twickenham. Navy beaten by Harlequins. Went to Farnham.

24

25 **Tues.** At Farnham.

26 Mainguy came to fetch me in Lawson's car. Broke down about 4 miles outside Farnham.

Pushed the car back 2.4 mi. to a garage. Hired a Ford to take us to Portsmouth. Went to Carnival at Assembly Rooms with the Lawsons, Evie &.

27 Mainguy & I went to town where we met G.C. Jones.

28 In Town.

29 Went to Farnham.

JAN 1, 1924

C.B. of C. Halifax $411.00
B. of M. $642.00
Wentz $500.00
War loan $600.00
C. B. of C. London £50 & 4.40.

30 Farnham.

31 Farnham.

1 Farnham.

2 Farnham.

3 Farnham.

4 Farnham.

5 Farnham.

6 Farnham. Froyle.

7 Farnham.

8 Farnham.

9 Left for Portsmouth 4:29 P.M.

JANUARY 1924

Jan. 9th Left at 2:55 P.M. for Deal. Arrived 9:15 P.M.

10 At P.T. School, Royal Marines Deal. Capt. Connybeare Supt. Left at 4:25 for London. Went to Brighter London at the Hippodrome. Stayed with Brett, 61 Warwick St.

11 Returned to Portsmouth.

12 Rugger march v. Bournemouth.

13

14.

15

16 Went to Aldershot. Met by Queenie & Olie.

17 Visited Army School of Physical Training.

18 Returned to Portsmouth in evening.

19 Rugger match cancelled. Dancing at Assembly Rooms in evening.

20 Lunch in Resolution.

21 Railway strike so couldn't go to Shotley.

22 Dancing with Eve.

23

24 Dance at R.N.B. Eve K.

25 Table

26

Mon. Feb. 4th Went to Dartmouth. Arrived at 7:30 P.M.

5th Went over Dartmouth. Very fine buildings. About 488 Cadets now that Osborne had been done away with. Good gym and about 10 fields all together. Cadets play soccer & rugger. P.T. 2 hours per week. Swim team, 3 hours per 2 weeks. Not enough. Lt. Comm. Baker No. 1 & P.T. Left Dartmouth at 3:40 P.M. Arrived London 10:50 P.M. Charing Cross Hotel.

6 Caught 11:50 train for Cambridge. Played back U.S. v. Cambridge. WE lost 32-5. Tea & dinner with Mary & Roberts.

Feb. 7th Returned to Portsmouth. Dancing at Assembly Rooms with Eve.

8 Fri. Went up to Town with Mont Haes. He was fencing at Bertrands. Returned 11 P.M.

9 Sat. Up to Town 11:50 with U.S. II. Played Civil Service at Richmond and won, 18-12. Dinner at Canadian Club with Brett, Mainguy, Bidwell & H.T. Grant. Good show. Went to Brett's club afterwards. Danced until 4 A.M.

March 1st 1924 Left London 11:50 A.M. for Liverpool. Arrived 4 P.M. Went aboard "Montrose" sailed at 5 P.M.

Sun. 2nd At Sea.

Mar. 3rd At Sea. Play on deck, dances, etc. Jim & Cecil Smith, Spragge, Anderson, Eaton, Arthur Lane.

4

5

6

7

8

Hockey team – Dutchy second from left, back row

9   Arrived St. John [Saint John] 1 A.M. Got ashore about 10 A.M. Went to Royal Hotel.

Jim & Cecil Smith & Mrs. Smith there.

10th   Caught 7:10 train for Halifax, arrived at 5:30. Dad met me. P. Bangs delighted. Mother & I went to hockey match, Wanderers v. Dartm. Dartmouth won.

11 Tues.   Report at Barracks. I am C.O. Festubert & P.&R.T. Officer.

12 Wed.

20   Officers R.C.N.B. v. Army Officers at ice hockey at the Arena. We won 15-3. Ice very soft.

28   Trying to get a store establishment for the gym. Dance at Dr. Cunningham's. Reid & I went with the Symons sisters. Got car mil. 11385.

29   At Dentist in morning. Squash in P.M.

May 10th   Soccer match, Navy v. R.C.A. We won 3-0. Turned in old Chev. for new one, got $185.00 for it. Price of new one $855.00. Paid $358.58 & monthly payments of $21.00. Mother said that they would buy this one for at least $400.00 when I left.

11th Sun.   Harry, Mother & I went to Windsor to see Muriel.

12th Mon.   Day on.

AUGUST 1924

Aug. 11th Start of N.S. Provincial tournament at South End.

Sat. 23 Butler & I beat Grant & Allen for N.S. doubles.

24 M. Currie & I beaten in challenge round for mixed doubles 6-7, 6-8, 6-4.

Sept. 18th 1924 Proceeded at 0600 in Festubert for Baddeck, patt. VI target in tow. Very heavy weather, steering gear carried away. All RCNVRs dead to the world. Speed 4-5 knots.

19th Sighted County Island L at 0900.

20th Anchored at Kelly Cove.

21st Arrived at Baddeck.

22 At Baddeck.

23 Patriot arrived. Dinner at Casey Baldwin's.

24

25

26

27

28

29 Towing target for Patriot.

30

Oct. 1st

2nd

3rd Proceeded through Bar[r]a Strait to Great Bras D'Or, towing target for Patrick. Firing 12 pr.

4

5 Towing target etc.

6

7

8

9

10

11

12

Oct. 16th Sailed for Halifax at 12:35. Fine weather.

17th Very heavy weather, sea & wind. Difficulty in steering. Speed anything 7-3 knots. Decks leaking badly. Up all night.

Rugby team – Dutchy centre front

18 Arrived Halifax 7 A.M. Up all night. Played rugby for Wanderers v. Dalhousie, won 15-3.

19 Patriot arrived 6 P.M.

20

21

22

23

24

25 Played rugger v. Dalhousie, won.

Dec 24th Drove to Sarag[u]ay in cars. Roads very icy-awful driving. Christmas tree. Two S. M.MacI., E.J., E. P., H.R., F.H., J.E.

Dec. 25th Christmas Day. Dinner at home. Dance at Lola Hury's.

26th

27

28

29

30

Dutchy playing hockey, top centre   *Dutchy playing hockey, facing off on left*

31 Comm. Grant, E.M. & myself dinner dance at Halifax Hotel. Grant's car frozen up. Finished up at Cambridge Library.

Jan. 1st 1925 Called at Gov. Ho., Army Mess, Bishop's etc. Rec'd. callers in P.M. Dance at Ashburn. V.G. Party.

Jan. 2nd M. sailed. V. bad cold.

3rd, 4, 5th, 6th

> About 18th started the hockey team.
> Played v. Bank of Montreal at South End Rink & lost.
> Played v. A.S.C. Glassy Barracks won 14-3.
> Played v. Artillery, draw 4-4.
> Played v. Bank of Montreal, won 7-3.
> Played v. Morris Ltd., drew 5-5.
> Played v. Artillery, lost 2-1.

1925

> Navy v. R.C.R., won.
> Navy v. Hopgoods, won.
> Navy v. Bank of Montreal, won 3-2.
> Navy v. Imperial, won 5-4.

Feb. 13th Dance at Ashburn. D.S.

Feb. 14th Played Bank of Montreal at Arena.

Feb. 15th

Feb. 19

Feb. 20th Skating Club. South End Rink.

Feb. 21st Sat. Played Squash with Murray.

Feb. 22nd Went out to Surfdale. D.S.

Feb. 23rd

March 17 Mainguy & Duncan arrived on way through. D.S. in evening.

March 18 Party at Inspectors.

March 19 Mainguy left.

March 20 Badminton tournament started at Armouries. I was defeated by Sparling S.J. Dot & I beaten in mixed doubles by Major & Mrs. Scott. Dr. Woodbury & I beat two people & were defeated by Grant & Mercer.

March 21 Badminton in P.M. Harry arrived. Finals of Tournament in P.M. Dance later. Commissioned the car again. 3737.

March 22 Dot left on O.L. for Victoria. Day on.

April 8th Played badminton. Party at the Hibbard's.

April 9th Swimming class. Dinner in "Patriot".

Aril 10th Good Friday.

April 11

April 12

April 13 MacMechan's

April 14 Officers played Ship's Co Baseball – Admiral House Grounds.

April 15

April 16 Coaled "Festubert" 50 tons.

April 17

April 18 Navy defeated R.C.R. soccer 2-1. Kinsley gave part at Barracks. Quite good show.

April 19 Called on Jefferson's.

April 20 About 6" snow. Harry left for Montreal. Weight stripped 162 lbs.

April 21 Meeting of South End Committee.

May 1

May 2

May 3 Out at Surfdale. P.D., M.S., E.P., Taylor, Haughton.

May 4

May 5 Commissioned Festubert.

May 6 Swinging Festubert.

May 7 Sailed for Liverpool, N.S. with Hibbard, Barnes, Gunner, to blow up wreck of Cap D'Or. Arrived 9 P.M.

May 8 Blowing up wreck of Cap D'Or. Depth charges, 16¼ lb. charges.

May 9 Blowing up wreck of Cap D'Or. Sailed for Shelburne, arrived 10 P.M. Bad cold.

May 10 At Shelburne. Went fishing with Barnes.

May 11 Fog, at ↓.

May 12 Sailed for Halifax. 5 A.M. Arrived 9 P.M.

May 13 Played tennis.

May 14 At Sea with R.C.N.R. class.

May 15

May 16 Navy beat Crescents 4-1. Took Taylor to Grand Lake. Supper at Rupe. Woods. Danced at Aud. with Margaret McL.

May 17 Went out to Surfdale.

May 18 Mon. Played tennis.

May 19 Tues. Coaled 90 tons. Played tennis.

May 20 Sailed for Chester 9 A.M., arrived 4 P.M. Played golf with Miles.

May 21 Sailed for Hubbards.

May 22 Sailed for Halifax. Played tennis.

May 23 Played tennis. Party at Surfdale. M.M., E.J., M.S., E.P., D.R.N.T., H.E.R., F.L.N. Met Margaret McLean at Station.

May 24 Sunday.

21 Sun. Went out to Ashburn with D. Alan Creery played golf.

22 M.

23 Tues.

24 Wed.

25 Th.

26 Fr.

27 Saturday

28 Sunday. Went to Chester with Dr. Woodbury, Hilda Douglas & Winnie McFetridge. Played golf.

29

June 30 Raining. Movies with Marion Douglas.

July 1 Barnes & I went out to Surfdale. Played tennis in P.M. at Rupe. Woods in evening.

July 2 Went out to Bedford. Played tennis with Jimmy Butler.

Aug. 20th Played Jimmy Butler in finals of N.S. singles and won 6-4, 6-3, 6-2. Butler & I won doubles from Wiswell & Allen 6-2, 7-5, 6-3. Butler & Dot Symons beat W. McFetridge & myself.

Aug. 21 Played Hazen Short N.B. champ. & won 7-5, 6-4, 6-3 for Maritimes singles. Butler & I beat Short and Hallisey 6-2, 4-6, 5-7, 6-2, 6-3.

26 Played Comty Academy in A.M. were defeated 8-5.

Sept. 27 Went to Chester to play golf. D.S., E.J., C.R.H.T. & myself. Lovely day.

28 At sea, training after.

> To sell the Dummy
>
> The timing is the whole essence of the thing. Any player can pretend to pass the ball to one side or the other and go on running, but if he does so at the wrong time not even a bad player is deceived.
>
> The best dummy of all is that which is armed, say for a pass to the right simultaneously with a dodge off the right food towards the left.
>
> The Intercept
>
> Do not make for corner flag if you get through, but run towards the full back and get him standing still. When about 6 yards from him swerve to right or left. He (the F.B.) is standing still & You have a flying start.

1925

Sept 29th 1925 Practice rugger match. Hurt my left foot.

30 X-ray – broken bone – Dr. Curry.

Oct. 1

Oct. 2 Had foot put in plaster cast Camp Hill Hospital by Dr. Curry. Marge, Dot, Mother & I went to Surfdale.

Oct. 3 Wanderers beat Dalhousie 5-3. Dinner party in Wistaria in evening.

Oct. 4 Sun. Taylor, Miles, Barnes & Dot came to tea.

5 M.

6 T. M., Dot, Rastus & myself to Surfdale.

7 W. Went to "School For Scandal" with Mother & Muriel.

8 Th.

Oct. 17 United Services vs. Wanderers. Wanderers won 14-4. Raining hard. Quite good game. Wanderers scored about three tries in last 10 minutes.

Tart & McRae	835 View St., Victoria 1693
W.D. Tait	1419 Haultain, Victoria 5292X
B.D. Robinson	445 Admirals Road, Esquim. 3800
Nairn Robertson	930 Pemberton Road 576
J.S.H. Matson	875 Dunsmuir Rd. Esqui. 260
Dr. E.W. Boak	1070 Joan Crescent, Victoria 3249
	204 Jones Building 3562
G. P. Haddon	1021 Deal St., Oak Bay 1713Y1
J.G. Brown	1205 Fernwood Road, Vict 2147R
F. B. Pemberton	601 Foul Bay Road 559

C.B. Innes	1236 Sunnyside 3638R
A. R. Wolfenden	522 Head St., Esquimalt 3286R
Mrs. Croft	Mt. Adelaide, Dunsmuir Rd
E.A.E. Nixon	Hill Farm, Wilkinson Road, Colquitz.
E.E. McCallum	
Mrs. O. M. Jones	Metchosin P.O., BC

Oct. 20 U.S. played Dalhousie at Studley. Dal. won 17-7. Dal scored three tries in 1st 15 minutes.

Snow			
Vokes	Timothy	MacDonald	Andrews
Gilham			
Thompson			
Hart			
Wearing	Johnson		
Whittle	Jean	Margard	
Barnes	Mitchell		
Shawcross	77 Hamilton Terrace St. John's Wood London NW8		
Jackie	c/o Mrs. Troughton, "Silver Birches" Chalfort St. Giles, Bucks near Uxbridge		

Oct. 24th Dalhousie beat Wanderers 5-0 at Studley. V. bad game. The Harts, M., Rastus, D. & myself out to S___dale.[102]

25th

Oct. 31 Dal. beat U.S. 14-3. V.G. game.

Nov. 10

Nov. 11th Church in morning. Drive in P.M.

Nov. 12 Played bridge at D.'s bad cold.

Nov, 13

Nov. 14 Sat 1925. Wanderers won City rugby championship by beating Dalhousie 10-8. Taylor gave a birthday party in Patriot.

Nov. 25th 1925 C.B. of C 823 Roy B. 70

B. of M. 370 B. of NS 41

U/Lo 2300 After ded. 90.00 Mess B (50) Ex. total 30

Raisin Wine

Take 2 lbs. of raisins, a lemon & a lb. of white sugar & 2 gallons of boiling water. Pour into a stone jar & stir daily for 6 or 8 days.

Strain, bottle & put in cool place for 10 days or so. The wine will be ready for use.

---

102 Surfdale, the Edwards property at Purcell's Cove, Halifax.

Loganberry Wine
To 4 quarts berries add 5 qts. of clear cold water. Let stand 48 hours. Strain & add 5 lbs. granulated sugar. Let ferment two weeks. Cover mouth of crock with thicknesses of brown paper. Prick holes in paper with point of scissors. Bottle and pour into a crock.

Cherry Wine
Equal part of cherries & water. Ferment for 3 days. Strain. Pour into a cask & add 3 lbs. of sugar for each gallon of juice. Ferment for 10 or 12 days then seal up in bottles as required.

END OF JOURNAL THREE

JOURNAL FOUR
January 27, 1926 – September 13, 1929

Series of Italian stamps that commemorate the Franciscan order, issued January 30, 1926

JOURNAL FOUR
January 27, 1926 – September 13, 1929

In which Dutchy Edwards continues as Commanding Officer of HMCS Festubert, *marries Dorothy Elizabeth Symons, returns to Malta where he joins HMS* Valiant *patrolling around the Mediterranean, is transferred to HMS* Malaya *and returns to Halifax via England, takes command of HMCS* Champlain, *patrols the Caribbean, loses a daughter (the letter took some time to get to him), and returns to patrol the east coast of North America.*

Jan. 27 Dentist Dr. Fluke. Teeth cleaned. Got car from Nova Motors $59.43. Paid $25.00. Skating club in evening.

28 Thurs. V. cold. Blizz. and temp. 0°. Badminton.

29 Fri. Basketball, Daymen beat Seamen 17-13. Hockey match v. Chronicle, score 5-5.

Craig, Wurtele, Murray, Edwards, Bidwell, MacDonald. no subs. Took car out & turned it over to Bidwell.

30 Badminton in P.M. Day on in evening. Paid Life Ass. $18.25 and balance on car.

31 Lunch at Henry's. Supper at Dr. A. Curry.

Feb. 1, 1926 Played Imperial Tobacco Co. at Dartmouth, they won 6-4. V.G. game. Adams, Wurtele, Murray, Edwards, Bidwell & MacDonald, no subs.

Feb. 2nd More snow, about 3 or 4 ft. of snow. Went skiing with Dot & Barnes. Crescents beat Wanderers 6-2.

Feb. 3rd Skiing with Barnes at Golf Links. Skating club in the evening.

Feb. 4th Blizzard. Refereed Basketball game. Snow very deep.

Feb. 5th Blizzard. More snow. Letter from G.S. Jones.

Feb. 6th Blizzard. More snow. Played Royal Bank at Arena. They won 5-2. Very good game.

Feb. 7th Sun. Shovelling snow. Supper at Henry's.

Feb. 8th Mon. Basketball. Cold day. Played Badminton at Military Gymnasium.

Feb. 9 Attending the opening of N.S. Parliament. Badminton in evening at Armouries. Carol McInnes & I beat Mrs. Blamet & H. Roper also C. Mitchell & Miss Weston.

Feb. 10 More snow & cold weather, Rec'd. payment from Bidwell for car. $475.00. Ordered 5 1943 5% bonds & one Brompton @ $30 from Johnson & Ward. Skating club. Played hockey v. Bank of Montreal and won 6-1. Adams, Murray, Wurtele, Bidwell, Edwards, MacDonald.

Feb. 11th Navy v. Cranes Ltd. 9 P.M. Dartmouth Arena. Navy won 4-3. V. Good game. Heard from Ottawa that I am going to England in "Alaunia".

Feb. 12th Day on. Seamen beat Officers in Basketball 12-8.

(E) Sat. Feb 13th Very fine day, Badminton – C. McInnes & I beat G. Wyler & D. Page and are now in finals. Holms arrived from England to relieve me.

(E) Feb. 14th Lola Henry's for supper.

Feb. 15th Mon. Played Badminton at Military gym for Elkins Cup.

Feb. 16th Tues. Hockey at Dartmouth v. Imperial Tob. Co. They won 7-4. Went to hockey match Crescents v. New Glasgow, Crescents won 3-2.

(E) Feb. 17th Holms relieved me. Tea at Henry's. Skating club in evening.

Feb. 18th Went on leave. Badminton.

Feb. 19th Fri. Raining hard. Streets in v. bad condition. Dinner at R.C.N.B. for Hibbard G.M. Hurt my left foot.

Feb. 20th At home all day.

(E) Feb. 21st Sunday. Supper at Lola's.

Feb. 22nd Mon. Played hockey Navy v. Herald. Foot very sore. Had a hard time getting home. Cataloguing the library.

Feb. 23rd Went to see Dr. Curry.

Feb. 24th X-ray on Left foot at V.G. Hospital. Very bad cold.

Feb. 25th Dinner at Dorothy's. Lola H. D. & I went to hockey match, Crescents v. Truro. Truro won 3-0. Swales re P.T. job.

Feb. 26th

Feb. 27

(E) Feb. 28 Tea at D.'s.

March 1st Dinner at barracks. Petch dined with me. Rec'd. pay $160.00.

2nd Cataloguing the Library. Movie in evening. Bad cold.

3rd Cataloguing the Library.

4th

5

(E) 6

7

(E) 8 Cataloguing. Movie. Rain. Wrote Swailes.

9 Cataloguing.

10 Wed.

11 Thurs.

12 Fri.

13 Sat.

14 Sun. Went out to Surfdale.

15 Mon.

16 Tues.

17 Wed. Tea at D.'s. Majestic. Went to Station to meet Marge at 2 A.M. She did not arrive.

18th Met Marge at Station. Played Badminton.

19 Dot & I gave a party at Inspector La Nauge's. Closed Parliament.

20

21

22 At Barracks in forenoon. Movie in Evening.

23 Tues. Went on unofficial leave. Badminton in evening with Marge.

24 W.

25 T. Patriot arrived. Harry arrived.

30 At Barracks in evening.

March 31 Lunch at Inspector La Nauge's. Squash.

April 12 Sailed in Alaunia for Liverpool. All the chaps came down to see us off.

Ap. 20th Landed Liverpool. Went to London, Charing Cross Hotel.

21 In London. Went to Admiralty. Show etc.

22 Went down to Portsmouth in P.M.

23 Joined RN.B. – P.T. School.

24

May 17th D. & I went to Southampton. Caught the night boat to Havre.

18th Arrived Havre 7 A.M. Paris, noon. Shopping etc. in Paris. Left at 10:25 for Rome.

19 Modane 10 A.M.

20 Arrived Rome 8 A.M. Did a Cook's tour in forenoon around the Forum etc. St. Peter's etc. in P.M. Left at 6 P.M. for Syracuse.

21 Arrived Syracuse 3 P.M. Great difficulty with luggage; they put it off at wrong station. Cost 80 Lire to get on board Lubiana in which we sailed at 4 P.M.

HMS Valiant

22 Arrived Malta at 1:00 A.M. Rupert & Mrs. Wood met us, went to St. James Hotel.

Joined the "Valiant" in morning.

23.

24. Moved in to flat, 1 Strada Miratore, Floriana. Saw Lt. Com. B., assistant Fleet P. & R. T. O. Sent to C.B. of C. from War Loan $16.63.

June 3 Sent to C.B. of C. from 1923 reciprocity Loan $12.50 (Series 22 No. 12985 (A12))

June 8 Sent to C.B. of C. from 1926 reciprocity Loan $12.50 (Series 22 No. 13466 (A12))

June 5 O.O.D. D. came onboard, was inoculated.

June 6 Sunday. Tennis at Marsa with Hotham, Packer, Loveband & myself.

June 7 At Malta. Castille, etc.

June 8 At Malta. Played Tennis Else, Crashe, Elkins & myself.

June 9 Outside for exercises. Tennis with P.M.O. Eng. Cdr. Else & myself.

June 10 To sea for exercises. Sent cheque for £1-0-0 from W. Annesley to Nat. Prov. Bank. Day on.

June 11 Returned to Malta. Secured to 7 & 7A Buoys. De-ammunitioning ship. Tennis with Commander, Chief, P.M.O.

June 12 De-ammunitioning in forenoon. Tennis with Eveleigh & Markan. D. & I dined with Surg. Comm. Cameron. Dance at Sliema Club.

June 13th Tennis at Marsa.

June 14th De-ammunitioning. Castille in A.M. Tigné bathing in P.M.

JUNE 1926

15th O.O.D. Cutter dropped when hoisting.

16th Played tennis with Packer, Eveleigh, Lane. Boat pulling. Dance in Frobisher.

17 Thurs.

18 Fri.

19 Sat. Played Tennis with Eveleigh at Marsa.

20 Sun. Day off. Supper at the Wood's.

21 Mon. Corrodino in Morning to watch Water Polo in P.M

22 Tues. Morning watch. Played tennis with Packer.

23 Wed. Forenoon 1st. D. & 1st.

24 Thurs. Dockyard, Played Borg the Pro in tennis: score 3-6, 8-6, 6-1, 3-6.

25 Fri. 2nd Day on.

26 Sat. Played tennis with Packer at Marsa. Small earthquake at 20:45. Shook the flat a bit.

27 Sun. Played tennis with D. at Marsa.

28 Played tennis with Greig, Hemstead, Jones, Lanet, Packer at Marsa.

29 Tennis with Parker – Marsa.

30th Tennis with D. – Marsa.

JULY 1926 H.M.S. VALIANT AT MALTA

July 1st Thurs. Day on. Hotham was promoted.

July 2nd Tennis at Marsa with Packer.

July 3rd Sat. Day on.

July 4th Swim at Tigné. Tennis at Sliena. Batemans came to supper.

July 5 Tennis at Marsa with Col. Giles.

July 6th Getting new Water Polo pitch at Ricasoli Breakwater fixed up. Swim at Tigné. Tea with Rutherford's.

JULY 1926

July 7 Played tennis with Borg. Regatta dinner by G.W. Dickenson at Union Club. Corrodino in morning.

July 8 Tennis with D. Crash & Borrett. Dinner with Captain Walwyn in evening.

July 9 Day on.

July 10 Tennis with Commander, Havers, D. & myself. One set with Borg.

July 11 Day on. Dinner with Commander Hynes. D. came off to Cinema.

July 12 Went into No, 4 drydock at 9 A.M. Tennis in P.M. with Col Giles, Hamstead, Jones, Packer, etc.

July 13 Commander Hynes leaving ship. Hotham to relieve him. Tennis with Packer.

July 14 New job as boat officer. Played tennis with Hemsted at Marsa in P.M.

July 15 Day on. Dined Commander Hynes. Went to Melita with Walker & the Adams. Went for a swim afterwards at _____. Got back 03:45.

July 16th Tennis with Miss Walwyn, Packer, D. & myself at Marsa.

July 17th Swimming at Tigné. Dinner & dance with Packer at Sliema Club.

July 18th Tennis with Moss. King at Sliema. Bathe afterwards.

July 19th Day on. Very hot.

July 20th Played cricket at Corrodino, Valiant v. R.A.S.C. Was 11th man in, rec'd. one ball made 1 run when other man was out. Very hot.

July 21 Marsa in forenoon marking out ground for Gymk[h]ana. Tennis with Parker in P.M. & was very bad. 2-5, 3-6, 1-6.

July 23rd Donkey gymk[h]ana at Marsa. I did not go as I was C.O. Went to dance in evening at R.A.M.'s. R. Ad. Campbell.

24 Went for a swim Delamara with Sims & Packer. Tennis with Packer 2-6, 3-6. 8-6.

25 Havers came to lunch. Tennis with Borg. 6-8, 6-3, 4-4.

26 Tennis with Col. Giles, Greig, Phinney & Hemstead at Marsa. Woods came in to bridge in the evening.

27 Day on.

28 Boats; Tennis with Col. Giles, Mts. Unuim, D. and myself at Sliema – bathe.

29 Boats; To Manoel Isl. in P.M. to see Destroyer Football ground. Tennis with Hernsted & Mrs. ___.

30 Tennis with Packer. 7-5, 6-2, 6-1.

AUGUST 1926

1st Sunday. Church & bw. Tennis with Packer. 6-2, 6-2, 3-6, 6-6.

2nd Mon. Tennis at Marsa. Doubles with the Boys.

3rd Tues. Finishing off Water Polo at Ricasoli Breakwater. Swim at Tigné. Else, Sims, & Gilbert came to dinner.

4th Wed. Day on.

5th Thurs. Boats, etc. Tennis at Marsa. Parker & I played Cl. Giles & Finney & won 7-9, 6-3, 6-3, 6-2. Packer came to dinner & we went to Sliema afterwards.

6th D. & I went to Tea party in U.S.S. Touchey.

7th Sat. Tennis with Packer, 6-8, 6-2, 7-5. Packer came to dinner & we went to Sliema afterwards.

8th Sun. Tennis with D. at Marsa.

9th Mon. Day on.

10th Tues. Packer & I played Finney & Giles & beat them 9-11, 11-9, 6-3.

11th Wed. The Fleet arrived back from 1st half of Summer Cruise. Tennis with Packer 6-3, 7-5, 6-1.

12th Thursday.

13th Fri. Went out to 3 & 3A buoys.

14th Sat. Marsa with D.

15th Sunday. Swim at Tigné in forenoon. Played Eng. Comm. Eveleigh in P.M. 6-0, 6-3, 6-3. Doubles with Moore.

16 Mon. Commenced ammunitioning.

17 Tuesday. Felt a bit ill. MALTA DOG. The Woods in to play bridge.

18 Wednesday.

19 Thurs.

20 Friday. Dorothy quite ill. Day on, but managed to get ashore in the evening.

21 Sat. Tennis in P.M. D. still quite ill. Anchored outside the Breakwater. Advanced Dorothy £14-0-0 for September. Advanced Dorothy £5-0-0 for Emergencies.

22nd Sunday. Tennis in PM. with Packer, Eveleigh, Giles, Furney, Maham.

23rd Mon. Sailed at 0730 in company Warspite, Resolution, Royal Oak, Barham, Eagle, Hermes, 2 carrier Squadrons & destroyers.

24th Exercises. Saw aeroplane taking off & flying on "Eagle". Quite a heavy sea.

25th Still blowing hard. H.A. gun firing at Sleeve target for Aeroplanes. First watch. Search light exercise (poor). Manoeuvring by Fixed Light Signals. to star. Flashed number of tens of degrees.

H.M.S. VALIANT 1926 1ST B.S. MED.[103]

August 26 Arrived at Gavrion Bay which is near entrance to the Doro

---

103 First Battle Squadron Mediterranean.

Channel. Blowing very hard from off the land. Could not lower any racing boats so I took the crews in P.T. in dog watches, also the Midshipmen.

27th At Gavrion Bay. General drill. Boat pulling in skiff.

28th O.O.D. Still blowing hard. Training regatta crews.

29th Still blowing hard. Cold.

30th At Gavrion Bay. Bad cold.

31st Sailed at 0700 in company Barham, Resolution, Royal Oak for Skiathos. Arrived 1830. Bad cold. Weather still rather chilly. H.A. Firing.

SEPTEMBER 1926

Sept. 1st Wednesday. We were going to sea for torpedo firing & full power trial but it was cancelled at last moment. Went out & did some sub calibre instead. O.O.D. Cold v. bad. Rec'd. $46.00 from Income Tax Dept.

2nd Thurs. We were going to sea at 0800 but did not go. Very bad cold.

3rd Proceeded at 0745. Forenoon watch. Carried out Torpedo firing. 4 Torpedoes (GT. 12) & 6" firing. Afterwards carried out Full Power Trial 23½ Knots. Returned to harbour at 1530. Weighed at 1915, carried out star shell, searchlight & torpedo firing. Returned to harbour at 2300. Still have a bad cold.

4th Saturday. Went away in the skiff in the afternoon with Havers, Else, Crashe, Blundell—swim. Fine day. Still have a cold.

5th Sunday. O.O.D. Date due for promotion to Lieut.-Commander. Doled out fizz.

H.M.S. VALIANT SEPTEMBER 1926

September 6th Mon. At Skiathos.

September 7th Tues. Sailed at 1330 in company Barham, Resolution, Royal Oak & destroyers. Carried out an exercise and later parted company. Valiant proceeding to Deuthero Cove. Middle watch.

September 8 Wed. At Deuthero Cove. Moored.

September 9 Thurs. O.O.D. Held a ship's practice regatta in the afternoon.

September 10 Friday. Held a few cutters & whalers & gigs races to time.

September 11 Saturday. Went ashore in P.M. for a walk with Derry & Grant.

September 12 Sunday. Pansey & I went ashore with regatta boats' crew's picnic part. Quite a good wharf at Deuthero Cove, old military one, old touches & military road. Small refugee village. Tobacco grown largely.

13th O.O.D.

14th Sailed at 1900 for Volo[s].

15th Had Morning watch. Joined up with Warspite, Reso. & Royal Oak & rest of fleet. Carried out torpedo firing & proceeded to Volo[s], arriving there at 1800. Moored.

16 Went over to Warspite to see Evans in the morning. Went ashore with Walker in Volo[s] in afternoon. A very funny place & old.

17th Fri. O.O.D. Came on to blow very hard in the night for a couple of hours.

18th Sat. Examined Water Polo referees in the morning in the Frobisher with Neams & Mr. Hals. Bull Wood came to dinner with me. Heard about S. I. stolen.

19th Sun. Went for a walk with Bull Wood ashore in Volo[s]. Watched football match.

Sept. 20th Mon. 1st day of the Regatta. We did badly in forenoon. Lost the greatest number of points in the whaler's races. Barham getting a good lead in these events. They have 4 whalers to our two to practice with. Our gigs V.G. The crews which did P.T. training lasted better than the others. Marines cutter won. We won Officer's gig race in P.M. Stokers crew except cutter – poor.

Stroke for gig
Stroke for Cutter
Stroke for Whaler
Stroke for Skiff

Sept. 21st Tues. O.O.D. We lost a lot of points in Seamen's cutter. Won the Boy's cutters in A.M. P.M. we won the first race O.A. & E.A.S. gigs but Barnham went ahead on points. We won the all comers which was a great achievement.

Centipede gig
Barham's skiff steering from Ford & raised thwart aft won.
Barham won the Cock, Valiant 2nd, Reso. 3, Warspite 4th, Royal Oak 5th.

Sept. 22nd Fleet regatta commenced. Valiant won the Officer's gig. Did not win any of the other races. Went to concert in Warspite in evening.

23rd More Fleet regatta races. Went sailing in 2nd whaler with Mids. Preparing for general drill.

24th General Drill. "Everybody For'd", "Everybody Aft", "Away first engine", "Away Stream Anchor", "Fire a rocket". We did very well and were ahead. Went over see F.R.O. in afternoon. 10 of Warspite's dined with us in the evening.

H.M.S. VALIANT

Sept. 25th Sat. O.O.D.

Sept. 26th Sunday. Sailed at 1830 from Volo[s]. Warspite had turns in her cable when unmooring and joined up late.

Sept. 27th In company with the fleet did TD.11' at 2100-2300. Our search lights weren't a success. Duty Boys off watch 630-700.

Sept. 28th Parted company with Warspite, Resolution, Royal Oak. Carried out an approach exercise. Searchlights much better. Dirty Boys off watch 630-700. T classes 1115-1145. Off. Bayonets in Dog Watches.

Sept. 29th At sea in comp. Barham. Stopped for swim.

Sept 30th Arrived off Malta 0730. Did sub calibre. Entered harbour 1000. Nearly went ashore. Made a bad shot at securing to 7 & 7A buoys, nearly ramming the floating dock. Finally secured at 1330. Raining. When I got home I found that D. was ill in bed with sand fly fever.[104]

Oct. 1st Fri. Rain. Lunch in Egmont with Cordeaux.

Oct. 2nd I am carrying out duties of F.R.O. Allocations of grounds & W.P. pitches. Marsa ground unfit until 1st Nov. Played tennis with Packer & Capt. Marines. Could not hit anything.

3rd Sunday O.O.D. D. came off to Movies on board.

4th Mon. Proceeded at 0900 and after sub calibre anchored off B.J. Played tennis with Col. Giles, Phinney, Gregg, Capt. Marines.

5th Barham & Valiant carried out 6" shoot against the Agamemnon who was controlled by W/T. She made smoke screens. We got 27 hits. Returned to Malta. Tennis with D.

Oct. 6th Tennis with Captain Marines. Bit of rain.

Oct. 7th Havers, Heaton & myself went out in forenoon to look for new bathing place. Tennis with Packer in P.M. at Marsa. I won 6-3, 6-3, 3-6.

Oct. 8th O.O.D. D. & I had lunch with the Captain on board.

Oct. 9th Sat. Packer & I played Capt. Mariners and Col Giles. WE won 6-3, 3-6, 3-6, 6-3, 6-1. We were not playing very well.

Oct. 10th Sunday. D. & I went to Tigné to bathe in the forenoon. In the afternoon, went to Marsa and played Borg. I won 6-2, 6-2, 6-6.

Oct. 11th O.O.D.

Oct. 12th Tues.

Oct. 13th Wed. Tennis with Borg.

---

104 Sandfly fever is an acute mild viral disease characterized by fever, malaise, eye pain, and headache occurring mainly during the warm weather in many parts of the world. It is caused by Phleboviruses and is transmitted by sandflies. Sandfly fever is also known as pappataci fever, phlebotomus fever, and three-day fever.

Oct. 14th Thurs. Day on.

Oct. 15th Fri. Played tennis with Packer, Mrs., Packer & D.

Oct. 16th Sat.

Oct. 17th Sun. D. came off to church. Played tennis with the Everett's. Woods in to supper.

Oct. 18th Mon. Tennis with Packer, Giles, Greig, Mrs. King. To the gym in the afternoon.

Oct. 19

Oct. 20 Packer & I played Finney and Greig. They won 3-6, 6-3, 6-3, 6-3, 6-3.

Oct. 21 Thurs.

Oct. 22 Fri. Dinner with Capt. & Mrs. Walwyn on board Valiant.

Oct. 23 Sat. Day on.

Oct. 24 Sun. Went for a picnic with Captain & Mrs. Walwyn, Crashe, Elkins & some mids.

Oct. 25th Mon. Warspite, Resolution, Royal Oak & Malaya arrived at Castillo. Tennis with Borg.

Oct. 26th Packer & I played Finney & Greig. 2 sets all.

Oct. 27th Wed. Day on.

Oct. 28th Thurs.

Oct. 29th Fri. Rigging Katamarans at Fleet Bathing Place in forenoon for Fleet swimming races. Mixed doubles with the Packers.

Oct. 30th Fleet swimming races in the forenoon at Ricasoli. Went out to Marsa in P.M. Went to the Sliena dance in the evening with the Packers.

Oct. 31st Lent D. £7-0-0; total £13-0-0. Day on.

NOVEMBER 1926

Nov. 1st Monday. In company Malaya proceeded out of harbour for G. & T. exercises. Blowing quite hard.

Nov. 2nd Meeting of P. & R.T. Officers at Castille in forenoon. Played tennis D. & I v. Capt. Manners & Mrs. Rodgers. They won 6-5, 6-4. Went off to the ship for searchlight exercise. Two Japanese cruisers arrived. Dinner in the gun room.

Nov. 3rd Gunnery – 6". Fired 4 torpedoes. Returned to harbour. Played tennis with Captain Manners singles. I won 6-1, 6-5, 6-3, 6-2. Party.

Nov. 4th Day on. Went home in the evening.

Nov. 5th Castille in forenoon. Played tennis in P.M. with Capt. Manners, Packer, Moore, Brook-Shortt. Draw for tennis tournament up.

Nov. 6th The tennis tournament was to have started today but it poured with rain, so play was cancelled until Monday.

Nov. 7th Day on. D came off tea. Havers looked out for me. Supper at Woods.

Nov. 8th Tennis tournament at Marsa commenced. I played Eng. Comm. Turner +3. I am -3. I won 6-1, 6-0.

Nov. 9th Packer & I beat Parkinson & Dyer 6-3, 6-1. Also Surg. Comm. Hole & Turner in the handicap 7-5. 6-0.

Nov. 10th Tournament. Went out to do firing. Anchored outside B.W.

Nov 11th Agamemnon firing 6". Returned to harbour afterwards.

Nov. 12th Day on but torps looked out while I played Strickland. He is +15 & I am -3. I won in two sets. Boxing at Canteen. 7 of our people won cups.

Ord. Sea. Watson (Valiant) beat A.B. Barry (Malaya)
Ld. Sea. Virgoe (Valiant) beat Marine Davis (Malaya)
Marine Maloney (Valiant) beat A.B. Rendelson (Venetia)
Marine Lamphill (Valiant) beat P.O. Callahan (Malaya)
Ord. Sea. Cross (Valiant) beat Stoker Platt (Barham)
Ld. Sea. Woods (Valiant) beat Stoker Boyce (Barham)
Stoker Mann (Valiant) beat A.B. Ogilvie (Malaya)

Nov. 13th Saturday. Played tennis.

Nov. 14th Sun. Played two mixed doubles & won. D. & I played Rapkin & Mrs. Wright. They won the first set 6-2 and were 6-5 40-love, then we won the game and the set 9-7 & next set 6-2.

Nov 15th Parker & I beat Ryde & Basset 6-2, 6-3. D. & I beat Mrs. Duman & Wood in the open 6-2, 6-2. Evans came to dinner.

Nov 16 Played two rounds in the tennis tournament.

Nov. 17

Nov. 18 Was beaten by Gilbride in the handicap singles. Also in handicap mixed. Dance on board.

Nov. 19 D. & I beat Mrs. Unwin & Andrews. Packer & I were beaten by Everett & Parker in handicap doubles. Cruise cancelled.

Nov. 20 D. & I were defeated by Miss Harrison & Moore 6-1, 10-8. Packer & I were beaten by Moore & Land 6-1, 2-6, 7-5, 7-5. Packer sprained a ligament in his foot in the first set.

Nov. 21 Sunday. Day on.

Nov. 22 Mon. Arbothnot trophy meeting in the Barham. Dorothy & Mrs. Unwin won ladies doubles.

Total money received by us for tennis prizes £7-0-0.

Nov. 23 Boxing meeting on board. I have taken over the training of the Marathon team. Pawsey organizer & Bundell. Went for a 5 mile walk.

Nov. 24th Played tennis with Borg.

Nov. 25th Day on.

Nov. 26th

Nov. 27th Played tennis with Finney, Moore, Giles. Dinner at the Packer's.

Nov. 28th Day on.

29th 3′ Mid Miers 18m 35 s. Heavy track. Commenced on Novices Boxing meeting at Corrodino theatre. 11 bouts.

30th Tennis with Captain Manners & Finney at Marsa. 5-7, 2-6.
Novices boxing meeting at Corradino

Dec. 1st Tennis with Captain Manners & Lane.

Dec. 2nd Rec'd. Pay. £44-0-0 M.B. £5-3-8. Tennis mixed D. & I v. Finney & Mrs. Cooke. Dinner with Captain & Mrs. Walwyn on board. Bad cold.

Dec. 3rd Day on. Refereed boxing at Corradino in evening.

Dec. 4th Saturday. Tennis with Dorothy in the afternoon. Cold still very bad. Rain in night.

Dec. 5th Sunday. Stayed in bed all day. Had a bit of a temperature. Raining.

Dec. 6th Mon. Day on.

Dec. 7th Tues. Tennis with Borg. 2 sets all. Pawsey and Bedall came to dinner and bridge.

Dec. 8th Wed. Run with Marathon team in the afternoon.

Dec. 9th Thurs.

Dec. 10 Day on. But went to boxing meeting at Corradino in the evening.

Dec. 11 Sat. Tennis with Packer at Marsa.

Dec. 12 Sun. D. came off to church. Packer & I played Moore & Lane & won 3-6, 6-4, 6-3, 6-4, 6-2.

13 Mon. Went to sea at 1530. Run with Marathon team. Search Light exercise in the evening. Went home afterwards. Anchored outside the BreakWater. Sent E. Leckie 12/6 for L.A.E. for December.

14th Tues. Proceeded at 0900. Sub calibre. Aeroplane attack in afternoon. Anchored at 1500. Proceeded at 1700, Search Light & star shell.

Dec. 13th Mon. Went to sea. Anchored off Breakwater for night.

14th Tues. Gunnery & Torp. Exercises.

15th Wed. Gunnery & Torp. Exercises.

16th Thurs. Returned to Harbour. Played tennis with Moore. Dance at C. in C.

| MARCH | TUESDAY 30 | (89-276) | 1926 |

Dec 26th Marathon trial 8'

27th Commenced the Med. Fleet Novices Flat boxing at Conradino in afternoon & evening. Teams of 8

28th Novices boxing in afternoon & evening

29th Children's party in the afternoon commencing at 1500. Rained hard. — Shoots from Boat Deck to Q.D. Aerial Railway. After Capstan, Coryunio, Movies etc. Marathon trial 8' in afternoon. Finals of Novices boxing in the evening. Valiant 24. Royal Sov. 21. Warspite 20 etc.

31 Played tennis with Borg at Marsa. The Hertons, Packers & Moore came to dinner with us and we went on to the fancy dress dance at the Union Club afterwards.

| | WEDNESDAY 31 | (90-275) | |

JANUARY 1927

Jan 1st Sat. Marathon Trial Intarfa — Conradino. I rode back on a push bike. 8' time of 1st man about 46 min.

Jan 2nd Inspection by V.A. — Tennis in P.M.
Jan. 3 " " — General Quarters.
Jan. 4 " " " Drill. Out all boats. Out fire engine. Out Steam Anchor. Away Fire Engine. Shift Lower Booms etc.

Jan 5th Wed. Battleships Arbuthnot Trophy Competition Intarfa to Conradino Football Grounds. Teams of 10. Barham came first. Warspite, Valiant. Royal Sovereign. Royal Oak, Malaya, Eagle.

Journal page December 26, 1926 to January 5, 1927

17th Friday Navy v. Army tennis match at Marsa.

Myself, Moore, Packer, Captain Manners, Lane, Rapkin

Gregg, Finney, Jones Giles, Morrison.

I played Gregg in singles; he won 6-4, 4-6, 6-4. Very dark day. He chops everything. Parker hurt his foot again & I played with Brook-Shortt in doubles. We beat Jones & Giles 6-4, 6-4.

18th Brook-Shortt & I beat Jones & ? 6-4, 6-4, also Gregg & Finney, 6-4, 6-4.

19th Sunday Rain.

20th Monday Proceeded to sea at 1630. Carried out Search Light exercises from 1800-2330. Various problems (1) Last ship dazzling enemy (2) (3) Effect of gunfire on search lights. Rec'd. letter from D. enclos. £1-0-0.

21 Tues.

22

23

24

25 Went onboard V. in forenoon. Packer's in the evening. It had been raining in the forenoon which made the course difficult. Wind behind the runners. They all came in very close together. Our team: ? Butler, Clarke, Peatfield, White, Southwood, James, Merlam, Miers, Blundell, Wise. 1st man home 42 min. 27 sec. Miers collapsed just before the finish. Blundell came to dinner.

December 26th Marathon trial 8'

27th Commenced the Med. Fleet Novices Team boxing at Corrodino in afternoon & evening. Teams of 8.

28th Novices boxing in afternoon & evening.

29th Children's party in the afternoon commencing at 1500. Rained hard. Shoots from Boat Deck to Q.D. Aerial Railway. After Capstan, Conjurers, Movies etc. Marathon trial 8' in afternoon. Finals of Novices boxing in the evening. Valiant 24, Royal Sov. 21, Warspite 20 etc.

31 Played tennis with Borg at Marsa. The Heatons, Packers & Moore came to dinner with us and we went on to the fancy dress dance at the Union Club afterwards.

JANUARY 1927

Jan 1st Sat. Marathon on Trial Imtarfa-Corrodino. I rode back on a push bike. 8' time of 1st man about 46 min.

Jan. 2nd Inspection by V.A. – Tennis in P.M.

Jan. 3 Inspection by V.A. – General Quarters.

Jan. 4 Inspection by V.A. – General Drill. Out all boats. Out fire engine. Out Stream Anchor. Away Fie Engine. Shift Lower Booms, etc.

Jan. 5th Battleship Arbuthnot Trophy Competition Imtarfa to Corrodino Football grounds. Teams of 10. Barham came first, Warspite, Valiant, Royal Sovereign, Royal Oak, Malaya, Eagle.

Jan. 6th Thurs.

7

8 Played tennis with D. Went to a Marathon dinner at White Ensign Club. Woods came to dinner. Capt. wrote to Admiralty re my appointment.

9. D. & I played in a Mixed Double American handicap tennis tournament at the Marsa. We were leading when rain came down. You play 7 games. Start level, the loser of the 1st game gets +15 in a 2nd game & if they still lose, +30, and if they win they +15 etc. Supper at the Woods. Gregales.[105]

Jan. 10 Sailed at 1600 in company The Fleet less Eagle. Blowing quite hard outside.

11 Exercises.

12 15" Throw off Firing with Barham. Exercises. T.D.s T.D. No. 8. Fog. Royal Sov.[106] lost a man overboard, picked up by Warspite, but was dead due to having hit his head. A Stoker hung himself in R.O.[107]

Jan. 13th Morning Watch. Arrived at Athens at 10 A.M. Anchored at Phaleron Bay. The Acropolis is plainly visible from the ship.

14th Went to Warspite in morning. Landed at 1330 with Packer & went to the Athens Lawn Tennis Club. They have a very nice club, 10 courts clay. Had a very good game. The club is near the Temple of Zeus. Returned to ship at 1900. We have a lawn Tennis Match against them tomorrow. The club is very hospitable supplying new tennis balls for us.

15th Played a Lawn Tennis match v. The Athens Club. The courts were wet as it rained during the forenoon. We won by 5 to 1. I played No. 1 & won my single against Mr. Chrysisalas 6-2, 5-1. Packer & I won our double. They had a dance afterwards which was a very good show & lots of eats. etc. even hamburger cheese buns. They presented us with a cup & a medal for the Captain. Our Launch went ashore but no damage done. The 1st C.S. Frobisher, Delhi, Danae, Dragon, Dauntless ordered to Malta at 18 knots, then to China.

16th Sunday. Day on.

17 Monday. Blowing very hard. Could not land.

18 Tues. Packer, Surg. Cdr. Dean & myself played tennis at Athens Club. I had 3 sets of singles with the Greek chap who beat Packer. I won 6-4, 6-2, 6-2. Dinner in the royal Sovereign with Orr Ewing.

---

105 The Gregale is a Mediterranean wind that can occur during times when a low-pressure area moves through the area to the south of Malta and causes a strong, cool, northeasterly wind to affect the island.
106 Royal Sovereign.
107 Royal Oak.

Jan. 19th Wed. Heaton & I went and saw the Acropolis which is a wonderful place, situated as it is in practically the centre of Athens. Afterwards we went to the Museum, which is also very fine indeed. Contains old statues, pottery, etc.

Went to a dance at the Russian Restaurant. The dance commenced at 10:30. We came back at 1230 arriving on board at 0330. The Captain had a letter from Captain Ford saying that I would be transferred to the Malaya when Valiant returned to England.

Jan. 20 Sailed at 1000 in Company with the Fleet for Oxia Island.[108] Warspite going to Salonika. Quite a heavy sea. T.D.s cancelled.

Jan. 21st At Sea. Called in at Navarino Bay for oil from R.F.A. Montenol.[109] Proceeded to Oxia Island.

Jan. 22nd Anchored at Oxia Island at 0900. Quite a number went duck shooting on the marshes and got about 10 duck.

Jan. 23rd At Oxia Island. Raining, did not go ashore.

Jan. 24 At Oxia Island. Sent $24.50 B. of N.S. cheque to Great West Life Assur. Co. Halifax.

Jan. 25 At Oxia Island. Went shooting in P.M. but did not shoot anything. Party went off in the Canteen M.B. in the direction of Draganesti & got 10 Woodcock. Saw some snipe & ducks. Remitted £2 to Geo. Spencer and £2 to Nat. & Prov. Portsea deposit account. Cash.

Jan. 26 At Oxia. Dined in G. Room, with Myers.

Jan. 27 Sailed for Malta. R.V. with Royal Sov., Royal Oak & Malaya. £12 not contained in envelopes labelled & in purse.

Jan. 28th At sea.

29th Arrived off Malta at 0800. Did a sub calibre shoot & entered harbour at 0930. Morning Watch.

30th Played tennis with the Packer's.

31st

Feb. 1st Tues. Played Tennis with Packer.

2nd Wed. Ship went into No. 4 dock. Got my appointment to the "Malaya". Am very disappointed that I am not going to England in the Valiant. Soulsby came to dinner.

3. Thurs. Played tennis with Packer. Lunch there. Soulsby came to dinner.

4. Friday Came out of dock. Secured to 3 & 3A Buoys. The Heaton's came to dinner & bridge.

5 Sat.

---

108 Oxeia Island is the current name.
109 Royal Fleet Auxiliary. This ship was used to oil other ships in the fleet.

6th Sun.

7 Mon.

8 Tues.

9 Wed.

10 Thurs.

11 Fri. Packing up my gear.

12. Sat. Joined H.M.S. Malaya. Tennis with Packer. Packer's to dinner.

13 Sun. Gin up in Val. Farewell dinner party by Captain Walwyn.

MARCH 1927

1st March Tuesday Still blowing quite hard. Various exercises all day. "Equal Speed" Turning in the wake of next ahead. & the usual battle. Night defence stations.

2nd March –

3rd March Exercise with Atlantic Fleet. Malaya represented a Battle Cruiser, Med. Fleet, Blue Fleet, Atl. F. Red Fleet. Red Fleet endeavour to make contact with some of its forces from Balearic Islands.

4th March Arrived Gib. at 10:00 A.M. Went alongside detached Mole. Tennis with Capt. of Marines. Dinner with Hibbard in Cyclops.

5th March Tennis with Moore, Lane, Laing & me at Sand Pits Club.

6th March Tennis with Eveleigh. Supper with Edden in Eagle.

7th Mon. Tennis with Brooke-Shortt at Sand Pits, also Moore Eveleigh. Most of the Atlantic Fleet are at Lagos.

8th Tues. Sailed at 2000 in company with most of Med. Fleet. The Exercise (Tactical) is as follows: Med. Fleet is Blue Fleet; A.G. is red. Red's home ports are up north near Arctic. Blue is Balearic Isls. Red has a base at Gib. & has a Colony X about 400' from Gib. Blue has sent troops to X supported by a detached fore consisting of a Battle Cruiser & cruisers. Red Fleet is just superior to Blue. Blue has reinforcement in Med. which are coming up from Base at Balearic Isls. Red tries to cut off Blue's detached force & the Red Fleet being about 600' away. Blue goes to sea and endeavours to meet her detached force making a R.V. with them & at all costs joining up with them & not letting them be cut off. Red goes to sea & sails in Southly direct., telling my detached force to go behind Red's force and make a R.V. Blue give the impression to Red that the detached forces are to Southward etc.

9th At Tactical Ex. with A.F.

Steering Southerly Co. Attacked by Red. Torpedo planes & hit by two torpedoes. Our speed reduced 4 knots. Very good shadowing of enemy's battle fleet by Cardiff. P.C.O. at Defence Stations. 1st Watch.

10th Had another daylight battle with A.F. Returned to Gib. P.M. and anchored outside the B.W.

11. Tennis with Brooke-Shortt, playing very badly. Dinner with Miles in the Defender.

12. Played the A.F. at tennis on the hard courts at N.O.P. B.S. & I, Moore & Lane, Eveleigh & Newsome. We won 5-4. I was not playing very well. We were defeated by Glover and Warburton Lee. Concert & at home in "Revenge"

March 13th Sunday Tennis at Sand Pits with Comdr. Spooner, Glover, Eveleigh. Dinner in Marlborough with Soulsby.

14 Day on. Dined at Capt. Ashly-Rushton & concert afterwards. Every division gave a turn—it was quite a good show.

15th Tennis in P.M. Rec'd. a letter from Dad telling me of "Peter Bangs'" death. It was an awful shock to me to hear of it. The wonderful "Black and Tan" dog. I was so fond of him and he was almost human, that I can hardly believe he is gone.

16th Wed. Tennis with Glover, Brooke Shortt, Warburton Lee & Capt. MacDonald at Sand Pits. Feel very depressed over Peter Bangs' death.

17th Thurs. Discussion on Fleet Exercises. A few of the points were: The need of lots of cruisers. The value of Battle Cruisers. Aircraft spotting submarines. The great value they were in doing this as they could see alteration of course to a depth of 80 feet. Submarines should be painted black.

Tennis with Brooke-Shortt. Watched hockey. Abelson the N.1 got concussion. Hibbard dined with me on board.

18 Fri. Went ashore to watch the rugger. Blowing hard. Dined the W.O.s

19 Sat. Ralhs & I walked to top of the Rock, about 1,300 feet. Shopping & buying leather cushion covers etc.

20th Sunday Blowing hard. Day on.

21st Sailed at 0820 for Toulon, in company Warspite Barham, Coventry. Blowing hard with rough seas.

March 22nd 1927 Tues. Gib.-Toulon. Control parties 0930-1200. T.D.'s 1430-1600. At 1600 Warspite took us in tow. The evolution lasted 2 hours as she did not come close enough. Our compressor slip broke & came flying up through Navel pipe breaking one man's hand. At 2000 went to Night action stations, searchlights & starshells.

23rd At Sea Gib.-Toulon. Exercises, etc.

24th Arrived Toulon at 1000. Secured to buoy. Tennis party at Tennis Club. It rained so we danced. Tremendous number of invitations received for various parties.

25th Friday At Home in Bretagne. Did not go. Went to Hyerés & played tennis at Christobello Hotel. Dinner & dance n Evening at Commander Corssion, 13 Rue del la Republic.

26th Saturday Went to dance Préfect de la Maritime. 4 AM.

27 Sun. Watching a football match at Hyerés. Dinner at Christobello. Dance at Casino in evening. 4 A.M.

28 Sailed for Ville Franche & arrived at 1730. Very nice spot.

29 Went to Juan-Les-Pins in morning. Arrived late, was scratched in singles. Went to Cannes in evening. Had lunch at the Carlton Pension at Juan-Les-Pins. Cannes is very pretty and of course very clean & fine shops. Went to the Casino.

30 Went to Juan-les-Pins in forenoon. Played in a handicap single. I was 15-2 & gave ½ of 15. Was defeated 6-2, 3-6, 8-6. Saw some V.G. tennis. Louis (Worm) Chapin of Sweden was playing also Mrs. Satherwaite etc. Returned to ship at 1900. Went to Nice in evening with Holford.

31st Thursday. Went to Monte Carlo in the afternoon with Walker. To the Casino & lost some money at the tables. It is as very pretty place i.e. Monte Carlo, also Monaco. Did some shopping. Dance in Warspite but I did not go.

April 1st Fri. Played tennis at the Bristol Hotel Beaulieu, with Hillyard, Mrs. Satherwaite & the pro. Went to Nice with Buriel in the evening.

2nd Played tennis in morning with J. Hillyard at the Bristol Hotel. Day on.

3rd Tennis at Bristol with Hillyard. He and Mrs. Satherwaite (c/o Queens Club, Earls Court) came off to dinner. All England Club.

April 4th Sailed at 10:30 A.M. for Malta. Warspite sailed at 0800 for Naples. Very fine day. No ships in company. They are having a proper dust up in China.[110] There is a rumour that we may go out there.

5 At sea. Ville Franche – Malta.

6th Wed. At sea. Ville Franche – Malta. 1st D. S.

---

110 The Chinese Civil War was a civil war in China fought between the Kuomintang (KMT)-led government of the Republic of China (ROC) under Chiang Kai-shek and the Communist Party of China (CPC) under Mao Zedong lasting intermittently between 1927 and 1949. The war is generally divided into two phases with an interlude: from August 1927 to 1937, the KMT-CPC Alliance collapsed during the Northern Expedition, and the Nationalists controlled most of China. From 1937 to 1945, hostilities were put on hold, and the Second United Front fought the Japanese invasion of China with eventual help from the World War II Allies. The civil war resumed with the Japanese defeat, and the CPC gained the upper hand in the final phase of the war from 1945–1949, generally referred to as the Chinese Communist Revolution.

The Communists gained control of mainland China and established the People's Republic of China (PRC) in 1949, forcing the Republic of China to retreat to the island of Taiwan. A lasting political and military standoff between the two sides of the Taiwan Strait ensued, with the ROC in Taiwan and the PRC in mainland China both officially claiming to be the legitimate government of all China. No armistice or peace treaty was ever signed, and the debate continues as to whether the civil war has legally ended.

The Shanghai Massacre of Communists was one week after this entry—on April 12.

7 **Thurs.** Arrived Malta at 0945. Secured to No. 3. Ashore in P.M. New flat no. 21 Str. Meyzodi is very nice. D. has been ill.

8. **Fri.** Sports training at Corradino.

9 **Sat.** Tennis with Brook-Shortt, Finny, Jones & Newsome at Marsa. Sport training later.

16th Bought a "Jowett" car for 845 from Capt. Thomas (Proctor). Played tennis.

17th

18th April To sea for exercises. G. & T. Anchored outside B.W.

19 April To sea for exercises. G. & T.

20 April To sea for exercises. G. & T.

21 April

22 April Returned to harbour.

23 April Ships sports at Corradino A.M. & P.M. Started at 1000. Ran off everything in the day. They went well.

24 **Sun.** R.A. won Cassar Cup defeating the Malaya 4-2. Supper at Captain Usborne's.

25 **Mon** Proceeded to sea at 0845. We are representing the Invincible in the film of the "Battle of The Falkland Islands". Barham represents Inflexible. Coventry with Dummy funnels the Scharnhorst. It was rather amusing.

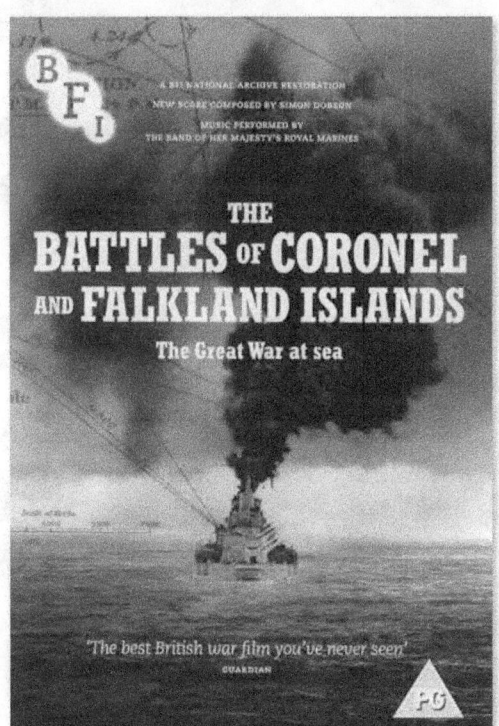

"The Battles of Coronel and Falkland Islands" video in which Dutchy's ship played one of the combatants

26th Full power trial. I stayed ashore.

27th Wed. Played tennis with Brook-Shortt, Miss Robinson, D. & myself. Corradino in evening.

28th Thurs. Tennis, Corradino in the evening.

29 Fri. Tennis with B.S., Gibs & Eveleigh.

30 Sat. Spring dawn Tennis Tournament commenced at Marsa.

[No entries for this time]

12 Thurs. Heats.

Fri. 13 At sports Gr. Heats for Battleship meeting. Bromet beat us in Hdcp.[111]

Sat. 14th Played Moore & Lane in doubles & won 6-0, 6-4. D. & I beat Moore & Miss Harrison 6-3, 6-4. B.S. & I beat Giles & Philips.

Sun. 15

May 16th Fleet sports. Battleships & Cruisers at the Marsa. Barham, R. Sov., Warspite, Malaya, Eagle, Egmont in that order. Cardiff, Calypso, Ceres, Concord. Sports went off very well.

May 18th Championship heats at Marsa. Finals of Lawn Tennis Tournament at Marsa. Brook-Shortt & I played Major Finny & Jones & we won 7-5, 3-6, 6-3, 6-4. I sprained my ankle in the second set. I then played Finny in Singles & won 6-2, 6-1, 6-3. Dot & I. beat Major Jones & Miss M. Strickland 6-4, 3-6, 6-0. Ankle hurt a great deal. Faulkner was married. Dance in Malaya.

19th Went on sick leave ashore – in bed.

20 Went on sick leave ashore – in bed.

21 Went on sick leave ashore – in bed.

22

23

24

25

27 Went out to Calafrana R.A.F. display.

28

29th At 0800 Rec'd. signal saying to be ready to sail P.M. Spent forenoon getting my gear on board. Sailed at 1800 in Company Barham & Royal Sovereign.

30 Malta-Alexandria. I am 2nd in command of A Company. Serving out equipment, etc. drilling & forming companies. General Organization.

---

111 Handicap.

31 May May pay £25-0-0. Malta-Alex. 14 knots, serving out equipment, rations, etc. to the companies. Very hot.

June 1, 1927 Arrived at Alexandria at 0530. Not so much excitement although the political situation has been a bit intense over the demands of Egyptian government to increase its army & do away with the Sirdar. Went ashore in P.M. with Johnson & went out to Sporting Club, entered a tennis tournament commencing June 7th. Still drilling, etc.

June 2nd 3rd Day On. Went for staff ride around Alexandria looking at the places we would have to take over in the event of Trouble. Dressed ship.

June 4 Went to a dinner at Mr. I. Rolo.

5th Swim & L. Tennis at Sporting Club. Supper at _ _ _.

6th Skipper had a tea party to which I went.

June 7th Played in the handicap singles at Sporting Club. I beat Chessman who was +15. I was -15.1. Non swimmers.

June 8th Wed. Played tennis at Sporting Club.

June 9th Thurs. Day on.

June 10th Fri. Played Allen +15.7 & I won 6-2, 6-3. Dinner with the Consul General Heathcote-Smith. Went out to the R.A.F. Depot at Aboukis & watched the boxing which was good. They have an open air ring.

June 11th Played in a double with Steinthall, Edwards & Wilkinson.

June 12th Inspection by V.A. Kelly in forenoon. Had a single with Steinthal in P.M. 7-5, 5-7. Rec'd. cheque for diff. of Pay Oct 26-Dec 1926 £4-1-10.

June 13 Mon. Inspection by V.A. Gen. Quarters. Played Yabu & won in 3 sets.

14. Tues. Inspection by V.A General Drill. Played Gérsole & was defeated 3 sets. I played very badly. It lasted 2 hours. Very hot.

15. Wed. Day on.

16. Thurs. Had a game of tennis with the Pro.

17. Fri. Had a game of tennis with the Pro in forenoon. Went to the R.A.F Depot Aboukis. Played tennis. We won the match 5 games to 4. Also two ship's company cricket teams & a billiard team went up.

18 Caught the 715 train to Cairo arriving at 1030. Went to Museum in the forenoon with Best, Hunt, Fleming. Very interesting especially all the things from King Tutankhamun's tomb. Very hot. Had lunch at the Continental & went to see three Mosques in P.M. Mohammed Ali, Blue Mosque, etc. Then went to the Bazaars & bought some things including a shawl. Things are very cheap as this is the off season. Returned to Alex. at 2250.

19th Sunday Played tennis in P.M. with Steinthall, Edwards & Hammond (Pro). V.G. game. Had supper with the Steinthall's.

Naval officers on camels by the Sphinx and the Pyramids – Dutchy in centre

20th June Monday As the Egyptian crisis is over, we sailed for Malta at 0900, 14 knots. Fine weather but hot.

21st June Tues. At sea Alexandria-Malta, 13 knots. V. hot.

22 June Wed. At sea Alexandria-Malta.

23 June Thurs. Arrived Malta at 0700. Played tennis in P.M.

24 June Fri. At Malta. Dinner with Faulknors.

25 June Sat. Tennis. Went to Delemara for a swim. V.G. Sliena Club dance in evening.

26 June Sun. Tennis – Delemara.

27 June Mon. Sailed at 0530 in company Barham, Eagle & Ceres & destroyers for 1st half of Summer cruise to which I don't look forward to at all. We got to Navarin Bay first. Day On & last day.

28 Tues. Very hot. We are carrying out a Tactical Exercise. We are part of Blue Fleet trying to make a junction with the other half & return to our base. Red Fleet whose base is Malta is trying to cut us off.

Wed. 29

Thurs. 30 Arrived at Navarin Bay at 0700. Cdr. Barrett promoted.

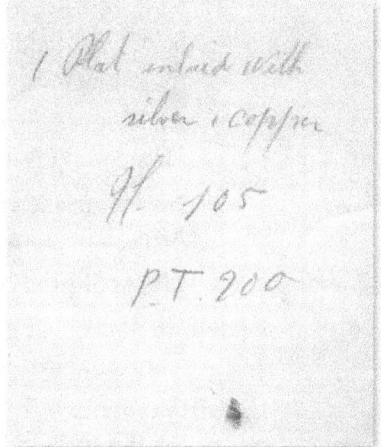

(upper) Business card from Cairo – front and back

(left) Italian five lire note

Fri. 1 JULY 1927 At Navarin.

2nd July Practice landing of Royal Marine Striking Force.

3rd July Sunday Day on.

4th July Practice landing of R.M. Striking Force. F.R.O. All.

5th July

6 July

7 July Trieste Cup Sailing – won by Whitehall's K. Whaler.

July 8th

July 9 Sailing race for Cup. Not much wind. In Warspite all day.

July 10 Went ashore for a walk at Navarin.

July 11 Monday Sailing race for C. in C.'s Cup in the forenoon. Won by Coventry's DX Cutter Cdr. Ridley. Lunch in Warspite with McGrane. In the P.M. Sailing Race for Beresford Cup (Midshipmen) won by Mid. Tancred R.A.N. Royal Sovereign in DX Cutter. Dined Captain Usborne.

Navarin Bay is the bay where the big battle was in ? .[112] It is a very fine bay & will hold a large fleet. Has narrow entrance, seems a bad spot for sailing races.

July 12th Proceeded at 0630. Submarines exercised an attack on us in forenoon. H.A. firing in P.M. No Night Exercise.

July 13th Aeroplane attack in P.M. with torpedo planes. Sub calibre in P.M. Arrived Skiathos at 1430 & anchored. Mail.

July 14th At Skiathos.

July 15th Proceeded to sea at 0800, 15" Sub Calibre. M.S.C. (Master Ship Control). Fired 9 Torpedoes. Returned to Skiathos. Day on.

July 16th Saturday. Tried to hold the Iron Duke Trophy Sailing Race in the P.M. But the wind dropped when the leading boats had got nearly once around. I was in the Royal Sovereign as one of the judges.

July 17th Sunday. Went ashore with Brunelle for a walk. This is quite a pretty place with sandy beaches.

July 18th Monday At sea – Sub Calibre.

July 19th Tues. Proceeded at 0800. 6" M.A.C. 60 rounds. Anchored at 1330. Boat pulling in the gig.

July 20th Sailing race for Iron Duke Trophy. A very good breeze about 30 M.P.H. Several boats capsized and lost masts, etc. This is a team race, 1st boat counting 28 points, next 27 and so on. Malaya won trophy, Royal Sovereign second. I was judging in the Royal Sovereign. Concord proceeded to Malta with sick Midshipmen.

June (sb July) 21st We were going to sea at 0715 for 15" concentration but weather was too bad for targets. Fire ashore, each battleship landed 65 men. Day on. Regatta practice.

June (sb July) 22nd Weather bad. Finally went to sea at about 1545. Got in position for firing etc. when Royal Sovereign's W.T. broke down. Shoot was cancelled and we returned to harbour.

June (sb July) 23rd

 Saturday Proceeded at about 0830 to carry out 15" concentration. The shoot was V.G. except that the gun was shooting over owing to super elevation from not being shipped. Returned to harbour.

Sunday July 24th Went for a picnic at one of islands.

Mon. 25th Sailed at 1300 hours for Port Skutari by ourselves. Ceres & Concord arrived.

---

112 The Battle of Navarino was a naval battle fought on 20 October 1827, during the Greek War of Independence (1821–32), in Navarino Bay (modern Pylos), on the west coast of the Peloponnese peninsula, in the Ionian Sea. Allied forces from Britain, France, and Russia decisively defeated Ottoman and Egyptian forces trying to suppress the Greeks, thereby making much more likely the independence of Greece.

Tues. 26th Arrived Port Skutari which is a bay which is not very far from Cape Matapan. Open to the S.E. A small village. Regatta practice – Raced G.R. gig & beat them. Dinner in the G.R. with Glass.

Wed. 27th Regatta practice. P.T. at 0900 for Seaman Racing Boat's crews. Remainder of hands go to P.T. at 1550 & going to bathe at 1620. Day on.

Thurs. 28th At Port Skutari. Regatta practice gig.

Fri. 29th At Port Skutari.

Sat. 30 Heard that Malaya would probably arrive in England by 31st of August.

Sun. 31 Went ashore with Burrell for a walk. Very uninteresting. The village is an awful place, absolutely filthy & no roads but there are very fine bathing beaches.

H.M.S. MALAYA AUGUST 1927

1st August 1927 Monday Regatta practice etc. Boats crews at P.T. Swimming etc.

2nd August Tues. At Port Skutari.

3rd August Wed. Swim ashore. Gig.

4th August Thurs. Gig.

5 August Sailed at 0300 for Argostoli. R.V. with the Fleet. Exercise at 0700 to determine the best disposition of submarines with the Battle Fleet.

6 August Arrived at 1430 at Argostoli in company with the fleet. Moored ship. Mail. Dinner with Pog. Havers in the Valiant. Not many of the old commission in the ship.

7th Aug. Regatta practice. Went ashore for a walk at Argostoli in P.M.

8th Aug. Went over to Warspite in forenoon to find out where I am going when Malaya goes to England. Heard that I will probably go to Valiant. Although I asked if I could go to England in the Malaya and come out in October in the Q.E.

9th Battle Squadron and Cruiser Regatta. We did not do well in the W.R. officers gig race. We came in next to last. Perhaps the stroke was too slow for us, as with a following wind it appears better to have a stroke of about 33 or 34. Talbot cox (coxswain). Westmacott, Leggett, Higham, Edwards, Fleming, Hollebone. Malaya did not do very well. Warspite and Barham very close. Warspite stokers' cutter disqualified for crossing out stokers' cutters bows.

Aug. 10th 2nd day of regatta. We won subordinate officers' gig, Marine Whalers, P.O.'s cutters. Barham just won the cock by 3 points from Warspite. Show in Warspite which was good. Middles Watch. Have not heard definitely as to my movements yet.

Aug 11th Fleet Cup Races
  0950 Duke of Edinb. Seamen's cutters 3' – Barham
  1000 Royal Sov. Officers' gigs 1' – Warspite, Valiant
  1045 Ramilles Cup Marine's cutters 2' – Valiant
  1130 Subordinate officers' gigs 1' – Malaya, R. Sov.
  1400 Renown Cup Stokers' cutters 2' – Warspite
  1430 Benbow Warrant Officers' gigs 1' - R. Sov., Malaya
  1500 Bosphorus Boys' cutters – Val.

Aug 12 Fleet Cup races. Admiralty sent signal saying that Malaya would leave for England September 3rd & asked for C. in C.'s concurrence. Elliot came to dinner. A big party of manned the launch illuminated by a cup & went round the fleet: Bryony, Barham, Malaya & Eagle. Big party.

August 12th Fleet Cup Races.
  0900 Illustrious Cup – Open Cutter 3'
  *1000 Cambrian Cup – Open Gigs 2' – Malaya
  1100 Orion – Open Whalers
  1700 Funnel – All Comers 3' – Ceres, Cardiff.
  *This was won by our Officers crew, 1st time on record. All comers won by 16 oared centipede gig – about 42 strokes per min.
  About 32 gigs stroke
  About 34 cutters

Aug. 13th 1927 Prize giving for Fleet Cup Races in Warspite in forenoon. Went for a walk with Westmacott in afternoon. Captain gave a dance in the evening.

Aug 14th Day on.

Aug 15th Mon. Unmoored. Went for walk & swim with Westmacott in P.M. Very nice sandy beach.

Aug. 16th Tues. Sailed for Malta at 0730. Exercise N.N. which is one repelling submarine attack. Tactical Drills nos. Deploying etc. & searching exercise at night until 2330. Darkened ship.

17 Wed. Various Exercises.

18 Thurs. Arrived Malta – went alongside Somerset wharf. I am going back to the Valiant. Very hot. Tennis & swim at Delamara.

19th Warspite in forenoon. Tennis with Leggett. Harold Grant to dinner.

20th Sat. Day on but Burnell looked out. Tennis with Leggett and Walkey. Walkey to dinner.

21 Sun. Day off. Tennis with D. & swim.

22 Mon. Tennis.

23 Tues. Tennis with D.

24 Wed. Tennis at Sliema with D. Water Polo Malaya v. Valiant

August 25 Thurs. Heats of B.S. Swimming races at Ricasoli.

Aug 26 Fri. Day on. Water Polo.

Aug. 27 Sat. Swimming heats at Ricasoli & final of the relay race won by Eagle. Tennis at Marsa with Eveleigh, Finney & Jones. Harold Grant came to dinner.

Aug. 28th Sun. Played tennis with Eveleigh. Wing Cdr. Bromet & Surg. Cdr. Quinton to supper. Vin D'honneur[113] in Malaya.

Aug. 29 Mon. Fleet Water Polo semi-finals at Ricasoli. Tennis with D.

Aug. 30 Tues.

Aug. 31st Fleet swimming and Water Polo finals at Ricasoli. H. Grant to dinner.

Sept. 1st Joined H.M.S VALIANT at 1345. Tennis with Dorothy.

Sept. 2nd Sailed at 0700 in company with the fleet. T.D.s & 15" Throw off firing in P.M.

Sept. 3rd At Sea. Various T.D.s etc.

Sept. 4 At Sea. Various T.D.s etc.

Sept. 5 At sea. Parted company with Royal Oak.

Sept. 6 At sea. Arrived at Rhodes at 1830. Anchored about ¾ of a mile from Torm. Rhodes is Italian.

Sept. 7th Went ashore with the Marathon team for a walk. Rhodes is quite a clean place, good roads. Quite a number of hotels and some good buildings. The Italian Military Club is very nice & has one tennis court – lighted.

8 Played tennis with Miers at the Military Club.

9 Played tennis with Miers at the Military Club. Very hot. Sharks reported in the vicinity so we have to stop bathing. General Drill.

10 Went to the Museum and visited the old fortifications which was very interesting. The fortifications are about 7' long & go all around the Old town. the Knights of St. John had the place. The various sections of the town & walls were divided up amongst the nations represented. The Museum is very good indeed. The statue of Colossus stood at Rhodes and was very big being about 170' high. The Turks took the place the Knights of St. John being given very good terms were allowed to go to Malta with all their possessions. Italy has had the Island since 1912.[114]

---

113 Vin d'honneur literally translates from French to "Wine of honour" and is akin to a prolonged social celebration after an official ceremony like a marriage.
114 In 1947, Rhodes, together with the other islands of the Dodecanese, was united with Greece.

11 Played tennis.

12 Played tennis. Went to the Albergo Des Roses. STAG HUNT

13 Dance at the Circolo Italia which was very good fun. Dinner with Elliot (of Cairo) at the Grand Albergo Des Roses. Took the Boys Division to the Museum and Fortifications. Official Tea Party on board.

14 Tennis. We gave a dance on board which was quite good and very amusing.

15 Played tennis with Selby, Quinton, Walker. Sailed at 1815 for Salonika.

16 At sea. Rhodes – Salonika.

17 At sea. Rhodes – Salonika. O.O.W. manoeuvring the ship. Arrived at Salonika at 1600.

18 **Sunday** Went ashore to see the Hercule Football Ground etc. Ground is quite good, it has a running track around it.

19 **Monday** Went ashore with Capt. Consul & wife KING & Mrs. Menzies. Went for a swim.

20 **Tues.** Played football W.R. V. G.R. We won 4-3.

21 **Wed.** Went to the Greek Lawn Tennis club which is near the British Consul's; they have 4 courts which are quite good. The club has just been opened. We were met by Mr. Helias who works at British Consulate.

22 **Thurs.** Played tennis with Quinton, Selby, Barcroft at the Donaldson's. They have one court. Salonika is a pretty filthy place, all the sewers & drains go into the sea, so the smell is not pleasant. The fire in 1917 destroyed most of the town but it is being built up now with quite good buildings. We cannot bathe here as the water is too dirty.

SEPT. 1927 H.M.S. VALIANT

23rd Went ashore with Stokes for a run at 0630. Had a game of tennis with Miers. Watched the football match & Marathon party.

24. Went ashore with Miers to watch the tennis at the Greek Club which was quite good as they had the chaps from Athens playing, the champion of Greece, etc. Went to the Industrial Fair afterwards.

25 **Sunday** Day on.

26th Played Chamenes & won 6-2, 6-1. Also played Europilios from Athens & won 6-2, 6-6; also played a double.

27th **Tues.** Dinner at the Menzies'.

28th **Wed.** Took the boys (42) to the Exhibitions.

29th **Thurs.** Tennis at Jewish Club. Dinner at the Menzies' in the evening.

30th **Fri.** Landed at 0730 for 3' Marathon Run Inter Part. About 120 landed, having gone to breakfast at 0545. Owing to the fact that the markers misdirected the runners, the result was not satisfying although they had a very good run. Stokers were in front. Time of race 0800 was a success.

At home on board in the afternoon.

OCTOBER 1st Heavy rain during the night. Went out to the Greek club but there was no play. Watched football match Greek Army v. Val. We lost 6-2. We had practically a second team out.

OCTOBER 2nd Sunday I stayed on board – looked out for Leggett.

OCTOBER 3rd Sailed at 0600 10 kn. for Alexandria.

OCTOBER 4th At sea. We have General Spinks (Sirdar of Egypt)[115] on board as a passenger.

OCTOBER 5th At sea.

OCTOBER 6th Arrived at Alexandria at 1030. Dorothy came on board having come from Malta in a trooper. Staying at the Regina Palace. On board most of the day, waiting for various Sports Officers to call.

7th Very busy arranging games, etc. Lt. McKinnon Gray, Royal Scots came down from Cairo to see me about games.

8th Sat. Played tennis 2 sets. Conquest, Cyclops & S of M.'s arrived.

9th Sun. Meeting on board of sports officers to arrange Cairo trip.

10th Monday Tennis with Wilkinson.

11th Dance at San Stefano given by Mrs. Carver & the British Community at Alex.

12th Caught the 0900 train to Cairo arriving at 1220. Went to the Victoria Hotel. Was met at station by Gray. Tennis at Gezira Club[116] with D. & the Pro. Lt. Dow R.T.C. came to dinner, afterwards we went to see the Pyramids by moon light (Met the LIMIT) & the Mena House.

13th Tennis at Gezira. Bazaars in the morning. Dinner with the Grays. Watched the Pelotta Basque which was very good.

14th Played our tennis match v. the Army which we lost by one match. Our team; myself, Capt. Stevens, Webber, Selby, Cdr. De Burgh & Miers. I played Capt. Moore R.A.O.C. & won 7-5, 6-2. I felt very poorly in the first set. The Navy team lost at Soccer. Went to the Boxing in the evening at Abassia. We only won one fight.

15th Dorothy caught the 0700 train to Port Said as she is returning to Malta in the Trooper "City of Marseilles". I went to the Bazaar & in afternoon

---

115 Sirdar, a variant of Sardar – was assigned to the British Commander-in-Chief of the British-controlled Egyptian Army in the late 19th and early 20th centuries. The Sirdar resided at the Sirdaria, a three-block-long property in Zamalek which was also the home of British military intelligence in Egypt. Spinks was Sirdar 1924 to 1937.

116 The Gezira Sporting Club is the largest multi-sport facility in Egypt. It was founded in 1882 and was originally called Khedivial Sporting Club. It is located on the island of Zamalek in Cairo.

played tennis with Hatton. I am staying at the R.E. & R.T.C.[117] mess Abassia (Haking House).

16th Sunday Played tennis in the afternoon in our little Davis Cup. Hatton & I played Hon. Cecil Campbell & Greenwood and we lost 3-6, 14-12, 6-4. We next played Egypt Waheed & T.... We lost 4-6, 7-5, 5-7. I caught the 1930 train arriving Alex. 2250.

17th Monday

18th Tues. Tennis with the Miss Alexandroff & Rhys (Tel Rawlib 567).

19th Wed. Played the R.A.F. Aboukir in tennis & won 5-4. Our team Cdr. Deburgh, Webber, myself, Miers, Barcroft, Leggett. Boxing afterwards. Arrived on board at 0230.

20th Tennis with Zelandia. Dance on board.

21st Sailed at 1430 for MALTA.

22nd At sea Alex. – MALTA in company with Royal Oak.

23rd Sun. Alex – MALTA.

24th Mon. Carried out 15" and 6" throw off shoots on Warspite & destroyers respectively. I was in H.S. top spotting for line with sextant 6°.

25th Tuesday Ramillies carried out a 15" throw off shoot on us. Arrived Malta at 1430 to no. 3 & 3A Buoys.

26th Wednesday Hibbard & H. Grant to dinner.

27th Thurs. Tennis with Brook-Shortt.

28th Fri.

29 Sat. Tennis with D. Pog Havers to dinner.

30

31

NOVEMBER 1927

1 Tennis with Jones, Bocquet, Eveleigh etc.

2

3 Tennis with Eveleigh.

4 Day on. L. Tennis handicap meeting at Union Club. The Moncriefs came in to bridge.

Nov. 6th 1927 Queen Elizabeth arrived at 0900. Singles with Brook-Shortt. Watched football match, Navy V. Civilian Team at E.S.G. Navy won 1-0. Dinner with Capt. Carrington on board Valiant. Movies.

7th 1927 At Castillo in A.M. Tennis with Army etc. Singles with Packer.

8th 1927 Castille in forenoon. Played tennis with Major & Mrs. Bocquet.

---

117 Royal Engineers & Royal Tank Regiment.

9th Castille in forenoon. Day on.

10th Morning watch. Castille. Tennis with the Bromets. Very windy. Boxing at Corrodino Canteen. 12 fights. V. good. No rain yet, there hasn't been any except for one day since April. Country & grounds needs it very badly.

11th ARMISTICE DAY. 2 min. silence. Massed bands played on the Barraca. Went in to the Quinton's in the evening. Morning watch. Tennis with the Brometts.

12th Sat. It rained a little bit during the night. Quite chilly. Tennis with BS. Major Bowle & Borg. Called on the Fletchers. Quintons in. H. Grant & Hibbard to dinner.

13th Sun. Raining hard. Called on Q.E. Packer's in evening.

14th Monday AUTUMN LAWN TENNIS Tournament commenced at Marsa. I played Capt. Simpson R.M. +15.3. I am -15.3. I won 6-2, 6-2. Marg. Bromet & I -15.2 were defeated by the Brookings +15 6-3, 3-6, 6-3.

15th Tuesday D. & I beat Eveleigh & Mrs. Carter 6-2, 7-5 in open mixed.

16 Wed. Tennis tournament.

17 Thurs.

18 Fri.

19 Sat.

20 Sun.

> I have heard rumours that I am taking a Destroyer out to Canada but nothing official.

DECEMBER 1927

Dec. 4

Dec. 5

Dec. 6th

Dec. 7th Frobisher & 1st C.S. arrived back from China. Pro. Boxing. R.W. Wood easily won.

Dec. 8th

Dec. 9th Weighing in the boxers for Novices competition in forenoon. Dinner party Quintons, Moncriefs. Went to the Cyclops' concert.

DECEMBER 10th 1927 Went to a lecture in the War Game room in forenoon. Played tennis with Borg in afternoon.

Dec. 14 Dance on board Valiant. Rain.

Dec. 15 Dance at R.A.M.'s Admin at Campbell.

Dec. 16

Dec. 17 Watched football match Navy V. St. George's at E.S.C.

Dec. 18 **Sunday** A day's leave.

Dec. 19 Played tennis with Packer at Marsa. V. cold day.

Dec. 20th Played tennis with Evans.

Dec. 23rd Dinner with the Everett's.

Dec. 24th Watched soccer match, Navy V. Hyduk at E.S.G. Badminton with H. Grant. The Quintons, Grant & Hibbard to dinner.

Dec. 25th CHRISTMAS. Church on board Valiant went around the mess decks. etc. Hockey match (in funny rigs) in P.M. Dinner with the Packers.

Dec. 26th BOXING DAY. Day on but managed to get ashore to have a game of Badminton with H. Grant. Tickie & Dot came on board to dinner.

Dec. 27th BOYS BOXING meetings at 1415 & 2015. Went to the Eagles' dance.

Dec. 28 Tennis with Borg. Boxing meeting in evening (Boys).

29 Tennis with Packer. Dinner with the Quintons. Went to dance given by Gov. Sir J. Du Cane[118] in P.M.

30 Went for a run with the Marathon team.

31 Tennis. At house.

JAN. 1ST 1928

Jan. 1 **Sunday** Day's leave. Lunch with Packers. We were going to play tennis but it rained.

Jan. 2nd

Mon. 2nd Saw in the paper that Canada is getting two destroyers also Torbay[119] & Toreador.[120]

Tues. 3rd

Wed. 4 Jan. Tennis with Major Bowle.

Thurs. 5th Jan. Played tennis with Packer.

6 Fri.

7 Sat. Had a couple of sets of tennis with Borg, then watched the football math United Services V. Hadjacks – a draw 0-0. Barcroft & Pelham Kent came to dinner.

---

118 General Sir John Philip Du Cane, GCB (5 May 1865 – 5 April 1947) was a British Army officer. He held high rank during the First World War, most notably as Major General Royal Artillery at General Headquarters in 1915 when the Du Cane was appointed Master-General of the Ordnance in 1920 and then General Officer Commanding-in-Chief for Western Command in 1923. He was General Officer Commanding-in-Chief for British Army of the Rhine from 1924 until 1927 when he became Governor and Commander-in-Chief of Malta. He was also Aide-de-Camp General to the King from 1926 to 1930. He retired in 1931
119 HMS *Torbay* was renamed HMCS *Champlain* when she was loaned to the RCN.
120 HMS *Toreador* was renamed HMCS *Vancouver* when she was loaned to the RCN.

8 Sunday A day's leave played tennis in forenoon with the Quintons. Lunch at the Marsa. Played in an American mixed double tournament sealed handicap. D. & I won 4 games out of 42 but owing to handicap could not possibly win the prize. Watched the movies on board "Coronel & the Falkland Islands".

9 Mon. Smoke shells trial. The idea is to blank off ourselves from our enemy so that we can concentrate on them.

Tues. 10

Wed. 11

Thurs. 12 The Quintons, Massey Goolden & Forrest came to dinner.

Fri. 13 Tennis with Evans. Went to Bulldog Drummond with the Quintons.

Jan. 14th 1928 Navy V. Army tennis match at Marsa. Navy won by 7 matches to 2. Eveleigh & Packer, Brook-Shortt & myself, Loveland & Tottors. B.S. & I won all our matches. Letter forwarded to C. of N.S. for two weeks leave in the South of France.

Jan. 15th Sunday Day on. Asked the Captain if I could go to Alex. in the Q.E. Movies in evening.

16 Mon. Approved to go to Alex. but they wanted to send me in Warspite. Finally I had it altered & so am going in the Q.E.

17 Tues. Sailed in Q.E. for Alex. at 1145.

18 Wed. At sea. Malta – Alex. Exercise N.P. Viceroy had collision with Sandhurst.

19 Thurs. At sea. Blowing hard, rain. Caledon had collision with Italian steamer in Doro Channel.

20 Fri.

21 Sat. Arrived Alex. at 0700. went ashore to Sporting Club to see Major Goodchild and fix up some matches.

22 Sun. L. Tennis match V. a sporting club team (doubles). I played with Mid. The Hon. Cairns. Navy was beaten 5-4.

1928

Jan. 23rd Monday A very fine day. Packer & I played tennis at the sporting club in the afternoon.

Jan. 24th Tues. Packer & I & the remainder of the tennis team caught the 0900 train to Cairo arriving there at 1220. Met by McKinnon Gray. Packer & I stayed at the Somersets' 13th Regt. at Kaiser-El-Nil Barracks. Nearly all the regiment is out at camp. Played the Army in Cairo at tennis in the P.M. & were beaten 7-2. P. & I won two, Hatton & ---- are V.G. pair. Dinner at the Shiera Club given by the British Community, dance afterwards at the Continental Savoy.

Jan. 25th Wed. Went to the Museum in forenoon. Played Hatton and the No. 1 pro in afternoon & beat them. Dance at the Semiramis Hotel. Miss Percival. Went to the Pelota Basque afterwards.

Jan. 26th Thurs. Bazaars in forenoon. Tennis at the Gezira. Left Cairo 1930 arrived Alex., 2280.

Jan. 27th Fri. Tennis match V. Alex. sporting club. Packer & I played together & won 3 matches score 5-4 against. Dance on board. Good show. Lord Lloyd attended.

Jan. 28 Sat Went ashore at 1000. Had a game with the Pro. Hammond. Then played Rye in P.M. & won. Dinner at the E.T.C. Mess with Wilkinson in the evening.

Jan. 29 Sun. Sailed at 1700 for Malta.

30 At Sea – Bad weather.

31 At Sea – Bad weather.

Feb.1 1928 Exercise with the Fleet.

Feb. 2 1928 Arrived Malta 1000.

Feb. 3 1928 At Castillo. Rec'd. a chit from Admiralty saying that I was to be discharged to await passage to Canada and to arrive there about 10th April. H. Grant came in. He gave us a V. fine brass tray.

5 Feb. Sent letter to V.A. re leave at Beaulieu & course in England.

6 Feb. Valiant, Warspite, Q.F. sailed for exercises. I did not go but remained behind, working at Castille.

7 Feb. Cold & rain.

8 Feb. At Malta.

9 Feb. At Malta.

10 Feb. At Malta.

11 Feb. Sat. Rec's. from Ottawa re returning to Canada & that I am going in command of H.M.C.S. Torbay on completion of foreign service leave i.e. about the end of May.

Sat. 18th Feb. Marathon eliminating race in afternoon. Quintons, K. Warren, Blundell dined with us & went on to the arrival at the Opera House.

March 3rd Sailed in M/V Stella Polaris for Monaco.

March 4 Sunday At sea. Malta – Monte Carlo.

March 5 Mon. Arrived Monaco at 0700. Drove to Mentone in taxi. Room at Hotel De Paris for 65 per day each. Went up to tennis club.

6th Played Dr. Buss & was beaten 6-4, 6-1. Won a Handicap against Youill. My handicap is +15.

7. Wheatcroft & I beat Peters & Harris. Saw some V.G. players. Cochet, Van Tuley, Lorenzo, etc. Stefani.

MARCH 1928

Wheatcroft & I were beaten by Dr. Russ & Menzel. I played badly. Won a handicap single & D. & I beat Miss Morill & Brace in mixed doubles. Miss Morill beat Betty Nuttall 6-3, 6-3.

9. Played a mixed v. Ostley & Fran ?. Lost 6-0, 3-6. 6-1.

10 Played Cuthbertson in handicap singles & won 6-1, 6-3. Cochet, Von Ruby, D'Alverez, Eileen Bennet etc. playing.

11 **Sunday** Played Martino in final of handicap single & won 6-1, 6-0. I am +15. Prize 500 Francs. Went to Sospel in a car. A very pretty drive in the mountains. A very good Golf hotel at Sospel.

12th **Mon.** Went to Mil. Played Barker & won 6-3, 6-2, 6-3.

13th **Tues.** Went to Hotel Bristol at Beaulieau-Sur-Mer. They took us for 90 Francs each. A very fine hotel.

14 **Wed.** Playing at Nice was defeated by Makoloff.

15 **Thurs.** At Nice.

16 **Fri.** D. & I played the King of Sweden & Fran Aussen. We had to give them 15.3. They won.

17 **Sat.** Had a tennis lesson with Karl Kozerlach. He is very good. 120 Francs per hour.

18 **Sun.** Lesson with Kozerlach. Battle of Flowers at Beaulieu.

19 **Mon.** Went to Cannes, The Elysée Palace Hotel, Route D'Antibes. 60 Francs each. A good pub.

MARCH 1928

20 **Tues.** Played Donner & won 6-2, 6-4. Beat Van der Byl 6-0, 6-0. Played a handicap & won against Dr. Lupper 6-3, 6-3.

21 **Wed.** Rain in morning. played Sol. Evers & won 6-4, 8-6, 6-2.

21 (sb 22) **Thurs.** Rain. 24 Rain.

23 **Sat.** (sb Fri.) Played Art. Hunter. won 6-4, 6-0.

24 **Sun** (sb Sat.) Rain.

25 (sb 26) **Mon.** Played McGrane & won 6-3, 6-4. D. & I beaten by Acheslemon & Fraulein Aussen. Played 2 Handicap singles & 2 doubles.

26 (sb 27) **Tues.** Played Dr. Lupper (Romanian) in finals & won 6-3, 6-3, 5-7, 3-6, 6-0. Very tired after 5 matches yesterday. Scratched from Handicap singles.

27 (sb 28) **Wed.** Beansite Tournament at Bean Site Hotel, Cannes. I played Williams & won 6-2, 13-11. Played Cochet & lost 4-6, 6-3, 6-4. Had a very good game that I enjoyed very much.

28 (sb. 29) **Thurs.** Hamilton & I won a doubles and then lost to Acheslemon & Donner.

29 (sb 30) **Fri.** Played a H'cap mixed and H'cap single.

30 (sb 31) **Sat.** Was beaten in 3rd round of H'cap singles by Villiers. I was scratch and he was +15. Lunch with Col. Mayes at Grand Parc Hotel.

1 **Sun.** D. & I beaten in H'cap mixed. We had to give up +15.4. Mayes won singles. Cochet scratched.

Caught the 1523 train for Calais. 2nd class.

2 April Arrived Paris at 0825, Calais, 1330, over, 1530, London, 1800. Went straight to Portsmouth, Carlton Hotel.

3 April Went to Whale Island and short Gun control course. Tea, Mainguy.

4 April Portsmouth. Rain & cold.

5 April Portsmouth. Went to R.N. Barracks.

6 April **Good Friday** Squash with Mainguy. Tea at Barracks.

7 April **Sat.** The Mainguys took us up to London in their car. Lunch at Simpson's in the Strand. Went to the Zoo. Dinner with the Mainguys at "The Maison Basque". Saw "Clowns in Clover" at the Adelphi. Very good show.

8 Returned to Portsmouth.

9. Played tennis with D. at U.S.

10. **Tues.** Tennis in morning. Commercial signal course in P.M. D. went to visit Mrs. Carrington at Botley. "Blue Eyes" at Kings in P.M. with Sam Worth.

11. **Wed.** At signal school.

12 **Thurs.** –

13 **Fri.** At signal school. Dined with De Wolf in the Champion.

14 **Sat.** –

15 **Sun.** D. & I went over the Victory, then up to Town.

16 **Mon.** Went out to Roehampton. Played Whitehead & won. Very cold.

Fri. 4 At Burlington Hotel. A game with Toogood & Harris. Watched Spence beat Cochet. Lacoste beat Col Mayes.

Sat. 5 Left Bournemouth at 0830. Arrived S'hampton, 930. Did some shopping and caught the tender off to the "Pennland" at noon. Alf O'Leary, Norcross, Dr. Buel, & the ___Smiths on board. Also the Williams. Fine weather.

Sun. 6

Mon. 7

Tues. 8

Wed. 9

Thurs. 10th Foggy. Passed big ice bergs.

Fri. 11th At Sea. Foggy.

Sat. 12th May Arrived Halifax at 1700. Busy getting my gear through the Customs etc. Mother, Marge, Mr. Symons, Art & Harry met us. Dinner at the Alexandra. We are staying there. At home in the evening. Went to Admiralty House later on.

Sun. 13 Called on Champlain & S.N.O. in the morning.

Mon. 14 On leave.

Tues. 15 On leave. Sent Curtiss P.O. for £3-16-3.

Wed. 16 Dinner.

Thurs. 17th

Fri. 18th On board Champlain, preparing to take over. Played Baseball at exhibition grounds. Officers V. ship's co. of the Barracks. Dinner party in Champlain. Danced at Admiralty House.

Sat. 19th Mustering C.B. Books. Went to Hubley's Lake with D., Marge & George Mitchell. Stayed at the Symons' camp. Fishing. Caught four.

Sun. 20th At Hubley's Lake. Fishing. Early and late. Not many fish. May flies, black flies. Returned to Halifax at 2150.

May 21st Monday. Relieved C.T. Beard in command of H.M.C.S. Champlain. Turning over.

22 Tuesday. On board. Sent Grieve M.O. for £2-0-0.

23 Wed. On board. Reid to lunch.

June 7th Squash with Taylor. Went to Ashburn Dance. Then to Admiralty House.

June 8th Sat. In forenoon Rec'd. box shipped by H. Grant. In P.M. played tennis at the South End. Bought from C.B. of C. on $100 1943 Bond Refunding Loan.

June 9

June 10

June 11

June 12

June 13

June 14

June 15 Dinner at Saraguay. M. McInnis.

June 16 Tennis at South End & Cambridge.

June 17 Church at St. Mark's. Tennis with Martin in Dockyard. At home in the evening. Took a flat.

June 18 **Monday.** Sailed at 0930 for St. John [Saint John]. Fine weather. 14 knots. Survey ship before leaving. Experienced strong tide set in entrance to Bay of Fundy according to tide arrows.

June 19 **Tues.** Arrived at St. John 1030 as it was an hour before slack water experienced strong tide going alongside. No. 4 Berth West St. John. Called on Brig. Gen. Hill, G.O.C. at Armouries. Sam Harris, Col Williams & Capt. Makaly came on board.

June 20 Proceeded at 1330 with Navy League delegates on board. Returned at 1500. Gave them tea etc. They seemed quite pleased. Dinner at the Admiral Beatty Hotel, guests of the Navy League. Dorothy & Marge arrived from Halifax by car and stayed at the Admiral Beatty.

21. Tennis at Rothesay.

June 22nd At St. John.

June 23rd

June 24th Trinity Church. Tennis with Shortt & Hudson at Rothsay.

June 25th Sailed at 0830 for Halifax. Fog came down shortly after leaving St. John. Sighted the Luncher Lt. Vessel.

26th Arrived Halifax at 1315. Dense fog until we got near Mayor Beach Lt. Ho. Went alongside Patriot to embark oil from her. Called on Admiral Robertson U.S.N. in Wyoming. Tennis at South End.

27 Delayed sailing on account of fog until 1000. Dense fog outside Halifax. Tried to go through Gut of Canso but too foggy.

28th Foggy until 1800.

29th Arrived Quebec at 1800. Went to No. 20 berth in Louise Basin. The tug which was sent out was a nuisance. Dinner at Chateau with Miles.

30th **Sat.** Called on G.O.C. Col Benoit, Mayor & Lt. Gov. Rain. Dinner at Quebec Garrison Club.

July 1st

July 10th At Montreal. Tennis at Mount Royal.

July 11th

July 12 Tennis at the Mount Royal Club with Leslie. Marge & I had dinner with Leslie. Later to the Ritz Carlton. Car broken open and my tennis gear and 2 Queen rackets and a Burke Bros. Racket stolen. Car was locked. Reported loss to the Police. John Annesley on board brought down by Mrs. Fenton.

13

14 Tennis with C.W. Aikman – c/o Sun Life. The Bannantynes & Dot Campbell came to dinner.

15 Sun. Dorothy and Marge left for Halifax. Tennis at Mt. Royal in P.M. with C.W. Aikman. Good game, I won. Went out to Bannantyne's in evening for supper. Cornwall St.

16 Mon. Slipped & proceeded at 0700. Had some difficulty in getting ship bow out. Secured alongside the oiling jetty. Slipped at 1500 and proceeded down River to Three Rivers.[121] Good passage. Arrived 3 Rivers at about 2000. Went alongside Quai Bureau near Signal Station.

July 17th At Three Rivers. Called on The Mayor. Lunch with Dr. Rousseau at the Chateau Bois. Went over the International Paper Mill with Woolcombe. Dinner with D. Rousseau at his house near Champlain village. Dance afterwards.

July 18th Slipped and proceeded at 0630. Down River. Good passage. Arrived at Québec at 1140. Set C.P.O. Hardy to Military Hospital. Proceeded at 1230. We were going through the North Channel but heavy rain storms prevented passage. Bit misty in places in Traverse & tide sets all over the place. Anchored in Murray Bay for the night. Went ashore with Woolcombe, had dinner with the hotel.

July 19th Weighed and proceeded at 0630. Anchored off Little Metis for two hours. Apparently there is good anchorage there south near the Big Boulders near the Hotel. Chief and Woolcombe went ashore. Proceeded at 1630 for Gaspé.

July 20th Arrived Gaspé at 0730 & anchored between two inner lights. Very pretty place. Went ashore & played "Heave staff" tennis at the Jopling's.

July 21st Played tennis at the Joplings in the P.M.

22nd At Gaspé.

23rd At Gaspé.

24th Sailed at 1800 for Charlottetown. Quite rough outside.

25th Arrived at Charlottetown at about 1030 and went alongside the "Marine" wharf. Considerable tide sets across the entrance. Buntain met me & I went up to Lieut. Governor Heartz to call. Had a game of tennis at the tennis club, Victoria Park. Dined the governor.

26th July Dance in the evening at Government House, about 300 people. Buntain and party came down to the ship afterwards.

---

121 More commonly known today by the French name of Trois-Rivières.

27th July Fri.

28th July Sat. I was going to play tennis but it rained.

29th Went on a picnic to Beach. Met the Stewarts. C. Mercheson, D. Hollings, etc.

30th Mon. Sailed for Halifax at 1000. Carried out 1" A.R. practice. Passed through the Gut of Canso.

Aug. 1st At Halifax. Moving into a flat, Webster Apartments, 294 Gottingen Street.

[No entries for August 2 to August 12. Dutchy likely on leave as he and Dot were moving into a new apartment.]

August 13th Oiled & then anchored off the dockyard. We were going to take Sir Henry Thornton around the harbour but he didn't arrive. Sailed at 1600 for Digby.

14th Arrived Digby at 1030. Came through Petit Passage on the way. Anchored.

15th At Digby.

16th At Digby. Picnic at Sandy Cove with Richardson, etc.

17th Sailed at 0700 for Yarmouth. Thick fog when off Yarmouth so we anchored about 1½'[122] from Forchu.

18th Proceeded into Yarmouth harbour at 0800. Not much room in there. Went alongside Baker's Wharf but a dredger was there so had to shove off and go to Killem's Wharf. Called on Col. J. L. Ralston, the Minister of National Defence. He then came down and inspected the ship. Col. Ralston & Mayor (Waterman) to dinner on board.

AUGUST 1928

19th August Sunday Church in morning, A memorial service at Tusket in P.M. Went for a dive with Captain Brown. Dinner at Meteghan.

20 August Mon. Lunch at Rotary club. Tennis with Hanes. Sailed at 1630.

21 Arrived Halifax 0845. Alongside no. 3 wharf. Houghton's wedding at St. Paul's. Went to the reception at Tuft's Cove. Miles & I decorated Houghton's car and weren't very popular.

22 H.M.A.S. Australia arrived at 0630 and went alongside No. 4. Played tennis with Carr, MacMahon & several others. Went to a dinner given by the Hon. Minister of National Defence at the Halifax Club for Rear Admiral Hyde and Officers of the Australia.

23rd Lunch at R.A. & R.C.E. Mess. Reception on board Australia. Marge gave a dinner at Ashburn. Dance at Government House.

---

122 The normal sign for "feet" is used here for miles.

24th Australia sailed at 0600. Tennis with Martin.

25th Sailed at 1030 for Lunenburg. Arrived Lunenburg at 1400. Went alongside Zwicker's Wharf West side. Not much room to manoeuvre a ship in. Wharf is very short. Government wharf is under repair.

26th Church in morning. The Mayor A.H. Schwartz took Miles & I for a motor drive to Mahone, Bridgewater & down the LeHave River. Very pretty scenery. Tea at the Zwicker's.

27th Dorothy & Marge motored down from Halifax. We went to Chester and had a game of golf. Dance given by the Mayor & council.

28th Sailed at 1600 for Liverpool. It is advisable to manoeuvre at High water when leaving Lunenburg. Arrived at Liverpool 1900, anchored off the New Pulp Mill. Buoy off the pier in Breakwater appears to be out of position i.e. further to the Westward.

29th At Liverpool. Several drills – out kedge. V.G. swimming water, about 70°. Went ashore in P.M. & Ottawa evidently sent a telegram to the Mayor saying that our visit had been cancelled.

30th At Liverpool. Called on the Mayor. Played tennis in P.M.

31st August Sailed for Shelburne A.M. Arrived P.M. Anchored off the Government Pier (which is quite large and suitable to go alongside).

1st September At Shelburne.

2nd September Sailed at 1130 for Clark's Harbour. Arrived about 1700 & anchored outside the entrance to buoyed channel. It is suitable to anchor between the two light buoys. Mayor Nickerson & council came off to call.

Sept. 3rd, 1928 The Gunner & I landed at 0930 to watch the Labour Day Celebrations at Clark's Harbour. Motor Boat races, Greasy Pole & Swimming races. They were to stage a parade in P.M. but it rained and fog came down. Proceeded at 1900 for Halifax. Dense fog after leaving ↓age.

Sept. 4th Arrived Halifax at 0930. Went alongside Imperial. Then no. 4.

Sept. 10th Sailed for Baddeck at 1800, after embarking oil fuel from Patriot. Had a V.G. game of tennis in P.M. before sailing. Patt VI target in tow. Speed 14 knots.

11th Arrived Baddeck 0700 & anchored.

12th Carried our 1" A.R. At anchor. Festubert arrived.

13th Carried out 1" A.R.

14 Carried out 1" A.R.

15 Big Lake Commissioning Shoot.

16

17 Several drills.

18 Proceeded to Sydney at 20 knots to launch S.P.O. Melhuish for Operations. Tennis with W.N. Reid.

Sept. 19th Sailed from Sydney to Bras D'or Lakes. Carried out 1" A.R. Exercised Night Action stations.

Sept. 20th 20" G.C.O.'s short 8 rounds per gun.

Sept. 21 4" full calibre short. Night Action, firing star shell. Killed a horse belonging to Mr. Dan McNeil.

Sept. 22 Proceeded to Baddeck.

Sept. 23 Motor drive to Margaree.

Sept. 24 General Drill.

Sept. 25

Sept. 26 4" Full Calibre Firing.

Sept. 27 Preparing Torpedoes for morning.

Sept. 28 Carried out Long Range Torpedo Attack. 4 Torpedoes. Failed to recover one torpedo.

Sept. 29 In company Festubert, searching for lost torpedo.

Sept. 30 Searching for lost torpedo.

Oct. 1 Searching for lost torpedo.

Oct. 2 Carried out Long Range torpedo attack on Festubert. Sailed for Sydney. Arrived Sydney.

Oct. 3 Embarked S.N.O. and carried out 4" Full Calibre and Torpedo Firing. Returned Sydney. Wisteria in.

Oct. 4 At Sydney.

Oct. 5 At Sydney.

Oct. 6 Sailed for Halifax.

Oct. 7 Carried out Reporting Exercise with Ypres.

Oct. 8 Arrived Halifax.

Oct. 9th Halifax. Rugby practice.

Oct. 10th

Oct. 11th

Oct. 12th

Oct. 13th

Oct. 14th

Oct. 15th

Oct. 16th

Jan. 12 1929 Heavy & thick snow which delayed sailing. I sailed at 1615 for Bermuda-18 knots. Quite a swell outside.

13th At 0530 mainmast snapped at heel. Rescued it with extra guys etc. Wind & sea increasing. Very heavy wind & confused sea in the evening. Wind blowing from N.W. Turned & steamed more or less into it at 6-8 knots. Very uncomfortable. Ship rides very well.

14th Wind & sea eased down a bit about noon so turned & ran at 16 knots with sea on quarter.

15th Better weather. Arrived Bermuda at 1600. Went alongside Oiling wharf which is North end of the South Basin. Colombo & Capetown here. Capt. C.C. Dobson (Colombo) is S.N.O. Dinner with the Dobsons at Borg Isl. We are very much upset as we found that the C. in C. has arranged a gunnery & Torpedo program for us commencing straight away. As we have just lost all our A.B.s it is bit poor.

Jan. 16th Wed. At Bermuda. Very busy training control parties, etc. Dinner with the Dobsons. Went to ship's co. dance at Spar Yard.

Jan. 17th Played in a handicap mixed tennis tournament at Somerset Island with Potly.

Jan. 18th Proceeded at 0830 outside the Narrows. Sub Calibre & Test Runs (2) Torpedoes. Did a Full Calibre 4" Shoot at B.C. Target towed by St. Affs. Not so good—as I expected as guns crews and control are very green, some never having been at a gun before.

In the evening did as Night Firing Full Calibre at B.C. Target towed by St. Affs. Had to do it in 3 mins. Searchlight Poor. Anchored in 5 fathom hole for the night.

Jan. 19th Proceeded into harbour at 0700. Secured alongside North End of South Basin. Shipping new mainmast. Played tennis with Major Newnham at Admiralty House & beat him 8-6, 6-2. Tea at Government House with Sir Louis Bols.

Jan. 20th 1929 Played tennis at Government House with Newnham, Hyde or Ryde, P. ? VG. game which I enjoyed very much.

Jan. 21st Colombo and Capetown sailed at about 1000. We waited for a Conf. Mail so did not sail until 1345. Went on to 20 knots & caught the cruisers up. Took part in a rangefinder & Inclination exercise. Moderate seas.

Jan. 22nd Early A.M. did a dummy day torpedo attack which we got congratulated upon. Then target ship for cruiser 6" Sub Calibre concentration throw off. Another Range finder and Inclination Exercise. After Dark we went on ahead to carry out a Dummy Night Torpedo attack.

Jan. 23rd We were the target line for Cruisers' Torpedo Firing. Picked up 4 out of 8. Our ship's crew did very good work towing a 21" MK IV about the ocean. Capetown lost a torpedo & we all spent the day searching for it. After dark we went ahead in order to carry out a night torpedo attack which was very successful. Fired 2 torpedoes. Both crossed the target line. Went on ahead of the Cruisers at 17 knots.

Jan. 24th We were target ship for a 6" F.C. concentration Throw off of Colombo & Capetown. The fuses blew at the beginning but afterward everything was O.K. Weather was too bad for any other exercises.

Jan. 25th Arrived Kingston at about 1530 & anchored. Ships were rather in the way. Went ashore with the Captains of Colombo & Capetown to call on the Governor Sir Stubbs[123] at Kings House, also Colonial Sec. Jeffs, Chief Justice. The K.H.M. Commander Dix, R.N. ret'd. took us about in his car. Dance at the Myrtle Bank in the evening.

Jan. 26th Played tennis at the Col. Sec. Jeffs. Dance at the Bournemouth Baths in the evening.

Jan. 27th Sun. Prayers on board. Swim at Bournemouth Baths. Tennis.

Jan. 28th Tennis at Military Club. Up Park Camp.

Jan. 27th At home Brig. Glazebrook Military Club. Played tennis V. the Army & won.

Jan. 28th

Jan. 29 Tennis at St. Andrews with DeWolf, Alexander Arnott & Beamish. Dance at Bournemouth Baths.

Jan. 30 Tennis at Lindos with Arbuthnot, Imppen & Heath.

Jan 31st 1929

Feb. 1st Tennis at St. Andrews with Alexander, Cargill, Brett, Mrs. Beswick, Miss Da Costa, Capt. Duncan and De Wolf. Dance at Kings House in P.M.

Feb. 2nd Tennis at the Brigadier & Mrs. Graychook. Exhibition match. Dance at the Royal Jamaica Yacht Club. Good show.

Feb. 3rd

Feb. 4th Monday Tennis at St. Andrews with DeWolf. Dance at Myrtle Bank.

Feb. 5th Tues. Played ? at Liguanal tournament & I won 6-4, 6-2. Got very hot & could not get to the bounce of the balls. Dinner in Capetown with Capt. Durrand. Dance at Jamaica club which went on to 0430.

Feb. 6th Proceeded at 1715. Picked up Capt. Temple at Port Royal. Then went out through the Eastern Channel. We were target for Shoe S/L. Anchored then came in & went out again. Pretty poor going through

---

123 Sir Reginald Edward Stubbs.

the channel with S/Ls blazing on you. Anchored at 0430. Proceeded to Bull Bay to make a landing demonstration. Put our S/L/ on for a bit.

Feb. 7th Rejoined Colombo & Capetown at Old Harbour at 0815. We did not land a party but Cruisers landed the Argyle & Sutherlands who were supposed to be making a raid on Kingston. Returned to harbour at 1400 approx. and anchored at Kingston. Rec'd a cable from Marjorie re the Baby.[124]

Feb. 8th Went to the Colonial Secretary's Mr. Jelf Vale Royal. Tennis.

Feb. 9th Played Lake (H.A.) in Open Singles at Liguanal & won 4-6, 6-2, 6-1. Was nearly cooked in the middle of first set. Dance at St. Andrews club.

Feb. 10th Sunday Tennis with DeWolf & Brett at St. Andrews. Supper with the Kindersley's at the Sec's house Liguanal Club.

12 Sent D. B. of N.S draft no. 71555 for $50.00 for March. Went alongside Capetown at R.M.S.P. wharf. Rain in P.M. Dance on board.

13 Went to oiling jetty at 0700. Very poor jetty as only about 6" long & catches in our guard rails. Navy & Army played Jamaica in doubles & lost. Mr. Cargill's team.

14 Played a mixed double. Miss Squires & I were defeated by B.M. Clark & Miss Strathern. Dinner at Manor House with Miss Janet Bonnets.

15 Played H. Philpotts in open singles & won 6-1, 6-3. Very tired.

Feb. 16th 1929 Feeling a bit poor in A.M. Went ashore looking for old furniture with Mrs. Kindersley. Bought a Chest of Drawers for £3-10-0 & a mirror for £2-0-0. Went sick with fever, a temp of 101.4. I had to scratch in the finals of the Open Singles against B.M. Clarke.

17th In bed all day.

18th Sailed at 1500 to Portland Rock where we carried out 2 rounds per gun live ammo firing. In company Colombo sailed for Dominica. Weather bad.

19th At sea. DeWolf ill or very sea sick. Head sea – bumpy.

20 At sea.

21

22 Arrived at Dominica at 0700 & anchored off the town of Roseau. Durban here. Called on the Administrator & Mrs. Eliot. Tennis match v. the club. Dinner & dance a Government House.

23rd Dinner & dance in Durban.

24 Tennis at the Administration G.C Eliot. Church parade A.M. Supper with Edden in Durban.

---

124 Dutchy's wife Dorothy delivered a still-born daughter on February 7, 1929. She was named Susan Elizabeth and was buried in Halifax.

Feb. 25 Tennis with Archer a Gov. Ho. Dinner with Capt. Dobson in Colombo.

Feb. 26th Sailed at 0620 in company Colombo. Sea rougher. Carried out 4" F.C. Throw off. Arrived St. Vincent 1745. Dinner at Administrator's (acting). Patterson Acting Administrator.

Feb. 27th Captain Dobson & myself called on Administrator at Gov. House & on Chief Justice Bulloch. Adm. returned call in Colombo Guard officers. Salute on leaving. Dance at Gov. House in evening.

28th Watched football Champlain V. St. Vincent; 4-1 for St. Vincent. Dance at Mrs. Otway given by the Ladies of St Vincent.

March 1

March 2nd At Home in Colombo in which we shared Administrator, Mrs. ?, Mrs. Parry, Miss Minion, Col Sec. Granada Mr. Furguson on board for cocktails. Colombo's concert in the evening.

March 4 Lunch in the Colombo with Capt. Dobson. The Administrator & his wife (Mad) Patterson, Mrs. Parry, Miss Minion. Pretty sticky show. Weighed & proceeded at 1630. Carried out 4" F.C. Throw off on Colombo 9 R.P.G. 22 knots. Colombo 17. then Pom Pom and Lewis gun.

March 5th Went on ahead & at 0700 carried out Long Range Torpedo attack on Colombo at 10000 yds. Torpedoes ran very well. One hit, one missed ahead, both came up together. Arrived Port of Spain at 0900 & anchored. Called on Gov. Sir Hor[ace Archer Byatt]. Warner & I dined ashore at Paris Restaurant.

6th Called on Col. Sec. Jackson & Chief Justice. Went to Gov. House to stay for a couple of days. Tennis – awful, no back net. Dinner.

7th

8 Fri. Tennis St. Clair Club. Dinner onboard.

9 Sat. Watched the tennis final at the Tranquility club. Richie beat Tindall 6-3, 6-2. Played in a doubles. Dinner with the Alston's at the Paris Restaurant.

10th Sunday Church on board. Art. of War. Tennis in P.M. at Gov. House. Played Dr. Ritchie a single, he won 6-3, 4-3. Lady Diana Bridgeman there & others.

11th Mon. Bought a table from Dearles Ltd. for $27.50. Tennis with Dr. Ritchie at Tranquility Club. I won 7-5, 3-4. Dined Captain Dobson, Eng. Cdr. Smith, Pay Cdr. Condé Williams, Lt. Cdr, Warner, Eng. Lt. Cdr. Heath onboard. Presented them with an Umbo. Took them back in the Motor Boat as they were sailing at Midnight. The Chief couldn't start the engine. Guard at drill.

12th We were to oil at 8 A.M. from a barge but it did not arrive owing to a breakdown so in the end we went to Point a Pierre which is 25' from Port of Spain. Went alongside at about 1645. Inside berth North side.

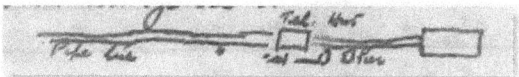

Sailed at 2145 for Barbados.

13th Arrived Barbados at 1430 & anchored off Engineer's Wharf or as it now the Barbados Aquatic Club. H. Master Cdr. Wynne (ret'd.) & Health Officer came off.

14th Called on Governor Sir W. Robertson[125] at Gov. House. Also the Bishop, Chief Justice, Att. Gen. Pilot & I went to play tennis at Yacht Club. Bowry is Pres. Lunch in Lady Drake with Capt. Armiat.

Dinner at G.H. in P.M.

15th March Lunch with Mrs. Miles at Club. Swim at Yacht club. Tennis at Gov. House. It rained a bit. Played with Austin, Challoner, Dr. Hudson. Dinner at Marine Hotel with Armiat & Mrs. Wilson, Mrs. ---. Danced afterwards at Aquatic Club.

Our troops had three dances arranged here for them, also Laing of Y.M.C.A. is very good. Football matches & water polo. The troops have been a bit discontented up to date.

17th March Sunday Barbados. Landed 25 Ratings & one officer to attend church Barbados Volunteer forces annual church parade. Went out to the Cooks (G o) Sam Lords' Castle for lunch and a bathe. Supper with Mr. Miles, Mgr. The Canadian Bank of Commerce.

18th Went ashore in P.M. & bought some furniture: 2 chairs 10/- each, 1 table 16/- from Mrs. Prince, washerwoman. Also 1 chest of drawers $15.00, 2 tables $27.00.

Sailed at 2000 for Grenada. Provisions from Da Costa – Mr. Foster.

March 19th Arrived Grenada at 0830 and anchored off Fort St. George. Called on the Governor Sir Frederick Seeton-James [Seton James]. Major Donaldson is the A.D.C. & very nice. Very pretty place. Tennis at the club. Dinner at G.H.

March 20th Tennis at G.H.

March 21st Tennis sat the Club with Gentle, Patterson, De Wolfe etc. Cocktails at Mr. Furgueson the Colonial Secretary. Easton had dinner aboard. Dance at the club. Franco. Troops had 2 Rifle shooting matches & 2 football matches. People ashore anxious to see baseball played. Very good bathing beach here. Major Turner (Ex R.C.N. W.N.P.) in charge of

---

125 Sir William Charles Fleming Robertson.

police. Mr. Easton, Director of Education, arranges entertainment for the troops, etc.

March 22nd Sailed at 0630 for Bermuda. Went up to leeward of the Island. Rough. Fan fell on my table top & broke it.

23rd At Sea. Still rough, Sombrero Isl. Lt. at 1430.

24 At Sea.

25 At Sea.

26 Sighted Gibbs Hill Lt. at 0330. And anchored at 5 fathom hole Nr. Narrows at 0630 to await the Tug & Target. Weighed at 1000 & carried out 4" F.C. shoot 8 R.P.G. Proceeded to Dockyard & secured alongside at 1230. Dorothy was on jetty & had lunch with me. Went to Inverurie Hotel & staying there.

27th March

28th March Paying bills etc. before end of financial year. Very busy all day. Inverurie in P.M.

29 Good Friday. Took day off. Bathing & game of tennis.

30th Sat. On board in forenoon. Bathing in P.M. Went to Bermudiana in evening—very amusing.

31st Sunday Easter Church in forenoon at Paget church.

April 1st Easter Monday Bermuda.

9th Dot & Marge sailed in the S.S Bermuda for N.Y. & Halifax at 1000. I went over to see them off. Tennis at the Gilberts at Somerset. Dinner at Government House—Sir Louis Bols in P.M.

10th On board getting accounts etc. squared up Dinner in Hamilton at New Wicker.

11 Sailed at 1430. Exercises 4" Night Firing. Sailed at 2145 for Halifax.

12th Fine day.

13th Very cold. Heavy sea. Snow in P.M.

14 Arrived Halifax 1430. Dorothy & Marge arrived by O.L.

Fri. June 14th Rain in A.M. "At Home on Capetown". Progressive Dinner Party. Soup in Festubert, Fish in Ypres & remainder of dinner in Champlain. The chief produced a bevy of people afterwards. Frankie. Smith.

Sat. June 15th Tennis in P.M. at Sydney Club with W.N. Reid, McCann, Vought. Sailed at 1900 for Quebec.

Sun. 16th Heavy rain in middle & fog nearly all day. On bridge the whole time.

Mon. June 17th Fine Day coming up River North Channel. Pretty sticky just

South of Island of Orleans. Arrived Quebec at 1600, I went to bed. Went to Chateau with Miles & had our annual dinner. Met some of the 9th Royal Rifles.

Tues. June 18th Sailed at 0680 for Montreal, arrived at 1800. Went alongside Victoria Pier.

Wed. 19th Tennis with Leslie.

Thurs.

Fri.

Sat. 22 Played Percy in Quebec championships & won 6-2, 6-2.

Sun. 23 Tennis at West Hill with R. McCoy, O'Shaunessy, Scriver, O'Brien. Rained. Supper at Bannantynes.

24 Played Yashiri.

25

26

27

Went to Ottawa. Dinner with Beard & Oland at Henri's. Stayed at Chateau Laurier. Played a mixed double, Myself & Mlle Gadbois V. Aikman & Mrs. Beer. We lost 6-2, 6-3.

June 30 Grants Eric & Harold. At Cupies in P.M.

July 1st At Bannantynes. Grants came out. Played tennis in P.M. Saw Grants off. Dinner on board to Bannantynes. Dance at Mount Royal.

July 2nd Tues. Sailed at 0800 for Three Rivers. Had some difficulty getting out as wind was blowing us on, and numerous tugs, etc. in the way. Arrived Three Rivers at 1330. Went alongside Quai Bureau. Fulford and his party from Yacht called – Went over to the Yacht & Monsieur Beariau.

July 3rd Went out for a drive to Shawinigan Falls. Lunch with Dr. Rousseau.

July 4th Rained all day. Dr. Rousseau's in afternoon.

July 5th Sailed for Quebec at 0900. Arrived at 1400 & went into Outer Basin near shed 20. Pettigrew & DeLaze called. My birthday.

6th Played tennis with Henri Colomb at Québec club & won 6-2, 6-3.

Played tennis at Jacques Cartier club.

9th

10 I was going to play tennis but it rained, Dinner at G.O.C. Brig. Benoit.

11th July Lunch at Chateau given by R.C.N.V.R. Went out to Ste. Anne de Beaupré. Dance at Chateau. At 9th R. Rifles mess afterwards. Margaret Marquis.

```
DECEMBER              FRIDAY 31            (365)         1926
```

July 3rd Went out for a drive to Shawinigan Falls.
     Lunch with Dr Rousseau.

July 4th Rained all day – Dr Rousseau in afternoon.

July 5th Sailed for Quebec at 0900. Arrived at 1400 & went into
     Outer Basin reg shed 20. Pettigrew & DeLage called.
     My birthday.

6th Played tennis with Henri Colomb at Quebec club & won 6-3 6-3

    Played tennis at Jacques-Cartier club.

9th

10   Was going to play tennis but it rained. Dinner at G.C.C. Brig. Benoit.

11th July Lunch at Chateau given by R.C.N.V.R. went out to Stamme St Baupré. Dance at
     Chateau – At 9th R. Rifles mess afterwards.   Mrs Margaret Marquis
12th July Sailed for St Rivière du Loup at 1030 Arrived at 1200.
     Major called.
13th Called on Major Dubé – 30 People came off to see the ship
     & have tea onboard, All quite a good time & I think they
     all enjoyed themselves. Le Moine came onboard.
14th Sunday Prayers onboard Landed at 1330 & were taken
     for motor drive around the Town. Tea party for us at The
     Bungalow. Dinner at hotel in evening in our honour at
     which we all had to make a speech. Went to Mrs
     Sutherland's afterwards and the party all came onboard.

Journal page July 3, 1929 to July 14, 1929

12th July Sailed for Rivière-du-Loup at 1030. Arrived at 1700. Mayor called.

13th Called on Mayor Dubée. 30 people came to see the ship & have tea onboard. Quite a good time & I think they all enjoyed themselves. LeMoine came onboard.

14th Sunday. Prayers onboard. Landed at 1330 and were taken for motor drive around the Town. Tea party for us at The Bungalow. Dinner at hotel in evening in our honour at which we all had to make a speech. Went to Mr. Sutherland's afterwards and the party all came on board.

15th July Sailed for Metis at 0900. Arrived at 1430 & anchored off Boule Rock. Went ashore in P.M. Dinner at Harris. Went to Baldwins in evening.

16th July Lunch on board H. & Mr. B. Tennis in P.M. with John Bogert at Cascade club. Picnic in P.M. It rained. Hole, Molson, Seagram, Matheson. Went to Mrs. Baldwin's in P.M. Mrs. Molson.

17th Lunch on b. H.H., Hazel Molson, Mrs. Baldwin. went to Wilson.

18th Took some children around ship. Tennis with Durrant. Dinner at Miss Blues. Went to Molson's in P.M.

19th We were to have sailed for 7 Islands but had two ratings sick. Went ashore in afternoon. Tea at _____. Dinner party on board. Went to the Molson's afterwards.

July 20 Sailed for 7 Islands Bay at 0800. Fine weather. Arrived at 1700. Exercised dropping seaboat twice. Anchored off the Village of 7 Isl.

July 21st Prayers on board. Landed R.C.s. Went to Clark City in P.M. A R.R. runs up from Norié Pt. Has old engines & flat cars. Had to wait for train 1½ hours. Arrived Clark City & found that the sports were all over so we had a baseball game. Came back on a Gradene trolley arriving back in ship at 2100.

22 On board all day. Blew quite hard in P.M. Unable to land. A poor place this.

23rd At 7 Islands. On board all day.

24th Sailed at 0400 for Percé. Arrived at 1500. Did some 1" A.R. Percé a very pretty place although not very good for bathing. Sailed at 1900 for Charlottetown. Good weather.

July 25th 1929 Arrived Ch'Town at 1030. Difficult going alongside as there was a strong flood tide setting & a pontoon just ahead of the ship. Called on Lt. Gov. S Heartz. He returned the call. Had a seaman guard of 12. Went to tennis club in afternoon with Pullen. Played with Mr. Hutcheson. In evening Buntain, the Two Longworths, Miss Fisher, Holly.

July 26th Tennis in afternoon. Dance at Lt. Governor's. Dinner party onboard.

July 27th Saturday Tennis at Club with Hutcheson.

July 31   Sailed for Halifax. – at near St. Peter's Bay for a few hours whilst we had looked at The Canal.

Aug. 1st   Arrived Halifax, Oiled. Went alongside. Was ordered to proceed at Midnight as "There was no dense fog in the Harbour". Anchored off No. 2 as the visibility was about 60 feet.

Aug. 2nd   Proceeded at 0500 17 knots for R.V with Capetown off Lurcher Lt. Vessel. Carried 4" F.C. Shoot, speed 25 knots. Afterwards Capetown carried out 6" F.C. shoot on us. On conclusion shaped course for Bar Harbo[u]r Maine.

Aug. 3rd   Arrived Bar Harbo[u]r at 0600. Clocks put back 2 hours. U.S.S. Richmond and Cincinnati here. Heliotrope arrived from Yarmouth at 0700. Not a great deal of room in the harbour. Official calls. Tennis match in P.M. for International Lawn Tennis Cup. Startin & I played in the doubles & were beaten. I played Howard in singles & won 6-2, 6-0. Dance at swimming club in P.M.

Aug. 4th   Big lunch party at --- . Tennis with Howard. Dinner in Rockwood with Howard.

Aug. 5th 1929   Motor drive with Capt. --- & Vice Admiral. Can C.N.S. Atlantic Fleet to Belfast, Maine. Lunch with the Admiral.

August 6th   Sailed at 0700 for Halifax.

Aug. 7th   Arrived Halifax 0700.

Aug. 8th   Carnival Curri.

Aug. 9th   Went to N.W. Arm. Illuminated ship. Ypres & Festubert also here. Mayor & 50 guests onboard in P.M. I could not go to Wolfville to play in the N.S. Tournament as I could not get leave although I had hired a car. Dot won mixed doubles and runner up in singles.

10   Returned from Arm. Went to Wolfville to see Maritime Tennis. McLennan won singles beating Babbit. D. & Cliff mixed.

Sept. 5th

Sept. 6th   Tennis S. End. Oiled in A.M. Lunch on board Despatch with Cdr. Harrison Hodge. Dance in Despatch.

Sept. 7th   Tennis at S. End then at Cambridge Library V. Despatch. Dinner Admiralty House for Officers PRIMAUGUET.

Sept. 8th   Sailed for St. John 14 knots. Thick & rain.

Sept. 9th 1929   Arrived St. John at 0600 & went alongside at No. 4 Berth West St. John. Called on G.O.C. Brig.-Gen. F.W. Hill. In P.M. went to Rothesay in car and called on Lt. Gov. Hugh McLean.[126] G.O.C. came onboard to play bridge in evening.

---

126 Hugh Havelock McLean.

Sept. 10th Tues. Called on Mayor White & Premier Baxter[127] in A.M. In P.M. weather was foggy so Despatch with C. in C. Sir Cyril Fuller was delayed & could not enter harbour. Lt. Gov. onboard was H. McLean.

C. in C. Eveleigh, Bower & Sec. came off to Champlain in the barge. We went on to dinner at Gov. House. Reception afterwards. I drove Miles' car in from Rothesay after the reception.

Sept. 11th Despatch arrived at 0800. Unveiled monument at Fort Howe in P.M. to ----.

Dinner at G.O.C.'s Brig. Gen. Hill, Miss Hill, Webster, Mrs. Woods, Connolly, Pullen. Dance at Riverside Golf & Country Club given by Mayor White.

Sept. 12th Tennis at Riverside Club. Fairweather, Tilley. Dinner at Byng Boys Club in P.M. at Bungalow. Col. McLeod took us out.

Sept. 13th Friday Sailed for Liverpool, NS at 0600. Rained most of the day Arrived Liverpool at 2100 & secured off the New Pulp & Paper Mill.

END OF JOURNAL FOUR

---

127 John Babington Macaulay Baxter.

HMCS Niobe

APPENDIX A. SHIPS NAMED IN THE JOURNALS

PREFIX	SHIP NAME	INFORMATION
French cruiser	*Amiral Aube*	Built in the early 1900s for the French Navy, the *Amiral Aube* served in the English Channel and the Mediterranean during World War I.
French cruiser	*Jeanne d'Arc*	*Jeanne d'Arc* was launched in 1899 by the French Navy as an armoured cruiser. She became the flagship of French ships patrolling the Levantine coast and was then assigned to the French West Indies.
French cruiser	*Montcalm*	*Montcalm* was a Gueydon-class armoured cruiser built for the French Navy in the 1890s. The ship saw service during World War I in the Pacific.
French cruiser	*Primauguet*	*Primauguet* was a French Duguay-Trouin-class light cruiser built after World War I. During the Anglo-American invasion of French North Africa in 1942, she was burnt out and abandoned, having been subject to gunfire from a fleet led by the battleship Massachusetts, and repeated aerial attacks by SBD Dauntless dive bombers.
HMAS	*Australia*	*Australia* left Portsmouth for her namesake country on August 3, 1928 after completing sea trials. During the voyage, the cruiser visited Canada, the United States of America, several Pacific islands, and New Zealand before she reached Sydney on October 23.
HMAS	*Melbourne*	HMAS *Melbourne* was a Town class light cruiser. She was launched in 1912 and commissioned in 1913. At the start of World War I, *Melbourne* was involved in attempts to locate the German East Asia Squadron and participated in the capture of German colonies in the Pacific, before being assigned to the North America and West Indies Stations. In 1916, the cruiser joined the Grand Fleet in the North Sea, where she remained for the remainder of the war.
HMAS	*Yarra*	HMAS *Yarra* was a River-class torpedo-boat destroyer. Built in 1909, she was involved in wartime patrols on the Pacific and Southeast Asian regions from 1914 to 1917. She was then transferred to the Mediterranean for anti-submarine operations. She was eventually sunk as a target ship in 1921.
HMAT	*A70 Ballerat*	HMAT *A70 Ballerat* was owned by Pacific & Orient Steam Navigation Co Ltd, London and used pre-war to transport emigrants to Australia from the UK. She made four voyages from Australia before at 2:00pm on Apr 25, 1917 in the English Channel as an Anzac Day service was being held, when she was torpedoed by U-boat UB-32 sinking the next day.
HMCS	*Aurora*	HMCS *Aurora* was built as HMS Aurora, an Arethusa-class light cruiser launched on September 13, 1913. She was part of the Grand Fleet and was on hand at the surrender of the German High Seas Fleet in November 1918. She was paid off and was presented to the Royal Canadian Navy in 1920, along with 2 destroyers, and commissioned on November 1. After the 3 ships arrived in Halifax, Nova Scotia on December 21, they set out on a training cruise via the Caribbean to Esquimalt, British Columbia, returning to Halifax via the same route on July 30, 1921. A year later, drastic cuts in the naval budget made it necessary to pay off Aurora and she was paid off on July 1, 1922. Her weapons were placed ashore in training facilities and on other active ships. Her crew was reduced to non-manned, and much of her up-to-date equipment was salvaged for use in other Royal Canadian Navy warships. She lay at Halifax until 1927, when she was sold for scrap and broken up.

PREFIX	SHIP NAME	INFORMATION
HMCS	Canada	HMCS *Canada*, built in 1904, was originally a patrol ship in the Fisheries Protection Service of Canada. After the commencement of World War I, the ship was transferred to the Royal Canadian Navy. She underwent a refit and was recommissioned HMCS *Canada* on January 25, 1915 and operated on the Atlantic coast until 1919 when she was decommissioned. She was used as a training vessel for Canadian naval officers.
HMCS	Carnarvon	HMS *Carnarvon* was a Devonshire-class cruiser of 10,850 tons built for the Royal Navy in 1905. She served in various capacities prior to the start of the First World War, where she was assigned to Cape Verde Station to protect British ships. In October 1914, the *Carnarvon* was transferred to the South Atlantic where she was part of the Battle of the Falklands, December 1914. Throughout the rest of the war she continued to patrol against German raiders and escort convoys. In 1919, she became a training ship, before being sold for scrap in 1921.
HMCS	Champlain	HMCS *Champlain* was a Thornycroft S-class destroyer, formerly HMS Torbay built for the Royal Navy in 1917–19. She was transferred to the Royal Canadian Navy in 1928 and served primarily as a training ship until 1936.
HMCS	Festubert	HMCS *Festubert* was one of 12 Battle-class naval trawlers constructed for and used by the Royal Canadian Navy during the First World War. Following the war, *Festubert* remained in Canadian service as a training ship until 1934.
HMCS	Florence	HMCS *Florence* was a commissioned patrol vessel of the Royal Canadian Navy that served in the First World War. Originally launched as the yacht *Czarina*, she was acquired by John Craig Eaton in 1910 and renamed *Florence*. Following the outbreak of war, Eaton donated the yacht to the Royal Canadian Navy. The ship had a short career and proved unsuitable for navy work and was paid off in September 1916. The vessel was subsequently sold to buyers in Martinique and was reportedly lost in the Caribbean in January 1917.
HMCS	Grilse	HMCS *Grilse* was a commissioned patrol boat of the Royal Canadian Navy during the First World War. Launched in 1912 as the private yacht *Winchester* of the American industrialist Peter Rouss, the vessel was constructed along the lines of a contemporary Royal Navy torpedo boat destroyer.
HMCS	Hochelaga	HMCS *Hochelaga* was a commissioned patrol vessel of the Royal Canadian Navy (RCN) that served in World War I and postwar until 1920.
HMCS	Margaret	CGS *Margaret* was the first vessel to be built specifically for the Canadian Customs Preventive Service. Delivered in 1914, she was transferred to the Royal Canadian Navy and served as HMCS *Margaret* during the First World War.
HMCS	Naden	HMCS *Naden* was built for the Dominion government in 1913 and was bought by the Naval Service while under construction. About 1918, she was loaned to the Naval College. The deck cabin was removed & she was commissioned as a tender to the Naval College at Esquimalt for training in sail. *Naden* was the tender to the College up to June 1, 1920 when she took over as depot ship for the shore barracks.
HMCS	Niobe	HMS *Niobe* was a ship of the Diadem class of protected cruisers in the Royal Navy. She served in the Boer War and was then given to Canada as the second ship of the newly created Naval Service of Canada as HMCS *Niobe*. The Naval Service of Canada became the Royal Canadian Navy in August 1911.

PREFIX	SHIP NAME	INFORMATION
HMCS	*Patrician*	HMS *Patrician* was a Thornycroft M-class destroyer that served in the British Royal Navy during World War I. The destroyer entered service in 1916 and served with the Grand Fleet. Following the war, the destroyer was deemed surplus and was transferred to the Royal Canadian Navy in 1920, renamed HMCS *Patrician*, and served there until 1928.
HMCS	*Patriot*	HMS *Patriot* was a Thornycroft M-class destroyer that served in the British Royal Navy. The destroyer entered service in 1915 during the First World War and saw service with the Grand Fleet. Following the war, she was declared surplus and in 1920, the ship was transferred to the Royal Canadian Navy and renamed HMCS *Patriot*.
HMCS	*Rainbow*	HMCS *Rainbow* was an Apollo-class protected cruiser built for Great Britain's Royal Navy as HMS *Rainbow* entering service in 1892. *Rainbow* saw time in Asian waters before being placed in reserve in 1909. In 1910 the cruiser was transferred to the Royal Canadian Navy for service on the west coast. During the First World War, *Rainbow* was the only major Commonwealth warship on the western coast of North America at the outbreak of war. Due to age, the cruiser was taken out of service in 1917 and sold for scrap in 1920 and broken up.
HMCS	*Stadacona*	HMCS *Stadacona* was a commissioned patrol boat of the Royal Canadian Navy (RCN) that served in the First World War and postwar until 1920.
HMCS	*Starling*	HMCS *Starling* was a Lockeport cold storage vessel acquired by the RCN as an auxiliary/patrol vessel.
HMCS	*Vancouver*	HMCS *Vancouver* was a Thornycroft S-class destroyer, formerly HMS *Toreador* built for the Royal Navy in 1917–1919. Seeing limited service with the Royal Navy, the ship was loaned to the Royal Canadian Navy in March 1928. The destroyer served primarily as a training vessel until 1936 when the vessel was discarded.
HMCS	*Ypres*	HMCS *Ypres* was one of twelve Battle-class naval trawlers constructed for and used by the Royal Canadian Navy during the First World War. The ship entered service in 1918, patrolling the east coast of Canada for submarine activity. Following the war, the ship remained in service as a patrol and training ship.
HMHS	*Britannic*	HMHS *Britannic*, the sister to White Star Line's RMS *Olympic* and RMS *Titanic*, was launched just before the start of World War I. Rather than being put into service as a transatlantic ocean liner, she was used as a hospital ship in 1915. On November 21, 1916, she hit a mine near the Greek island of Kea and foundered; 30 people were lost. She was the largest ship to be sunk in World War I.
HMS	*Abercrombie*	HMS *Abercrombie* was laid down 12 December 1914. The ship was originally named *Admiral Farragut* in honour of the United States Admiral David Farragut, but as the United States was still neutral, the ship was hurriedly renamed HMS M1 on May 31, 1915. She was then named HMS *General Abercrombie* on June 19, 1915, and then renamed HMS *Abercrombie* on June 21, 1915. She sailed for the Dardanelles on June 24, 1915 and provided fire support during the Battle of Gallipoli. She remained in the Eastern Mediterranean until returned to England in 1919.

PREFIX	SHIP NAME	INFORMATION
HMS	*Acheron*	HMS *Acheron* was an Acheron-class destroyer. She was launched on June 27, 1911 and served in the Grand Fleet, 1914–16; Devonport, Harwich or Dover, 1916–17 and to the Mediterranean by 1918. She was sold on May 9, 1921.
HMS	*Acorn*	HMS *Acorn* was an Acorn-class, designated H-class, destroyer. She was launched on July 1, 1910 and served in the Grand Fleet and the Mediterranean. She was sold in 1921.
HMS	*Agamemnon*	HMS *Agamemnon* was a Lord Nelson-class pre-dreadnought battleship. She was launched on June 23, 1906 and served in the Channel and Grand Fleet and then in the Mediterranean. She was sold in 1927.
HMS	*Alarm*	HMS *Alarm* was an Acorn-class destroyer. She was launched on August 28, 1910 and served in the Grand Fleet, and the Mediterranean. She was sold in 1921.
HMS	*Anemone*	HMS *Anemone* was a Flower-class fleet sweeping sloop. She was launched on May 13, 1915 and served in the Grand Fleet, at Queenstown, and in the Mediterranean. She was sold in 1922.
HMS	*Angora*	*Angora* was a minelayer, mercantile conversion. She was built in 1911 and fitted out at Blackwall. *Angora* was in service from February 27, 1915 to November 15, 1919.
HMS	*Apollo*	HMS *Apollo* was an Apollo-class minelayer (formerly a 2nd-class protected cruiser). She was launched on February 10, 1891 and was broken up in 1920.
HMS	*Archer*	HMS *Archer* was an Acheron-class destroyer. She was launched on October 21, 1911 and served in the Grand Fleet, 1914–16; Devonport, Harwich or Dover, 1916–17 and sent to the Mediterranean by 1918. She was sold on May 8, 1921.
HMS	*Ardent*	HMS *Ardent* was an Acasta-class destroyer. She was launched September 8, 1913 and was sunk on May 31, 1916 at Jutland.
HMS	*Ariel*	HMS *Ariel* was an Acheron-class destroyer. She was launched on September 26, 1911 and served in the Grand Fleet, 1914–16; Devonport, Harwich or Dover, 1916–17 and sent to the Mediterranean by 1918. She was mined in the North Sea on August 2, 1918.
HMS	*Arno*	HMS *Arno* was a unique destroyer of the Royal Navy that saw service and was lost during First Worldw War. She was under construction in Genoa, Italy for the friendly Portuguese Navy as Liz in 1914 when she was bought by the Royal Navy for service in the Mediterranean.
HMS	*Attack*	HMS *Attack* was an Acheron-class destroyer. She was launched on December 21, 1911 and served in the Grand Fleet, 1914–16; Devonport, Harwich or Dover, 1916–17 and to the Mediterranean by 1918. She was mined on December 30, 1917 off Alexandria.
HMS	*Badger*	HMS *Badger* was an Acheron-class destroyer. She was launched on July 11, 1911 and served in the Grand Fleet and also at Devonport, Harwich, or Dover. She was also deployed in the Mediterranean. She was sold on May 9, 1921.
HMS	*Barham*	HMS *Barham* was a Queen Elizabeth-class battleship launched on December 31, 1914. During the 1920s, she was assigned to the Atlantic, Mediterranean, and Home fleets. She was sunk on November 25, 1941 by U-331.
HMS	*Basilisk*	HMS *Basilisk* was a Beagle-class destroyer. She was launched on February 9, 1910 and served in the Mediterranean. She was sold in 1921.

PREFIX	SHIP NAME	INFORMATION
HMS	*Beaver*	HMS *Beaver* was an Acheron-class destroyer. She was launched on October 6, 1911 and served in the Grand Fleet and the Mediterranean. She was sold in 1921.
HMS	*Benbow*	HMS *Benbow* was an Iron Duke-class dreadnought battleship. She was launched on November 12, 1913 and served with the Grand Fleet. She was sold in 1931.
HMS	*Berwick*	HMS *Berwick* was one of 10 Monmouth-class armoured cruisers built in the first decade of the 20th century. She was assigned to the 2nd Cruiser Squadron of the Channel Fleet upon completion in 1903 and was transferred to the Home Fleet in 1906. She accidentally rammed and sank a British destroyer in 1908. *Berwick* was refitted in 1908–09 before she was transferred to the 4th Cruiser Squadron on the North America and West Indies Station later that year. She captured a German merchant ship shortly after World War I began. The ship patrolled for German commerce raiders and escorted convoys for the war. *Berwick* was assigned to the 8th Light Cruiser Squadron in 1919 before she was paid off and sold for scrap in 1920.
HMS	*Black Prince*	HMS *Black Prince* was a Duke of Edinburgh-class cruiser. She was launched November 8, 1904 and sunk on May 31, 1916 at Jutland.
HMS	*Blenheim*	HMS *Blenheim* was a first class protected cruiser launched in 1890. In May 1908, she joined the Mediterranean Fleet as a destroyer depot ship. She was sent to Mudros in March 1915 in support of the Mediterranean Expeditionary Force.
HMS	*Brisk*	HMS *Brisk* was an Acorn-class destroyer. She was launched on September 9, 1910 and served in the Grand Fleet, ending up in the Mediterranean. She was sold on November 15, 1921.
HMS	*Bristol*	HMS *Bristol* was an ex–2nd-class, Bristol-class light cruiser. She was launched on February 23, 1910 and served in the West Indies and South America and the Mediterranean. She was sold in 1921.
HMS	*Broke*	HMS *Broke*, a destroyer leader, was built in Chile as the Almirante Goni. She was purchased in August 1914 and served in the Grand Fleet and then at Dover. She was sold to the Chilean Navy in May 1920 as the *Almirante Uribe*.
HMS	*Bryony*	HMS *Bryony* was an Anchusa-class sloop of the Royal Navy, built at the yards of Armstrong Whitworth and launched on 27 October 1917. She was used to escort convoys during the First World War, and in common with other ships of her class, was disguised as a merchant vessel, known as a Q-ship. After the war she remained in service with the Royal Navy and was sold for breaking up in 1938.
HMS	*Bulldog*	HMS *Bulldog* was a Beagle-class destroyer. She was launched on November 13, 1909 and served in the Mediterranean. She was sold in 1920.
HMS	*Caesar*	HMS *Caesar* was a pre-dreadnought battleship, Majestic class. She was launched March 2, 1996 at Portsmouth. She served in the Channel Fleet at outbreak of war, later in war went abroad, most of class to Mediterranean, remained on foreign stations for some time, depot ship. She was sold November 8, 1921 and broken up in Germany.
HMS	*Calcutta*	HMS *Calcutta* was a Carlisle-class light cruiser. She was launched on July 9, 1918 and was sunk on June 1, 1941 off Crete.

PREFIX	SHIP NAME	INFORMATION
HMS	*Caledon*	HMS *Caledon* was a C-class light cruiser built for the Royal Navy during World War I. She was the name ship of the Caledon sub-class of the C class. She survived both world wars to be scrapped in 1948.
HMS	*Calgarian*	HMS *Calgarian* was an armed merchant cruiser of the Royal Navy. She was sunk by the U-boat U-19 off Rathlin Island, Northern Ireland on 1 March 1918.
HMS	*Calliope*	HMS *Calliope* was a Calliope-class light cruiser. She was launched on December 17, 1914 and served in the Grand Fleet. She was sold in 1931.
HMS	*Calypso*	HMS *Calypso* (D61) was a C-class cruiser. She was launched January 24, 1917 and sunk in 1940 by the Italian submarine *Alpino Attilio Bagnolini*.
HMS	*Cambrian*	HMS *Cambrian* was a Calliope-class light cruiser. She was launched March 3, 1916 and served in the Grand Fleet. She was sold in 1934.
HMS	*Cameleon*	HMS *Cameleon* was an Acorn-class destroyer. She was launched on June 2, 1910 and was part of the Grand Fleet. She also served in the Mediterranean. She was sold in 1921.
HMS	*Canterbury*	HMS *Canterbury* was a Calliope-class light cruiser. She was launched on December 21, 1915 and served in the Harwich Force and then the Mediterranean. She was sold on July 28, 1934.
HMS	*Capetown*	HMS *Capetown* was a Capetown or Carlisle-class light cruiser. She was launched on June 28, 1919 and sold in 1946.
HMS	*Cardiff*	HMS *Cardiff* was a C-class light cruiser. She was launched on April 12, 1917 and spent most of her career as a flagship.
HMS	*Ceanothus*	HMS *Ceanothus* was a Flower-class convoy sloop. She served with Grand Fleet in the Mediterranean as a decoy or Q-ship with concealed armament.
HMS	*Centurion*	HMS *Centurion* was a King George V-class dreadnought battleship. She was launched November 18, 1911 and served with the Grand Fleet. She was converted to a target ship in in 1920 and was sunk as a blockship in 1944.
HMS	*Ceres*	HMS *Ceres* was a C-class light cruiser. She was launched on March 24, 1917. She was sold in 1946.
HMS	*Chelmer*	HMS *Chelmer* was a destroyer ordered by the Royal Navy under the 1903 – 1904 Naval Estimates. Her armament was upgraded in 1906 and she patrolled British waters in her early years. In November 1914, she was deployed to the 5th Destroyer Flotilla in the Mediterranean Fleet where she remained until the end of the war.
HMS	*Cherryleaf*	HMS *Cherryleaf* (formerly *Persol*) was an Admiralty chartered red-ensign oiler. She was launched on November 9, 1916. She was later an RFA oiler/fleet attendant tanker, Leaf-class. She flew the red ensign until 1920, and later the blue ensign. She was sold in 1947 and renamed *Alan Clore*.
HMS	*Christopher*	HMS *Christopher* was an Acasta-class destroyer. She was launched on August 29, 1912 and served in the Grand Fleet, also in Portsmouth, Devonport, or Dover. She was sold on May 9, 1921.
HMS	*Chrysanthemum*	HMS *Chrysanthemum* was an Anchusa-class sloop launched on 10 November 1917. After service in the Mediterranean, in 1938 she became a drill ship with Royal Naval Volunteer Reserve and then the Royal Naval Reserve.
HMS	*Collingwood*	HMS *Collingwood* was a St Vincent-class dreadnought battleship. She was launched on November 7, 1908 and served in the Grand Fleet. She was sold in 1922.

PREFIX	SHIP NAME	INFORMATION
HMS	*Colne*	HMS *Colne* was launched in 1905 and was assigned to the China Station in 1914. After the fall of Tsingtso, she was redeployed to the 5th Destroyer Flotilla in the Mediterranean Fleet in November 1914 accompanying HMS *Triumph*, to support the Dardanelles campaign.
HMS	*Colombo*	HMS *Colombo* was a C-class light cruiser built for the Royal Navy during World War I. She was part of the Carlisle sub-class of the C class. She was launched on December 18, 1918 and survived both world wars to be scrapped in 1948.
HMS	*Comet*	HMS *Comet* was an Acorn-class destroyer launched in 1910 and sunk by an Austrian submarine in 1918.
HMS	*Concord*	HMS *Concord* was a C-class light cruiser that saw service during the First World War. She was launched on April 1, 1916 and was sold for scrapping in 1935.
HMS	*Constance*	HMS *Constance* was a Calliope-class light cruiser. She was launched on September 12, 1915 and served with the Grand Fleet. She was sold in 1936.
HMS	*Curlew*	Launched in 1917, HMS *Curlew* was a light cruiser built for the Royal Navy. The ship survived World War I to be sunk by German aircraft during the Norwegian Campaign in 1940.
HMS	*Danae*	HMS *Danae* was the lead ship of the Danae-class cruisers, serving with the Royal Navy between the world wars and with the Polish Navy during World War II.
HMS	*Dartmouth*	HMS *Dartmouth* was a Weymouth-class light cruiser. She was launched on December 14, 1910 and served in the East Indies and the Mediterranean. She was sold in 1930.
HMS	*Dauntless*	HMS *Dauntless* was a Danae-class light cruiser. She was commissioned on 22 November 1918.
HMS	*Defence*	HMS *Defence* was a Minotaur-class cruiser. She was launched April 24, 1907 and was sunk May 31, 1916 at Jutland.
HMS	*Defender*	HMS *Defender* was an Acheron-class destroyer. She was launched on August 30, 1911 and served in various sites including the Mediterranean.
HMS	*Defiance*	HMS *Defiance* was the last wooden line-of-battleship launched for the Royal Navy. She never saw service as a wooden line-of-battleship. In 1884 she became a school ship.
HMS	*Delhi*	HMS *Delhi* was a Danae-class light cruiser. She was launched on August 12, 1918 and was sold in 1948.
HMS	*Despatch*	HMS *Despatch* was a Danae-class light cruiser. She was launched on September 24, 1919 and sold in 1946.
HMS	*Devonshire*	HMS *Devonshire* was a Devonshire-class cruiser. She was launched on April 30, 1904 and served in North America and the West Indies 1916–1918. She was sold on May 9, 1921.
HMS	*Dragon*	HMS *Dragon* was a Danae-class cruiser built for the Royal Navy. She was launched in Glasgow, in December 1917, and scuttled in July 1944 off the Normandy beaches as part of the Arromanches Breakwater.
HMS	*Drake*	HMS *Drake* was launched in 1901 and served in many stations prior to World War I. The ship was refitted in October 1915 and then transferred to the North America and West Indies Station for convoy escort duties.

PREFIX	SHIP NAME	INFORMATION
HMS	*Druid*	HMS *Druid* was an Acheron-class destroyer. She was launched on December 4, 1911 and served with the Grand Fleet, then Devonport, Harwich or Dover and then in the Mediterranean. She was sold in 1921.
HMS	*Dryad*	HMS *Dryad* was a minesweeper and ex-torpedo gunboat. She was launched on November 22, 1893 and was attached to 10th CS in 1914–15 and to Lowestoft as a minesweeper until 1918. She was sold in 1920.
HMS	*Durban*	HMS *Durban* was a Danae-class light cruiser. She was launched on May 29, 1919 and served on the China Station. In 1928 she was transferred to the America and West Indies Station. She later served in the South Atlantic Division and the Mediterranean Fleet. She was sunk as a breakwater on June 9, 1944.
HMS	*E14*	HMS *E14* was a British E class submarine built by Vickers, Barrow-in-Furness. During the First World War, two of her captains were awarded the Victoria Cross, and a large number of her officers and men also decorated. HMS *E14* was laid down on December 14, 1912 and was commissioned on November 18, 1914. Her hull cost £105,700. She was sunk by shellfire from coastal batteries in the Dardanelles on 28 January 1918.
HMS	*Eagle*	HMS *Eagle* was built for the Chilean Navy as the Almirante Cochrane in 1913 and was purchased by the Royal Navy in early 1918. The ship was initially assigned to the Mediterranean Fleet and then later to the China Station. In 1924, she was converted to an aircraft carrier and was sunk on August 11, 1942 by U-73.
HMS	*Endymion*	HMS *Endymion* was an Edgar-class cruiser. She was launched on July 22, 1891 and served in the North Atlantic and the Mediterranean. She was sold in 1920.
HMS	*Egmont*	HMS *Egmont* was a harbour service base ship at Malta.
HMS	*Erebus*	HMS *Erebus* was an Erebus-class monitor. She was launched on June 19, 1916 and was based at Dover.
HMS	*Essex*	HMS *Essex* was a Kent-class cruiser. She was launched on August 29, 1901 and served in the West Indies and North America. She was sold in 1921.
HMS	*Europa*	HMS *Europa* was an ex–1st-class protected cruiser, Diadem-class cruiser. She was launched on March 20, 1897 and served as a depot ship in the Mediterranean. She was sold in 1920.
HMS	*Flat Calm*	HMS *Flat Calm* was an Admiralty wood drifter. She was delivered on June 3, 1918. She served as a minesweeper and was sold in 1920 and renamed Rowan Tree. She served as Rowan Tree in World War II.
HMS	*Flirt*	HMS *Flirt* was a C-class destroyer. She was launched on May 15, 1897 and, during World War I, patrolled in the Dover area. She was sunk October 27, 1916 in action in the Straits of Dover.
HMS	*Foresight*	HMS *Foresight* was a scout cruiser, launched in 1904. In 1915, she served in the Mediterranean and in July 1916 in the Aegean with her sister ship HMS *Forward* until the end of the war. In November 1916, she assisted the wounded survivors of HMHS *Britannic* and was paid off in June 1919. The ship was sold for scrap on 3 March 1920.
HMS	*Forester*	HMS *Forester* was an Acheron-class destroyer. She was launched June 1, 1911.

PREFIX	SHIP NAME	INFORMATION
HMS	*Forward*	HMS *Forward* was a Forward-class light cruiser. She was launched on August 27, 1904 and served on the Shetland Patrol then in the Mediterranean. She was sold in 1921.
HMS	*Frobisher*	HMS *Frobisher* was a Hawkins-class heavy cruiser of the Royal Navy. She was built at Devonport Dockyard and launched on 20 March 1920. She spent the majority of her career as a cadet training ship. She saw brief service during the Second World War being used for naval gunfire support.
HMS	*Fury*	HMS *Fury* was an Acorn-class destroyer launched in 1911 and sold in 1921.
HMS	*Galatea*	HMS *Galatea* was an Arethusa-class light cruiser. She was launched on May 14, 1914 and served with the Grand Fleet and was fitted for minelaying in 1917. She was sold in 1921.
HMS	*Gasconia*	HMS *Gasconia* was an Admiralty chartered collier. Built 1915, she was lost on Nov. 16, 1917 in the western Mediterranean.
HMS	*Gloucester*	HMS *Gloucester* was a Bristol-class light cruiser. She was launched on October 28, 1909 and served in the Mediterranean and other locations.
HMS	*Goshawk*	HMS *Goshawk* was an Acheron-class destroyer. She was launched on October 18, 1911 and served in the Grand Fleet, 1914–16; Devonport, Harwich or Dover, 1916–17, and sent to the Mediterranean by 1918. She was sold on November 4, 1921.
HMS	*Grasshopper*	HMS *Grasshopper* was a Beagle-class destroyer. She was launched on October 22, 1909 and served in the Mediterranean. She was sold on November 1, 1921.
HMS	*H4*	HMS *H4* was a British H-class submarine built by the Canadian Vickers Co., Montreal. She was commissioned on June 5, 1915 and sold November 30, 1921 at Malta.
HMS	*H5*	*H5* was an H1-class submarine, part of the 8th Flotilla. She was sunk on March 6, 1917 after a collision in the Irish Sea.
HMS	*Hannibal*	HMS *Hannibal* was a Majestic-class pre-dreadnought battleship. She was launched April 28, 1896 and served in the Channel Fleet and in the Mediterranean. She was sold in 1920 and broken up.
HMS	*Harpy*	HMS *Harpy* was a Beagle-class destroyer. She was launched on November 27, 1909 and served in the Mediterranean. She was sold in 1921.
HMS	*Heliotrope*	HMS *Heliotrope* was an Azalea-class sloop launched in 1915 and sold for scrapping in 1935.
HMS	*Hermes*	HMS *Hermes* was launched on September 11, 1919 and served briefly with the Atlantic Fleet before spending the bulk of her career assigned to the Mediterranean Fleet and the China Station. She was used as a training ship from 1938 and as an aircraft carrier from August 1939. She was sunk by Japanese aircraft on April 9, 1942.
HMS	*Heroic*	HMS *Heroic* was one of an additional group of ships requisitioned by the Admiralty during WW1 to augment the ships of the Royal Fleet Auxiliary.
HMS	*Highflyer*	HMS *Highflyer* was a Highflyer-Class cruiser that was launched in 1898. She spent most of World War I on convoy escort duties. She was scrapped in 1921.
HMS	*Hind*	HMS *Hind* was an Acheron-class destroyer. She was launched on July 28, 1911 and served with the Grand Fleet and ended the war in the Mediterranean. She was sold in 1921.

PREFIX	SHIP NAME	INFORMATION
HMS	*Hope*	The HMS *Hope* was a hired trawler built in 1903 as the Auk. She was in service November 1914 to November 1918 as a minesweeper. She also served as a Q-ship and was also known as *Ben Nevis, Claymore, Glen Afric, Lorne, St. Gothard,* and *Spika*. She was renamed the *Antic* in April 1918.
HMS	*Hornet*	HMS *Hornet* was an Acheron-class destroyer. She was launched on December 12, 1911. She served in the Grand Fleet and was then sent to the Mediterranean. She was sold in 1921 and broken up in 1922.
HMS	*Hydra*	HMS *Hydra* was an Acheron-class destroyer of the Royal Navy. She was launched in 1912, fought throughout World War I and was sold for breaking in 1921.
HMS	*Implacable*	HMS *Implacable* was a Formidable-class pre-dreadnought battleship. She was launched on March 11, 1899. She served in the Grand Fleet and in the Mediterranean. She was sold in 1921.
HMS	*Indefatigable*	HMS *Indefatigable* was an Indefatigable-class battlecruiser. She was launched October 28, 1909 and was sunk May 31, 1916 at Jutland.
HMS	*Invincible*	HMS *Invincible* was an Invincible-class battlecruiser. She was launched April 13, 1907 and was deployed to the South Atlantic. She was sunk May 31, 1916 at Jutland.
HMS	*Jackal*	HMS *Jackal* was a Royal Navy destroyer that served during World War I. She served in the Mediterranean in 1917–18 and was sold for breaking in 1920.
HMS	*Jed*	HMS *Jed* was a River-class destroyer. She was launched February 16, 1904 and served in China and the Mediterranean. She was sold in 1920.
HMS	*Kennet*	HMS *Kennet* was a Thornycroft type River Class Destroyer ordered by the Royal Navy under the 1902 – 1903 Naval Estimates. In November 1914, she was redeployed to the 5th Destroyer Flotilla in the Mediterranean Fleet, accompanying Triumph, to support the Dardanelles campaign. She remained in the Mediterranean for the remainder of the war.
HMS	*Kent*	HMS *Kent* was a Kent-class cruiser launched on March 6, 1901. She served in the Atlantic and was sold in 1920.
HMS	*King Alfred*	HMS *King Alfred* was a Drake-class cruiser. She was launched October 28, 1901 and was part of the Grand Fleet in 1914 and served in West Africa in 1915–17. She was sold on January 30, 1920.
HMS	*Lapwing*	HMS *Lapwing* was an Acheron-class destroyer. She was launched on July 29, 1911. She was part of the Grand Fleet 1914–16 and finished the war in the Mediterranean.
HMS	*Larne*	HMS *Larne* was an Acorn-class destroyer. She was launched on August 23, 1910 and formed part of the Grand Fleet and later the Mediterranean. She was sold in 1921.
HMS	*Laverock*	HMS *Laverock* (formerly *Herward*) was launched on November 19, 2013. She served around Harwich then Devonport or Portsmouth. She was sold in May 9, 1921.
HMS	*Liverpool*	HMS *Liverpool* was a Bristol-class light cruiser. She was launched on October 30, 1909 and served with the Grand Fleet and in the Mediterranean. She was sold in 1921.
HMS	*Lizard*	HMS *Lizard* was an Acheron-class destroyer of the British Royal Navy. She was launched in 1911 and scrapped in 1921.

PREFIX	SHIP NAME	INFORMATION
HMS	*Lord Nelson*	HMS *Lord Nelson* was a battleship launched in 1906 and completed in 1908. The ship was flagship of the Channel Fleet when World War I began in 1914. Lord Nelson was transferred to the Mediterranean Sea in early 1915 to participate in the Dardanelles Campaign. She remained there, becoming flagship of the Eastern Mediterranean Squadron, which was later re-designated the Aegean Squadron.
HMS	*Louvain*	Built in 1897, the SS Dresden was a British passenger ship which operated, as such, from 1897 to 1915. She was renamed HMS *Louvain* in 1915 and was used by the Royal Navy in World War I until her loss in 1918.
HMS	*Lowenstoft*	HMS *Lowenstoft* was a Birmingham-class cruiser that was launched on April 23, 1914. She served in the Mediterranean 1914–1916.
HMS	*Lychnis*	*Lychnis*, an Anchusa-class sloop, was launched in December 1916. During World War I, she served as a Q ship, a heavily armed merchant ships with concealed weaponry, designed to lure submarines into making surface attacks. This gave Q-ships the chance to open fire and sink them. She was renamed HMIS *Cornwallis* on her transferral to the Royal Indian Marine in 1921.
HMS	*Lyra*	HMS *Lyra* was an Acorn-class destroyer. She was launched on October 4, 1910 and served in the Grand Fleet, ending up in the Mediterranean. She was sold on May 8, 1921.
HMS	*M-15*	HMS *M15* was a First World War Royal Navy M15-class monitor. She was sunk off Gaza by UC-38 on 11 November 1917.
HMS	*Malaya*	HMS *Malaya* was a Queen Elizabeth-class battleship ordered in 1913 and commissioned in 1916. Shortly after commissioning she fought in the Battle of Jutland as part of the Grand Fleet. Other than that battle, and the inconclusive Action of 19 August, her service during the First World War mostly consisted of routine patrols and training in the North Sea.
HMS	*Marlborough*	HMS *Marlborough* was an Iron Duke-class dreadnought battleship. She was launched on October 24, 1912 and served in the Grand Fleet. She was sold in 1932.
HMS	*Marmora*	HMS *Marmora* was an armed merchant cruiser. She was built in 1903 and came into service on August 3, 1914. Her main areas of service were on patrol and convoy protection. She was sunk on July 23, 1918 south of Ireland by UB.64.
HMS	*Martin*	HMS *Martin* was an Acorn-class destroyer. She was launched on December 15, 1910 and served in the Grand Fleet, ending up in the Mediterranean. She was sold on August 21, 1920.
HMS	*Medina*	The HMS *Medina* was an Admiralty R-class destroyer, originally launched on March 8, 1916 as *Redmill*. She served in the Grand Fleet with some time in the Mediterranean. She was sold on May 9, 1921.
HMS	*Medway*	HMS *Medway* was an Admiralty M-class destroyer. Launched as *Redwing* on April 19, 1916 and renamed *Medora* temporarily, she served in the Grand Fleet. She was sold in 1921.
HMS	*Melampus*	HMS *Melampus* was an ex-Greek M-class destroyer. She was purchased in August 1914 and was sold in 1921.
HMS	*Mischief*	HMS *Mischief* was an Admiralty M-class destroyer. She was launched October 12, 1915 and served with the Grand Fleet and later the Mediterranean. She was sold in 1921 and broken up in 1922.

PREFIX	SHIP NAME	INFORMATION
HMS	*Monarch*	HMS *Monarch* was an Orion-class dreadnought battleship. She was launched on March 30, 1911 and served in the Grand Fleet. She was sunk as a target off Scilly in 1925.
HMS	*Neptune*	HMS *Neptune* was a Neptune-class dreadnought battleship. She was launched September 30, 1909 and served in the Grand Fleet until 1916, then 4th Battle Squadron. She was sold in 1922.
HMS	*Nereide*	HMS *Nereide* was an Acorn-class destroyer. She was launched in 1910 and served in the Mediterranean during World War I. She was sold in 1921.
HMS	*Nereus*	HMS *Nereus* was an Admiralty M-class destroyer. She was launched on February 24, 1916 and served in the Grand Fleet with some time in the Mediterranean. She was sold on November 15, 1921.
HMS	*Nubian*	HMS *Nubian* was a Tribal-class destroyer. She was launched April 20, 1909 and was disabled by a torpedo off the Belgian coast on October 27, 1916.
HMS	*Nymphe*	HMS *Nymphe* was an Acorn-class destroyer launched January 31, 1911. She served in the Grand Fleet and finished the war in the Mediterranean.
HMS	*Osiris II*	*Osiris II* was a fishing trawler built in 1898. She was requisitioned by the Admiralty in 1917 for Fishery Reserve, commissioned and flew the white ensign; and continued commercial fishing under naval control.
HMS	*Paragon*	HMS *Paragon* was an Acasta-class destroyer. She was launched February 21, 1913 and served around Portsmouth, Devonport and Dover. She was sunk on March 18, 1917 by a destroyer torpedo in Dover Straits.
HMS	*Parthian*	HMS *Parthian* was an Admiralty M-class destroyer. She was launched on July 3, 1916 and served as part of the Grand Fleet and later in the Mediterranean. She was sold in 1921.
HMS	*Pelorus*	HMS *Pelorus* was a Pyramus-class light cruiser. She was launched on December 15, 1896 and served in the Bristol Channel and then the Mediterranean. She was sold in 1920.
HMS	*Petrel*	HMS *Petrel* was built as a fishery patrol vessel in 1892 but did not see saltwater until 1905. Between 1914 and 1918 she was employed frequently as a patrol or examination vessel on the east coast.
HMS	*Phaeton*	HMS *Phaeton* was an Arethusa-class light cruiser and later minelayer. She was launched on October 21, 1914 and was part of the Grand Fleet, then 1st LCS. She was sold in 1923.
HMS	*Phoenix*	HMS *Phoenix* was an Acheron-class destroyer of the British Royal Navy. She is named for the mythical bird and was the fifteenth ship of the Royal Navy to bear the name. She was the only British warship ever to be sunk by the Austro-Hungarian Navy.
HMS	*Pincher*	HMS *Pincher* was a Beagle-class destroyer. She was launched on March 15, 1910 and served in the Mediterranean. She was wrecked on July 24, 1918 on the Seven Stones.
HMS	*Prince Edward*	HMS *Prince Edward* (formerly HMS *Prince of Wales*) was a paddle netlayer. She was built in 1887 and was purchased by the Royal Navy on January 28, 1915. She served in the Dardanelles and was sold in 1920.
HMS	*Queen Elizabeth*	HMS *Queen Elizabeth* was the lead ship of her class of dreadnought battleships built in the early 1910s and was often used as a flagship. She served in the First World War as part of the Grand Fleet. Between the wars she was the flagship of the Atlantic Fleet from 1919 to 1924.

PREFIX	SHIP NAME	INFORMATION
HMS	Queen Mary	HMS *Queen Mary* was a Lion-class battle cruiser. She was launched March 20, 1912. The ship was part of the Grand Fleet from 1914. She was sunk May 31, 1916 at Jutland.
HMS	Queen Victoria	HMS *Queen Victoria* was a paddle netlayer. She was built in 1887 and was in service from January 28, 1915. She was purchased by the Royal Navy in August 1915 and served on the Belgian Coast and at the Dardanelles. She was sold in 1920.
HMS	Racoon	HMS *Racoon* (or *Raccoon*) was a Beagle-class destroyer launched in 1910 and wrecked in 1918.
HMS	Raleigh	HMS *Raleigh* was a Hawkins-class light cruiser. She was launched on August 28, 1919 and was wrecked in Belle Isle Strait, Labrador on August 8, 1922.
HMS	Redpole	RMS *Redpole* was an Acorn-class destroyer launched in 1910 and scrapped in 1921.
HMS	Renard	HMS *Renard* was a Beagle-class destroyer launched in 1909 and sold in 1920.
HMS	Renown	HMS *Renown* was a Renown-class battlecruiser. She was laid down as a Royal Sovereign-class battleship and was launched on March 4, 1916. She served in the Grand Fleet and was sold in 1948.
HMS	Resolution	HMS *Resolution* was launched on January 14, 1915. Resolution spent the 1920s and 1930s alternating between the Atlantic Fleet and the Mediterranean Fleet. She also saw service in World War II and was sold for scrap in 1948.
HMS	Ribble	HMS *Ribble* was a River-class destroyer. She was launched on March 3, 1904 and served in the Mediterranean. She was sold in 1920.
HMS	Rifleman	HMS *Rifleman* was an Acorn-class destroyer built by J. Samuel White & Company, Cowes, completed on 4 November 1910 and sold for breaking up on 9 May 1921.
HMS	River Clyde	HMS *River Clyde* was an ex-mercantile, assault ship.
HMS	Roxburgh	HMS *Roxburgh* was a Devonshire-class cruiser. She was launched on January 19, 1904 and served in North America and the West Indies from 1916–1918. She was sold on November 8, 1921.
HMS	Royal Oak	HMS *Royal Oak* was launched on November 17, 1914 and was part of the Grand Fleet. After the war, she saw service in the Atlantic. Mediterranean, and Home fleets. She was sunk on October 14, 1939 by *U-47*.
HMS	Royal Sovereign	HMS *Royal Sovereign* was a Revenge-class battleship. She was laid down in January 1914 and launched in April 1915; she was completed in May 1916. She served with the Grand Fleet for the remainder of the First World War but did not see action. In the early 1930s, she was assigned to the Mediterranean Fleet and based in Malta.
HMS	Ruby	Launched in 1910, HMS *Ruby* was one of twenty destroyers of the Acorn class.
HMS	Sandhurst	HMS *Sandhurst* was the former civil ship *Manipur*, hired in November 1914 and purchased in 1915. She served as the dummy battleship Indomitable before being converted to a fleet repair ship.
HMS	Scandinavia	HMS *Scandinavia* was a fleet messenger She was built in 1905 and was in service from November 9, 1914 to October 5, 1919. She flew the red ensign.
HMS	Shark	HMS *Shark* was an Admiralty S-class, destroyer. She was launched on April 4, 1918 and served in the Grand Fleet, Harwich, and in the Mediterranean. She was sold in 1921.

PREFIX	SHIP NAME	INFORMATION
HMS	*Skirmisher*	HMS *Skirmisher* was one of two Sentinel-class scout cruisers which served with the Royal Navy. She was completed in 1905 and served through World War I. She was scrapped in 1920.
HMS	*Sparrowhawk*	HMS *Sparrowhawk* was an Acasta-class destroyer. She was launched October 12, 1912 and was sunk on May 31, 1916 at Jutland.
HMS	*Spear*	HMS *Spear* was a Scott-class destroyer. She was launched on November 9, 1918. She was sold in 1926.
HMS	*Speedy*	HMS *Speedy* was a Thornycroft S-class destroyer. She was launched on June 1, 1918. She was sunk on September 24, 1922 in a collision with a merchant ship.
HMS	*Spindrift*	HMS *Spindrift* was an Admiralty S-class destroyer. She was launched on December 30, 1918 and was sold in 1936.
HMS	*Sportive*	HMS *Sportive* was an Admiralty S-class destroyer. She was launched on September 19, 1918. She was handed over on September 25, 1936, to Ward. Inverkeithing in part payment for the liner *Majestic*.
HMS	*St. George*	HMS *St. George* was an Edgar-class, 1st-class protected cruiser conversion sea-going depot ship. She was launched on June 23, 1892 and was converted to a depot ship in March 1910 and served in the Mediterranean from 1915–1918. She was sold in 1920.
HMS	*Staunch*	HMS *Staunch* was an Acorn-class destroyer. She was launched October 29, 1910 and served in the Grand Fleet and the Mediterranean. She was sunk by *UC38* off the coast of Palestine on November 11, 1917.
HMS	*Stuart*	HMS *Stuart* was a Scott-class destroyer. She was launched on August 22, 1918. She was sold in 1947.
HMS	*Suffolk*	HMS *Suffolk* was one of 10 Monmouth-class armoured cruisers built for the Royal Navy in the first decade of the 20th century. Upon completion she was assigned to the 3rd Cruiser Squadron of the Mediterranean Fleet and was then assigned to the 5th Cruiser Squadron in the Mediterranean in 1909 after a lengthy refit. She returned home for another refit in 1912 and became the flagship of the 4th Cruiser Squadron on the North America and West Indies Station in 1913. After the beginning of World War I in August, *Suffolk* became a private ship and searched for German commerce raiders while protecting British shipping. She captured a German merchantman shortly after the war began.
HMS	*Superb*	HMS *Superb* was a Bellerophon-class dreadnought battleship. She was launched on November 7, 1907 and served in the Grand Fleet and in the Mediterranean. She was sold in 1922.
HMS	*Sutlej*	HMS *Sutlej*, a Cressy-class cruiser, was launched on November 18, 1899. She served in West Africa, was renamed *Crescent II* in 1920, and was sold in 1921.
HMS	*Swallow*	HMS *Swallow* was a Scott-class destroyer. She was launched on August 1, 1918. She was handed over to Ward, Inverkeithing in part payment for the liner *Majestic* on September 24, 1936.
HMS	*Swiftsure*	HMS *Swiftsure*, a pre-dreadnought battleship, was launched January 12, 1903 as Chilean Constitucion. She was purchased by the Royal Navy on December 3, 1903 and served in the East Indies until 1915 then was deployed in the Mediterranean. She was sold on June 18, 1920.

PREFIX	SHIP NAME	INFORMATION
HMS	*Temeraire*	HMS *Temeraire* was a Bellerophon-class dreadnought battleship. She was launched on August 24, 1907 and served in the Grand Fleet and in the Mediterranean. She was sold in 1921.
HMS	*Theseus*	HMS *Theseus* was an ex–1st-class protected cruiser, Edgar-class cruiser. She was launched on September 8, 1992 and served in the North Atlantic and the Dardanelles. She was sold in 1921.
HMS	*Tigress*	HMS *Tigress* was an Acheron-class destroyer of the Royal Navy that served during World War I. She was built under the 1910–11 shipbuilding programme by R. W. Hawthorn Leslie & Company of Hebburn, was launched on 20 December 1911 and was sold for breaking on 9 May 1921.
HMS	*Tilbury*	HMS *Tilbury* was an Admiralty S-class destroyer. She was launched on June 13, 1918 and served as part of the Grand Fleet and later in the Mediterranean. She was sold in 1931.
HMS	*Tipperary*	HMS *Tipperary* (the former Chilean *Almirante Riveros*) was purchased in August 1914 and launched on March 5, 1915. She was sunk on June 1, 1916 at Jutland.
HMS	*Torch*	HMS *Torch* was a Yarrow S-class destroyer. She was launched on March 16, 1918. She was sold in 1929.
HMS	*Triad*	HMS *Triad* was a hired yacht. She was built in 1909 and served as an HQ ship from February 19, 1915 and was purchased on June 16, 1919. She served as a Special Service Vessel from January 1, 1920 and was sold in May 1933.
HMS	*Tribune*	HMS *Tribune* was an Admiralty S-class destroyer. She was launched on March 28, 1918 and served in the Mediterranean. She was sold in 1931.
HMS	*Tryphon*	HMS *Tryphon* was a Yarrow S-class destroyer. She was launched on June 22, 1918. She was sold in 1920.
HMS	*Tumult*	HMS *Tumult* was a Yarrow S-class destroyer. She was launched on September 17, 1918. She was sold in 1928.
HMS	*Turbulent*	HMS *Turbulent* was a Talisman-class destroyer. She was launched as *Ogre* on January 5, 1916 (name was changed in February 1916) and was sunk on May 31, 1916 at Jutland.
HMS	*Unity*	HMS *Unity* was an Acasta-class destroyer. She was originally going to be named *Kinsale*. She was launched on September 18, 1913 and served around Portsmouth, Devonport and Dover. She was sold on October 25, 1922.
HMS	*Usk*	HMS *Usk* was a River-class destroyer. She was launched July 25, 1903 and served in the China Station and in the Mediterranean.
HMS	*Valiant*	HMS *Valiant* was a Queen Elizabeth-class battleship built for the Royal Navy during the early 1910s. She participated in the Battle of Jutland during the First World War as part of the Grand Fleet. Other than that battle, and the inconclusive Action of 19 August, her service during the war generally consisted of routine patrols and training in the North Sea.
HMS	*Valorous*	HMS *Valorous* (formerly the *Montrose*) was an Admiralty V-class destroyer. She was launched on May 8, 1917 and was Grand Fleet Leader 1917–19. She was sold in 1947.
HMS	*Venetia*	HMS *Venetia* was an Admiralty V-class destroyer. She was launched on October 29, 1917 and served in the Grand Fleet and Harwich force. She was mined on October 19, 1940 in the Thames estuary.

PREFIX	SHIP NAME	INFORMATION
HMS	*Verbena*	HMS *Verbena* (1915) was an Arabis-class sloop launched in 1915 and sold for scrap in 1933.
HMS	*Vernon*	HMS *Vernon* was a shore establishment or "stone frigate" of the Royal Navy. *Vernon* was established on April 26, 1876 as the Royal Navy's Torpedo Branch also known as the Torpedo School, named after the ship HMS *Vernon*, which served as part of its floating base.
HMS	*Viceroy*	HMS *Viceroy* was a W-class destroyer that was launched on November 17, 1917. She saw service in the final months of World War I and also in World War II. She was sold in 1947 or 1948 for scrapping.
HMS	*Wallflower*	HMS *Wallflower* was a Flower-class, Arabis-type, fleet sweeping sloop, built on merchant ship lines. She was launched on November 8, 1915. She served in the Grand Fleet, in the North Sea and the Mediterranean. She was sold in 1931.
HMS	*Warrior*	HMS *Warrior* was a Warrior or improved Duke of Edinburgh-class cruiser. She was launched on November 25, 1905 and foundered in tow on June 1, 1916 after being damaged at Jutland.
HMS	*Warspite*	HMS *Warspite* was a Queen Elizabeth-class battleship built for the Royal Navy during the early 1910s. Her thirty-year career covered both world wars and took her across the Atlantic, Indian, Arctic, and Pacific Oceans. She was decommissioned in 1945.
HMS	*Warwick*	HMS *Warwick* was an Admiralty W-class destroyer. She was launched on December 28, 1917 and served in the Grand Fleet and Harwich Force. She was sunk on February 22, 1944 by *U413* off North Cornwall.
HMS	*Wear*	HMS *Wear* was a River-class destroyer. She was launched on January 21, 1905 and served in the Mediterranean. She was sold in 1919.
HMS	*Welland*	HMS *Welland* was a River-class destroyer. She was launched on April 14, 1904 and served on the China Station and in the Mediterranean. She was sold in 1920.
HMS	*Weymouth*	HMS *Weymouth* was a Weymouth-class cruiser that was launched on November 18, 1910. She served in the Mediterranean and East Africa during the war and was sold in 1928.
HMS	*Whitley*	HMS *Whitley* was an Admiralty W-class destroyer. She was launched on April 13, 1918 and served in the Grand Fleet and Harwich Force. She was bombed and beached on May 19, 1940 on the Belgian coast.
HMS	*Winchester*	HMS *Winchester* was an Admiralty W-class destroyer. She was launched on February 1, 1918 and served in the Grand Fleet and Harwich Force. She was sold in 1946.
HMT	*Aragon*	HMT *Aragon*, originally RMS *Aragon*, was a Royal Mail Ship that served as a troop ship in the First World War. She was built in Ireland in 1905. In 1913 *Aragon* became Britain's first defensively armed merchant ship of modern times. In the First World War she served as a troop ship, taking part in the Gallipoli Campaign in 1915. On December 30, 1917 a German submarine sank her in the Mediterranean.
HMT	*Briton*	HMT *Briton* was originally built in 1897 for the Union Steamship Company and transferred to the Union Castle Line in 1900. She was scrapped in 1926.

PREFIX	SHIP NAME	INFORMATION
	Kashi	The *Kashi*, a Momo-class destroyer, was launched on December 1, 1916. Along with the other three destroyers in the Momo class, she served in Malta from August 1917 to the end of World War One in November 11, 1918. They were attached to the 15th Flotilla along with the cruiser Idzumo, assigned to protect convoys.
	Momo	*Momo* was a Momo-class Japanese destroyer, one of four in this class built in 1916–17. She was deployed in the Mediterranean until 1919.
MV	*Pacuare*	The MV *Pacuare* was built in 1905 and scrapped in 1936.
RMS	*Adriatic*	RMS *Adriatic* was an ocean liner of the White Star Line, launched in 1906. During World War I, *Adriatic* served as a troopship and survived the war without incident. After the war ended, she returned to passenger service.
RMS	*Alaunia*	RMS *Alaunia* was built by John Brown & Company in Scotland to augment the transatlantic passenger fleet of the Cunard Line. The ship entered service in July 1925 and was primarily employed on the Canadian route running from Southampton to Quebec and Montreal during the warm weather months and Halifax during the winter.
RMS	*Baltic*	RMS *Baltic* was an ocean line of the White Star Line that was launched in 1904. She assisted in the evacuation of Americans from Europe and hauling war materials from the US to Britain. In 1916, she was used in transporting the Canadian Expeditionary Force from Halifax to Britain.
RMS	*Caronia*	RMS *Caronia* was launched in 1904 for the Cunard Line. She was briefly placed on Cunard's Boston service in 1914, but the start of the First World War caused her to be requisitioned as an armed merchant cruiser. She was stationed off New York on contraband patrol. In 1916, she became a troopship and served in that role for the duration. Her last duties were the repatriation of Canadian troops in 1919.
RMS	*Durham Castle*	RMS *Durham Castle* was a passenger ship built for the Union-Castle Mail Steamship Company in 1904.] In 1939, the Admiralty requisitioned her for use as a store ship. She sank on 26 January 1940 after hitting a mine probably laid by the German submarine *U-57*.
RMS	*Empress of Britain*	RMS *Empress of Britain* was a transatlantic ocean steamer launched in 1905. Owned by the Canadian Pacific Steamships, she carried passengers between Canada and Europe. In 1914, she was re-fitted to become one of the Admiralty's Armed merchantmen. In May 1915, she was recommissioned as a troop transport and carried more than 110,000 troops to the Dardanelles, Egypt and India. She also carried Canadian and US expeditionary forces across the North Atlantic.
RMS	*Franconia*	RMS *Franconia* was an ocean liner operated by the Cunard Line. She was launched on 23 July 1910. After several years' service primarily in the North Atlantic, she was taken into service as a troop transport in early 1915. On 4 October 1916, while heading for Salonika, she was torpedoed and sunk by the German U-boat *UB-47* 195 miles east of Malta.
RMS	*Magdalena*	RMS *Magdalena* was a British steamship that was built in 1889 as a Royal Mail Ship and ocean liner for the Royal Mail Steam Packet Company. In the First World War she served as the troop ship HMT *Magdalena*. After a long and successful civilian and military career she was scrapped in 1923.

PREFIX	SHIP NAME	INFORMATION
RMS	*Olympic*	RMS *Olympic* was an ocean liner of the White Star Line that was launched in 1911. Unlike her sister ships, *Britannic* and *Titanic*, she had many years of service until 1935. She was converted to a troop transport ship in 1915.
RMS	*Saxonia*	The first RMS *Saxonia* was a passenger ship of the British Cunard Line. Between 1900 and 1925, *Saxonia* operated on North Atlantic and Mediterranean passenger routes, and she saw military service during World War I.
RMSP	*Chaleur*	RMSP *Chaleur* was built in 1893 as Gaul and purchased from the Union Castle Line and renamed *Sabor*. In 1908, she was transferred to Jenkins's Shire Line and renamed Carmarthenshire. In 1913, she reverted to the Royal Mail Steam Packet Co and was renamed *Chaleur*. She operated between Canada and the West Indies. She was scrapped in 1927.
SMS	*Breslau*	SMS *Breslau* was a Magdeburg-class cruiser of the Imperial German Navy, built in the early 1910s.
SMS	*Frauenlob*	SMS *Frauenlob* was a Gazelle-class light cruiser. She was launched on March 22, 1902 and was sunk on May 31, 1916 at Jutland.
SMS	*Goeben*	Several months after her commissioning in 1912, *Goeben*, with the light cruiser *Breslau*, formed the German Mediterranean Division.
SMS	*Lutnow*	SMS *Lutnow* was a Derfflinger-class battlecruiser. She was launched on 29 November 1913, but not completed until 1916. She was scuttled after severe damage at the Battle of Jutland, June 1, 1916.
SMS	*Mecklenburg*	SMS *Mecklenburg* was the fifth ship of the Wittelsbach class of pre-dreadnought battleships of the German Imperial Navy. Laid down in May 1900, she was finished in May 1903.
SMS	*Pommern*	SMS *Pommern* was a Deutschland-clan battleship. She was launched on December 2, 1905 and sunk on June 1, 1916 at Jutland.
SMS	*Rostock*	SMS *Rostock* was a Karlsruhe-class light cruiser. She was launched on November 12, 1912 and was scuttled at the Battle of Jutland, May 31 and June 1, 1916.
SMS	*Wiesbaden*	SMS *Wiesbaden* was a Wiesbaden-class light cruiser. She was launched on January 20, 1915 and was sunk on June 1, 1916 at Jutland.
SS	*Ascania*	SS *Ascania* was originally laid down as *Gerona* for the Thomson Line, prior to being taken over for completion by Cunard as *Ascania*. *Ascania* was used on Cunard's fortnightly service to Quebec and Montreal. During the First World War, the *Ascania* was used as an AMC sailing across the North Atlantic, but on the eastbound voyages all the third class was occupied by Canadian troops on their way to the battlefront in France. In May 1918 the *Ascania* also carried a detachment of the US 119th Infantry from Hoboken, New Jersey, first to Halifax, Nova Scotia, and then made up a transatlantic convoy to their destination at the port of Liverpool. They were attacked by submarines on the night of 26 May but arrived safely at Liverpool on 27 May 1918. The *Ascania* was wrecked during the night of the 13/14 June 1918 in the Breton Strait, 20 miles east of Cape Ray, Newfoundland. The keel of the vessel was broken so she could not be refloated and was declared a total loss. All hands were saved.

PREFIX	SHIP NAME	INFORMATION
SS	*Ayrshire*	SS *Ayrshire* was a refrigerated cargo ship. She was launched on August 28, 1903 and was abandoned on November 28, 1926 after fire broke out on a voyage from Brisbane to the UK with tallow, frozen meat & general cargo. She sank on December 2, 1926, 200 miles SW of Cochin, India.
SS	*Bellerophon*	SS *Bellerophon*, built in 1906, was used for cross-channel transport of troops from August 1914 to Jan 1917, then for the transport of Portuguese troops from Jan to Oct 1917, then troop transport to the Mediterranean from October 1917 to March 1918.
SS	*Bermudian*	SS *Bermudian* was as passenger and refrigerated cargo ship built in 1904. In 1915, she was purchased by Canada Steamship Lines Ltd.
SS	*Cameronia*	This ship was launched in 1911 and was owned by the Anchor Line. She was used as a troop ship and was torpedoed on April 15, 1917 in the Mediterranean and sank 250 miles east of Malta with 2,650 soldiers on board. Most were able to make their way to lifeboats and were rescued.
SS	*Chagres*	This passenger ship was torpedoed and sunk in the Mediterranean Sea 62 nautical miles east north east of Cape Drepano, Crete, Greece by SM *UC-74* (Imperial German Navy) with the loss of one life.
SS	*City of Marseilles*	This steam merchant was built in 1913 for the Ellerman Lies. Ltd. of London. During the First World War, the ship was shelled by a German U-boat but escaped.
SS	*Corsican*	SS *Corsican* was launched in 1907 for the Allan Line. She was leased by Canadian Pacific Line and transported two thousand British Home Children/Child Migrants to Canada between 1908 and 1911. In 1914, she shifted to transporting troops. In 1917, she was taken over by Canadian Pacific and returned to transatlantic passenger service. In 1922, she was renamed *Marvale* and was wrecked on May 21, 1923 near Cape Race.
SS	*El Kharia*	Unable to find any information on this vessel.
SS	*Hebburn*	SS *Hebburn* was an Admiralty chartered collier. She was built in 1908 and was lost on September 25, 1918 in St George's Channel.
SS	*Inventor*	SS *Inventor* was built in 1910 and was a steel screw steamer.
SS	*Lady Drake*	The dual cargo and passenger steam ship *Lady Drake* was built by Cammell Laird & Company of Birkenhead, England in 1928. *Lady Drake* was owned by the Canadian National Steamships Limited of Montreal.
SS	*Lady Sybil*	SS *Lady Sybil* was built in Scotland in 1908 for passenger & cargo services between the Magdalen Islands and Canadian mainland.
SS	*Lapland*	SS *Lapland* was a passenger ship launched on June 27, 1908. She sailed the Liverpool-New York City crossings under the British flag while under charter to Cunard Line. In April 1917 she was mined off the Mersey Bar Lightship but managed to reach Liverpool and in June 1917 she was requisitioned and converted to a troopship.
SS	*Laurentic*	S.S. *Laurentic* was a British ocean liner of the White Star Line. She was completed in 1909 and was converted to an armed merchant cruiser at the onset of World War I. She sank on January 25, 1917 after encountering two mines north of Ireland.

PREFIX	SHIP NAME	INFORMATION
SS	*Lorenzo*	The *Lorenzo* was an American freight steamship.
SS	*Matutua*	Owned by the Red Star Line, *Matutua* was a cargo liner built in 1904. She was used as a cargo ship during World War I. In 1916 she had a serious fire on board while in Canadian waters and the master, Captain Louis B. Gillman was killed.
SS	*Mégantic*	SS *Mégantic* was an ocean liner built by Harland and Wolff, of Belfast, and operated by the White Star Line
SS	*Metagama*	SS *Metagama* was launched in 1914 and entered Canadian Pacific's North Atlantic service with a 26 March 1915 maiden voyage from Liverpool to Saint John, New Brunswick. She was a sister ship to *Missanabie*. *Metagama* remained in CP's service during World War I, although she often carried Canadian troops in her third-class accommodations on eastbound crossings. She was broken up in 1934.
SS	*Mexican Prince*	*Mexican Prince* was built in 1893. She was an oil tanker which remained with the Prince Steam Shipping Company until 1919.
SS	*Missanabie*	SS *Missanabie* was a defensively armed British Passenger Liner of the Canadian Pacific Line built in 1914. On the September 9, 1918 when en route from Liverpool for New York she was torpedoed by German submarine *UB-87* when 52 miles SE from Daunts Rock, Ireland with 45 lives lost.
SS	*Pancras*	This passenger and cargo ship was completed in September 1911 and was broken up in 1932.
SS	*Pennland*	SS *Pittsburgh* was a transatlantic ocean liner. It was built by Harland and Wolff in Belfast for the American Line. Initial construction began in 1913, but was delayed by World War I. The ship was completed in 1920 and made its first voyage in 1922 for the White Star Line. In 1925, as *Pennland*, it commenced operations for the Red Star Line. The ship was refitted as a troopship for the Allies in World War II. The ship was bombed April 25, 1941 in the Gulf of Athens and sank.
SS	*Queen Louise*	The S.S. *Queen Louise* was a cargo ship that was launched on February 5, 1912. On March 31, 1917, she was torpedoed 3 miles north of Cap Barfleur while carrying steel billets and locomotives. She was broken up in 1924.
SS	*San Rito*	This cargo ship was launched in 1916 and was sunk on February 15, 1918 in the Aegean Sea when she was torpedoed by the German submarine *UC37*.
SS	*Scandinavian*	The SS *Scandinavian* was a steamship ocean liner built at Harland & Wolff in Belfast which entered service in 1898. The ship changed names and owners several times; she was originally built for the Dominion Line and was known as New England. In 1903 she was transferred to the White Star Line and renamed Romanic.
SS	*Scotian*	This ship was launched on May 7, 1898 as the *Statendam* of the Holland America Line. In 1911, she was acquired by the Allan Line and renamed the *Scotian*. She was used as a troop ship in 1914.
SS	*Southland*	Built as *Vaderland* in 1900, she sailed the Southampton-Cherbourg-New York line. In 1915 she was requisitioned as a troopship and renamed *Southland* and on 2nd Nov.1915 was torpedoed in the Aegean Sea but reached port and was repaired. She returned to White Star-Dominion Liverpool-Quebec-Montreal service in Aug.1916 but on 4th Jun.1917 was torpedoed and sunk by the German submarine *U-70* off the Irish coast with the loss of four lives.

PREFIX	SHIP NAME	INFORMATION
SS	*Spreewald*	The Spreewald was a German Hamburg-America line steamer that had been outfitted as an armed cruiser.
SS	*Thor*	The SS *Thor* was a Norwegian tramp steamer.
SS	*Tibor*	SS *Tibor* was a French cargo ship launched in 1900. On January 10th, 1918, the French steel cargo ship *Tibor*, with a cargo of benzine, was lost in a fire at Port Said.
SS	*Volumnia*	SS *Volumnia* was a British Cargo Steamer of 5,608 tons built in 1911 by Russell & Co, Port Glasgow for Gow Harrison & Co, Glasgow. On the 8th December 1929 she foundered in the middle of the North Atlantic and sank.
TSS	*Themistocles*	TSS *Themistocles* was a passenger ship launched on September 22, 1910, sailing on the London to Australia via Cape Town route. She served as a British troopship during World War I and survived a number of convoy duties during World War II. She was scrapped on August 24, 1947.
USS	*Cincinnati*	USS *Cincinnati* was the third Omaha-class light cruiser, originally classified as a scout cruiser, built for the United States Navy. She was launched on May 23, 1921 and was scrapped in 1946.
USS	*Richmond*	USS *Richmond* was an Omaha-class light cruiser, originally classified as a scout cruiser, of the United States Navy. She was launched on September 19, 1921 and was sold for scrap in 1946.
USS	*Wyoming*	USS *Wyoming* (BB-32) was the lead ship of her class of dreadnought battleships. She was launched May 25, 1911, was used as a training ship through the 1930s and was sold for scrap in 1947.

APPENDIX B. PLACE NAMES IN THE JOURNALS

See pages 299–301 for maps, which show a number of the places mentioned in this table.

COUNTRY	PLACE	DESCRIPTION
Bahamas	Nassau	Nassau is the capital of the Bahamas. It lies on the island of New Providence.
Barbados	Ragged Point Lighthouse	Ragged Point is a village in Saint Philip Parish in Barbados. The lighthouse is located at the easternmost point of the island.
Barbados		Barbados is an eastern Caribbean island and an independent British Commonwealth nation.
Bermuda	Hamilton	Hamilton is the capital city of Bermuda, a British island territory in the North Atlantic.
Canada	7 Islands, QC	7 Islands (Sept-Îles) is a city in eastern Québec, Canada. It is among the northernmost locales with a paved connection to the rest of Québec's road network.
Canada	Agassiz, BC	Agassiz is a small community located in the Eastern Fraser Valley region of British Columbia, Canada, about 61 miles east of Vancouver.
Canada	Aspy Bay, NS	Aspy Bay is a bay of the Atlantic Ocean near the northern tip of Cape Breton Island.
Canada	Baddeck, NS	Baddeck is a village in Victoria County, Nova Scotia, Canada. This village is situated on the northern shore of Bras d'Or Lake on Cape Breton Island.
Canada	Bedwell Harbour, BC	Bedwell Harbour is located on South Pender Island.
Canada	Biggar, SK	Biggar is a town in central Saskatchewan.
Canada	Bridgewater, NS	Bridgewater is a town in Lunenburg County, Nova Scotia, at the navigable limit of the LaHave River.
Canada	Brier Island, NS	Brier Island is an island in the Bay of Fundy.
Canada	Cabot Strait, NS	Cabot Strait is a strait in eastern Canada approximately 110 kilometres wide between Cape Ray, Newfoundland and Cape North, Cape Breton Island.
Canada	Cape Egmont, PE	Cape Egmont, an unincorporated area, is located in Prince County in the western portion of Prince Edward Island. The lighthouse was erected in 1883–84.
Canada	Cape Forchu, NS	Cape Forchu is a Canadian fishing community and headland of the same name in Yarmouth County, Nova Scotia.
Canada	Cape Ray, NL	Cape Ray is a headland located at the southwestern extremity of Newfoundland.
Canada	Centreville, NS	Centreville is located on Digby Neck.
Canada	Charlottetown, PE	Charlottetown is the capital city of the province of Prince Edward Island. It is on the southern coast of the island.
Canada	Chester, NS	Chester is a village on the Chester Peninsula, Mahone Bay, Nova Scotia.

COUNTRY	PLACE	DESCRIPTION
Canada	Clark's Harbour, NS	Clark's Harbour is a town on Cape Sable Island in southwestern Nova Scotia.
Canada	Colwood, BC	Colwood is a city located on Vancouver Island to the southwest of Victoria.
Canada	Cordova Bay, BC	Cordova Bay is a part of the District of Saanich. It is located on the east coast of Vancouver Island.
Canada	Crofton, BC	Crofton is a small community on Vancouver Island, nestled into the shoreline of Osborne Bay and overlooking Salt Spring Island.
Canada	Digby, NS	Digby is a town in southwestern Nova Scotia, Canada. It is situated on the western shore of the Annapolis Basin near the entrance to Digby Gut, which connects the basin to the Bay of Fundy.
Canada	Duncan, BC	Duncan is a city on southern Vancouver Island in British Columbia, Canada. It is in the heart of the scenic Cowichan Valley.
Canada	Edmonton, AB	Edmonton, the capital of Alberta, sits on the North Saskatchewan River.
Canada	Esquimalt, BC	Esquimalt is a municipality at the southern tip of Vancouver Island, in British Columbia. It is home to Canadian Forces Base Esquimalt, Canada's Pacific Coast naval base.
Canada	Fort Howe, NB	Fort Howe was built by the British during the American Revolution shortly after the American Siege of Saint John (1777), to protect Saint John from further American raids
Canada	Fulford Harbour, BC	Fulford Harbour is a residential community on the southeast side of Salt Spring Island, British Columbia, located near the island's southern end.
Canada	Ganges, BC	Ganges is a community on Salt Spring Island, clustered around the Ganges Harbour. It is located in the middle of the Island.
Canada	Gaspé, Québec	Gaspé is a city at the tip of the Gaspé Peninsula in eastern Québec.
Canada	Gorge Waterway, Victoria, BC	The Gorge Waterway is a narrow tidal inlet that connects Victoria Harbour to Portage Inlet. Past generations of Victorians would spend summer days swimming, sunbathing, canoeing, rowing and generally relaxing.
Canada	Grand Manan, NB	Grand Manan Island is a Canadian island, and the largest of the Fundy Islands in the Bay of Fundy.
Canada	Grand Passage, NS	Grand Passage is a body of water located between Brier Island and Long Island off the northeast coast of Nova Scotia. To the south is St Mary's Bay and to the north, the Bay of Fundy.
Canada	Grand-Pré, NS	Grand-Pré is a Canadian rural community in Kings County, Nova Scotia. The community was made famous by Henry Wadsworth Longfellow's poem "Evangeline."

COUNTRY	PLACE	DESCRIPTION
Canada	Halifax, NS	Established in 1749, Halifax is the capital of the Canadian province of Nova Scotia. It was in World War I that Halifax came into its own as a world-class port and naval facility. The strategic location of the port with its protective waters of Bedford Basin sheltered convoys from German U-boat attack prior to heading into the open Atlantic Ocean. Troops for overseas left from Halifax and the injured returned there.
Canada	Harbour Island, NL	Little Bay Islands is a town in Newfoundland and Labrador, Canada. It consists of Little Bay Island, Macks Island, Goat Island, Harbour Island, and Boatswain Tickle Island.
Canada	Hubbards, NS	Hubbards is an unincorporated rural community on the South Shore of Nova Scotia.
Canada	Ingonish, NS	Ingonish is a rural community in northeastern Nova Scotia. Located along the northeast coast of Cape Breton Island, Ingonish is situated on the Cabot Trail.
Canada	Island of Orleans, PQ	The Island of Orleans (Île d'Orléans) is located in the Saint Lawrence River about 5 kilometres east of downtown Québec City.
Canada	Letang, NB	Letang is located on the east coast of New Brunswick on the Bay of Fundy.
Canada	Liverpool, N.S.	Liverpool is a community located along the Atlantic Ocean of the Province of Nova Scotia's South Shore.
Canada	Londonderry, NS	Londonderry is an unincorporated community located in Colchester County, Nova Scotia, Canada, formerly called Acadia Mines. Commodore Edwards was born there.
Canada	Lunenburg, NS	Lunenburg is a port town in Lunenburg County, Nova Scotia, Canada. Situated on the province's South Shore.
Canada	Mahone Bay, NS	Mahone Bay is a town on the northwest shore of Mahone Bay along the South Shore of Nova Scotia.
Canada	Malahat Drive, BC	Malahat is mostly known for the portion of British Columbia Highway 1 that traverses the community, locally known as 'The Malahat' or 'The Malahat Drive'. The roadway has a mix of 2, 3 and 4 lane cross-sections.
Canada	Maple Bay, BC	Maple Bay is a seaside community located in the Cowichan Valley of southern Vancouver Island.
Canada	Margaree, NS	Margaree is a small community in the Canadian province of Nova Scotia, located on the Cabot Trail on Cape Breton Island.
Canada	Metchosin, BC	Metchosin is a small, coastal community in Greater Victoria on the southern tip of Vancouver Island.
Canada	Miramichi, NB	Miramichi is the largest city in northern New Brunswick, Canada. It is situated at the mouth of the Miramichi River where it enters Miramichi Bay.
Canada	Montreal, QC	Montréal, the largest city in Québec, is set on an island in the Saint Lawrence River and named after Mt. Royal, the triple-peaked hill at its heart.

COUNTRY	PLACE	DESCRIPTION
Canada	Mount Robson, BC	Mount Robson is the most prominent mountain in the Rocky Mountain range; it is also the highest point in the Canadian Rockies.
Canada	Mutton Bay, NL	Mutton Bay is located on the shore of a protected bay, surrounded by forested mountains. It is a charming, picturesque fishing village with distinct outport-style architecture.
Canada	Nanaimo, BC	Nanaimo is a city on the east coast of Vancouver Island, BC.
Canada	Neil's Harbour, NS	Neil's Harbour is a small fishing village in northern Cape Breton Island.
Canada	New Westminster, BC	New Westminster is a city in the Lower Mainland region of British Columbia located on the Fraser River.
Canada	North Sydney, NS	North Sydney is a community on Cape Breton Island. It is located on the north side of Sydney Harbour, along the eastern coast of Cape Breton Island,
Canada	Northwest Arm, Halifax, NS	The Northwest Arm, originally named Sandwich River, is an inlet in eastern Canada off the Atlantic Ocean in Nova Scotia's Halifax Regional Municipality.
Canada	Ottawa, ON	Ottawa is Canada's capital. It is located on the Ottawa River in the east of southern Ontario, near the city of Montréal and the U.S. border.
Canada	Parrsboro, NS	Parrsboro is a Canadian community located in Cumberland County, Nova Scotia.
Canada	Pender Island, BC	Pender Island is one of the southern Gulf Islands located in the Gulf of Georgia. It consists of two islands, North Pender and South Pender, which are separated by a narrow canal and connected by a one-lane bridge.
Canada	Percé, QC	Percé is a small city near the tip of the Gaspé Peninsula in Québec.
Canada	Port aux Basques, NL	Port aux Basques is located at the extreme southwestern tip of Newfoundland fronting on the western end of the Cabot Strait.
Canada	Preedy Harbour, BC	Preedy Harbour is close to Thetis Island.
Canada	Qualicum Beach, BC	Qualicum Beach is a town located on the east coast of Vancouver Island, BC.
Canada	Quamichan, BC	Quamichan Village is a small community in the Cowichan Valley.
Canada	Québec City, QC	Québec City is the capital city of the province of Québec It is one of the oldest European settlements in North America and the only fortified city north of Mexico whose walls still exist.
Canada	Rivière-du-Loup, QC	Rivière-du-Loup is a small city on the south shore of the Saint Lawrence River in Québec.
Canada	Rocky Mountains	The Rocky Mountains stretch 3,000 miles from British Columbia and Alberta in Canada through Idaho, Montana, Wyoming, Colorado, and down to New Mexico in the U.S.

COUNTRY	PLACE	DESCRIPTION
Canada	Rothesay, NB	Rothesay is a town located in Kings County, New Brunswick. It is adjacent to the City of Saint John along the Kennebecasis River.
Canada	Saint John, NB	Saint John is the coastal port city of the Bay of Fundy.
Canada	Salt Spring Island, BC	Salt Spring Island is one of the Gulf Islands in the Strait of Georgia between mainland British Columbia and Vancouver Island.
Canada	Sansum Narrows, BC	Sansum Narrows is a strait or channel between Vancouver Island (W) and Saltspring Island (E) in the Southern Gulf Islands region of British Columbia, Canada.
Canada	Sarnia, ON	Sarnia is a city in Southwestern Ontario. It is the largest city on Lake Huron.
Canada	Sault Ste. Marie, ON	Sault Ste. Marie is a city in Ontario on the St. Marys River, north of the U.S. border, near three of the Great Lakes.
Canada	Scatarie Island, NS	Scatarie Island is an island in Nova Scotia, located off the coast of Baleine, Cape Breton Island.
Canada	Shawinigan, QC	Shawinigan is a city located on the Saint-Maurice River in the Mauricie area in Québec
Canada	Shawnigan Lake, BC	Shawnigan Lake is a lake on southern Vancouver Island, located to the west of Saanich Inlet and to the south of the Cowichan Valley region.
Canada	Shelburne, NS	Shelburne is a town located in southwestern Nova Scotia.
Canada	Sidney, BC	Sidney is a town located at the northern end of the Saanich Peninsula on Vancouver Island
Canada	St. Lawrence Bay, NS	St. Lawrence Bay is located on Cape Breton Island, Nova Scotia.
Canada	St. Paul Island, NS	St. Paul Island is a small uninhabited island located approximately 24 km northeast of Cape North on Cape Breton Island and 71 km southwest of Cape Ray on Newfoundland; it is along the boundary between the Gulf of St. Lawrence and the Cabot Strait.
Canada	Sydney, NS	Sydney is a harbour town on Cape Breton Island, Nova Scotia.
Canada	Thetis Island, BC	Thetis Island is an island and unincorporated community off the coast of British Columbia, Canada, lying between Vancouver Island, which is to the west across Stuart Channel, and the west from the north tip of Galiano Island, from which it is separated by Trincomali Channel.
Canada	Toronto, ON	Toronto, the capital of the province of Ontario, is located along Lake Ontario's northwestern shore.
Canada	Trial Island, BC	The Trial Islands are a group of islands located off the southeastern tip of Vancouver Island off Victoria, part of the municipality of Oak Bay.
Canada	Trois-Rivières, Quebéc	Trois-Rivières is a city in Québec, Canada, at the confluence of the Saint-Maurice and Saint Lawrence rivers, on the north shore of the Saint Lawrence River.

COUNTRY	PLACE	DESCRIPTION
Canada	Tuft's Cove, NS	Tuft's Cove is an urban neighbourhood in the Dartmouth area of Halifax, Nova Scotia, Canada. It is situated on the eastern shore of Halifax Harbour in the north end of Dartmouth.
Canada	Valcartier, QC	Valcartier (now CFB Valcartier) was originally erected as a military training camp in August 1914 as part of the mobilization of the Canadian Expeditionary Force at the onset of World War I.
Canada	Vancouver, BC	Vancouver is a bustling west coast seaport in British Columbia, set against a backdrop of mountains.
Canada	Victoria, BC	Victoria, the capital of British Columbia, sits on the craggy southern end of Vancouver Island.
Canada	Whitehead, NS	Whitehead is a small community in Nova Scotia, located in Guysborough County.
Canada	Winnipeg, MB	Winnipeg is the capital of the province of Manitoba. It is centred around The Forks, a historic site at the intersection of the Red and Assiniboine rivers.
Canada	Yarmouth, NS	Yarmouth is a port town located on the Bay of Fundy in southwestern Nova Scotia.
Cape Verde Islands	St. Vincent	Saint Vincent is a volcanic island in the Caribbean. It is the largest island of the country Saint Vincent and the Grenadines. It is located in the Caribbean Sea, between Saint Lucia and Grenada.
Colombia	Cartagena	Cartagena is a port city on Colombia's Caribbean coast.
Crete	Souda Bay	Souda Bay is a bay and natural harbour near the town of Souda on the northwest coast of the Greek island of Crete.
Croatia	Fiume	Rijeka, formerly known as Fiume, is a city located in the northern tip of the Kvarner Gulf in the northern Adriatic. It was an independent free state between 1920 and 1924 and is now part of Croatia.
Cuba	Cape Maysi	Cape Maysi is a cape at the eastern extremity of Cuba, projecting into the Windward Passage.
Curacao	Wilhamstad	Wilhamstad is a port city in Curacao.
Curacao		Curacao is a Lesser Antilles island in the southern Caribbean Sea. It is part of the Kingdom of the Netherlands.
Cyprus	Pyrgos	Pyrgos is a village east of the town of Limassol, Cyprus.
Demerara	Georgetown	Georgetown was the main town of Demerara in 1916. It is now part of Guyana.
Demerara		Demerara is a historical region in the Guianas on the north coast of South America which is now part of the country of Guyana. It was a Dutch colony until 1815 and a county of British Guiana from 1838 to 1966. It was located about the lower courses of the Demerara River, and its main town was Georgetown.
Denmark	Bornholm Island	Bornholm is a Danish island in the Baltic Sea off the south coast of Sweden.

COUNTRY	PLACE	DESCRIPTION
Denmark	Copenhagen	Copenhagen, Denmark's capital, sits on the coastal islands of Zealand and Amager.
Dominica		Dominica is an island country in the West Indies. It is part of the Windward Islands in the Lesser Antilles archipelago in the Caribbean Sea.
East Prussia	Memel	Memel, at the time of this journal, was in East Prussia. It is now called Klaipda and part of Lithuania on the Baltic coast.
Egypt	Abassia	Abassia is now part of Cairo.
Egypt	Alexandria	Alexandria is a Mediterranean port city in Egypt.
Egypt	Cairo	Cairo, Egypt's capital city, is located on the Nile River.
Egypt	Gaza	Gaza is on the east coast of the Mediterranean Sea. It was under Ottoman rule until the years following World War I, when the Ottoman Empire collapsed and Gaza formed part of the League of Nations British Mandate of Palestine.
Egypt	Kantara	Kantara is a northeastern Egyptian city.
Egypt	Port Said	Port Said is a city that lies in north east Egypt extending about 30 km along the coast of the Mediterranean Sea, north of the Suez Canal.
England	Aldershot	Aldershot is a town in the Rushmoor district of Hampshire, England. It is known as the home of the British Army.
England	Avonmouth	Avonmouth is a port and outer suburb of Bristol, England facing two rivers: the reinforced north bank of the final stage of the Avon which rises at sources in Wiltshire, Gloucestershire and Somerset; and the eastern shore of the Severn Estuary.
England	Babbacombe	Babbacombe is a district of Torquay, Devon, England.
England	Basingstoke	Basingstoke is the largest town in the modern county of Hampshire.
England	Beckenham	Beckenham is a district of London.
England	Bentley	Bentley railway station serves the village of Bentley in Hampshire, England. It is situated on the Alton Line, between Farnham and Alton.
England	Bridport	Bridport is a market town in Dorset, England, 1.5 miles inland from the English Channel near the confluence of the River Brit and its tributary the Asker.
England	Bristol	Bristol is a city straddling the River Avon in the southwest of England. It has a prosperous maritime history.
England	Brookwood	Brookwood is a village in Surrey, England.
England	Cambridge	Cambridge is a city on the River Cam in eastern England.
England	Cawsand	Cawsand and Kingsand are twin villages in southeast Cornwall, England.

COUNTRY	PLACE	DESCRIPTION
England	Dartmouth	Dartmouth is a town and civil parish in the English county of Devon.
England	Devonport	The largest naval base in Western Europe, Devonport has been supporting the Royal Navy since 1691. The vast site now covers more than 650 acres and has 15 dry docks, four miles of waterfront, 25 tidal berths and five basins.
England	Dorchester	Dorchester is a town of Dorset, England.
England	Farnham	Farnham is a town in Surrey, England, in the Borough of Waverley. The town is 34.5 miles southwest of London in the extreme west of Surrey, adjacent to the border with Hampshire.
England	Faversham	Faversham is a market town and civil parish in the Swale district of Kent, England.
England	Folkestone	Folkestone is a port town on the English Channel, in Kent, south-east England.
England	Froyle	Froyle is a village and civil parish in the East Hampshire district of Hampshire, England. It is 3.6 miles northeast of Alton. The nearest railway station is 2 miles east of the village, at Bentley.
England	Grantham	Grantham is a town in the South Kesteven district of Lincolnshire, England.
England	Haslar	Haslar is on the south coast of England, at the southern tip of Alverstoke, on the Gosport peninsula, Hampshire.
England	Liverpool	Liverpool is a maritime city in northwest England, where the River Mersey meets the Irish Sea.
England	Lyme Regis	Lyme Regis is a town in West Dorset, England, 25 miles west of Dorchester and 25 miles east of Exeter.
England	Maidstone	Maidstone is a large, historically important town in Kent, England, of which it is the county town. It lies 32 miles east-south-east of London.
England	Marefield	Marefield is a hamlet and civil parish in the Harborough district of Leicestershire, England.
England	Portsmouth	Portsmouth is a port city and naval base on England's south coast, mostly spread across Portsea Island. It's known for its maritime heritage and Portsmouth Historic Dockyard. It is sometimes called Pompey.
England	Princetown	Princetown is a village in the Dartmoor national park in the English county of Devon.
England	Ringwood	Ringwood is a market town in Hampshire, England, on the River Avon.
England	Rodmersham	Rodmersham is a village and civil parish in the Borough of Swale in the north of the English county of Kent.
England	Roehampton	Roehampton is a large suburban district in southwest London.

COUNTRY	PLACE	DESCRIPTION
England	Royal Hospital Haslar	The Royal Hospital Haslar in Gosport, Hampshire, was one of several hospitals serving the Portsmouth Urban Area but had previously been the country's foremost – and ultimately last – military hospital.
England	Saint Helier	Saint Helier is one of the twelve parishes of Jersey, the largest of the Channel Islands in the English Channel.
England	Sheerness	Sheerness is a town beside the mouth of the River Medway on the north-west corner of the Isle of Sheppey in north Kent, England.
England	Sittingbourne	Sittingbourne is an industrial town situated in the Swale district of Kent in south east England, 17 miles from Canterbury and 45 miles from London.
England	Southampton	Southampton is a port city on England's south coast.
England	Tavistock	Tavistock is a market town in West Devon. It is the birthplace of Sir Francis Drake.
England	Teignmouth	Teignmouth is a large seaside town, fishing port and civil parish in the English county of Devon.
England	Torquay	Torquay is a seaside town in Devon, England.
England	Two Bridges	Two Bridges is an isolated location on the river West Dart in the heart of Dartmoor National Park in Devon, England.
England	Yelverton	Yelverton is a large village on the south-western edge of Dartmoor, Devon, In England.
England	Yeovil	Yeovil is an English town and civil parish in the district of South Somerset.
Finland	Helsingfors	Helsingfors, now known as Helsinki, was established as a trading town by King Gustav I of Sweden in 1550 as the town which he intended to be a rival to the Hanseatic city of Reval (today known as Tallinn).
France	Arras	Arras is an attractive town in the Nord-Pas de Calais region of France. It was much fought-over in World War 1 and is mainly visited by tourists travelling from or to the nearby ports of Calais and Boulogne. It is also a recommended place to travel from to visit the Canadian National Vimy Memorial.
France	Boulogne	Boulogne, now called Boulogne-sur-Mer is a city, known as a major fishing port, on the north coast of France.
France	Brest	Brest is a port city in Brittany, in northwestern France, bisected by the Penfeld river. It's known for its rich maritime history and naval base.
France	Calais	Calais is a city and major ferry port in northern France.

COUNTRY	PLACE	DESCRIPTION
France	Cambrai	Located in northern France, this city was occupied by the German forces during World War 1 and was the site of the Battle of Cambrai, a huge tank battle with many casualties on both sides.
France	Cannes	Cannes is a resort town on the French Riviera.
France	Cherbourg	Cherbourg was a city at the northern end of the Cotentin peninsula in the northwestern French department of Manche. It is now called Cherbourg-Octeville.
France	Ecoivres	Ecoivres is a hamlet lying at the foot of the hill, to the south-west and about 1.5 kilometres from Mont St Eloi on the Arras-St Pol line. The Ecoivres Military Cemetery is on the D49 road.
France	Juan-les-Pins	Juan-les-Pins is a town in southeastern France, on the Côte d'Azur. It is situated between Nice and Cannes.
France	Le Havre	Le Havre is a major port in northern France's Normandy region, where the Seine River meets the English Channel.
France	Marseilles	Marseilles is a port city in southern France that has been a crossroads of immigration and trade since its founding by the Greeks circa 600 B.C.
France	Modane	Modane is a commune in the Savoie department in the Auvergne-Rhône-Alpes region in southeastern France.
France	Mont-Saint-Éloi	Mont-Saint-Éloi is a commune in the Pas-de-Calais department in the Hauts-de-France region of France.
France	Nice	Nice is a city on the French Riviera. It sits on the pebbly shores of the Baie des Anges.
France	Paris	Paris is the capital city of France. It has been one of Europe's major centres of finance, commerce, fashion, science, and the arts.
France	Toulon	Toulon is a city in southern France and a large military harbour on the Mediterranean coast, with a major French naval base.
France	Ville Franche	Ville Franche is located on the French Riviera.
France	Vimy	Vimy is a commune in the Pas-de-Calais department in the Hauts-de-France region of France. It is located 3.8 kilometres east of the Canadian National Vimy Memorial dedicated to the Battle of Vimy Ridge and the Canadian soldiers who were killed during the war.
Germany	Kiel	Kiel is a port city on Germany's Baltic Sea coast.
Gibraltar		Gibraltar is a British Overseas Territory located at the southern top of the Iberian Peninsula. It is bordered to the north by Spain. The landscape is dominated by the Rock of Gibraltar.

COUNTRY	PLACE	DESCRIPTION
Greece	Argostoli	Argostoli is a town on the island of Kefalonia, Ionian Islands of Greece.
Greece	Athens	Athens is a historic city and capital of Greece. Many of Classical civilization's intellectual and artistic ideas originated there, and the city is generally considered to be the birthplace of Western civilization.
Greece	Cape Castro	Cape Castro is a town on the southwest coast of Greece,
Greece	Cape Matapan	Cape Matapan is the southernmost point of mainland Greece, and the second southernmost point in mainland Europe. It separates the Messenian Gulf in the west from the Laconian Gulf in the east.
Greece	Corfu	Corfu is an island off Greece's northwest coast in the Ionian Sea.
Greece	Corinth Canal	This is a man-made flat canal that crosses the Isthmus of Corinth joining the Gulf of Corinth in the northwest with the Saronic Gulf in the southeast.
Greece	Deuthero Cove	Deuthero Cove is a bay in East Macedonia.
Greece	Gavrion Bay	Gavrion Bay is a bay in the South Aegean Islands of Greece.
Greece	Gulf of Patras	The Gulf of Patras is a branch of the Ionian Sea in Western Greece.
Greece	Kasos	Kasos is a Greek island in the Aegean sea.
Greece	Kastro	Now known as Kastro-Kyllini, it is a former municipality in West Greece.
Greece	Kefalos Bay	Kefalos Bay (more commonly known as Kamari Bay) is situated at the south-western end of the Greek island of Kos. It is overlooked by the ancient cliff-top village of Kefalos.
Greece	Kondia	Kondia is a village on the Greek island of Lemnos, North Aegean.
Greece	Mavros	Mavros is an uninhabited Greek islet, in the Aegean Sea, close to the eastern coast of Crete.
Greece	Milo	Milo or Melos is a volcanic Greek island in the Aegean Sea, just north of the Sea of Crete. Milos is the southwesternmost island in the Cyclades group.
Greece	Mudros	Mudros is a town on the Greek Island of Lemnos. During the Dardanelles Campaign of the First World War, the town and its harbour were used as an Allied base,
Greece	Navarino Bay	The Bay of Navarino is a small, deep, and almost landlocked bay of the Ionian Sea in the southwestern Peloponnese, Greece. It is also known also as Pylos Bay.
Greece	Oxeia Island	Oxeia is a Greek island in the Ionian Sea.

COUNTRY	PLACE	DESCRIPTION
Greece	Pireaus	Piraeus is a port city in the region of Attica, Greece. Piraeus is located 12 kilometres southwest of the City of Athens core.
Greece	Port Trebuki	Port Trebuki is a coastal indentation in central Greece.
Greece	Salonika	Salonika (Thessaloniki) is a Greek port city on the Thermaic Gulf of the Aegean Sea. Evidence of Roman, Byzantine and Ottoman history remains.
Greece	Samothraki	Samothraki (also known as Samothrace or Samothracia) is a Greek island in the northern Aegean Sea.
Greece	Skiathos	Skiathos is a Greek island in the northwest Aegean Sea and is part of the Sporades archipelago.
Greece	Skyros Island	Skyros is a Greek island in the Aegean Sea, part of the Sporades archipelago.
Greece	Syros	Syros or Siros or Syra is a Greek island in the Cyclades, in the Aegean Sea. It is located 78 nautical miles south-east of Athens.
Greece	Volo	Volos is a coastal port city in Thessaly situated midway on the Greek mainland, about 330 kilometres north of Athens and 220 kilometres south of Thessaloniki.
Greece (now)	Dedeagatch	Dedeagatch (now called Alexandroupoli) was founded as a small fishing village in the early 19th century. The name was changed when the area came under the control of Greece.
Grenada	St. George's	St. George's is the capital city of the Caribbean island of Grenada.
Grenada		Grenada is a country in the West Indies in the Caribbean Sea at the southern end of the Grenadines island chain. Grenada consists of the island of Grenada itself plus six smaller islands which lie to the north of the main island.
Grenadine Islands	Martinique Channel	The Martinique Channel is a strait in the Caribbean Sea that separates Saint Vincent and the Grenadines from Grenada.
Grenadine Islands		The Grenadines are a chain of small islands that lie on a line between the larger islands of Saint Vincent and Grenada in the Lesser Antilles.
Ireland	Coningbeg Light Vessel	Coningbeg, off the Saltee Islands, 14 km from the County Wexford coast, was established in 1824 and replaced on 26 February 2007 with a "Superbuoy".
Ireland	Lough Swilly	Lough Swilly in Ireland is a glacial fjord or sea inlet lying between the western side of the Inishowen Peninsula and the Fanad Peninsula, in County Donegal.
Ireland	Queenstown	Now called Cobh, Queenstown was the major seaport for ships leaving for North America and other ports.
Ireland	Rathlin Island	Rathlin Island is an island off the coast of County Antrim, Northern Ireland, and the northernmost point of Northern Ireland.

COUNTRY	PLACE	DESCRIPTION
Italy	Borghese Garden, Rome	The Borghese Garden is a landscape garden in the naturalistic English manner in Rome, containing a number of buildings, museums and attractions.
Italy	Brindisi	Brindisi is a port city on the Adriatic Sea, in southern Italy's Apulia region.
Italy	Florence	Florence is the capital city of the Italia region of Tuscany.
Italy	Leghorn	Leghorn, known as Livorno in Italian, is a port city on the Ligurian Sea on the western coast of Tuscany, Italy.
Italy	Messina	Messina is a harbour city in northeast Sicily, separated from mainland Italy by the Strait of Messina.
Italy	Montenero	Montenero is a small hill-top town in Italy.
Italy	Naples	Naples, a city in southern Italy, sits on the Bay of Naples.
Italy	Rome	Rome is the capital city of Italy.
Italy	Stromboli	Stromboli is a small island in the Tyrrhenian Sea, off the north coast of Sicily, containing one of the three active volcanoes in Italy.
Italy	Syracuse	Syracuse is a city on the Ionian coast of Sicily, Italy.
Italy	Taranto	Taranto is a coastal city in southern Italy.
Italy	Vallona	Vallona is a city located in northern Italy on the Adriatic Sea.
Jamaica	Kingston	Kingston is the capital and largest city of Jamaica, located on the southeastern coast of the island. It faces a natural harbour protected by the Palisadoes, a long sand spit.
Jamaica	Morant Point	Morant Point Lighthouse is on the easternmost tip of Jamaica.
Jamaica	Port Royal	Port Royal is a village located at the end of the Palisadoes at the mouth of the Kingston Harbour, in southeastern Jamaica.
Jamaica		Jamaica is an island country in the Caribbean Sea. It is the fourth-largest country island in the area.
Lesser Antilles	Mount Pelée	Mount Pelée is a volcano at the northern end of Martinique, an island and French overseas department in the Lesser Antilles island arc of the Caribbean.
Malta	Bighi Hospital	The Royal Naval Hospital Bighi also known as Bighi Hospital, was a major naval hospital located in the small town of Kalkara on the island of Malta. It opened in 1832 and closed in 1970.
Malta	Calafrana	Calafrana, more commonly known as Kalafrana, is a town on the southern tip of Malta. Between 1917 and 1946, it was the location of RAF Kalafrana, a marine aircraft base and aircraft maintenance facility.

COUNTRY	PLACE	DESCRIPTION
Malta	Imtarfa	Imtarfa (also known as Mtarfa) is a small town in the Northern Region of Malta.
Malta	Manoel Island	Manoel Island is a small island which forms part of the municipality of G ira in Marsamxett Harbour, Malta.
Malta	Marsa	Marsa is a town in the South Eastern Region of Malta, with a population of 4,401 people as of March 2014. The name Marsa means "the harbour."
Malta	Marsa Scirocco	Marsa Scirocco is a fishing village, located in the south-east area of Malta.
Malta	Sliema	Sliema is a resort town on the east coast of the Mediterranean island of Malta.
Malta		Malta is an archipelago in the central Mediterranean between Sicily and the North African coast. It's a nation known for historic sites related to a succession of rulers including the Romans, Moors, Knights of Saint John, French and British.
Martinique	Fort-de-France	Fort-de-France is the capital of France's Caribbean island of Martinique.
Martinique		Martinique is a rugged Caribbean island that is part of the Lesser Antilles.
Monaco	Monte Carlo	Monte Carlo is one of the four sections of Monaco. It is situated on an escarpment at the base of the Maritime Alps along the French Riviera, on the Mediterranean, just northeast of Nice, France.
Monaco		Monaco is a tiny independent city-state on France's Mediterranean coastline
Nassau	Great Inagua	Inagua is the southernmost district of the Bahamas, comprising the islands of Great Inagua and Little Inagua.
Northern Ireland	Belfast	Belfast is a port and the capital city of Northern Ireland.
Northern Ireland	Fanad Lighthouse	Fanad, the location of the lighthouse, is a peninsula that lies between Lough Swilly and Mulroy Bay on the north coast of County Donegal in Ireland.
Palestine	Haifa	At the beginning of the 20th century, Haifa emerged as an industrial port city and growing population centre. It is now part of Israel.
Portugal	Azores	The Azores, an autonomous region of Portugal, are an archipelago in the mid-Atlantic.
Portugal	Lagos	Lagos is a town in southern Portugal's Algarve region.
Portugal	Lisbon	Lisbon is the capital city of Portugal.

COUNTRY	PLACE	DESCRIPTION
Russia	Sevastapol	Sevastopol is the largest city on the Crimean Peninsula and a major Black Sea port.
Russia (in 1919)	Libau	Now called Liepāja and part of Latvia, Libau was a seaport on the Baltic Sea.
Saint Lucia		Saint Lucia is an Eastern Caribbean island nation with a pair of dramatically tapered mountains, the Pitons, on its west coast.
Scotland	Dumfries	Dumfries is a market town located near the mouth of the River Nith into the Solway Firth.
Scotland	Dunfermline	Dunfermline is a town and former Royal Burgh, and parish, in Fife, Scotland, on high ground 3 miles from the northern shore of the Firth of Forth.
Scotland	Edinburgh	Edinburgh is the capital city of Scotland and is located on the Firth of Forth's southern shore.
Scotland	Inverkeithing	Inverkeithing is a town and a royal burgh, and parish, in Fife, Scotland, located on the Firth of Forth.
Scotland	Queensferry	Queensferry, also called South Queensferry or simply "The Ferry", is a town to the west of Edinburgh, Scotland.
Scotland	Rosyth Dockyard	Rosyth Dockyard is a large naval dockyard on the Firth of Forth at Rosyth, Fife, Scotland which formerly undertook refitting of Royal Navy surface vessels and submarines. Before its privatization in the 1990s, it was formally the Royal Naval Dockyard Rosyth.
Spain	Balearic Islands	The Balearic Islands are an archipelago off eastern Spain, in the Mediterranean. Mallorca (Majorca) is the largest island.
Spain	Linea	La Línea de la Concepción is a town in Spain which lies on the eastern isthmus of the Bay of Gibraltar, north of the Gibraltar–Spain border, which lies north of the British overseas territory of Gibraltar, with which it has close economic and social links
St. Vincent	Kingstown	Kingstown is the capital, chief port, and main commercial centre of Saint Vincent and the Grenadines.
Sweden	Björkö	Björkö is an island in Lake Mälaren in eastern-central Sweden.
Sweden	Sandhammaren Light	Sandhammaren is a low and sandy point at the southeastern extremity of Sweden.
Trinidad	Port of Spain	Port of Spain, on Trinidad's northwest coast, is the capital city of Trinidad and Tobago.
Trinidad		Trinidad is the larger and more populous of the two major islands of Trinidad and Tobago. The island lies off the northeastern coast of Venezuela and sits on the continental shelf of South America.
Tunisia	Biserta	Biserta is the northernmost city in Africa. It is one of the oldest cities in the region, having been founded around 1100 B.C.

COUNTRY	PLACE	DESCRIPTION
Turkey	Cape Aliki	Cape Aliki is a point and is south of Ovacık, southeast of E elek and west of Aphrodite Point.
Turkey	Cape Helles	Cape Helles is the rocky headland at the southwesternmost tip of the Gallipoli peninsula, Turkey. It was the scene of heavy fighting between Ottoman Turkish and British troops during the landing at Cape Helles at the beginning of the Gallipoli Campaign in 1915.
Turkey	Chanak	Chanak refers to Çanakkale, a city at the Anatolian side of the Dardanelles Strait.
Turkey	Constantinople	Constantinople, known formerly as Byzantium and now as Istanbul, is the most populous city in Turkey and the country's economic, cultural and historic centre. It is a transcontinental city in Eurasia, straddling the Bosporus Strait (that separates Europe and Asia) between the Sea of Marmara and the Black Sea.
Turkey	Dardanelles	The Dardanelles, formerly known as The Hellespont, is a narrow strait in Turkey that links the Aegean Sea with the Sea of Marmara. Control of shipping in the area was critical to the Allied efforts in World War I. The closing of the Dardanelles brought the Ottoman Empire into the war as a German ally at the end of October 1914. An Allied campaign in 1915–16 was a disaster with huge loss of life. By the time this journal was written, a second assault was underway, with more favourable results.
Turkey	Imbros	Imbros is the largest island of Turkey.
Turkey	Ismid	Ismid (now called Izmit) is a Gulf in Turkey. It is located in the Sea of Marmara.
Turkey	Kumkale	Kumkale is a village in Çanakkale Province, Turkey.
Turkey	Kusu Bay	Kusu Bay is off the island of Imbros.
Turkey	Suvla	Suvla is a bay on the Aegean coast of the Gallipoli peninsula in European Turkey, south of the Gulf of Saros.
Turkey	Tenedos	Tenedos is an island of Turkey in the northeastern part of the Aegean Sea. It was under Greek administration between 1912 and 1923. During the World War I Gallipoli Campaign, the British used the island as a supply base and built a 600m. long airstrip for military operations. Tenedos was ceded according to the Treaty of Lausanne to the new Turkish republic that emerged with the dissolution of the Ottoman Empire in 1923.
United States of America	Bar Harbor, Maine	Bar Harbor is a town on Mount Desert Island along Maine's Frenchman Bay.

COUNTRY	PLACE	DESCRIPTION
United States of America	Cape Henry, Virginia	Cape Henry is a cape on the Atlantic shore of Virginia located in the northeast corner of Virginia Beach. It is the southern boundary of the entrance to the long estuary of the Chesapeake Bay.
United States of America	Chesapeake Bay, Maryland	Chesapeake Bay is an estuary in the U.S. states of Maryland and Virginia.
United States of America	Florida Strait	The Straits of Florida, Florida Straits, or Florida Strait is a strait located south-southeast of the North American mainland, generally accepted to be between the Gulf of Mexico and the Atlantic Ocean, and between the Florida Keys (U.S.) and Cuba.
United States of America	Nantucket light ship, Massachusetts	The Lightship Nantucket or Nantucket Shoals was the name given to the lightvessel that marked the hazardous Nantucket Shoals south of Nantucket Island.
United States of America	Sandy Hook, NJ	Sandy Hook is a barrier spit in Middletown Township, Monmouth County, New Jersey. The barrier spit, approximately 6 miles in length and varying from 0.1 to 1.0 miles wide, is located at the north end of the Jersey Shore.
Venezuela	La Guaira	La Guaira is the capital city of the Venezuelan state of Vargas and the country's main port.
Venezuela	Orquilla Island	Orquilla Island is one of the seven islets of the Los Hermanos Archipelago off the coast of Venezuela.
Venezuela	Pico Island	Pico Island is one of the seven islets of the Los Hermanos Archipelago off the coast of Venezuela.
Wales	Caerleon	Roman Wales was the farthest point west that the Roman Empire in Roman Britain extended to, and as a defence point the fortress at Caerleon, built in AD 75, was one of only three permanent Roman Legionary fortresses in Roman Britain.
Wales	Caerphilly	Caerphilly is a town and community in South Wales, at the southern end of the Rhymney Valley.
Wales	Cardiff	Cardiff is a port city on the south coast of Wales, where the River Taff meets the Severn Estuary.
Wales	Ladyhill Golf Course, Newport	The Ladyhill Golf Club opened as a 9-hole course in March 1903 and was co-designed by Harry Vardon; it was extended to 18 holes in 1905 and was closed by 1923.
Wales	St Woollos church, Newport	St. Wolloos is an ancient church. A stone church was built on the site of an early 5th-century wooden church in the 9th century. It was extended in the 12th, 15th, and 20th centuries. It is located in Newport, Wales as is known today as Cathedral Church of St. Woolos King & Confessor.
Wales	Wyndecliff	The Wyndcliff (sometimes spelled Wyndecliffe) is a steep limestone cliff rising above the western bank of the River Wye in Monmouthshire, Wales.

MAPS: *Which include a selection of the places named in the journals.*

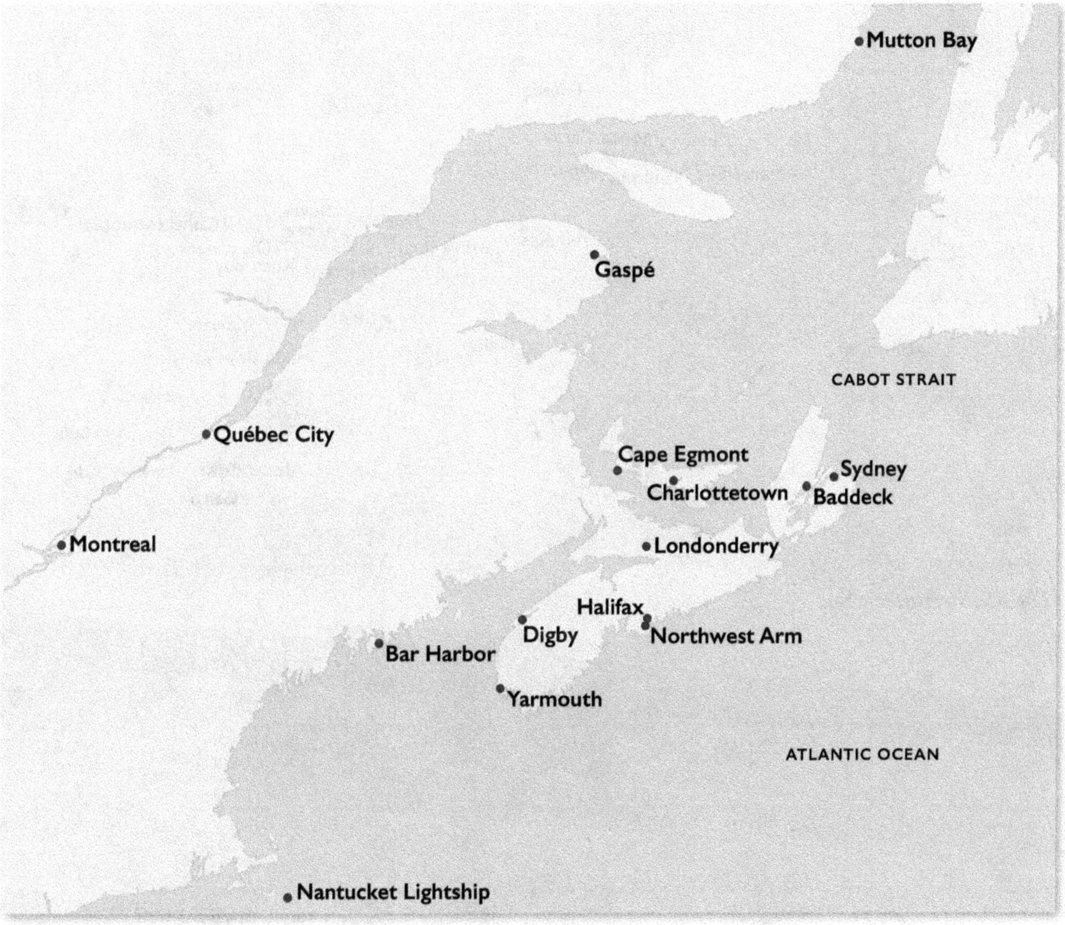

East Coast of North America

West Coast of Canada

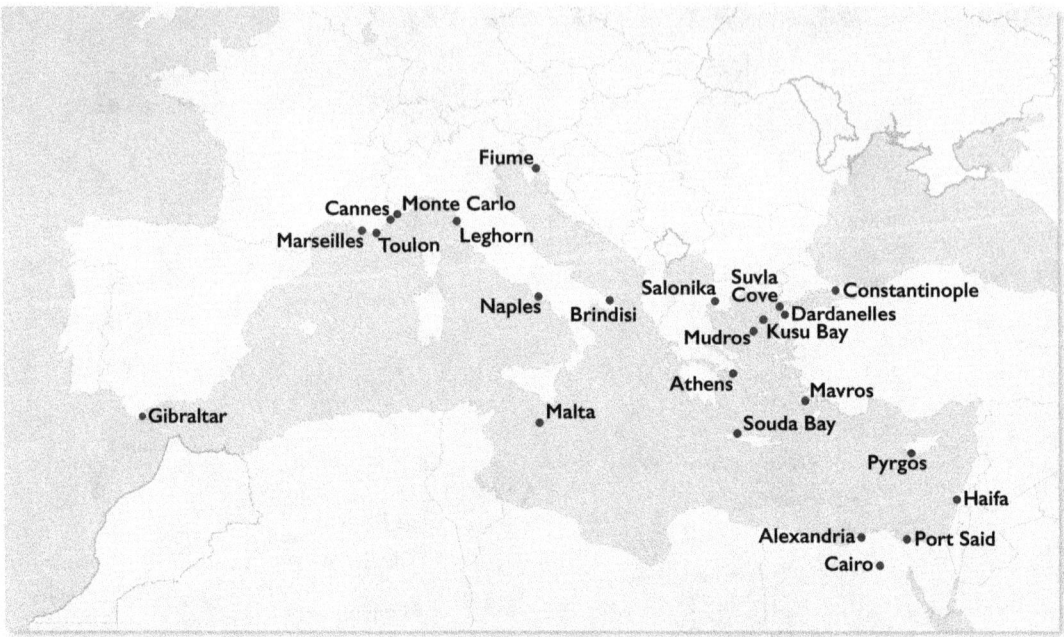

The Mediterranean Sea

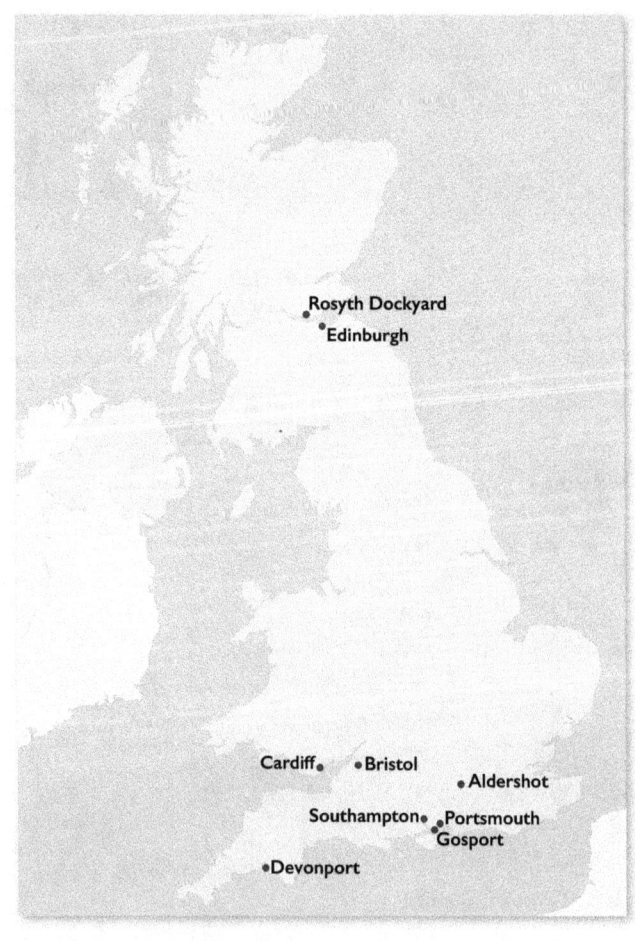

The British Isles

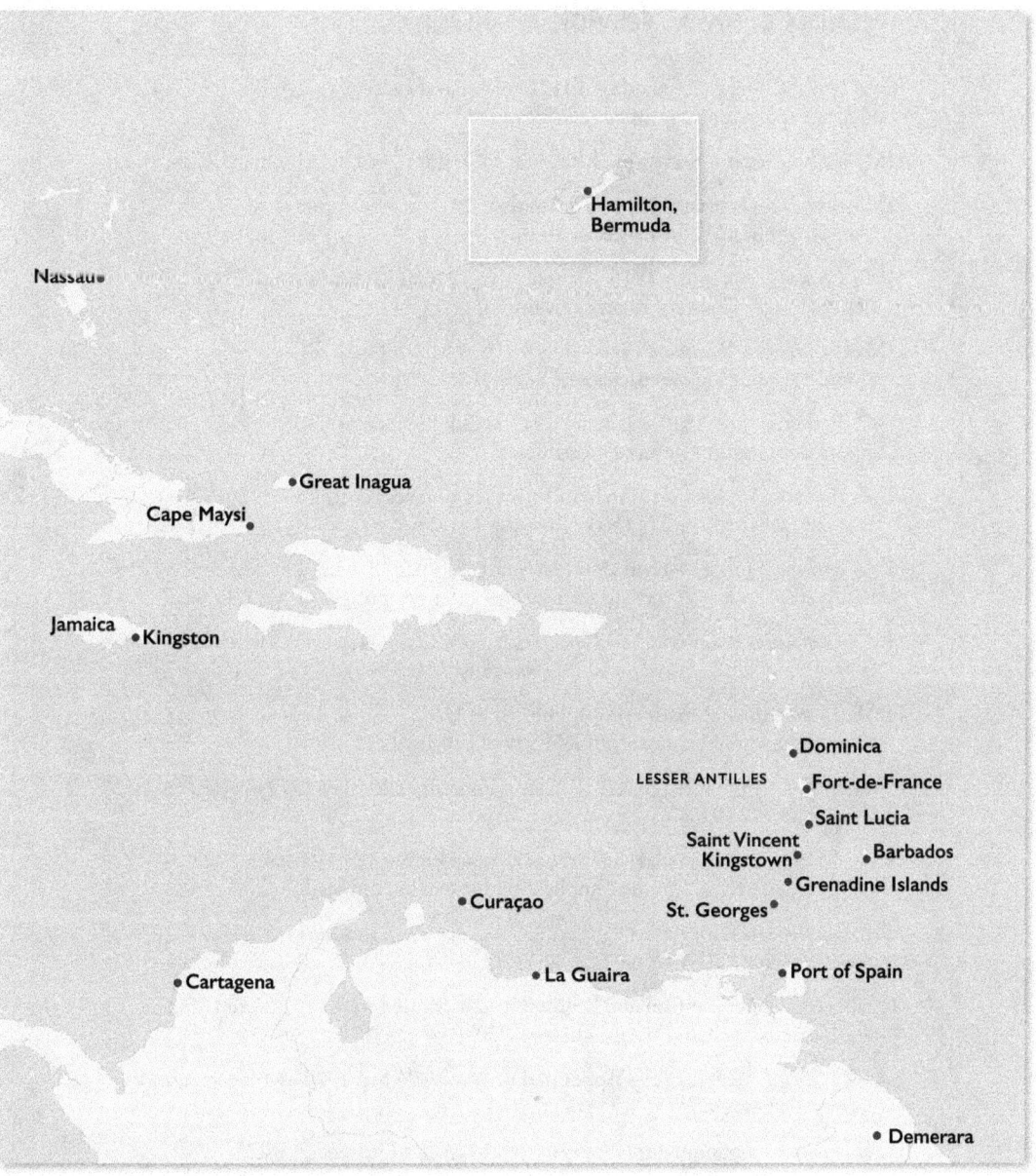

The Caribbean Sea and Bermuda

APPENDIX C. NAVAL SERVICE, 1912–1950

Royal Naval College of Canada – 1912–1914, naval cadet.
(Source: application for master certificate)

HMCS *Shearwater* – Served in Shearwater for training as a Midshipman, RCN.

HMS *Berwick* – February 1914 to September 1915 as Midshipman, RCN.
(Source: application for master certificate)

HMS *Caesar* – September 1915 – January 16, 1916 as Midshipman, RCN.
(sSource: application for master certificate)

HMCS *Canada* – February 1916 – July 1916 as Midshipman, RCN.
(Source: application for master certificate)

HMS *Berwick* – July 1916 – January 1917 as Sub Lieutenant, RCN.
(Source: application for master certificate)

HMS *Archer* – Appointed to Archer (Torpedo Boat Destroyer) 24 Feb 1917 as a Sub Lieutenant, RCN (Navy List Aug 1918)

HMS *Lychnis* (Q ship) – Loaned as Navigator, February 21, 1918 to March 17, 1918 Returned to Archer at the end of this time. (Source: journals of J.C.I. Edwards)

HMS *Cameleon* – Appointed to *Cameleon* (Acorn Class Destroyer) 11 Sep 1918 as an Acting Sub Lieutenant, RCN (Navy List Mar 1919)

HMS *Thames* (for submarines) – Appointed to HMS *Thames* 25 Feb 1919 as an Acting Sub Lieutenant, RCN (Navy List May 1919)

HMS/m *R-1* – Appointed to R-1 (R Class Submarine) 26 May 1919 as an A/Lt, RCN (Navy List Oct 1919)

HMS *Galatea* (Arethusa-class light cruiser) – September 1919 – March 1920 as Lieutenant, RCN. (Source: application for master certificate)

HMS *Calliope* (Calliope-class light cruiser) – Appointed to *Calliope* 25 Mar 1920 as a Lieutenant, RCN (Navy List Jul 1920)

Royal Naval College of Canada, Esquimalt – Appointed to RNCC 28 Jun 1920 as a Lieutenant, RCN (Navy List Nov 1920)

HMCS *Guelph* (depot ship) – Appointed to *Guelph* 06 Sep 1922 as a Lieutenant, RCN (Navy List Dec 1922)

HMS *Victory* – Appointed to *Victory* 06 Jan 1923 as a Lieutenant, RCN (Navy List Sep 1923)

HMCS *Festubert* – Appointed to *Festubert* (Battle-class naval trawler) 10 Mar 1924 as a Lieutenant, RCN, Commanding Officer (Navy List Jul 1924)

HMCS *Stadacona* (depot ship) – Appointed to *Stadacona* 10 Mar 1926 as Lieutenant, RCN (Navy List Feb 1926)

HMS *Valiant* – Served in *Valiant* (Queen Elizabeth Class battleship) 22 Apr 1926 – 11 Feb 1927 (Source: journals of J.C.I Edwards)

HMS *Malaya* – Appointed to *Malaya* (Queen Elizabeth Class battleship) 12 Feb 1927 as a Lieutenant Commander, RCN (Navy List Jul 1927)

HMCS *Champlain* (Thornycroft S-class destroyer) – Appointed Commanding Officer 21 May 1928 as a Lieutenant Commander, RCN (Navy List Jul 1928). 3rd Commanding Officer 21 May 1928 – 26 Dec 1929

RCN Naval Barracks Esquimalt – Appointed to RCN Naval Barracks Esquimalt 17 Jan 1930 as a Lieutenant Commander, RCN (Navy List Jan 1931)

RCN Naval Barracks Halifax – Appointed to RCN Naval Barracks Halifax, Additional for Headquarters Ottawa, Assistant to Director Naval Reserves 21 Dec 1931 as a Lieutenant Commander, RCN (Navy List Jan 1932)

RCN Naval Barracks Halifax – Appointed to RCN Naval Barracks Halifax 20 Jun 1934 as Lieutenant Commander, RCN (Navy List Sep 1934)

RCN Naval Barracks Esquimalt – Appointed to RCN Naval Barracks Esquimalt 06 May 1936 as Lieutenant Commander, RCN (Navy List Aug 1936). Appointed Commander, RCN seniority 01 Dec 1938 (Navy List Apr 1939)

HMC Dockyard, Esquimalt – Appointed to HMC Dockyard Esquimalt 26 Aug 1939 as Commander, RCN, Extended Defence Officer and Commanding Officer Auxiliary Vessels based at Esquimalt. (Navy List Oct 1939)

RCN Naval Barracks Halifax – Appointed to RCN Barracks Halifax 26 Dec 1939 as Cdr, RCN, Commanding Officer (Navy List Apr 1940). Appointed Acting Captain, RCN (Navy List Dec 1940)

HMCS *Prince Henry* – Appointed Commanding Officer 20 Dec 1941 as a Captain, RCN (Navy List Apr 1942). 2nd Commanding Officer 20 Dec 1941 – 31 Dec 1942

HMCS Cornwallis – Appointed to Cornwallis 21 Jan 1943 as a Captain, RCN, Commanding Officer (Navy List Aug 1943)

HMCS Naden – Appointed to Naden 11 Mar 1946 as a Captain, RCN, Commanding Officer (Navy List Apr 1946). Appointed Commodore seniority 01 Jan 1949 (Navy List Jan 1949) Appointed OIC RCN Depot Esquimalt (Navy List Jan 1950)

RCN Barracks Esquimalt – Appointed to RCN Barracks Esquimalt as additional 14 Feb 1950 (Navy List Jul 1950)

Retired from the RCN as a Commodore on 11 Oct 1950 (Navy List Jan 1951)

SOURCES

Wikipedia

Royal Navy ships of World War I at https://www.naval-history.net/WW1NavyBritishShips-Dittmar2.htm

https://www.militaryfactory.com/ships/ww1-german-navy-warships.asp

https://en.wikipedia.org/wiki/List_of_ships_of_the_Imperial_German_Navy

https://uboat.net/allies/commanders/1197.html

https://www.naval-history.net/index.htm

http://www.gov.pe.ca/placefinder

https://www.historicplaces.ca

Maps at: https://www.google.ca/

https://novascotia.ca/archives/

http://www.norwayheritage.com

https://uboat.net/allies/merchants/ship/1098.html

http://discovery.nationalarchives.gov.uk/

https://search.findmypast.com/

National Library of Scotland at https://deriv.nls.uk/dcn23/9203/92030545.23.pdf

French Navy, World War I at http://www.naval-history.net/WW1NavyFrench.htm

Flickr at https://www.flickr.com

https://www.wrecksite.eu/

Norway heritage at http://www.norwayheritage.com

https://www.cunardshipwrecks.com

http://www.tynebuiltships.co.uk/

https://uboat.net/

Australian Library at https://birtwistlewiki.com.au/

British Home Children at http://britishhomechild.com

Golf's Missing Links at https://www.golfsmissinglinks.co.uk/

https://www.naval-encyclopedia.com

Galatea ship log found at: https://www.naval-history.net/OWShips-WW1-06-HMS_Galatea.htm

Government of Canada ship's histories at https://www.canada.ca/en/navy/services/history/ships-histories/

For Posterity's Sake at http://www.forposterityssake.ca/Navy/HMCS_NADEN.htm

Ships of the Royal Canadian Navy at http://readyayeready.com/ships/

CRD at https://www.crd.bc.ca/education/our-environment/harbours/

William Harbeck's 1907 video at williamharbeck1907.ca/

The *Daily Colonist* at http://britishcolonist.ca/index.html

Medicine Net at https://www.medicinenet.com/

INDEX to the JOURNALS

7
7 Islands. See Sept Îles

A
Alder, William and family,
    1936 Hampshire Road, Victoria, B.C., 132
Alexandria Club, 156, 162, 163, 164
Annesley, John, 112, 185, 188, 245

B
Bahamas
    Great Ianagua, 26
    Nassau, 26, 42, 126
    New Providence Island, 25, 42
Baker, Capt. L. Clinton, 30
Baldwin, Casey, 195
Barbados, 34, 36, 128, 253
Bartlett, Tim, 69
Beech, William James Robert, 145, 152, 153, 154, 155, 160, 166, 178
Bell-Irving, Nora, 160
Bermuda, 12, 23, 24, 25, 43, 44, 45, 46, 47, 50, 131, 132, 249, 254
    Gibbs Hill Light, 254
    Hamilton, 24, 47, 152, 254
Boak, Eric W. and family, 1070 Joan Crescent, Victoria, BC, 141, 146, 160, 163, 170, 200
Bridgman
    Jock, 180
    Montague, 141, 144, 154, 184
Browning, Admiral Montague Edward, 47
Bugno, Dicky, 112
Butler, Jimmy, 199

C
Canada
    Alberta
        Edmonton, 132
    British Columbia
        Agassiz, 151
        Bedwell Harbour, 148
        Chemainus, 155, 169, 170
        Cordova Bay, 147
        Cowichan Bay, 146, 148, 151, 166
        Crofton, 147
        Duncan, 133, 134, 159, 164, 169
        Esquimalt, 5, 12, 133, 134, 135, 136, 141, 145, 146, 147, 148, 149, 156, 164, 165, 166, 173, 201
        Fulford Harbour, 145, 146, 147, 165, 166, 168
        Ganges, 147, 148, 166, 168
        Gorge Waterway, 149, 169
        Malahat Drive, 133, 134, 168, 169
        Maple Bay, 134, 147
        Metchosin, 133, 134, 135, 147, 155, 157, 160, 161, 162, 164, 165, 201
        Mount Robson, 132
        Nanaimo, 168
        New Westminster, 132, 141, 151, 152, 155
        Pender Island, 133, 148
        Preedy Harbour, 148
        Qualicum Beach, 168, 169
        Quamichan, 146, 159
        Rocky Mountains, 132
        Salt Spring Island, 134, 136, 147, 152, 154
        Sansum Narrows, 147, 148
        Shawnigan Lake, 137, 147, 149, 153
        Sidney, 133
        Thetis Island, 148
        Trial Island, 147
        Vancouver, 132, 141, 142, 147, 155, 157, 160, 161, 162, 164
        Victoria, 132, 133, 134, 136, 141, 142, 143, 144, 145, 147, 148, 149, 150, 151, 152, 155, 156, 158, 159, 160, 151, 152, 153, 168, 170, 173, 184, 200
    Manitoba
        Winnipeg, 132, 170
    New Brunswick
        Fort Howe, 259
        Grand Manan, 6
        Letang, 6
        Miramichi, 17, 19
        Moncton, 50
        Rothesay, 244, 259
        Saint John, 6, 7, 8, 10, 50, 177, 194, 244
        Welchpool, 5
    Newfoundland and Labrador
        Cape Ray, 15, 16
        Harbour Island, 14
        Mutton Bay, 14
        Port aux Basques, 16, 17, 20
    Nova Scotia
        Aspy Bay, 17, 18, 19, 20
        Baddeck, 195, 247, 248
        Bras d'Or Lake, 195, 248
        Bridgewater, 247

Brier Island, 10
Cabot Strait, 15
Cape North, 15, 16, 17, 18, 19
Centreville, 8
Chester, 171, 199, 200, 247
Clark's Harbour, 247
Dartmouth, 193, 194, 205, 206
Digby, 6, 7, 8, 246
Grand Passage, 5
Grand-Pré, 191
Halifax, 5, 8, 9, 10, 11, 12, 21, 22, 24, 27, 38, 39, 40, 41, 45, 49, 50, 52, 58, 67, 73, 75, 77, 114, 120, 132, 134, 141, 140, 154, 170, 171, 174, 177, 182, 192, 194, 195, 196, 199, 201, 205, 243, 244, 245, 246, 247, 248, 251, 254, 258
   St. Paul's Anglican Church, 50, 177
Hubbards, 199
Ingonish, 20
Kentville, 8
LaHave River, 247
Liverpool, 247, 259
Londonderry, 11, 27
Lunenburg, 172, 247
Mahone Bay, 247
Margaree, 248
Neil's Harbour, 15
North Sydney, 15, 16, 18, 19
Petit Passage, 7, 246
Seal Island Light, 50
Shelburne, 45, 198, 199, 247
St. Lawrence Bay, 15, 16
St. Paul Island, 17, 18, 19, 20
Sydney, 12, 13, 15, 16, 18, 19, 20, 21, 248, 255
Truro, 21, 206
Tuft's Cove, 246
Whitehead, 12
Windsor, 114, 194
Wolfville, 258
Yarmouth, 5, 7, 8, 9, 10, 246
Ontario
   Ottawa, 137, 144, 170, 255
   Sarnia, 170
   Sault Ste. Marie, 170
   Toronto, 132, 170
Prince Edward Island
   Cape Egmont, 17
   Charlottetown, 245, 246, 257
Québec
   Gaspé, 19, 245

   Little Métis, 245
   Montreal, 114, 132, 198, 244, 255
   Percé, 257
   Québec City, 114, 132, 244, 245, 255
   Rivière-du-Loup, 257
   Sept Îles, 257
   Shawinigan Falls, 255
   Trois-Rivières, 245
Saskatchewan
   Biggar, 132, 170
Cap D'Or shipwreck, 198
Cape Verde Islands
   St. Vincent, 36, 37, 38, 41, 252
Carmichael family, 133, 153
Carr, Rupert, 170
Chetwoode, Captain D., 69
Colombia
   Cartagena, 33, 34
Constant Spring Hotel, 33, 42, 43, 44, 130, 131
Creery
   Alan, 199
Crete
   Suda Bay, 64, 69, 70
Critchley
   Sankey, 5, 6, 8, 9, 10, 11, 12, 17, 50, 51, 111, 112
Cuba
   Cape Maysi, 26, 45, 131
Curaçao
   Wilhamstad, 34

D

Demerara
   Georgetown, 40
Denmark
   Bornholm Island, 118
   Copenhagen, 104, 117, 118, 120
Dominica, 251
Douglas
   Hilda, 199
   Marion, 199

E

East Prussia
   Memel, 118
Easton
   Mrs., 12
   Polly, 11, 12, 21, 22, 41, 42, 50, 114
Edwards
   Arthur Wellesley, 132, 170, 243
   Emily Frances, 67, 50

Emily Susan (Crispo) – Mother, 21, 38, 40, 41, 42, 75, 169, 171, 172, 174, 194, 200, 243
Grace Gwendolyn, 40, 48, 67, 132, 141, 160, 170
Harold Leckie, 21, 40, 48, 50, 132, 170, 171, 177, 194, 198, 207, 243
Joseph Plimsoll – Father, 9, 11, 21, 22, 40, 50, 117, 160, 177, 194, 223
Joseph Plimsoll "Joe", 25, 38, 41, 59, 123, 172, 177
Muriel Katherine Annesley, 21, 171, 194
Susan Elizabeth, 251
Egypt
  Abassia, 236
  Alexandria, 67, 228, 229, 235, 240
  Cairo, 77, 92, 228, 229, 235, 240
  Gaza, 71, 73
  Kantara, 92
  Port Said, 68, 72, 72, 74, 77, 78, 92, 94, 236
Empress Hotel, 132, 135, 141, 143, 146, 156, 165
England
  Aldershot, 62, 111, 114, 121, 178, 189, 193
  Avonmouth, 53, 64
  Babbacombe, 186
  Basingstoke, 114, 179
  Beckenham, 85
  Bentley, 52
  Bournemouth, 192, 243, 250
  Bridport, 186
  Bristol, 53, 111
  Brookwood, 114
  Cambridge, 193
  Dartmouth, 193
  Devonport, 5, 52, 54, 55, 56, 58, 59, 61, 62, 64, 65, 111, 112, 120, 127, 128
  Dorchester, 186
  Dover, 57, 123
  Falmouth, 55, 57, 59, 60, 61, 66
  Farnham, 52, 62, 111, 113, 114, 120, 187, 191, 192
  Faversham, 180, 181
  Folkestone, 123
  Froyle, 52, 62, 112, 182, 183, 192
  Grantham, 117
  Guildford, 120, 184
  Liverpool, 56, 57, 59, 96, 114, 116, 193, 207
  London, 51, 57, 61, 62, 111, 112, 116, 123, 127, 178, 181, 183, 190, 192, 201, 207, 242
  Lyme Regis, 186
  Maidstone, 119, 180, 181
  Marefield, 180
  Plymouth, 52, 55, 56, 57, 58, 61, 109, 111, 112, 113, 114, 116, 128
  Portland, 57, 59, 61, 121
  Portsmouth, 5, 51, 52, 60, 120, 121, 122, 126, 141, 178, 183, 185, 186, 188, 189, 192, 193, 207, 242
  Princetown, 113
  Ringwood, 186
  Rodmersham, 179, 180, 182
  Roehampton, 242
  Saint Helier, 113
  Saltash, 61, 62, 112
  Sheerness, 120
  Sittingbourne, 123, 179
  Southampton, 178, 186, 188, 191, 207
  Spithead, 120, 122
  St. Budeaux, 113
  Taunton, 113
  Tavistock, 113
  Teignmouth, 186
  Torquay, 186
  Two Bridges, 113
  Weymouth, 113, 121
  Yelverton, 58
  Yeovil, 113

F

Finland
  Helsingfors, 119
France
  Amiens, 123
  Arras, 123
  Boulogne, 123
  Brest, 56, 64, 97
  Calais, 242
  Cambrai, 94
  Cannes, 241, 242
  Cherbourg, 55, 178
  Ecroivres, 123
  Juan-Les-Pins, 224
  Le Havre, 207
  Marseilles, 18, 80, 178
  Modane, 207
  Mont St. Eloi, 123
  Nice, 224
  Paris, 207, 242
  Toulon, 80, 223

Ville Franche, 224
Vimy, 56, 123
Fredrickson, Frank, 141
French cruiser *Amiral Aube*, 50
French cruiser *Jeanne d'Arc*, 41
French cruiser *Montcalm*, 41
French cruiser *Primauguet*, 258

G

Galt, Muriel, 137, 145, 166
Gauvreau, Leon Joseph Maurice, 16, 18, 22, 112
German vessel *Neptune*, 118
Germany
  Kiel, 104
Gibraltar, 18, 64, 97
Gore, Frances, 62, 113
Grant, John Moreau "Jack", 79, 80, 81, 82, 83, 94, 105, 106, 114, 127, 132, 133, 134, 137, 144, 145
Greece
  Argostoli, 231
  Athens, 76, 220, 221, 234, 235
  Cape Castro, 72
  Cape Matapan, 231
  Corfu, 69, 78, 81, 90
  Corinth, 90
  Corinth Canal, 76, 78, 90, 94
  Dedeagatch, 95, 96
  Deuthero Cove, 212
  Gavrion Bay, 211, 212
  Gulf of Patras, 78
  Kasos, 74
  Kastro, 75, 91
  Kephalo, 66, 75, 96
  Kondia, 74
  Mavros, 70
  Milo, 72, 73, 74, 78
  Mudros, 64, 65, 66, 69, 70, 71, 72, 74, 75, 76, 90, 91, 92, 95, 96, 102, 106, 108, 109
  Navarino Bay, 221, 230
  Oxeia Island, 221
  Pireaus, 76, 90
  Port Trebuki, 67, 68, 70, 74
  Pyrgos, 90, 91
  Salonika, 66, 67, 68, 72, 74, 96, 221, 234
  Samothraki, 90
  Skiathos, 212, 230
  Skyros Island, 67, 73
  Syros, 72
  Volo, 212, 213, 214

Grenada, 35, 253
Grenadine
  Martinique Channel, 34

H

Haddon, Lieutenant G. P., 132, 134, 141, 146, 151, 153, 155, 157, 158, 160, 162, 165, 200
Haking, General Sir Richard, 118, 119, 120
HMAS *Australia*, 60, 247
HMAS *Melbourne*, 25
HMAS *Yarra*, 89
HMAT *Ballerat*, 57
HMCS *Aurora*, 133, 144, 145, 148, 149, 166, 176, 177
HMCS *Canada*, 5, 6, 7, 8, 10, 12, 13, 15, 16, 17, 18, 19, 20, 22, 50, 51, 54, 121
HMCS *Champlain*, 205, 238, 243, 245, 252, 254, 259
HMCS *Festubert*, 141, 194, 195, 198, 205, 248, 254, 258
HMCS *Florence*, 6, 7, 8, 10, 15
HMCS *Grilse*, 12, 19, 20, 21, 45
HMCS *Hochelaga*, 10, 13, 15, 17, 18, 19, 20
HMCS *Margaret*, 5, 7, 12, 13, 15, 16, 19, 20, 22, 24
HMCS *Naden*, 133, 135, 136, 141, 145, 146, 147, 148, 149, 151, 155, 160, 165, 166, 168
HMCS *Niobe*, 5, 9, 10, 11, 12, 21, 22, 50
HMCS *Patrician*, 144, 145, 148, 166, 172, 173
HMCS *Patriot*, 144, 145, 146, 149, 166, 172, 176, 177, 195, 196, 198, 201, 207, 244, 247
HMCS *Rainbow*, 5, 12, 17
HMCS *Stadacona*, 7, 10, 12, 13, 14, 15, 16, 18, 20
HMCS *Starling*, 5, 8, 10
HMCS *Ypres*, 248, 254, 258
HMHS *Britannic*, 42
HMS *Abercrombie*, 70
HMS *Acheron*, 52, 55, 58, 59. 96, 102, 104, 106
HMS *Acorn*, 109, 111 113
HMS *Agamemnon*, 90, 96, 102, 106, 214, 216
HMS *Alarm*, 81
HMS *Angora*, 67
HMS *Apollo*, 113
HMS *Archer*, 52, 53, 54, 55, 56, 58, 59,

60, 61, 62, 63, 64, 65, 66, 67, 68, 71, 72, 73, 74, 75, 76, 77, 78, 79, 81, 82, 83, 87, 91, 94, 95, 108
HMS *Ardent*, 15
HMS *Ariel*, 54, 55, 61
HMS *Arno*, 75
HMS *Attack*, 52, 55, 58, 59
HMS *Badger*, 60
HMS *Barham*, 122, 211, 212, 213, 214, 216, 220, 223, 225, 226, 227, 229, 232
HMS *Basilisk*, 66, 67
HMS *Beaver*, 79, 80, 81, 82, 89, 102
HMS *Benbow*, 111
HMS *Berwick*, 5, 21, 22, 23, 24, 25, 26, 27, 29, 30, 31, 32, 33, 34, 35, 36, 37, 38, 39, 40, 41, 42, 43, 44, 45, 46, 47, 48, 54, 87
HMS *Black Prince*, 15
HMS *Blenheim*, 65, 69, 70, 71, 76, 80, 82, 83, 90, 94, 95, 108, 109
HMS *Brisk*, 52, 54, 55, 61
HMS *Bristol*, 69
HMS *Broke*, 57
HMS *Bryony*, 232
HMS *Bulldog*, 65
HMS *Caesar*, 47, 95
HMS *Calcutta*, 53, 132, 158
HMS *Caledon*, 239
HMS *Calgarian*, 9, 23, 56
HMS *Calliope*, 87, 127, 128, 129, 130, 131
HMS *Calypso*, 226
HMS *Cambrian*, 158
HMS *Cameleon*, 77, 87, 94, 102, 105, 107, 108, 109, 110, 111, 112, 114
HMS *Canterbury*, 56, 103
HMS *Capetown*, 249, 250, 251, 254, 258
HMS *Cardiff*, 226
HMS *Carnarvon*, 9, 22, 47, 49, 112
HMS *Ceanothus*, 79
HMS *Centurion*, 111, 112
HMS *Ceres*, 226, 229, 231, 232
HMS *Chelmer*, 70, 76, 77
HMS *Cherryleaf*, 132
HMS *Christopher*, 60
HMS *Collingwood*, 111
HMS *Colne*, 75, 76, 105
HMS *Colombo*, 249, 250, 251, 252
HMS *Comet*, 76
HMS *Concord*, 226, 230, 231
HMS *Constance*, 131
HMS *Curlew*, 5
HMS *Danae*, 220
HMS *Dartmouth*, 82, 193
HMS *Dauntless*, 220
HMS *Defender*, 82, 223
HMS *Defense*, 15
HMS *Defiance*, 57, 62
HMS *Delhi*, 119, 220
HMS *Despatch*, 258, 259
HMS *Devonshire*, 45, 58
HMS *Donegal*, 37
HMS *Dragon*, 114, 120
HMS *Drake*, 11, 21, 45, 52, 70
HMS *Druid*, 92, 106, 108, 113
HMS *Durban*, 59, 251
HMS *Dyad*, 122
HMS *E14*, 76
HMS *Eagle*, 211, 220, 222, 226, 229, 232, 233, 238
HMS *Egmont*, 17, 214 226
HMS *Endymion*, 91
HMS *Erebus*, 119, 120
HMS *Essex*, 37
HMS *Europa*, 64, 76, 82, 108
HMS *Flat Calm*, 121
HMS *Flirt*, 39
HMS *Foresight*, 76, 77
HMS *Forester*, 80, 81, 92
HMS *Forward*, 102
HMS *Frobisher*, 209, 213, 220, 237
HMS *Fury*, 65, 67, 68, 70
HMS *Galatea*, 87, 115, 116, 118, 121, 122, 123, 127
HMS *Gasconia*, 37
HMS *Gloucester*, 82
HMS *Goshawk*, 53, 54, 55, 56, 80, 108
HMS *Grasshopper*, 65
HMS *H4*, 80
HMS *H5*, 53
HMS *Hannibal*, 68
HMS *Harpy*, 64, 66
HMS *Heliotrope*, 258
HMS *Hermes*, 211
HMS *Heroic*, 78
HMS *Highflyer*, 24, 37, 59
HMS *Hind*, 102, 108
HMS *Hope*, 90, 91, 105, 109, 128
HMS *Hornet*, 80, 92, 102
HMS *Hydra*, 68, 70, 71, 82, 83, 102
HMS *Indefatigable*, 15
HMS *Invincible*, 15, 225
HMS *Jackal*, 52, 61, 70, 71, 72, 80, 82, 95, 96, 102, 108, 146
HMS *Jed*, 70, 77
HMS *Kennett*, 75

HMS *Kent*, 37
HMS *King Alfred*, 37
HMS *Lapwing*, 55, 57, 58, 61, 91, 96, 105
HMS *Larne*, 90, 91, 95
HMS *Laverock*, 62
HMS *Liverpool*, 96
HMS *Lizard*, 52, 55, 56, 57, 59, 61, 73, 74, 75
HMS *Lord Nelson*, 74, 75, 102
HMS *Louvain*, 68, 71, 75, 97
HMS *Lowenstoft*, 82
HMS *Lychnis*, 77
HMS *Lyra*, 52, 55
HMS *Magdalena*, 36, 37
HMS *Malaya*, 184, 185, 205, 215, 216, 220, 221, 222, 225, 226, 230, 231, 232, 233
HMS *Marlborough*, 111, 223
HMS *Marmora*, 57
HMS *Martin*, 52
HMS *Medina*, 61
HMS *Medway*, 37
HMS *Melampus*, 51
HMS *Mischief*, 111
HMS *Monarch*, 121
HMS *Neptune*, 116
HMS *Nereide*, 76, 77, 78
HMS *Nereus*, 60
HMS *Nubian*, 39
HMS *Nymphe*, 82
HMS *Osiris II*, 65
HMS *Paragon*, 55
HMS *Parthian*, 53, 105, 109
HMS *Pelorus*, 64
HMS *Petrel*, 5
HMS *Phaeton*, 118, 120
HMS *Phoenix*, 58, 59, 64, 65, 67, 68, 77, 80
HMS *Pincher*, 71
HMS *Prince Edward*, 92
HMS *Prince of Wales*, 114, 120
HMS *Queen Elizabeth*, 121, 237
HMS *Queen Mary*, 15
HMS *Queen Victoria*, 96
HMS *Raccoon*, 76
HMS *Raleigh*, 158, 159, 160
HMS *Redpole*, 71, 91, 109, 111
HMS *Renaud*, 74, 76
HMS *Renown*, 114, 120
HMS *Resolution*, 193, 211, 212, 214, 215
HMS *Ribble*, 94
HMS *Rifleman*, 68, 71, 108, 109, 111

HMS *River Clyde*, 9679, 91
HMS *Roxburgh*, 44, 45
HMS *Royal Oak*, 211, 212, 213, 214, 215, 220, 233, 236
HMS *Royal Sovereign*, 121, 220, 227, 230
HMS *Ruby*, 53, 59, 61, 71, 72, 77, 109
HMS *Sandhurst*, 117, 239
HMS *Scandinavia*, 22
HMS *Shark*, 109
HMS *Skirmisher*, 102
HMS *Sparrowhawk*, 15
HMS *Spear*, 111
HMS *Speedy*, 111
HMS *Sportive*, 111
HMS *St. George*, 108
HMS *Staunch*, 71
HMS *Stuart*, 111
HMS *Suffolk*, 9, 10, 60, 77
HMS *Superb*, 102, 109,
HMS *Sutlej*, 37
HMS *Swallow*, 111
HMS *Swiftsure*, 37, 56
HMS *Temeraire*, 95, 96, 97, 102
HMS *Theseus*, 94
HMS *Tigress*, 54, 55, 58, 75, 94, 95
HMS *Tilbury*, 105
HMS *Tipperary*, 15
HMS *Torbay*, See HMCS *Champlain*
HMS *Torch*, 111
HMS *Toreador*, See HMCS *Vancouver*
HMS *Triad*, 79, 91
HMS *Tribune*, 95, 109
HMS *Tryphon*, 111
HMS *Tumult*, 111
HMS *Turbulent*, 15
HMS *Unity*, 56, 61
HMS *Usk*, 80
HMS *Valiant*, 205, 208, 209, 210, 211, 212, 213, 214, 216, 219, 220, 221, 231, 232, 233, 234, 237, 238, 240
HMS *Valorous*, 118, 120
HMS *Venetia*, 216
HMS *Verbena*, 73
HMS *Vernon*, 5, 51, 52
HMS *Viceroy*, 239
HMS *Wallflower*, 79
HMS *Warrior*, 15
HMS *Warspite*, 211, 213, 214, 215, 219, 221, 223, 224, 226, 230, 231, 232, 233, 236, 239, 240
HMS *Warwick*, 127
HMS *Wear*, 65, 67, 68, 69
HMS *Welland*, 90

HMS *Weymouth*, 47, 82, 113, 121
HMS *Whitley*, 118
HMS *Winchester*, 62, 118, 191
HMT *Aragon*, 67, 68, 690
HMT *Briton*, 69, 72
Hobday, Bun, 141
Horan, H. E., 60
Hose, Captain Walter, 144, 145, 168, 170

I

Innes, Charles B. and family, 142, 146, 151, 153, 154, 155, 156, 158, 160, 161, 162, 163, 164, 168, 169, 201
Ireland
   Belfast, 58, 59
   Coningbeg Light Vessel, 54
   Fanad Light House, 58
   Lough Swilly, 58
   Queenstown, 53, 54, 55, 56, 58, 114
   Rathlin Island, 76
Italy
   Brindisi, 79, 80, 81, 82, 83, 89, 90, 91, 92, 94
   Durazzo, 82
   Genoa, 82, 89
   Leghorn (Livorno), 82, 83, 84, 87, 88, 89
   Messina, 80, 90, 95
   Montenero, 88
   Naples, 224
   Pisa, 84, 87
   Rome, 88, 207
      Borghese Garden, 88
   Stromboli, 90
   Syracuse, 207
   Taranto, 69, 76, 83
   Vallona, 82

J

Jamaica, 26, 33, 41, 42, 43, 45, 140, 250, 251
   Kingston, 33, 41, 42, 43, 44, 130, 250, 251
   Morant Point, 26
   Port Royal, 41, 42, 43, 44, 131
James, Sir Frederick Seton, 253
Janish, Dr. and family, 5, 7, 8, 9
Japanese destroyer *Kashi*, 104
Japanese destroyer *Momo*, 79, 104
Jones
   Dr. Thomas J., 133, 134, 135, 136, 141, 153
   Ticky, 153, 157, 158, 160, 164, 165, 169, 177

L

Lambert, Rear Adm. Cecil, 90
Leckie, Edith, 121, 127, 217
Lesser Antilles
   Mount Pelée, 35
Lindsay, Donald St. George, 7, 13, 14, 21, 22 25, 35, 38, 40, 41, 42, 44, 47, 48, 49, 52, 145
Luxton, Arthur P. and family, 132, 156

M

Malta, 64, 76, 77, 78, 79, 82, 87, 89, 95, 96, 101, 102, 105, 106, 109, 111, 205, 208, 214, 220, 221, 224, 225, 227, 228, 229, 230, 232, 233, 234, 235, 236, 238, 239, 240, 241
   Calafrana, 226
   Manoel Island, 210
   Marsa, 77, 79, 104, 208, 209, 210, 211, 214, 215, 216, 217, 219, 220, 225, 226, 233, 237, 238, 239
   Sliema, 79, 106, 208, 210, 211, 233
Manning, Sir William, KGB, 42
Martinique, 35, 41
   Fort-de-France, 35, 36
Matson, John and family, 134, 136, 141, 142, 143, 144, 145, 146, 147, 148, 149, 150, 153, 154, 155, 156, 157, 158, 159, 160, 162, 163, 164, 166, 168, 169, 170, 200
Maunsell family, 134, 135, 136, 141, 144, 150, 155
McFetridge, Winnie, 199
McInnes, Carol, 205, 206
Milliard, Rodney C., 24, 35, 36, 43
Mitchell, George, 243
Monaco
   Monte Carlo, 224, 240
Montizambert, Alex and family, 133

N

Nichol, Lieutenant Governor Walter, 143
Nixon, Commander Edward Atcherley Eckersall, 50, 135, 137, 150, 201

O

O'Leary, Michael Daniel, 17, 18, 90, 91, 243
Oak Bay High School, 144, 157, 163
Orchard, Robert, 182

P

Packenham, Vice Admiral Sir William, 159, 160
Palestine
  Haifa, 92
Pasco, Captain Frederick Claude Coote, 7, 8, 12, 13, 14, 15, 18, 19
Pears, Admiral Edmund Ratcliffe, 144
Pemberton, Frederick B. and family, 133, 134, 136, 141, 143, 154, 160, 164,169, 200
Peter Bangs (Gordon setter), 154, 157, 165,170, 173, 177, 194, 223
Pooley, Robert H. and family, 133
Portugal
  Azores, 127, 128

R

Reid, Howard Emerson, 52, 55, 57, 58, 178. 179, 180, 182, 194, 243
Reynolds, Ned, 62
RMS *Adriatic*, 9, 114
RMS *Alaunia*, 206, 207
RMS *Baltic*, 9
RMS *Coronia*, 9, 10
RMS *Empress of Britain*, 9, 22
RMS *Franconia*, 36
RMS *Olympic*, 9, 10, 11, 59
RMS *Saxonia*, 56, 59
RMSP *Chaleur*, 38, 49, 50
Robertson
  Nairn, 152, 1567, 164, 165, 166, 170, 189, 200
  Sir William Charles Fleming, 244
Russia
  Libau, 117, 118, 120
  Sevastopol, 104

S

Sayward, Joseph A. and family, 132, 134, 157
Scotland
  Dunfermline, 116, 117
  Dumfries, 117
  Edinburgh, 116, 117
  Inverkeithing, 117
  Queensferry, 117
  Rosyth Dockyard, 116, 117
Shawcross, Tony, 179
Simonds, Cicely, 134, 136 141, 142, 143, 144, 145, 146, 147, 149, 150, 154, 155, 157, 160, 162, 163, 166
SMS *Breslau*, 74, 75
SMS *Frauenlob*, 15
SMS *Goeben*, 74, 75, 76, 96, 108
SMS *Lutzow*, 16
SMS *Pommern*, 15
SMS *Rostock*, 16
SMS *Weisbaden*, 15
Soulsby, Henry William Stephens, 7, 13, 21, 22, 25, 33, 37, 39, 44, 49, 52, 70, 71, 79, 80, 82, 83, 95, 96, 108, 221, 223
SS *Ascania*, 54, 61
SS *Ayreshire*, 56, 59
SS *Bellerophon*, 64
SS *Bermudian*, 48, 73, 96
SS *Cameronian*, 22
SS *Cape Breton*, 18
SS *Chagres*, 78
SS *City of Marseilles*, 22, 236
SS *Corsican*, 58
SS *El Kharia*, 74
SS *Hebburn*, 87, 123, 124, 125, 126
SS *Inventor*, 64
SS *Lady Drake*, 253
SS *Lady Sybil*, 17
SS *Lapland*, 56
SS *Laurentic*, 58
SS *Lorenzo*, 30, 31
SS *Matatua*, 7
SS *Megantic*, 114
SS *Metagama*, 56, 58
SS *Mexican Prince*, 74
SS *Olympic*, 9, 10, 11, 59
SS *Pacuare*, 72, 73
SS *Pancras*, 79
SS *Pennland*, 242
SS *Queen Louise*, 55
SS *San Rito*, 9, 73, 74
SS *Scotian*, 22
SS *Southland*, 56
SS *Spreewald*, 26, 27, 30, 31
SS *Thor*, 30
SS *Tibor*, 74
SS *Volumnia*, 67
St. Lucia, 30, 31, 35, 36, 37, 38, 39, 40
Streatfield, Kenneth, Helen, and Betty, 135, 143, 148, 150
Stubbs, Governor Reginald Edward, 250
Surfdale, 172, 176, 197, 198, 199, 200, 201, 207
Sweden
  Björkö, 118, 119
  Reval, 118, 119
  Sandhammaren Light, 118

Symons
    Dorothy Elizabeth, 177, 182, 194, 198, 199, 205, 207, 226, 238, 246, 254, 258
    Marjorie Gertrude, 177, 194, 200, 243, 254
    Rupert Martell, 243

T
Tanner, Dr. Albert H., 134
Taylor
    B.A., 60
    Cuthbert Robert Holland, 52, 55, 56, 67
Thornton, Sir Henry, 246
Tingley, Harold Reed, 10, 13, 14, 15, 17, 51, 52
Tomalin, Tommy, 144, 150
Trinidad, 45, 127, 128, 130, 132
    Port of Spain, 128, 130, 252, 253
TSS *Themistocles*, 53
Tunisia
    Biserta, 95
Turkey
    Aliki Bay, 65, 66
    Cape Aliki, 65
    Cape Helles, 96, 109
    Constantinople, 76, 102, 108
    Dardanelles, 5, 64, 65, 66, 70, 72, 75, 76, 87, 90, 91, 96, 106, 108
    Imbros, 65, 90, 91
        Kephalo Bay, 66, 96
    Ismid, 96, 97, 102, 106, 108
    Kusu Bay, 74, 75, 108
    Suvla, 65, 75, 90
    Tenedos, 65, 66, 70, 90
    Zusu Bay, 65, 66

U
United States of America
    Florida
        Florida Strait, 44, 45
    Maine
        Bar Harbor, 258
    Maryland
        Chesapeake Bay, 22, 23
    Massachusetts
        Nantucket Light Vessel, 37
    Virginia
        Cape Henry, 23
    Washington
        Seattle, 141, 143, 144, 144, 160, 161, 162, 169

USS *Cincinnati*, 258
USS *Richmond*, 258
USS *Wyoming*, 244

V
Venezuela
    La Guaira, 34
    Orquilla Island, 34
    Pico Island, 34
Victoria High School, 136, 143, 156, 161

W
Wales
    Caerleon, 63
    Caerphilly, 63
    Cardiff, 63, 179
    Holyhead, 54, 56, 59
    Newport, 62, 63, 64, 65
        Ladyhill Golf Course, 63
        St. Woolos, 62, 63
    Wyndecliff, 63
Wolfenden, Arthur R. and family, 133, 135, 137, 152, 158, 161, 164, 168, 169, 201
Wood, Rupert and Maurine, 134
Wurtele, Alfred, 149, 205, 206

ACTION BETWEEN "RIFLEMAN"—"LYCHNIS" AND AN ENEMY SUBMARINE.

Diagram showing position of convoy and escort when attacked.

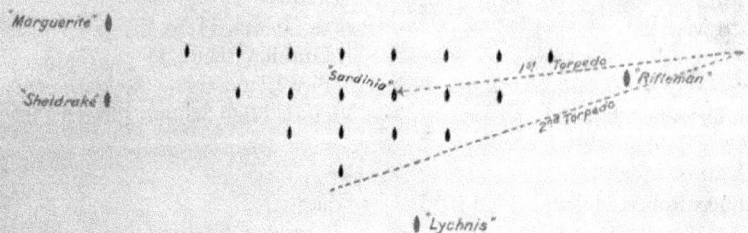

"Sardinia" torpedoed (but reached harbour).

Time and date	19.40, 4th Feb.	Sea		Calm, phosphorescent.
Designation of convoy	HE 5.			
Number of ships	19.	Visibility		Dark, very clear.
Position	36° 30′ N., 00° 56′ W.	Was submarine seen		Yes.
Course and speed	S. 76° W., 10 knots, zigzagging.	Was track of torpedo seen		Yes.
Weather	Fine.			

PLAN OF ATTACK ("Lychnis")

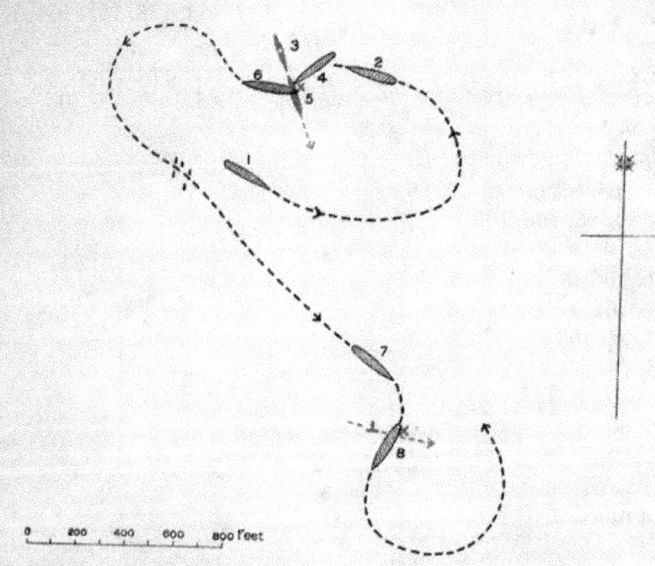

NOTE—Distances are approximate.

- ---- Track of H.M.S. "Lychnis."
- ⋰⋱ Abandoned boats of S.S. "Sardinia."
- ⊥ Periscope showing large feather.
- ⬬ Submarine.
- × Depth Charges dropped.

1. "Lychnis" at 21.10. From 20.30 till 21.10 ships stopped transferring passengers. "Lychnis" and "Sardinia" proceeded under way 21.10.
2. "Lychnis" and (3.) conning-tower of submarine when first sighted at 21.15.
4. Stem of "Lychnis" passing over stern of submarine.
5. Submarine just visible under water.
6. "Lychnis" helm hard aport, depth charge dropped, 21.16.
7. "Lychnis" when periscope sighted.
8. "Lychnis" when depth charge was let go, 21.21.

Diagram of action between HMS Rifleman, HMS Lychnis and an enemy submarine

www.ingramcontent.com/pod-product-compliance
Lightning Source LLC
Chambersburg PA
CBHW080437170426
43195CB00017B/2811